THE FIRE SPREADS

The Fire Spreads

Holiness and Pentecostalism in the American South

Randall J. Stephens

HARVARD UNIVERSITY PRESS

Cambridge, Massachusetts · London, England · 2008

LIBRARY OF CONGRESS CATALOGING-IN-PUBLICATION DATA

Stephens, Randall J., 1973–
  The fire spreads : holiness and Pentecostalism in the
American South / Randall J. Stephens.
    p. cm.
  Includes bibliographical references (p.) and index.
  ISBN-13: 978-0-674-02672-8 (alk. paper)
  ISBN-10: 0-674-02672-1 (alk. paper)
    1. Pentecostalism—Southern States—History. 2. Southern States—
Church history. I. Title.
  BR1644.5.U6S74 2008
  280'.40975—dc22   2007021436

For Solveig Elisabeth Stephens

and John Wesley Stephens

Contents

Acknowledgments

I could never have completed this book without the help of so many friends, family members, and colleagues who offered their support, advice, and constructive criticism. I thank my mentor, Bertram Wyatt-Brown, for all his marvelous assistance. Bert is a superb writer and an outstanding scholar. He helped me hone my skills considerably. Several readers did much to shape my work: Fitz Brundage, David G. Hackett, Paul Harvey, John Sommerville, Grant Wacker, Daniel Woods, and Ted Ownby. Their keen insight has been critical.

A number of archivists and researchers also aided me along the way, pointing me toward rare manuscripts and newspapers and guiding me in my research. Charles Edwin Jones of Oklahoma City; William Kostlevy and Bill Faupel, formerly of Asbury Theological Seminary; Harold Hunter and Erica Rutland at the International Pentecostal Holiness Church Archives; Wayne Warner, Darrin Rodgers, Glenn Gohr, and Joyce Lee at the Flower Pentecostal Heritage Center; David G. Roebuck of the Dixon Pentecostal Research Center; and Stan Ingersol, Meri Janssen, and Willie Rice at the Church of the Nazarene Archives offered tremendous assistance.

Colleagues at Eastern Nazarene College and the Historical

Society have given constructive feedback. Joe Lucas, Lou Ferleger, and Scott Hovey have been wonderful colleagues at THS. Carla Lovett and Donald Yerxa of ENC's history department were especially encouraging as the project neared completion. Students at ENC also provided helpful insights. Friends and family members listened to me prattle on about theologies of the Spirit and regional religion for much longer than seems humanly possible. Delvyn Case, Eddie Couchenour, Noel George, Karl Giberson, Beatrice Stephens, Brian and Jenny Ward, Bland Whitley, and Bryan Zimmerman all lent their ears and offered advice when possible. For that I am thankful. Now and then the guys in Jetenderpaul and Scott Hatch helped me escape dusty archives and the blinding glare of a computer screen. Mary Ellen Pryslak's generosity helped me get in and out of Boston and Cambridge, where I walked the stacks of Widener Library and Boston University's Divinity School library. John Callison of Kansas City kindly allowed me to use his photograph of Thomas Hart Benton's *Lord, Heal the Child* for the jacket. It is a wonderful fit. Vernon Burton and graduate student participants in the 2001 Pew Younger Scholars Seminar, University of Notre Dame, offered useful guidance in the early stages of this work. Joyce Seltzer and Jennifer Banks at Harvard University Press cannot be thanked enough. Jennifer made sure I kept to a reasonable schedule, and Joyce offered excellent advice on writing style, argument, and so much more. Amanda Heller, a superb copyeditor, kept me from making numerous mistakes; she and Elizabeth Gilbert at the Press aided this project immeasurably in the last stages. My work has also benefited from a generous fellowship from the Louisville Institute. For that I am most grateful. Participants in a Tucker Society forum helped me think through some critical issues as well.

My long-suffering wife, Solveig Elisabeth, is a godsend. Beth read and reread drafts until her eyes crossed. She was a perceptive critic and an even better encourager. I also appreciate the support of my mother, Janice Stephens; Nicole and Phil White; David and Nicole Stephens; and my in-laws, William and Solveig Cagwin and Nora and Jared Whitcomb. My late father, John Wesley Stephens, was a constant source of inspiration, as was my late grandfather, Raymond Cecil Stephens. (The latter was a barnstorming holiness preacher in the Wesleyan Church. His long, passionate prayers could shake the tiles off roofs and break the hearts of listeners.) My father would certainly be proud to see this project come to completion. To him and Beth I dedicate this book.

THE FIRE SPREADS

Introduction

IN EARLY JANUARY 1907, southern men and women, black and white, ventured to Dunn, North Carolina. Hundreds made the pilgrimage from South Carolina, Georgia, Alabama, and Tennessee. They longed to experience their "Pentecost" and the "gift of tongues" they had recently read so much about in holiness newspapers, publications devoted to moral purity and spiritual empowerment. A rambunctious North Carolina holiness preacher by the name of G. B. Cashwell organized the event. Just weeks before, he had taken a train 2,500 miles west to attend a boisterous interracial revival held in Los Angeles. While there, he claimed to have received the gift of the Spirit, evidenced by speaking in tongues. What happened to the disciples in the Book of Acts, asserted Cashwell, was happening again. To the uninitiated, however, tongues speech was gibberish. A skeptical journalist in Los Angeles parodied the ravings of crazed "new apostles" and deluded zealots: "You-oo-oo gouloo-loo come under the bloo-oo-oo bo-loo."[1]

Cashwell had no time to listen to critics. He quickly returned to the South, rented a tobacco warehouse in Dunn, and held his heavily attended revival. It was something of a reenactment of the West Coast meeting. Congregants spoke in unidentifiable tongues and thrashed about in divine ecstasy. The Holy Ghost seemed to be available to all worshippers, regardless of age, color, or sex. Most of the southerners present were affiliated with the holiness movement, which emerged in northern cities after the Civil War. They had initially looked to the North for guidance from leading Methodist ministers and holiness divines, and they turned to the work of John Wesley, the father of Methodism, for further enlightenment. Southern seekers of perfection had come to expect ever greater spiritual blessings during the ten years leading up to the Dunn meeting. Believers thought that God was perfecting and refining them for better things. They stressed the spiritual work of "sanctification," or being purified, made sinless, and set apart. They also called it their "second work." Salvation or conversion was the "first work," but that, thought holiness folk, was not enough. Adherents focused on several key passages from the Bible, a favorite being 1 John 3:6: "Whosoever abideth in him sinneth not: whosoever sinneth hath not seen him, neither known him."[2] They also looked for guidance to Phoebe Palmer, a prolific author and one of the founders of the holiness movement. She devoted much of her life to explaining what it meant to be sanctified. In 1845 Palmer wrote that sanctification was "salvation from sin, a redemption from *all* iniquity." Roughly forty years later, and twenty years before the Dunn meeting, one black holiness preacher in South Carolina defined sanctification as the fulfillment of the Christian life. "Until it is sought and found," wrote J. Wofford White, "the whole duty is not performed, requirements of spiritual life are not met, the danger line still in sight, and indeed not passed; for sanctification means, if anything, not only the pardon of sins, assurance and the other divine evidences of acceptance; it includes also the idea of the change in our nature of a proneness, inclination or natural bent to do evil, to a proneness or natural bent in us to do that only which pleases God."[3] If, in an instant, God could turn believers into perfect, sinless Christians, He surely could do much more. So went the logic. Holiness disciples eagerly embraced the new message of tongues that Cashwell brought to the South. Those filled with the Holy Ghost, he said, could speak in languages that would allow them to spread the gospel around the globe. "I jerked so I shook the whole house, my tongue fairly flew, saying something I knew not what," claimed one minister at the Dunn gathering.[4]

To mainline southern evangelicals, the divine revelations such enthusiasts celebrated seemed eccentric at best, diabolical at worst. The faithful spoke of baptisms of fire, gifts of healing, and prophetic visions. Some observers were especially vexed by believers' end-of-the-world theology. Indeed, those who gathered at Dunn thought themselves to be at the center of a divine end-time drama. The miracles that initiates claimed to witness seemed to them clear signs that Jesus would soon return to earth and usher his saints into paradise. A group of outspoken adversaries scorned what they called the religious fantasies of these latter-day prophets. Some critics in the South and West wishfully predicted the movement's inevitable demise. It was a religious fad, argued observers such as C. W. Shumway, a University of Southern California graduate student. In 1914 Shumway estimated that the tongues revival would soon vanish into obscurity, much as other embarrassing millennial upheavals had before it.[5] He could not have been more wrong. Still, despite pentecostalism's staggering rate of growth in the twentieth century, later critics and scholars of religious history continued to ignore the massive impact such movements of the Spirit had on the lives of countless southerners.

The story of the origins of holiness theology and pentecostalism in the U.S. South from the last quarter of the nineteenth century to the early twentieth century remains untold, as does that of the larger significance of these movements in both the modern South and the nation as a whole. Yet they are hardly peripheral to modern American, and particularly southern, history. With millions of devotees in the South alone, holiness and pentecostalism now rank second only to Roman Catholicism among the world's Christian denominations. Moreover, the U.S. South is home to the headquarters of fifty-seven different pentecostal churches and sects—including those of the Assemblies of God, the Church of God in Christ, and the Church of God (Cleveland, Tennessee). These groups, and born-again Christians in general, have experienced phenomenal growth since the 1970s. Their numbers soared as liberal Protestantism in the South and elsewhere waned. Some observers have even called this upsurge in religious enthusiasm the Fourth Great Awakening. Moreover, the recent politicization of conservative evangelicals, of whom southern pentecostals make up a significant proportion, deserves special scrutiny.[6] Believers are now more visible than ever before. Devout southern pentecostals and those with roots in the tradition—including former attorney general John Ashcroft, conservative religious spokesmen Jim Bakker and John Hagee, country singers Tammy Wynette and Johnny Cash, and rock and roll innovators Jerry Lee Lewis, Little Richard, and Elvis Presley—are known throughout the world.

Although for many Americans pentecostalism is almost synonymous with southern-grown political and social conservatism, things were not always so. Despite the contemporary visibility and current incarnation of the movement, it first took root in the South among anonymous zealots on the cultural fringes of society. The religious innovations and unusual beliefs of first-generation adherents were once deeply offensive to genteel working-class and middle-class southerners. The unconventional attitude toward religious authority among those in the holiness and pentecostal movements, as well as their views on race and gender during the height of the Jim Crow era, set them on an uncharted and dangerous course in Christian social life.

These religious traditions first entered the South through the northern revival of perfectionism in the late nineteenth century and then through an exuberant 1906 revival in Los Angeles. Southerners who adopted the theology and religious practices of those outside the region suffered the scorn of mainline southern Protestants. Hence believers played profoundly countercultural roles in the South in this early period. Adherents espoused a host of unusual beliefs regarding the end of the world, gifts of the Holy Ghost, and ecstatic worship. By 1906 devotees in the South had come to embrace the theology of premillennialism, a doctrine that stressed the imminent return of Jesus Christ, who would rescue the faithful from a corrupt, irredeemable world. Highly popular among contemporary American evangelicals, it was a belief almost unheard of in the turn-of-the-century South. The faithful looked to the heavens for their salvation and exalted sinless perfection. They also expected to receive the same "gifts of the Spirit"—healing, prophecy, miraculous "tongues speech"—evident in the Book of Acts, available again in the last days.

In part because of their strange beliefs, ecstatic worship, marginal social status, and apparent anti-intellectualism, outside observers often dismissed holiness disciples and pentecostals as a dispossessed minority, uneducated and fanatical. As far back as the 1920s, journalist Duncan Aikman satirized the southern faithful in H. L. Mencken's *American Mercury*. Believers were mountebanks, illiterates, and perennial losers, Aikman charged. It was no wonder "Holy Rollers" achieved most of their success "in the Hookworm Belt." Aikman lampooned southern perfectionists in Menckenesque tones: "They believe that salvation, being merely forgiveness of sin, is scarcely more creditable to the saved sinner than a sentimental Governor's pardon to a convict, and that after it comes the really essential work of grace, to wit, sanctification or baptism by the Holy Ghost, . . . enables the saved to attain . . . perfect holiness." Over a decade later, in his study of labor unrest in Gaston County, North Carolina, the sociologist Liston Pope indicted holiness and pentecostal church leaders for not standing in opposition to the prevailing economic arrangements or fighting the harsh methods employed to preserve them. Pope thought that the "millbillies" who flocked to holiness and pentecostal churches were escapists of the highest order. "The poorest strata of the community are attracted into membership," he observed. These new sects offered little more than a thin fantasy in the face of crippling social and economic circumstances.[7] Other critics argued that this otherworldliness suppressed social protest and defused class hostilities. Yet such oversimplified, reductionist interpretations do not capture the depth and breadth of either movement.[8]

The best works on the roots of holiness and pentecostalism have largely been denominationally based, limited to either holiness or pentecostalism, or they have been broader surveys of the movement throughout the twentieth century.[9] Grant Wacker's 2001 book *Heaven Below* and Vinson Synan's classic *The Holiness-Pentecostal Tradition* are the best interpretations of first-generation pentecostalism. Yet their work does not deal with regional and chronological nuances.[10]

Sources for research in this area are extremely rich, if relatively untapped. The holiness and pentecostal press, diaries, church records, and denominational histories show how both groups constructed their religious communities and transmitted and sustained their countercultural vision. Holiness folk and early pentecostals were, of course, more concerned with saving souls than archiving their history. One leading first-generation pentecostal, reflecting on the nascent movement years later, lamented that more preachers did not keep diaries or other records of their activities. But this was not their primary focus. In fact, some even considered the mere storing of artifacts and mementos to be sinful, a sure sign of vanity. A prominent preacher affiliated with the Azusa revival went so far as to burn five hundred personal letters. Keeping them, he thought, might tempt him to think too highly of himself.[11] Fortunately, all did not reason similarly. There is still an abundant treasury of records available in denominational and college archives throughout the South. These sources reveal much about the distinctive qualities of holiness worship and pentecostalism in the region.

Writing in 1982, the musicologist Stephen R. Tucker noted that "few have considered the influence of pentecostal religion in shaping southern culture."[12] Indeed, to this day few have considered the regional aspect of holiness or pentecostalism. Even the question of whether there was a distinctly "southern" variety of either movement has remained largely unanswered.[13] This book analyzes the deep roots of pentecostalism and holiness in the South, offering clear theological and cultural reasons for believers' adversarial roles in the region. Conflict, dissent, and antagonism marked both early movements. In many ways, the first converts were religious mavericks, bent on challenging a variety of traditions and institutions in the region. Only in recent years, especially since the 1970s, have holiness adherents and pentecostals moved into mainstream American society, shedding many of their distinctive features in the process.

The later growth and prominence of these religious traditions is all the more surprising, given the obstacles they once faced. The holiness movement, which preceded pentecostalism, claimed amazingly few adherents in the mid-nineteenth-century South. Only a handful of initiates scattered across the region hoped for a revival of holiness. Of course, perfectionism and belief in a cleansing or empowering second work of grace thrived in the antebellum North. In the South, however, the regional commitment to slavery, opposition to northern reform, and the power of formal and vernacular Calvinism made it difficult, if not impossible, for perfectionism to thrive. Indeed, from 1847 to 1861, the chief scholarly publication of the Methodist Episcopal Church, South, did not cover the subject of sanctification at all. C. B. Jernigan, who would become a leading Texas holiness preacher in the late nineteenth century, exemplified the experience of many on the matter. Only as an adult, long after the Civil War, did he come in contact with perfectionism. Until then, he recalled, "I had never heard a sermon on holiness in my life, although a regular attendant at my church. We had a cultured pastor . . . but he did not know about the definite baptism with the Holy Ghost."[14]

In the post–Civil War years, Confederate defeat and the aggressive efforts of northern holiness missionaries brought the movement to the former slave states. Northern holiness literature flooded the region in the 1880s and 1890s. Perfectionists in the North saw the South as a land ripe for mission work. Through the efforts of these northern agents, or what might be called carpetbag holiness missionaries, an indigenous southern crusade soon took shape. By the last decade of the nineteenth century, a nascent southern holiness press was familiarizing tens of thousands of evangelicals both black and white across the land with the nomenclature and religious practices of perfectionism. Readers lent their support to the cause and testified to the purifying power of the Spirit in widely circulated and inexpensive pamphlets, magazines, and journals. At least twenty different perfectionist newspapers in the South served as imagined holiness communities in the 1890s. They advertised revivals and conventions from Kentucky to Florida, carried testimonies and sermons, and lambasted mainline evangelicals for their "lukewarmness."

Because holiness people were less bound by prevailing social codes than members of mainline churches, their meetings were frequently racially integrated, wild, and loud. At the same time, women assumed leadership roles often denied to them in other churches. This openness proved to be one of the most distinguishing marks of both the holiness movement and, later, pentecostalism in the South. One female initiate from North Carolina expressed the sentiments of many when she denounced evangelicals who preached patriarchy. "Oh, how wily the enemy of our soul is," she declared.[15]

By the end of the century, holiness dissenters had grown increasingly hostile to mainline southern denominations. In turn, denominational officials were dismayed by a perceived holiness hubris. These perfectionist disciples, their critics thought, were literally saying that they were holier than average southern Christians. Facing fierce opposition, enthusiasts resentfully left their mother churches by the tens of thousands. They formed new sects and independent congregations throughout the South. Adherents became convinced that mainline churches could never be reformed. Still worse, they thought that society was corrupt beyond redemption and most Americans were headed for eternal perdition. By the turn of the century, nearly every leader and layperson in the southern movement had embraced an end-time theology known as premillennialism. Influenced by protofundamentalists in the United Kingdom and the United States, the faithful expected Christ's return before the millennium, as predicted in the Book of Revelation, to carry the saints into heaven. Those left behind would suffer unimaginable torments. A number of holiness people came to reject social reform and politics of any kind, for according to the calculus of Armageddon, political activity made no sense. In 1899, three short years after William McKinley swept the presidential election, one radical holiness preacher expressed the views of countless others when he lamented, "The world will not stand the truth today, never did, never will, until Jesus sets up His kingdom." The minister had "long ago lost confidence in Aid Societies, Epworth Leagues, and prohibition parties." Nothing could make "this sinful world any better," he concluded, except Jesus.[16] What set the southern movement apart was the nearly unanimous adoption of this ominous eschatology and the wide acceptance of healing and other miraculous signs of the "latter days." Some radical believers in the South defended a host of new baptisms of the Spirit, each more elaborate than the last. Consequently, a climate of expectancy prevailed among the vast majority of southern converts at the dawn of the twentieth century.

In April 1906 an interracial revival meeting on Azusa Street in Los Angeles convened under the leadership of William J. Seymour, a black radical holiness preacher born in Louisiana. Participants spoke in tongues and received the power of the Spirit, Seymour and others declared, just as the Bible foretold of the "last days." Those who spoke in tongues, initiates believed, were channeling the very Spirit of God. Within months, the "Pentecost" in the West had captivated the attention of holiness folk in the South. Initiates from the West Coast revival transmitted the radical doctrines and practices of pentecostalism not only by re-creating the event in the South but also through an elaborate print culture. Literature spread the new message far and wide. Thousands of southern disciples read in newspapers, pamphlets, and books that this revival was the sign of the end they so eagerly anticipated. The miracles and equality of the Spirit reportedly taking place at Azusa attested to the revival's unparalleled significance. In theory and in practice, the Spirit did not discriminate by color or sex. Thousands of southern holiness people were drawn to the ecstatic new movement, entranced by its egalitarian message, the hope of the second advent, and the promise of Holy Ghost empowerment.

Some of the southern holiness faithful, however, refused to accept the doctrine of "tongues speech" and other "gifts of the Spirit." The new pentecostal message compelled converts to concede that their former holiness experiences were not just incomplete but inauthentic. As a result, a vocal minority of holiness pulpits, pamphlets, books, and newspapers issued a torrent of denunciations of "tongues people." Outsiders were unlikely to see what all the fuss was about. The bitter warfare between the two camps seemed to border on the pathological. Yet the stakes were high for those involved. In his classic study *Civilization and Its Discontents,* Sigmund Freud describes what he calls the "narcissism of minor differences," a term that refers to the warfare that envelops closely linked groups. Freud was struck by the constant feuding and bickering that plagued adjoining territories and countries that otherwise shared much more than a common border—like Spain and Portugal, northern and southern Germany, and England and Scotland. As non-tongues-speaking holiness folk and pentecostals berated each other, the intensity of the conflict only grew. In fact, as late as the 1920s there was still so much wrangling going on between pentecostals and their holiness opponents that the journalist Duncan Aikman took note. Judging from the "mutual damnations" regularly appearing in their literature, scoffed Aikman, one would think that all "Holy Rollers" were hell bound. Hostilities between the two camps remained high throughout much of the twentieth century.[17]

Of course, beleaguered holiness followers had reason to be dismayed. The new tongues-speaking pentecostals swept the southern holiness movement largely into their camp. Holiness fellowships in the region—including the Church of the Nazarene and the Wesleyan Methodist Church—registered losses to the exuberant pentecostals from 1906 forward. So strong was the Wesleyan-holiness element that an early leader in the Church of God (Cleveland) acknowledged that "there have been many instances of churches, not Holiness, receiving the Holy Ghost during this Latter Rain." Yet these were few "in comparison to the number of Holiness people who were ready to receive the blessing."[18] Indeed, a large percentage of radical holiness zealots in the South had come to identify the new premillennial sect as the sole bearer of gospel truth.

Such extravagant claims rarely went unchallenged. Pentecostals would face opposition from mainline evangelicals and other southerners. Thus the new movement took root in a storm of controversy, much like holiness before it. Fiercely antipentecostal southerners lashed out at the new converts' peculiar beliefs and practices. As "tongues" revivals spread across the South, journalists satirized the bizarre antics of the faithful, and Methodist and Baptist ministers warned their flocks of the malicious designs of "tonguers." In 1910 a skeptic from Gaston County, North Carolina, summed up the fears of many when he charged that questionable disciples who claimed to possess gifts of the spirit had descended on his village, leading men's wives astray. This was little more than hell-hatched hypnotism, he railed in a local paper.[19] For pentecostals' many breaches of racial, social, and religious etiquette, their meeting tents were frequently burned down, and they were shot at, abused in the press, and jailed. But enthusiasts rejoiced at their persecution. Far from dampening their spirits, it seemed to confirm their election and anointing. When no enemies rose up to oppose them, they actively drew mainline Protestants into debate.

Believers were typically antagonistic toward other evangelicals and whoever else stood in their way. Holiness and pentecostal devotees opposed anything they deemed worldly, formal, spiritually lifeless, or constricting. The roots of this religious movement, popularly considered quintessentially southern, actually lay outside the South. Northern holiness missionaries first acquainted many southerners, both white and black, with perfectionism, and pentecostals in the West subsequently introduced the formative doctrine of "tongues" to the region. Moreover, the beliefs of first-generation adherents in the South often had more in common with those of other initiates in the North and West than with those of their nonpentecostal southern neighbors. In addition, southern advocates seldom identified with the shibboleths of sectionalism. Their literature never championed the Lost Cause, so prominent in the secular and denominational press. Their almost progressive views on race and gender in the late Victorian South contrasted starkly with those espoused by others. Not surprisingly, holiness people and pentecostals came to think of themselves as part of a larger religious family or a translocal community that obliterated many sectional, class, and racial barriers.

This makes the twentieth-century social and religious pilgrimage of believers all the more fascinating. Southern holiness disciples and pentecostals still watched and waited for Jesus' return, yet they turned their energies to more conservative mainline pursuits. Over the course of the century, many white stalwarts transformed themselves from religious and social pariahs into middle-class Republicans. The faithful eventually came to identify theological modernism as the work of Satan and a clear sign of the world's end. Some found common ground with fundamentalists on the evolution controversy. Other, later pentecostals crusaded against communism and denounced the cultural and sexual revolutions of the 1960s. Scores entered the political arena in response to the legalization of abortion, the Supreme Court ban on school prayer, and a range of other moral issues.

The fragile sanctified interracialism of the early period had vanished by the 1920s. At the peak of the civil rights movement, most white followers either ignored or condemned Martin Luther King Jr. Even with the passage of the Voting Rights Act, African American adherents would largely remain apart from politics entirely. Meanwhile, the gender equality that seemed possible after Azusa did not materialize either. Southern pentecostals discarded many of their more distinctive beliefs and traits and moved slowly into the American evangelical mainstream. Following World War II they gradually became more like other conservative Protestants. Ironically, white followers would eventually identify with the same social and political conservatism they once bitterly denounced.

For all the political and cultural changes that took place over the twentieth century, many southern holiness folk and pentecostals are still, like early enthusiasts, remarkably innovative and confrontational. Unconstrained by tradition, they use the latest satellite and communication technology to spread their message worldwide. They were pioneers of both black and white gospel music. And more recently, since the 1990s, some in the South have even looked to their unconventional roots and reclaimed their interracial and egalitarian past. But how did these and other significant transformations take place, and what would they mean for the political and religious landscape of the South and the nation? The answers to those questions reveal the changing shape of the movement in the South over the last one hundred years.

ONE 🦋

Angels from the North

GEORGE WATSON FOUGHT for the Confederacy. An adventurous religious seeker, he drifted north after the war, where he received his ministerial training. Full of zeal, Watson returned south in the late 1860s and began working with the newly arrived northern Methodist Church. His northern contacts taught him the Wesleyan doctrine of holiness, how one might be free from sin in this life. Years later he vividly recalled the abuse unreconstructed Confederates heaped on him in those perilous years: "You have been down in South Carolina, and now you come back here and turn Yankee." Watson, a leading southern holiness preacher by the 1870s, had a cousin named George, whom neighbors called "white George." They called Watson "black George," he later remembered, "because I belonged to a 'black Republican church.'"[1] Watson's experience was not unusual. A native son, he had embraced a religious movement that numerous mid-nineteenth-century southerners considered alien, bizarre, even dangerous.

Although the holiness movement and its successor, pentecostalism, are often considered quintessentially southern, both originated outside the region. Holiness theology, in fact, gained

Virginia native and Confederate veteran George D. Watson
was an early promoter of holiness in the South.

no substantial southern following until the postbellum period.
Theological perfectionism and entire sanctification (the holiness doctrine of a postconversion, instantaneous second work
of grace that cleansed believers of sin) claimed amazingly few
adherents south of the Mason-Dixon line in the years between
1840 and 1885. Indeed, the modern holiness movement, which
grew out of the northern perfectionist upheaval of the Second
Great Awakening, developed deep sectional roots. Owing to
antagonisms over slavery, reform, and theology, the vast majority of southerners remained completely unfamiliar with holi-

ness or else openly hostile to it. As holiness took on different and new meanings, the movement made modest gains in the region, but only after the Civil War. Even these later gains, however, were curtailed by southerners' suspicions of the northern origins of holiness and a lingering sense of the foreignness of perfectionism. Cultural and religious factors that hindered and discredited holiness in the antebellum and Reconstruction years served as the background to later positive developments. The activities of northern missionaries and evangelists before and immediately after the war merit special attention. The crucial role played by a few adventurous southerners who came in direct contact with northern holiness proved critical to the budding southern holiness movement.

In late September 1872 the *Knoxville Daily Chronicle* heralded two events that illustrate the changing landscape of post–Civil War southern religion. The first was something of a northern invasion, albeit one inspired by religious, not military, goals. Northern Methodist ministers descended on Knoxville, wrote a wide-eyed reporter, to preach the "fundamental idea of Christian Holiness."[2] These eminent evangelists came south with the sole purpose of spreading the doctrine of entire sanctification. One might live above willful sin, claimed the newly arrived perfectionist preachers. In an instant God could cleanse the saved from all unrighteousness. Merely regenerate souls might become saints of God.

Although local observers were little troubled by what seemed to be novel theology, many were disturbed by what they feared were the invaders' political and ecclesiastical ambitions. Detractors worried that such emissaries of holiness were in fact paid agents of the government with more sinister designs in mind. Their anxieties were well warranted. Relations between the northern and southern Methodists had been strained since the General Conference of the Methodist Episcopal Church divided over the issue of slavery in 1844. Then after the Civil War the two denominations became locked in a rancorous battle over churches and souls. The East Tennessee Conference of the Methodist Episcopal Church, South (MECS), fought a protracted war to maintain its property and membership in the face of competition from an increasingly aggressive northern Methodism.

The northern National Holiness Association, founded in 1867, whose leaders organized the 1872 Knoxville meeting, immediately assumed the defensive. The president of the association, John Inskip, had served as a chaplain for the Union Army. But he took great pains to assure southerners that he held no sectional prejudices. The *Knoxville Daily Chronicle* concurred. One reporter suggested that the revival could go far toward eradicating regional animus.[3] A former Confederate officer in attendance seconded the reporter's opinion. Though skeptical at first, the ex-rebel eventually embraced the spirited revival. "This work has done more to bridge the 'bloody chasm,'" he claimed, "than all the acts of Congress, conferences, and synods." Their most pressing fears allayed, participants nearly forgot the gruesome conflict that had divided the nation not a decade before.[4]

The outdoor gathering attracted more than six thousand worshippers, both black and white. Northern and southern Methodists were present as well as some Baptists, Presbyterians, and a handful of Episcopalians. They traveled from as far away as Boston, Philadelphia, Ohio, Kentucky, Georgia, and South Carolina to participate in this intersectional and interdenominational event. Although the perfectionist message preached at Knoxville was unknown to the majority of southerners of all denominations, most were intimately familiar with the intense evangelical style of their northern exhorters. To the throngs of southern participants the revival resembled an old-

An 1864 print depicting the graves of Civil War dead, Knoxville, Tennessee.

style camp meeting, complete with emotional conversions and the sorts of spiritual exercises that had shaken the southern frontier roughly seventy years before. For some southerners the Knoxville revival resurrected in style if not in content these meetings of the distant past. When Asbury Lowrey, a Methodist divine from Ohio, took to the pulpit, one onlooker declared, "With this tall form towering over the concourse . . . we saw depicted in imagination the camps of the early pioneers of Methodism, when Peter Cartwright and his colleagues carried the banner of the cross into the wilderness."[5]

A few days after Lowrey's appearance, Peter Cartwright, known fondly as "God's plowman," died. The *Knoxville Daily Chronicle* reported this second major event with a strong sense of sorrow and a deep appreciation of Cartwright's ministry on the Kentucky frontier. His obituary reminded southerners of his countless converts and his ameliorating impact on an otherwise lawless, violent society. This once young, vigorous preacher had done much to Christianize the upcountry, his mourners recalled. Perhaps, too, they ruminated on the elderly Cartwright, the curmudgeonly, jeremiad-preaching patriarch who had boldly condemned slavery as sinful and more recently challenged the growing cultural materialism of Methodists, North and South. How could Methodists be good stewards, he once asked, while adorning their bodies "with all this costly and extravagant dressing?" He also lamented the neglect of family prayer gatherings and class meetings and yearned for the days when men and women at revivals had been uninhibited by false proprieties. In his autobiography Cartwright remembered the religious enthusiasm and bodily exercises that had obliterated class distinctions in the revivals half a century before. "To see those proud young gentlemen and young ladies, dressed in their silks, jewelry, and prunella, from top to toe, take the jerks" and fall to the ground had given him immense pleasure. But such ecstasies were no more. Like others of his generation, the aged prophet saw mammonism and moral decline all around him.[6]

Cartwright's disdain might appear to be little more than the bitter reflections of a patriarch near the end of his life. Yet his fears and those of his clerical colleagues were so closely correlated with the changing character of southern denominations, especially Methodism, that they must have been well founded. Beginning in the Jacksonian era, the Methodist Church in the South had undergone dramatic changes. The growing wealth of its members, the decline in church discipline, and the increasing distaste for impassioned revivals all contributed to the shift. By the 1830s, southern evangelicalism was well established throughout the region. Once on the radical margins of society, Baptist and Methodist sects rose to ascendancy and began claiming the same social status that once belonged solely to their sectarian betters. So sweeping was the transformation, argues historian Nathan Hatch, that by the 1840s Methodists "had undertaken their own pilgrimage to respectability."[7]

A Methodist minister from Georgia became one of the more ardent critics of the new southern evangelicalism. Lovick Pierce had been a wealthy slaveholder. Accordingly, his critique of Methodists was not that they had grown rich or that wealth in itself was wrong. What disturbed him deeply, rather, were the materialistic values now dominating the lives of believers. At the age of ninety-four, only a year before his death in 1879, Pierce published a scathing attack on southern Methodism. Like Cartwright, he castigated churchgoers for their aristocratic pretensions. A new upwardly mobile middle class within the denomination followed fashion, rented pews in church, and softened their stance on church discipline. What accounted for this rampant backsliding? Pierce declared that the southern Methodist Church had fallen away as soon as its members ceased to seek and profess holiness, or, more specifically, entire sanctification. Methodists had neglected the cardinal Wesleyan doctrine of a second work of grace or perfect love, which freed the individual from sin. The General Conference of the MECS confirmed the suspicions of Pierce and others. "We fear," declared church officials, "that the doctrine of perfect love . . . is too much overlooked and neglected."[8]

This was not just the state of things in the postbellum era. For years Pierce had held special morning holiness sessions at camp meetings in various southern states. At least since the 1840s these meetings had been poorly attended, a circumstance that increasingly angered him. No one showed interest in holiness any longer. Most of the southerners Pierce encountered were concerned only with what would keep them out of hell. As an example of how inattentive Methodists had become to entire sanctification, he recounted how one of his charges had ducked out of a morning holiness gathering. After refusing to attend several sunrise meetings, the layman had jumped at the chance to view a sideshow just down the road from the campsite, where he was treated to the spectacle of "a full grown monkey in fantastic dress" and a prancing Shetland pony.[9] Pierce was disgusted. Indeed, the cause of Christian perfection fared poorly when upstaged by banal curiosities.

Theological and cultural opposition to holiness in the South proved even more detrimental. The doctrine and practice of perfection met its greatest impediment when many Methodists and most other evangelicals in the region held that there was no complete salvation from sin in this life.[10] Pierce found such opposition particularly galling while he was living in a Hard-Shell Baptist stronghold of Georgia. His perfectionist doctrines were incredible to these conservative Calvinists, who stressed the power of sin, imputed righteousness, double predestination, and eternal security.[11] By the 1840s, the vast majority of southern Methodists, if they believed in sanctification at all, considered it a slow process. Sanctification, wrote the Methodist theologian Thomas L. Boswell, "is developed by a gradual growth under the gracious influence of the Spirit." This divine work, however powerful, did not eliminate a tendency to sin.[12] As a result of the prevalence of such views, the doctrine of holiness as a distinct second work of grace rapidly became a rarity in the South. Pierce eagerly attended the National Holiness meeting at Knoxville in 1872. He also threw his support behind northern efforts to revive holiness in the South. Yet in the last forty years of his life he witnessed little that lifted his spirits.

Prospects had not always been so bleak. In the days of Pierce's early ministry, holiness proponents were not uncommon. Prior to the 1840s, some southern participants in the Second Great Awakening recounted seeking and obtaining entire

Georgia Methodist and champion of Christian perfection Lovick Pierce.

sanctification. Methodists scattered from Mississippi to South Carolina described their "second blessing" experiences in their diaries and in denominational journals. Of course, since the dawn of American Methodism, the movement's pioneers, including Francis Asbury, Thomas Coke, and Jesse Lee, had encouraged followers to seek perfection after salvation.[13] Perfection, as John Wesley formulated it in eighteenth-century England, was the doctrinal cornerstone of the denomination.

Like most transplanted traditions, however, Methodism in the South developed to suit the circumstances of the region.

Frontier Baptist and Methodist preachers as well as laity modified their theology and practice according to the needs of an isolated rural society. Many southern evangelical ministers, especially in the upcountry, itinerated from one church to another so as to serve larger areas. With contact so infrequent between preacher and parishioners, discipleship as well as theological education lagged. Sporadic camp meetings were held, but they emphasized conversion to the exclusion of other religious works. Moreover, the evangelicalism promoted at such revivals avoided theological subtleties and simplified doctrine in order to win the largest possible number of converts. If the Cane Ridge revival was a great influence on southern evangelicalism, that was because its modus operandi had a pragmatic, ecumenical cast. At mass religious meetings ministers laid aside anything that divided their listeners and concentrated instead on the basic tenets of the faith. Conversion became the hallmark of homogenized southern evangelicalism. Life for the faithful was split into two distinct states, unsaved and saved.[14] In this religious atmosphere ministers and laity lost interest in more complicated schemes of salvation. Hence at century's end a Mississippi Methodist minister recalled once having heard his denomination's impassioned founding fathers preach the second blessing, but since then, he sorrowfully observed, "little was said of this 'great depositum of Methodism.'"[15]

Still other, broader religious and cultural factors impeded the spread of holiness in the Old South. Evangelicalism had been growing in numbers and influence since the beginning of the nineteenth century. By the 1830s the Baptist and Methodist denominations had outdistanced their religious competitors by converting the majority of southern Christians, black and white. The Baptist-Methodist hegemony amounted to an evangelical orthodoxy in the region.[16] Even those who were not particularly religious were nonetheless conversant with evangelicalism. "None of my father's family were members of the church," wrote one Georgian. "All, however, from force of their surroundings, affiliated with the sentiments and prejudices of the Baptists." The South became an evangelical culture in just such a broad sense. According to one historian of the region, individuals "who rarely attended church and who lived far outside the evangelicals' moral code found ways to express their belief in the virtues of the dominant religion."[17]

Some of the basic elements of this evangelical cultural system bear closer inspection. Broad commonalities between Baptists, Methodists, and Presbyterians tended to overshadow their theological and cultural differences. This was true not only for whites but for blacks as well. Collecting data on antebellum Mississippi in the early 1880s, Clarence Deming noted the ease with which African Americans switched from Baptist to Methodist churches. Theological and creedal considerations played little or no role in denominational allegiance, Deming surmised. There were no doubt significant differences between groups such as Antimission Baptists, Disciples of Christ, and primitive Methodists and their mainline counterparts. Yet these distinctions are less surprising than the overall similarities. Baptists and Methodists, both steeped in continental pietistic traditions, and to a lesser extent Presbyterians, elevated religious experience and emphasized conviction of sin. The fact of human sinfulness was taken for granted by most southern evangelicals. Southerners, whether Arminian or Calvinist, also maintained a strict interpretation of the Bible and an overarching theory of human depravity. This so shaped the collective religious consciousness of antebellum southern evangelicals that they grew increasingly suspicious of human agency and perfectibility.[18] Calvinistic southerners, soon on the defensive against the North over slavery, also maintained a pessimism about humankind that seriously inhibited perfectionism.

In the early 1940s the journalist and social critic W. J. Cash perceived a distinctive Calvinistic trajectory in the nineteenth-century South. Somewhat overstating his case, he asserted, "As the pressure of the Yankee increased, the whole South, including the Methodists, would move toward a position of thorough-going Calvinism in feeling if not formal theology." Embattled against abolitionist radicals and northern freethinkers, the South lashed out. Slavery locked Calvinism in place in the region. So, argued Cash, owing to both external and internal pressures, the white South committed itself to a religious system at odds with theological perfection. Few scholars today defend Cash's notion of a monolithic South.[19] But some of his most vehement criticisms are not without substance. His "savage ideal"—depicting southerners as bloodthirsty, rapacious barbarians—is far too sweeping, but his argument about the growth of inflexible southern Calvinism, if exaggerated, contains a kernel of truth.

A suspicion of human agency in political and social matters permeated southern evangelicalism from the onset of sectional strife at least until the emergence of the New South. Basic notions about society and the individual divided North from South. Opposition to northern methods of revivalism clearly illustrates this outlook. A number of southerners repudiated the "new measures" which Charles Grandison Finney, the leading evangelist of the nineteenth-century North, employed to conduct successful revivals. Finney's adoption of the "anxious bench"—which served as a sort of witness stand—his encouraging women to testify at meetings, and his highly rationalized, structured, time-bound revivals scandalized conservative southerners. Finney's theology, too, appeared novel, with its fusion of Calvinism and Arminianism. He stressed the omnipotence and moral government of God while preaching the perfectibility of human nature and society. Not only did the hyper-Calvinistic Hard-Shell Baptist fringe in the southern up-country reject Finney's methods, but so too did many mainline southern evangelicals, who worried that Finney's techniques relied far too heavily on human instrumentality, virtually ignoring the dependence of the faithful on God.

Mainline evangelicals voiced the same fears about voluntary associations which promoted human means. A Georgia pastor echoed others' criticisms of secular temperance organizations, which he thought relied exclusively on hollow associations, pledges, and legislation instead of the church and a sovereign God. Sectarian groups evinced a similar ethos. Antimission Baptists objected to northern benevolence on much the same grounds and denounced as unbiblical the new evangelicalism gaining adherents in the North. Hyper-Calvinists in the South embraced an intensely literalistic, deterministic theology that contrasted sharply with a growing northern Arminianism.[20] Differences over doctrine soon led to religious warfare.

In the antebellum years, southern Presbyterians quickly entered the fray. In the 1830s theological battles in the North raged between New and Old School Presbyterians. Adam's guilt, argued the New School camp, was not imputed to humanity. Guilt was personal and relative to each individual's sins. The New School also emphasized activism and a faith in the ability of humankind to alter history for the better. The conservative Old School, a powerful force in Dixie, countered by upholding the doctrine of original sin and a dire skepticism about human progress. Southern Presbyterians sided with the conservatives, whose theology was more compatible with the white South's social needs, especially the maintenance of slavery.[21] No one represents this point of view better than James Henley Thornwell, preeminent Presbyterian theologian and sectional apologist, whose beliefs typify the conservative theology of the South as well as its sociopolitical outlook. His writings brim with allusions to absolute human depravity and the weight of sin, a fatalism that is central to his work. "No man," he wrote, "can bring himself to feel the sinfulness of his own nature." Under the influence of the pessimists' Brothers Grimm, Thomas Hobbes and John Calvin, Thornwell was intensely skeptical about the inherent goodness of the human species and viewed various perfectionist schemes as disorderly at best and demonic at worst.[22] Millennial and utopian chimeras, proclaimed Thornwell, required either total ignorance or willful delusion on the part of their advocates.

Perhaps the starkest example of the role Calvinism played in the prewar South is evident in the region's justice system and in the rigid honor code that was so fundamental to the culture. Fears of social disintegration resulting from slave insurrection on the one hand and abolitionism on the other, though often more imagined than real, were omnipresent. Control and order were paramount in the slaveholding states. Key religious and political leaders employed a modified Calvinism to uphold the rigid social order. For instance, the influential Presbyterian theologian Robert Lewis Dabney's penal satisfaction theory of the atonement greatly influenced the retributive justice system of the South. Dabney emphasized the abiding perils of sin and the necessity of humble expiation. Transgressions, both religious and secular, had to be met with severe penalties. This being the case, antebellum southerners, much more so than northerners, enforced intense discipline in all areas of life. They distrusted human institutions and human nature, and that skepticism informed the region's legal doctrine.[23] The deep-rooted commitment of the white South to slavery and the moral uncertainties that plagued the peculiar institution made perfectionism seem ludicrous.[24] Far from being perfectible, society and the individual had to be morally policed with extreme vigilance.

The South's rigid code of honor also made it nearly impossible for the doctrine of holiness to thrive in the region. Southern white men, ready to meet any challenge to their character with violence and retribution, were not disposed to the subtle pieties of holiness.[25] Even southern evangelicals, who once offered a viable alternative to the dictates of musky chauvinism, reconciled with honor culture and reworked their faith to suit the demands of southern manhood. Second-generation evangelicals accepted that when necessary, violence was a legitimate recourse.[26] It is not surprising, then, that the early northern holiness movement met mostly with indifference or fierce opposition in Dixie.

While the theology and social viewpoints of most southerners became increasingly Calvinistic and patriarchal, much of evangelicalism in the North took on a remarkably different shape. The prewar northern holiness revival is indicative of this divergence. The success of northern holiness owes much to one woman, Phoebe Worrall Palmer. A devout Methodist from New York, Palmer struggled with the idea of perfection throughout the 1830s. Grieved by the death of three of her infant children, she sought solace in her quest for religious purity. Amid the expectant atmosphere of the Second Great Awakening, scores of other northerners—including Charles Grandison Finney, Asa Mahan, Theodore Dwight Weld, and Timothy Merritt—turned to the patriarchs of Methodism and to an assortment of perfectionist theories. John Wesley, John Fletcher, and more recently Adam Clarke proposed that believers could live above sin through asceticism and pietistic devotion. Although Wesley's theology was never systematic, and he held various opinions through his life on Christian perfection, he did eventually come to emphasize the instantaneousness of sanctification. In his *Plain Account of Christian Perfection,* later generations had what they found to be a clear exposition of immediate perfection.

Wesley was never as narrow, culturally or religiously, as future generations of Methodists would be. In fact, he read widely on religious and nonreligious subjects. He especially enjoyed the work of certain Roman Catholic theologians and drew inspiration from mystical devotional literature. What seems to have been most important for later Methodists, however, was Wesley's elevation of personal religious experience to new heights. The English divine came to the conclusion that believers could be so completely devoted to God as to experience a "total death" to willful sin. Yet Wesley never codified Christian perfection and, by the ambiguities of his interpretation, left room for a wide range of opinions.[27]

Phoebe Palmer altered Wesley's views. The optimistic and utilitarian environment of the post-Puritan North greatly influenced her work. Consequently, her popular doctrine of perfection took a pragmatic turn. Palmer framed holiness as a state immediately attainable by all believers through an act of faith. Gone was the long, anxious struggle Wesley envisioned leading up to sanctification. Palmer's practical "shorter way" to holiness, as it was called, involved a total devotion of one's self and possessions to God. Taking Jesus' words from Matthew 23:19, "the altar that sanctifieth the gift," Palmer imagined that anyone who offered a full consecration of self would be sanctified completely. It was a thoroughly logical, quid pro quo theological formulation that bore a marked resemblance to earlier New England covenantal theologies. Her practical theology was also novel. She employed a language of the Spirit and of Pentecost that stressed the urgency of the age and pressed men as well as women toward religious activism. Sanctification made believers useful and empowered them for service. Her theology was firmly rooted in a spirit of Yankee optimism amenable to social reform.[28]

In the 1830s and 1840s other pious northerners contributed to the holiness revival. Most of them believed that Christ would return to earth after a glorious millennium initiated by personal reform and the pursuit of social perfection. This postmillennialism encapsulated northern evangelicals' optimistic view of the world. Antebellum visionaries considered the millennium a period of time necessary for evangelical ascendancy to occur. And the millennium would be a clear sign of the progress of civilization.[29] The work of evangelicals also featured an immediatist message. At the same time that William Lloyd Garrison and other radical antislavery advocates were calling for the immediate abolition of slavery, northern perfectionists declared that Christians could be completely cured of sin in a single moment. In 1839 the Methodist preacher and writer Timothy Merritt began publishing the *Guide to Christian Perfection,* a paper devoted to the instantaneous attainment of sanctification. Also during this period Oberlin College emerged as a center of reformed holiness. Charles Finney, professor and then president of the college, emphasized the law of the gospel and the believer's duty to consecrate oneself fully to God. In this vein the Presbyterian minister William E. Boardman published his highly influential work *The Higher Christian Life* at the peak of the northern revival in 1858. Boardman's book, more than any other at that time, spread holiness doctrines broadly among non-Methodist evangelicals in the North and in England.[30]

Few traveled more widely or influenced more northern evangelicals than did Phoebe Palmer. From 1840 until her death in 1874, she conducted a prayer and fellowship meeting in her New York City home called the Tuesday Meeting for the

Promotion of Holiness. Here she taught her "shorter way" doctrine and helped foster an ever-growing community of holiness converts. Unlike John Wesley, Palmer contended that public testimony was critical to attaining entire sanctification. Strongly influenced by pietism, Palmer encouraged those at her Tuesday meetings to take the floor and make public the many failures and triumphs of their private religious lives.[31] Thomas C. Upham, a pioneer American psychologist and influential nineteenth-century philosopher, championed Palmer's meetings. Soon after experiencing entire sanctification under Palmer's ministry, Upham opened his home for the same kind of therapeutic meetings Palmer was holding. The seven books Palmer published between 1845 and 1865 received wide circulation, and she edited the influential holiness newspaper *Guide to Holiness* at the height of its popularity.[32] Holiness enthusiasm spread. It is little wonder that other major reformers flocked to Palmer's gatherings in pursuit of personal and social purity. The movement followed the paths of Yankee migration through western New England, upstate New York, western Ohio, and Michigan. It could be found in all the centers of northern reform.[33]

Although Palmer avoided direct participation in abolitionism and women's rights, her perfectionism was nonetheless politically explosive among her followers. Her theology of unlimited potential influenced scores of reformers in the North and in England, including Harriet Beecher Stowe, and later Catherine Booth and Frances Willard.[34] Palmer's views, understandably, were less offensive to southerners than were those of many of her more radical contemporaries. Still, she never gained a significant, cohesive following in the slave states. Certainly Palmer's easy, short path to perfection struck some southerners as overly simplistic and out of step with Wesley's teachings.[35] Roughly twenty years after her death, the southern Methodist

Popular author and teacher Phoebe Palmer (1807–1874). Palmer's magazine, *The Guide to Holiness,* and her Tuesday Meetings for the Promotion of Holiness, held in her New York City home, did much to usher thousands into the holiness movement.

editor W. P. Harrison recalled Palmer as a "remarkable woman" with noble intentions. Yet Harrison sensed fanaticism in her writings. She bordered on Pelagianism, he argued, emphasizing human agency over and against the divine. Accordingly, she gave "great and real cause for anxiety upon the part of those who watch over the welfare of the [southern Methodist] Church."[36]

Palmer did have scattered followers in the antebellum South, albeit meager in number by comparison to the North.[37]

One newspaper in particular—the *Weekly Message* of Greensboro, North Carolina—enthusiastically adopted Palmer's holiness theories. The southern Methodist minister Sidney D. Bumpass established the paper in the early 1850s. After his death, his wife, Frances, took up management of the weekly and continued publishing it until 1872. Articles outlining entire sanctification, the possibility of "freedom from sin," and the virtues of perfect love regularly filled its pages. Holiness, declared one writer in the paper, is attainable in this life. But he feared that many in the region did "not like the word *perfection*." It is doubtful that the *Weekly Message* ever reached as large a readership as did other mainline southern evangelical papers. Indeed, it was for the most part an anomaly in the slaveholding South.[38]

Holiness remained marginal owing to the movement's northern origins and emphases. The holiness revival in the North, essentially an urban movement, was without a cause in the rural antebellum South.[39] The widely dispersed holiness enthusiasts in the southern states never developed communities like those of Boston, Philadelphia, and New York. Advocates of holiness in the South, with the exception of Sidney D. Bumpass, also failed to publish a newspaper or journal that might have helped promote perfection in the region. Holiness gatherings were weak or nonexistent, and there were no prominent southern holiness authors comparable to northern ones. Reflecting on the holiness cause in Arkansas during the mid-1850s, a Methodist preacher reported the bleak situation to a northern holiness journal. "Not a single minister of God within this state," he lamented, "has yet attained this grace [of entire sanctification]." The minister yearned to "'sit in heavenly places in Christ Jesus' with all those who have enjoyed and do enjoy this blessing in Boston and New York."[40]

The sectional crisis looming over the horizon thwarted

such dreams. The Civil War would completely devastate the cause of holiness in the South. With the exception of the *Weekly Message,* perfectionism received scant attention in the region's embattled denominational press. Meanwhile, the war cut off Palmer's *Guide to Holiness* from its hundreds of southern subscribers and broke vital ties with northern holiness allies.[41]

Between 1840 and 1865 the South became an inhospitable place for northern ideas, especially those promoted by avowed abolitionists. The South did not quite impose an intellectual blockade, as Clement Eaton asserted, but most white southerners had little truck with the North's social utopian theories and its many "-isms."[42] For example, the *Quarterly Review,* the premier scholarly journal of the MECS, never once even mentioned the subject of entire sanctification in the fourteen years leading up to the Civil War.[43] Assailed by northern reformers, leading southern whites succeeded in censoring northern literature and concepts they deemed subversive, including perfectionism. "Suppression of antislavery materials in the mails, the denial of free speech in the academies, colleges, and pulpits, and the general suspicion of strangers and new ideas," writes the historian Bertram Wyatt-Brown, "were all part of the popular reaction to northern criticisms."[44]

There were obvious reasons for stifling free thought and new religious theories. The connection between the doctrine of entire sanctification and abolitionism was not merely imagined by fire-eating southerners. Christian perfectionism and the quest for personal and social holiness often undergirded ecclesiastical abolitionism. Antislavery ministers such as Luther Myrick, Beriah Green, and William Goodell viewed the abolition of slavery as a kind of metaphor for a larger program: the eradication of individual and social iniquities. Many evangelicals in the North came to regard social problems as simply the outcome of personal sin.[45] Opponents of such views, though, bristled at the pious presumptions of these moral purifiers. Consequently, dissension within American religious institutions prefigured the sectional crisis. Denominations split along abolitionist fissures. At a deep level the conflict revolved around perfectionism. And while the antislavery sects founded in the 1840s—Free Baptists, Unionists, Franckean Lutherans, and Wesleyan Methodists—differed on the basics of theology and church government, they were firmly united in their commitment to social and personal holiness.[46] They all actively sought the sanctification of society and the individual.

Moreover, abolitionism was not a distant, harmless curiosity in the mid-nineteenth-century South. Abolitionists within the region ignited conflicts wherever they ventured, while the southern press regularly published pieces on the perils of northern radicalism. When Wesleyan Methodist missionaries infiltrated North Carolina and Virginia in the 1840s and 1850s, the public uproar there rose to a fever pitch. The Wesleyan Methodists constituted a perfectionist protest against slavery and the Methodist episcopacy.[47] Of all the leading American denominations, Methodism had at one time taken the strongest stance against slavery. That changed, however, as the church grew more affluent in the American South and adapted to the customs and traditions of the region. A group of angry antislavery Methodists in New York voiced their disgust with the changing church and bolted from the denomination in 1843. Orange Scott, one of the founders of the new church, raged against complacent politicians and slaveholding Methodists. It was nothing to the nation's leaders, Scott claimed, "that two and a half millions of American citizens are groaning in chains! . . . What a paradox we are to surrounding nations—and what a stench in the nostrils of the Almighty!" America was crippled by sin, charged Scott. Soon after the Wesleyan Methodists organized their new church, leading ministers established a periodical titled *The True Wesleyan*. The journal promoted the abolitionist cause, condemned accommodationist Methodists, and called for bold missionaries to take the antislavery cause into the South.[48] Several northern ministers enthusiastically answered the call.

Adam Crooks, a young, ambitious Wesleyan pastor from upstate New York, traveled to North Carolina in 1847 to begin mission work in Guilford County. Crooks, who claimed entire sanctification in 1840, held meetings wherever he could and propagated a message of personal and social holiness. He shepherded a small yet devoted following. Quakers in this area had some history of antislavery activity, but their efforts scarcely matched in zeal and combativeness the work of the newcomers. Jarvis C. Bacon and Jesse McBride from New York and an Indiana native, Daniel Worth, came after Crooks and trekked through Virginia and North Carolina. All preached emancipation and temperance and distributed reformist literature among interested parties. As word of their activities spread, threats and mob violence dogged the missionaries from one community to another. Crooks, sneeringly described by one local paper as a "typical Yankee," was the first to face local hostility. Residents of Jamestown tarred and feathered his image just months after his arrival. Plans to lynch him and his compatriots, however, never materialized despite repeated threats.[49]

In lieu of extralegal retributions, county officials turned to the courts. More than a decade before, northern reformers and proslavery advocates in the South had clashed violently over the abolitionists' campaign to distribute literature through the mail. This struggle served to unify much of the southern clergy along anti-abolitionist lines.[50] Not surprisingly, then, powerful politicians and newspaper editors in Virginia and North Carolina reasoned that the best way to eliminate these sanctimonious missionaries would be to charge them with distributing malicious literature. Authorities arrested Jarvis Bacon for circulating antislavery sermons and Frederick Douglass's autobiography, while Daniel Worth was later charged with dispersing Hinton Helper's *Impending Crisis in the South* along with other incendiary publications.[51] Regardless of how damaging these charges were, the Wesleyans' cause was hurt most when local officials linked the missionaries' work to a Virginia slave insurrection which occurred in August 1851. Local papers anathematized Bacon and the others for provoking the violent revolt. Their radical perfectionist doctrines, observers believed, had instigated the episode. With the missionaries' work damaged beyond all repair, they retreated North in the years preceding the Civil War.[52]

Because radical perfectionist doctrines like those espoused by the Wesleyan Methodists were so closely tied to the antislavery cause, southerners were quick to reject both the political and the religious zealotry of their adversaries. The secular and spiritual goals of the northern abolitionists were foreign, they reasoned. Even worse, asserted southerners on the defensive, the abolitionists intended to remake southern society in the image of a "godless" urban reform utopia.

Protectors of the slaveholding South saw little that they thought qualified as genuine religion among northern reformers. Their beliefs were rank heresy as far as most white southerners were concerned. Abolitionists made reason their God and replaced the doctrine of original sin with a theory of universal human equality, their detractors declared.[53] The northern reformers' message was almost uniformly rejected. Abolitionists who intended to convince southern slaveholders of the sinfulness of slavery were overwhelmingly unsuccessful. Most slaveholders saw nothing fundamentally wrong with their peculiar institution. Moreover, since the 1830s key southern intellectuals and religious leaders had developed a sophisticated apology for the practice. This intellectual bulwark proved remarkably steadfast against northern onslaughts.[54] James Henley Thornwell reflected the robust conscience of his peers when he denounced abolitionists as "atheists, socialists, communists, red republicans, [and] jacobins," while defending slaveholders as "the friends of order and regulated freedom." Southern opposition peaked in the decade before the Civil War. From the pulpit and within the denominational press, proto-Confederates—including the Presbyterian ministers Benjamin Morgan Palmer and Robert Lewis Dabney, and the Georgia Methodist bishop George Foster Pierce—excoriated all northern theories of human perfectibility. The illusions of progress and perfection, wrote the Methodist minister Henry Bascom, were misleading millions.[55] On the eve of the Civil War, the *Macon Daily Telegraph* published a crude burlesque, "The New Catechism: Now Generally in Use in Northern Churches." The parody first appeared in the *Boston Post,* but its racist logic appealed equally to white Georgians: "Q—What do the Holy Scriptures teach? A—They teach us niggerhood to preach, It's nigger! to keep bawling. Q—Sanctification, what is that? What, when and how begins? A—It's niggerism, sir, throughout, And bides a host of sins."[56]

Such metaphysical Confederates profoundly influenced their contemporaries. Southern journalists employed the logic of religious fire-eaters when they responded to spiritualism. Southerners perceived that northern spiritualists, much like holiness advocates, allied themselves with the most radical and "irrational" Yankee reformers. Reporters in the South frequently attacked spiritualists, making little distinction between their theological and secular aims.[57] White southerners believed themselves to be under siege. Hence members of southern denominations fumed when religious outsiders offered moral instruction.[58] This spirit of suspicion and hostility prevailed up to and during the Civil War. What little existed of the southern movement had always been dependent on the ideas and resources of northern holiness advocates. With the onset of war, that support quickly dwindled away.

The Civil War was as disruptive to southern denominations as it was to other social structures. Church services became infrequent during the war, and episcopal supervision west of the Mississippi diminished. Federal troops seized the southern Methodist Church's central publishing house in Nashville in February 1862, and Union Army forces captured numerous other denominational presses in the years that followed. When the Civil War broke out in 1861, the MECS was the largest and wealthiest denomination in the region. By 1866 church membership had fallen by more than 100,000. Severe financial losses, damage to denominational colleges, and destruction of property put considerable strain on southern Methodists, Baptists, and Presbyterians in the immediate postbellum years.[59]

The hostilities that raged between northern and southern Methodists far exceeded those erupting between other denominations. Northern Methodists agitated southern Methodists long after the cessation of combat in 1865. If southern Methodists understood defeat as "God's chastisement" for greater purposes in the future, their northern brethren believed that victory had given them the moral authority to punish and reconstruct southern Methodism.[60] In 1864 Secretary of War Edwin M. Stanton gave bishops Mathew Simpson and Edward R. Ames the power to take over and fill the pulpits of wayward southern Methodist churches with northern loyalists. This "disintegration and absorption" policy toward southern Methodism was particularly acrimonious in the upcountry of Tennessee, Alabama, and western North Carolina, where northern missionaries found allies among southern Unionists.[61] The editor of New York's *Christian Advocate* summed up his coreligionists' thoughts on the matter when he expressed concern that the war had ended too soon for the good of the South. Former Confederates in the churches needed to be brought low. Not surprisingly, the militant strategies of northern agents failed to sway the majority of white southern Methodists.[62]

Northern Methodists were most successful at drawing African Americans away from southern Methodism.[63] A number of recently freed African Americans reasoned that the North was merely an instrument of God's judgment. Yet many came to believe that northern Methodists had demonstrated their moral superiority. Under the leadership of Bishop Gilbert Haven, the northern church reached out to African Americans with its own Freedmen's Aid Society, and in some cases seemed to do away with the "color line" for a period of time in the 1870s. Humiliated and enraged by northern encroachments, white southern leaders were all too aware of the northern threat. After the war the American Methodist Church was perhaps more sectionally divided than it had been in the antebellum years. Recognizing this, one southern minister writing in the Richmond, Virginia, *Advocate* in June 1869 considered "reunion neither possible nor desirable."[64]

Northern missionaries and evangelists were a source of great concern to white southern evangelicals. Considered religious carpetbaggers by southern denominational loyalists, these northern Baptist, Methodist, and Presbyterian agents moved south behind rapidly advancing Union forces as early as 1861. They began educational work among freed former slaves and, occasionally, sympathetic whites in federally occupied cities such as Baton Rouge and New Orleans, Louisiana; Murfreesboro, Nashville, and Memphis, Tennessee; Charleston and Beaufort, South Carolina; and New Bern, North Carolina. Most such missionaries, overwhelmingly from New England, carried with them neo-Puritan notions about education, uplift, and bourgeois propriety.[65] A select group among the thousands of devout who marched south also championed holiness.

These "carpetbag holiness" evangelists and social workers streamed into the conquered region following the post–Civil War revival of perfectionism in the North. Their efforts in the region were supplemented by southern seekers of holiness who came into direct contact with the northern revival. Similar to fundamentalism decades later, holiness theology was spread primarily by outsiders and their southern followers. Thus both fundamentalism and holiness, popularly imagined as rooted in the South, actually originated outside the region. Fundamentalism was first disseminated by a group of itinerants from the urban North who crisscrossed the South in the early twentieth century.[66] Postbellum holiness likewise emerged in northern cities, and only after years of southern mission work did it become a robust movement south of the Mason-Dixon line.

In the late 1860s a number of young northern Methodist divines, influenced by Phoebe Palmer and other popular holiness theologians, sought out new venues for the advancement of perfectionism. Leading Methodist ministers from New York, eastern Pennsylvania, and Boston—including John S. Inskip, J. A. Wood, and Alfred Cookman—called for a revival of primitive, unadorned Methodism. The war, they thought, had produced widespread demoralization. The popularity of novel reading and questionable urban amusements as well as the decline in religious discipline and the rise of high-church worship were enervating evangelicalism. A massive revival of holiness would cure the ills of church and society.[67] In mid-July 1867 these ministers conducted an enormous holiness revival in Vineland, New Jersey. For over ten days, thousands of enthusiasts from the North and West attended a series of meetings dedicated to entire sanctification and moral renewal. Shortly after this highly successful event, the leaders of the burgeoning movement organized the National Camp Meeting Association for the Promotion of Holiness (NCMAPH). This collection of laity and clergy orchestrated and advertised other mass revivals from the East to the West Coast in Palmer's *Guide to Holiness* and in the Camp Meeting Association's new northern journals, the *Christian Standard and Home Journal* and the *Advocate of Holiness*.[68] In addition to the Knoxville revival of 1872, the association held a second meeting in that city one year later and in 1880 sponsored revivals in Richmond, Virginia; Charleston, South Carolina; and Augusta and Savannah, Georgia. So successful were the Georgia meetings that enthusiasts held another in Augusta in 1885.

At roughly the same time that John Inskip and the northern evangelists of the National Holiness Association began holding occasional meetings in the South, one Methodist minister from the North settled in the region with more permanent goals. William Baker was one of the earliest carpetbag holiness evangelists to spread perfectionism among southerners. Baker moved south to McMinnville, Tennessee, shortly after the war to seek his fortune in land speculation and journalism.[69] Through his paper, the *McMinnville Enterprise,* and in various booster pamphlets on middle Tennessee, Baker extolled the virtues of an upcountry Eden. "Neither cholera nor yellow fever ever prevail here," he assured northern readers, and the atmosphere and natural conditions would ensure long life.[70] Like other carpetbaggers, Baker "combined the desire for personal gain with a commitment to reforming the 'unprogressive' South."[71] For a brief period he felt torn between heaven and earth. With the very real prospect of business failure (he had $2,000 invested in one teetering commercial venture) and an ever-growing spiritual anxiety, Baker experienced something like a breakdown. "My prayers and desires were pretty equally divided for a time between pecuniary success and to be delivered from the 'sin that dwelleth in us,'" he later recounted.[72] Baker turned religious entrepreneur after undergoing a "second work of grace" through the influence of northern holiness literature. Following his entire sanctification he established the South's first holiness journal, *The Home Altar,* in 1871. In 1875 he renamed the publication after Phoebe Palmer's widely read book *The Way of Holiness.* He also moved the paper to Spartanburg, South Carolina, and took on the South Carolina Methodist minister R. C. Oliver as co-editor. Oliver and Baker's monthly, *The Way of Holiness,* and their southern tract society soon reached hundreds of southern Methodists, who made up nine-tenths of their readership. They employed over one hundred field agents for the journal in every southern state except Florida.[73] Baker primarily featured excerpts from the Wesleyan canon along with writings of contemporary northern holiness authors such as John Inskip, Daniel Steele, J. A. Wood, Hannah Whitall Smith, and Alfred Cookman. But he also gave space to testimonies from southerners. The most prominent of these was the aged, irascible Lovick Pierce, who recounted his sanctification experience and denounced a spiritually corrupt southern Methodism.[74]

Baker's holiness message was simple. The authors he featured in his publication taught that believers could experience the old Methodist doctrine of entire sanctification. *The Way of Holiness* spoke in a plain-folk idiom familiar to white southerners. Absent from its pages were any allusions to radical politics or the expansionist goals of northern Methodists. This obviously made it much more palatable than antebellum perfectionism. War-weary southerners, according to Baker, could inaugurate a new religious epoch in their lives marked by perfect peace and salvation from doubt, fear, and all sin. In extremely unsure times, southerners might gain "perfect rest from all apprehension of future ill."[75] Although the message was well suited to its readers' needs, Baker struggled to keep the paper afloat. Holiness was still new to the South. And outside of the National Camp Meeting Association's assemblies in major southern cities, there were only a few regional evangelists in these early years who were preaching sanctification. When subscriptions lagged, Baker angrily assumed that "there is less interest taken in the circulation of holiness literature in the M. E. Church, South," than in the much more vibrant northern church. He was right. Finally, plagued by debt and the loss of his wife in 1886, Baker discontinued the paper.[76]

Other carpetbag holiness missionaries met with difficulties too. Those who worked among African Americans faced a myriad of challenges from local whites who scorned interracial efforts. Two white women missionaries from Illinois merit special attention. Joanna P. Moore, a Baptist schoolteacher from Belvidere, Illinois, and Adelia Arnold, from an abolitionist Wesleyan Methodist family in Mayfield, Illinois, both felt a strong calling to "go South" and "teach the emancipated slaves." Fearing for her safety, Arnold's parents prohibited her from venturing there. Years later, though, she would fulfill her calling through itinerant work on a gospel boat along the Mississippi and in a mission in Atlanta. Uninhibited by familial constraints, Moore became the first woman appointed by the American Baptist Home Missions Society. She was sent to a Union-occupied island near Memphis, Tennessee, in December 1863. In the years that followed, she labored in black communities throughout the South, aiding African American schools, setting up home missions, and publishing her influential periodical, *Hope*.[77] Before she journeyed south, Moore had experienced sanctification under the influence of Methodist holiness literature and through a Quaker holiness meeting she attended in Iowa. "I was taught," she later remembered, "that the old sinful nature could be taken out and the heart made pure."[78] Her periodical influenced thousands of African Americans in search of a deeper religious experience. While Moore published the paper in Helena, Arkansas, several local blacks were drawn to her holiness message. Among them were C. H. Mason, C. P. Jones, and Lizzie Roberson, who would later form the Church of God in Christ.[79]

Moore's holiness message seems to have transcended social barriers. Contrary to the canons of southern paternalist culture, holiness empowered African Americans as well as white women. Moore's views did not pass unnoticed by white supremacists. The notorious White League threatened and intimidated Moore and her associates on more than one occasion. While she was teaching at a black women's school in Baton Rouge, local adversaries challenged, "You are educating the nigger up to think they are equals of the white folks."[80] Indeed, Moore taught that anyone, regardless of color or caste, could receive the gift of sanctification, and moreover, that both sanctified and unsanctified deserved the advantages of good health and education.

Adelia Arnold faced similar challenges to her work among African American prisoners and in mixed congregations in late-nineteenth-century Atlanta. Arnold, affiliated with the Free Methodist Church, held a post-abolitionist view of racial equality that ran counter to prevailing southern sentiments.[81] At one integrated holiness meeting she held in a tent outside Atlanta, local white residents turned against her in fury. Arnold barely escaped a lynch mob intent on maintaining racial purity.[82]

African American and white evangelists and missionaries from the North who ministered primarily to African Americans met with far less opposition. Holiness evangelist Elijah Lowney, a former Methodist minister from Cleveland, Ohio, traveled to North Carolina in the 1890s and preached sanctification to large black congregations. One observer, stunned by Lowney's novel message and the force with which he preached it, described the evangelist as unusually powerful and remarkably popular.[83] Former slave and later holiness preacher Irving Lowery recalled the seminal missionary efforts of True Whittier, a white Methodist Episcopal Church (MEC) minister from Maine who zealously preached sanctification throughout upper South Carolina following the war. Lowery credited his adoption of holiness to Whittier. Through contacts like Whittier, Lowery joined the MEC and traveled north, where he briefly attended a Methodist school in Wilbraham, Massachusetts. Equally successful in the African American community were George and Laura Goings, a Baptist-affiliated husband-and-wife ministerial team who entered the South in the late 1890s. They joined Joanna Moore, then in Nashville, in social work, racial uplift, and the dissemination of the holiness message. The Goingses also united with white holiness advocates in California who maintained contact with missionaries and evangelists in the South and the Southwest.[84]

Hardin Wallace, a white peripatetic holiness enthusiast from Illinois, did more in the earliest years to link evangelicals from the Far West and Southwest with northern perfectionism than any other missionary. He experienced sanctification in an Illinois holiness revival that swept through rural parts of that state in 1870. Though an ordained northern Methodist minister, he spent much of his time in the 1870s preaching entire sanctification to southern Methodists and Cumberland Presbyterians in northern Texas. In 1877 he held meetings at Denton, Bremond, Marlin, Gainesville, and Ennis, Texas. Soon Wallace's northern Methodist associates traveled south from Illinois to aid him in his rambunctious revival meetings.[85] In nearly every town in which they held meetings, these preachers organized holiness bands, initiated Palmeresque Tuesday night prayer meetings, and took subscriptions for a radical ascetic paper they published in Illinois, *The Banner of Holiness.* Largely through the work of Wallace and his followers, the northern Free Methodist sect gained a foothold in the region.[86] In 1878 Wallace and his co-workers established the Texas Holiness Association, the first holiness organization in the South. In these early years, however, the movement was amorphous, less a chorus of voices than a cacophony of wild theories and syncretic theologies.

Wallace and company moved on to California in 1880, but not before provoking a fury of controversies among north Texas evangelicals. At a revival in Corsicana, Texas, the zealous Illinois holiness missionaries influenced a small group of pious Cumberland Presbyterian ministers. Led by N. J. Haynes and T. M. Goodnight, these preachers developed their own Adventist, apocalyptic theories and proclaimed a perfectionist salvation from death. Called the Corsicana Enthusiasts by their many detractors, the ministers went beyond entire sanctification and preached extra gifts and graces, including speaking in tongues, healing, and extraperceptual powers of discernment. Editors of a Texas Methodist newspaper bristled at the thought of such fanatics deluding the people of their southern Zion. They accused Haynes, Goodnight, and the rest of practicing Millerite Adventism and jeeringly compared them to the followers of Edward Irving, an English leader of a Christian restorationist sect.[87] The secular press joined the fray, lampooning Haynes and his fellow "enthusiasts" as well. These were lecherous charlatans, declared one local journalist. The editor of the Castroville, Texas, *Quill* called Haynes and Goodnight "social vampires" who brought shame to the state. Corsicana residents recoiled at the negative attention the local perfectionist sectarians brought their town. Focusing their anger on Haynes, a local mob ambushed him on a cold night and dunked him in a water tank until he lost consciousness from shock. Soon after he fled town.[88]

Leading southern Methodists in Texas thought the incident lamentable. Yet they had little trouble identifying the real culprits. These neo-perfectionists, argued H. Ashby in the *Texas Christian Advocate,* "date their reawakening to a certain sermon on 'new light, instantaneous sanctification,' preached by some visiting brother." Most even claimed they had "never heard the truth preached until this angel of peace flew down from the regions of snow" to the sunny South armed with the doctrine of "know-now-full-salvation." Ashby's argument resonated with his readers. Outsiders had deceived Texans with baroque religious theories. Sanctification did not make believers into better Christians. Instead, these northern doctrines made them lose their senses. Ashby charged that it caused men to become vain and intolerant and made women rough, boisterous, and immodest.[89] Whatever wreaked this much havoc on religious order and gender hierarchy surely had non-southern origins, reasoned Ashby and other outraged divines.

Since the Civil War, southern Methodists in Texas had contended with new, alien adversaries. Northern Methodist officials, who referred to their denomination as the "Mother Church," had achieved moderate success in drawing African Americans and some whites away from southern churches.[90] Was holiness not part of some larger conspiracy, wondered southern loyalists, since it entered the region at roughly the same time as aggressive northern Methodism? Similarly, southern evangelicals still felt threatened by the seemingly foreign, unorthodox theology of holiness. On more than one occasion, early holiness evangelists in Texas contended with local antagonists who mistook the new sect for Mormonism, an even greater bête noire of southern orthodoxy.[91] Other outside religions received much the same treatment. Southern denominational leaders initially responded to holiness as they did to the English-born Plymouth Brethren sect. The Brethren, a pietistic, millennialist religious faction, were uniformly denounced in the southern denominational press as dangerously unsound. Editorials in Methodist and Presbyterian papers labeled the movement a "fungus which appears after considerable religious excitement." The Brethren's perfectionism and antinomian tendencies also received sharp rebuke.[92] Perhaps worst of all, though, was the fact that this sect originated on foreign soil and seemed to threaten southern evangelicalism.

Not surprisingly, southern Baptists and Methodists in Georgia viewed the work of the northern-dominated National Camp Meeting Association with apprehension and concern. As in Tennessee and Texas before, some Georgia evangelicals worried that the northern-sponsored holiness revivals in their state would serve sectional goals. In the mid-1880s the prominent MECS minister Warren Candler harbored such fears. Even while encouraging and supporting holiness revivals in major Georgia cities, Candler worried that the presence of northern evangelists in Augusta and Atlanta would encourage sectional strife. What would be the result, he asked one holiness advocate, of the National Camp Meeting Association sending "into this region preachers only who agree with the views of the wing of our church they may think they can most likely secure?" The postbellum policies of northern Methodists were too recent to be forgotten. And it seemed likely to Candler that the same church "which once avowed a policy of disintegration and absorption" would now use holiness as a back door into the southern church. Fears of northern aggression lingered well after the Civil War and Reconstruction. The Union veteran and holiness evangelist M. L. Haney received a typically cold reception when preaching in Ennis, Texas, around the turn of the century. "Had we struck an iceberg in August it would hardly have been more apparent," he remarked. The Ohio native encountered one woman in the community who was particularly hostile to Yankee preachers. She had long believed, Haney recalled, that an epidemic that spread through Memphis resulted when "Chicago's people combined and sent them a barrel of arsenic to destroy them by poison!"[93]

Though not disposed to such fantasies, Georgia Baptists dreaded religious infiltration. And like Texas and Georgia Methodists, they questioned the legitimacy of sanctificationists. Several years after John Inskip held revivals in Savannah and Augusta, the Georgia Baptist Convention periodical, *The Christian Index,* discredited the movement for having recent northern origins. It was only a short time ago, wrote a skeptical observer, that Inskip had introduced the doctrine of holiness to the state. A religious theory so new to the region and championed principally by northerners was surely dubious.[94] A quarter century after the Civil War, a writer in the *Atlanta Constitution* reached a similar conclusion. A gaggle of questionable northern men and women had come forward "advocating perfectionism, adventism, vegetarianism, mesmerism, spiritualism, Grahamism, Fourrierism, free-loveism, Fanny Wrightism, nonresistance, no government, and anti-religion." All those northern lights had proved shockingly dim.[95]

The northern origins argument, as with others made in defense of southern orthodoxy, was only partly right. Northerners certainly bore much responsibility for the modern holiness movement in the South. Yet a handful of southerners adopted holiness views long before the National Holiness Association entered the region. More important, southern converts to holiness, who might be termed "holiness scalawags," proved much more instrumental to the growth and long-term success of the southern movement than their northern brethren. Although northern divines were the first to introduce holiness to the postwar South, the movement achieved coherence and numerical strength only through indigenous leadership.

After the war a handful of enterprising southerners looked to the North for solutions to the economic and social problems of their region. Newspaper editors such as Henry Grady and Richard Edmonds touted northern industrialism and material progress as a cure for the South's poverty, backwardness, and moral turpitude. The authors of the New South creed traveled widely above and below the Mason-Dixon line in search of new answers to vexing old problems.[96] Like them, the first southern converts to holiness, who came of age in a war-ravaged South, also looked north for answers to southern problems. In turn, they joined northern missionaries and evangelists in spreading perfectionism throughout the South.

Several of these ambitious figures distinguished themselves for their fervor and tireless commitment. Virginia preacher George D. Watson first encountered holiness theology while living in the North. After serving as a soldier of the Confederacy in his home state, the disaffected Watson enrolled in a northern Methodist school in Concord, New Hampshire. In close contact with a host of northern Methodists, he heard about and then attended the 1870 National Camp Meeting held at Oakington, Maryland. Watson's interest in sanctification grew. While pastoring in Delaware, he came under the influence of holiness leaders Alfred Cookman and Jacob Todd, who were in part responsible for Watson's sanctification in 1876. As a result Watson wrote about and preached holiness all over the South in the years that followed. Later in the century, from his home in Windsor, Florida, he was one of the most powerful influences over the southern wing of the movement.[97]

Like Watson, the Georgia Methodist and onetime Confederate chaplain A. J. Jarrell encountered holiness firsthand at a National Camp Meeting in the North. Jarrell seems to have had relatively few sectional biases and maintained close contacts with northern brethren. One such acquaintance, a New Jersey Methodist by the name of Ludlow, invited Jarrell to attend the holiness revival at Ocean Grove, New Jersey, in August 1879. Here Jarrell claimed sanctification and invited John Inskip to preach at his large church in Augusta, Georgia. From this period forward, the Georgia convert proved a tireless champion of the cause.[98]

No less committed was Jarrell's fellow Georgian and colaborer William Asbury Dodge. He too served as a chaplain in the Confederacy but inevitably looked outside the South for religious answers. Dodge came under the influence of George Kramer, a Maryland man who traveled between the North and the South in the years after the war. Kramer introduced Dodge to Phoebe Palmer's work and William Baker's journal *The Way of Life* and encouraged him to seek a second work of grace.[99] He followed Kramer's advice. Dodge's sanctification experience, as he recorded it in Atlanta in 1876, evinced a complete indebtedness to Palmer. He wrote of consecrating his whole being on the altar of God and offering all that he possessed in return for perfection.[100] The work of Dodge, Jarrell, Watson, and other southern-born stalwarts would eventually supplant that of their northern predecessors.

The National Holiness Association and carpetbag holiness evangelists had had some success in the years leading up to the 1880s. But most northerners' efforts were seriously impaired since southerners largely viewed them as strangers in Zion. Northern evangelists such as John Inskip, Alfred Cookman, and William McDonald preached only the occasional revival in the region, returning north afterwards. With little ongoing support in the South, early holiness efforts yielded meager results. Following the 1872 Knoxville meeting, no significant holiness organizations or publications emerged to unify and spread the movement. Other than Baker's mildly successful periodical *The Way of Life,* there were no indigenous media for the southern wing. In the late 1880s F. W. Henck, a fiery holiness evangelist from Tennessee, lamented that holiness adherents had failed to follow up on the Knoxville revivals of 1872 and 1873. As a result, only a few had maintained their sanctification, "while others had gotten in the dark."[101]

The cause of holiness fared even worse elsewhere in the South before the 1880s. Both black and white converts to holiness recalled that they had not heard holiness preached nor read holiness literature. "We had no idea what a sanctified man looked like," wrote the Texas holiness preacher "Uncle Bud" Robinson years later. Beverly Carradine, a young southern Methodist minister in Mississippi, was similarly in the dark. In his early ministry he had never worked with a sanctified minister or heard a sermon on perfection.[102]

In South Carolina during the mid-1880s Irving Lowery, the African American Methodist minister, testified to this lack of knowledge and experience throughout the black Methodist Episcopal Church. In one conference he estimated that as few as four out of eighty ministers professed sanctification. Most believed the experience impossible in this life. Lowery blamed the deficiency on his denomination's failure to publish and promote the doctrine vigorously enough. Another African American preacher from South Carolina who later embraced holiness reminisced despairingly of his youth in the postslavery years: "I never saw a holiness tract, paper, or sermon; I was never in the presence of a holiness layman, preacher or lady."[103]

These circumstances changed radically in the 1880s and 1890s. With the emergence of indigenous leadership and the related boom in southern holiness literature, thousands of southerners became aware of the movement. At the same time, new southern holiness adherents reshaped the movement to suit their plain-folk, largely rural religious needs. As a result the mainline understanding that holiness came from outside the South soon faded into obscurity. With this shift, scores converted to holiness and lent their support to the cause. As they did so, they distanced themselves from mainline southern churches and infuriated their rivals wherever they ventured.

Two 🔥

Holiness Strangers in
a Southern Zion

AROUND THE TURN of the century, the Texas holiness preacher "Uncle Bud" Robinson described his mother as an unrepentant Confederate. With dramatic flair, he linked her cultural and political commitments to her spiritual life. She had remained in a state of "rebellion" until she experienced sanctification at a Texas camp meeting. An adept sentimental folk preacher, Robinson stretched the analogy to its limits: "Lee surrendered in 1865, but it was years later when Mother Robinson surrendered." She still saw "the blue-coats and muskets in her dreams, until the year Bros. H. C. Morrison and Joe McClurkan held the Waco Holiness Camp Meeting, when mother got so happy in the experience of full salvation that she lost her little black bonnet, her handbag, and her prejudice, and hasn't seen the Mason Dixon line since." She was not alone. Once brought into the light of "full salvation," holiness stalwarts adopted new styles of dress, speech, and demeanor that often scandalized their neighbors. Some followers, like "Mother Robinson," came to shun sectionalism, while others denounced the vanities of the new middle class, condemned Jim Crow, or lauded women preachers.[1] Oddly enough, between 1880 and 1900 the prickly message and manners of holiness folk drew countless newcomers into the fold.

The holiness movement grew dramatically in these years. By the early twentieth century, no fewer than 250,000 believers identified with a movement that emphasized equally a kind of ostentatious righteousness and freedom from sin.[2] As many as half of the movement's new adherents lived in the South. Holiness preachers drew men and women, African Americans and whites to their ranks by condemning the "Sodom-like" luxuries of Victorian Methodism, denouncing Sunday newspapers, alcohol, and the theater, and calling for a return to the simpler, more emotional faith of a bygone era. Given that as late as the mid-1880s only a handful of believers scattered throughout the South claimed allegiance to perfectionism, these gains must have appeared quite remarkable. Still, the vast majority of southerners kept their distance from the movement, a growing number even rebuking holiness partisans. If most southerners, for one reason or another, held themselves aloof, larger questions remain unanswered. Just who joined the holiness ranks in the South? And perhaps more important, were there particular cultural and social factors that led some to ally themselves with the movement and others to oppose it?

Initiates attributed the movement's success to God. They seldom noted social factors, which they would have considered more mundane. Yet southern followers held distinct views concerning class, region, race, and gender. Individual temperament came into play as well. Adherents were often fiercely independent populists, and most were religious mavericks as well, ill at ease in a southern evangelical Zion. Thus the very "southernness" of the movement is questionable. Why did certain individuals gravitate toward the holiness movement while others turned away from it? Broader cultural differences between mainliners and perfectionists in the South provide some clues. Many white southerners of the era feared "race-mixing" and "mongrelization" as holiness people experimented with interracialism. In addition, while most southerners seldom traveled outside the state in which they lived, holiness enthusiasts were restless visionaries, crisscrossing the country in search of spiritual ecstasy. Sectional ideology hardened in southern denominations as holiness preachers and publications embraced transregionalism. And finally, the patriarchal views of southern Baptists and Methodists contrasted sharply with the relative gender equality that existed among holiness disciples.

Yet southern holiness believers do not lend themselves to casual generalization. There were numerous reasons why certain individuals identified with the movement. No one factor determined a seeker's acceptance of holiness religion or practice. Still, some contemporaries, and most historians and social scientists, have used class and status to define the southern movement narrowly. Observers often fail to understand believers as anything more than impoverished rubes. As early as the late nineteenth century, denominational officials found the lower-class-origins motif of great use. Thus holiness insurgents were impecunious, coarse apostles of indecency. The word "holiness," wrote one southern Methodist critic of the movement, had become "a by-word among the ignorant and profane."[3] A Baptist minister in Mississippi, threatened by encroaching perfectionists, reasoned that the movement succeeded wherever "poor and illiterate" blacks and whites could be found. Despite such denunciations, the social and economic status of holiness adherents constitutes a much more complicated picture.

Scholarly and popular views in the twentieth century followed a similar, if sometimes less biased, course. Beginning in the 1920s, the University of Chicago–trained historian Merrill

Elmer Gaddis concluded that economic and social deprivations after the Panic of 1893 were the chief agents that gave rise to southern perfectionism. The much more visceral critique of mid-century social critic W. J. Cash depicted followers with a mixture of disgust and contempt. His became the more popular and enduring view. According to Cash, as the modern South industrialized and the gulf between rich and poor widened, "Holy Rollers" gained ground "in the mill villages, in the poorest sections of the towns, and even in the countryside." Barefoot hill folk, infested with hookworm and beset by pellagra, longed for the indwelling of the Spirit. The "orgiastic," "otherworldly" religion of these "millbillies," claimed Cash, could be reduced to a matter of psychology and economics. "Thus the preachers of the frenetic sects," he observed, "ascribe their great success, next after the workings of the Holy Ghost, to the rising demands of the people for a place where they might worship without feeling ashamed of their clothes and manners, and a religion that would stress and give outlet to emotion."[4] They needed a religion, in other words, as poor and ignorant as they were.

Of course, there is much anecdotal evidence which suggests that a number of southern holiness people did come from the lower strata of society. In their autobiographies believers often referred to their poverty-stricken upbringing, their lack of any formal education, and the harsh, violent surroundings of their youth. Typical of these was the account of the folksy holiness preacher Uncle Bud Robinson, who described his early years in the Tennessee mountains as having been spent "in the very lowest depths of poverty." This was no exaggeration. The log cabin in which Robinson grew up had a dirt floor, a mud chimney, scant furniture, and no cooking stove.[5] The moral condition of his family only added to his misery. Robinson's father made a living as a moonshiner and squandered the family's

Bud Robinson as a young man in Texas, late nineteenth century. Uncle Bud, as he was later known, was a masterly holiness preacher who drew from rural imagery and plain-folk wisdom to craft his sermons and books.

small income on the "whiskey business." The Robinson children seldom attended church, and they did not receive any formal education. It was not until Bud Robinson was in his twenties, in fact, that he learned how to read. Other individuals in Georgia, Kentucky, and South Carolina who would later identify with holiness described similar conditions. Working in mills or on sharecropping farms, they experienced the same hardships as most other poor whites and blacks, who lived in abject poverty and received very little education. Joseph H. King, who later became a leading pentecostal author and minister, recalled his lower-class roots in his autobiography. His father worked as a tenant farmer near the Savannah River in Georgia. The King family lived in a series of cramped one-room houses and moved frequently in search of better work.[6]

Yet for nearly every story of the plain-folk origins of southern holiness people, there are other accounts of individuals situated in the New South's middle and even upper-middle classes. Outside observers often overlooked this pattern of diversity and ascribed the movement solely to the lower strata. Evidence suggests, though, that many key initiates, both black and white, were well off and held positions of power and authority within their churches and communities. For instance, the white southern holiness pioneer R. C. Oliver owned a large estate and commanded respect from both races among South Carolina's southern Methodists. At the time of his death in 1891, Oliver bequeathed over $50,000 to various charities and perfectionist causes.[7] N. J. Holmes, another prominent champion of holiness in the state, came from an elite slaveholding plantation family. Immediately after the Civil War, Holmes received training in law at the University of Edinburgh . In 1876 he married the daughter of South Carolina's governor, and he would later serve as pastor of an esteemed church in Greenville.[8] Beverly Carradine, a white holiness preacher from Mississippi, also came from a family of high social rank. Carradine rose in the Methodist Episcopal Church, South, as a respected minister, commanding some of the most influential pulpits in the denomination.[9] More typically, though, white holiness people derived from the southern middle classes, neither rich nor poor. In this sense they were like most other southern evangelicals of the era.[10] A significant percentage of the members of the Georgia Holiness Association, one of the region's largest perfectionist groups, were professionals. Such circumstances indicate the strong middle-class makeup of the new sect.[11]

Just as middle- and upper-class white holiness adherents were not the exception to the rule, scores of African American ministers and lay leaders were also members of the aspiring black middle class. Some black converts worked as railroad inspectors and teachers, and a number served as Baptist ministers, having graduated from schools such as Atlanta Baptist, Arkansas Baptist, Jackson Baptist, and Selma Baptist.[12] A few African American leaders even came from the black aristocracy. Robert White, a former African Methodist Episcopal preacher who affiliated with the holiness movement in Wilmington, North Carolina, owned a grocery store and was one of the town's wealthiest black businessmen.[13]

Although southern holiness folk came from a variety of social and economic backgrounds, they were united in their identification with the poor. For this reason critics too often confused the plain-folk style and biases of holiness people with their actual social status. Innumerable examples exist of holiness adherents proclaiming the virtues of the simple Jeffersonian farmer. Like their Populist contemporaries, believers imputed a natural goodness to the underclasses and attributed decadence and immorality to the Old and New South aristocracies. Preachers such as W. A. Dodge went out of their way to minister to mill workers and poor tenant farmers. Even while Dodge filled the pulpits of the largest, most prestigious churches in the North Georgia Conference, he still managed to conduct revivals and Sunday schools in poorer districts surrounding Atlanta.[14] Other ministers were more confrontational, flaunting their outreach to the poor in the face of an increasingly bourgeois church. In the early 1890s Bud Robinson barred "any of the rich people" from an outdoor meeting he held exclusively for the poor near Georgetown, Texas. Regardless, the curious wealthy arrived in their buggies to witness the popular preacher at work. Robinson excoriated these haughty onlookers who failed to understand the basic tenet of equality before God. Furious, Robinson "told them that if they did not get out of their carriages and sit down on the ground with the rest of us I would move my meetings over to the field and would not be bothered with them." They grudgingly acquiesced.[15] W. B. Godbey was perhaps even more ruthless with those he deemed the prideful rich. In the mid-1880s Godbey held one memorable meeting in Paris, Tennessee, at an "old, aristocratic, proslavery church." The ardent holiness minister raged at the congregants, shaking them "over Hell" for their wealth, "dead legalism, cold ritualism, lifeless formality and hollow hypocrisy."[16] It is little wonder that Godbey's egalitarian, low-church message met with little success in such environments. His approach did prove quite effective, however, among middle- and lower-class audiences. Evangelists in Texas, Tennessee, and Kentucky drew many converts from among the region's landless classes. A contemporary described one of the earliest separate holiness churches in Texas as made up primarily of this group: "Not a man in the whole number of charter members was a landowner."[17] Perhaps most evident of their commitment to plain-folk southerners, holiness groups met the urgent needs of the poor across the region.[18] They set up missions, orphanages, and homes for "fallen women" in Shreveport, Louisiana; Nashville, Tennessee; Atlanta, Georgia; Columbia, South Carolina; and Greenville, McKinney, Beaumont, Paris, Terrell, Dallas, Fort Worth, Gainesville, and San Antonio, Texas.

Holiness people from all over the South held clear views on class and wealth. Less clear, but no less important, was their understanding of region and place. On a basic level, regionalism played a vital role in the development of a southern holiness tradition. Historians, however, have paid little attention to this aspect of the movement. With the exception of a few insightful studies, what might be called the holiness movement's "southernness" has seldom been examined.[19]

Certainly regionalism always plays a critical role in any social or religious movement. In the nineteenth-century South, everything from a given political, social, or religious group's self-understanding to the way it challenged prevailing views often owed much to the folkways of place. Hence, as one historian notes, the roots of southern Populism lie in an upcountry tradition of republican dissent. Southern Populists developed their basic ideas about justice, independence, and obligation in response to encroaching free market values.[20] Antimission Baptists offer another example of highland protest. These southern sectarians disapproved of northern evangelicals' missionary endeavors in their region and lashed out at what they thought to be political, economic, and religious intrusions on their upcountry way of life.[21] Southerners from the Piedmont had long resisted the flows of plantation South opinion.

This regional legacy is also apparent in the lives and careers of prominent nineteenth-century southerners. Agrarian protesters in the late-nineteenth-century South were steeped in a long tradition of regional dissent. Political rebels like Tom Watson drew heavily from older Jeffersonian traditions.[22] Even those who remained within the two-party system borrowed much from this anti-aristocratic legacy. Thus the Republican Party took root in areas that were resistant to the dominant culture. Upland Republicans portrayed themselves as the successors to Unionism and champions of the common white man against Bourbon rule.[23] Farmers and laborers in the southern Piedmont and hill country had much to be dismayed about in the postwar period. Commercialization in that region was occurring at a much quicker pace and was far more detrimental to the interests of farmers than it was in the low country. As one historian puts it, "Increasing debt, decreasing self-sufficiency, and declining cotton prices combined to impoverish many small producers and to make them dependent on merchants for credit and supplies."[24] In the face of such brutal, rapid change, a number of southerners turned to alternative political and social movements in search of new answers.

Not only did the Republican Party and agrarian protest thrive in this region, but so too did religious dissent. This was an area that some scholars refer to as the "seedbed of sectarianism." Disciples of Christ, Baptist Landmarkists, and Cumberland Presbyterians dotted the landscape and made religious protest ubiquitous in Kentucky and Tennessee.[25] Mainline dissent also proved strong in the region. The northern Methodist Church gained its greatest following in the upcountry. Not surprisingly, by the late nineteenth century, areas where Union sentiment had prevailed—including east Tennessee, northern Alabama, and Appalachian Kentucky—contained the majority of the Yankee denomination's more than 72,000 members.[26] Southern culture was certainly not monolithic. Indeed, the late-century upper South remained rife with religious and social protest even as the rest of the former Confederacy was overwhelmingly Democratic and dominated by southern Baptist and Methodist denominations.[27]

Holiness adherents, too, came largely from the southern upcountry. The movement was strongest in north Georgia, northwest South Carolina, the western half of Kentucky, Tennessee, and northeast Texas. Typically—with the exception of Mississippi, which became a center for black holiness—the movement took hold in areas that had not contained a large slave population. What is referred to as the "Black Belt" South saw relatively little holiness activity.[28] In the early years Virginia, the southern half of Alabama, and most of Louisiana remained mostly untouched by the movement.[29] Holiness made its greatest gains in areas suffused with the republican ideology of the upcountry yeomanry. Accordingly the movement evidenced some of the same elements of dissent that characterized other traditions in the region. White holiness converts in the upcountry expressed themselves in terms remarkably similar to those of their self-consciously independent compatriots.

The backgrounds of several holiness leaders exemplify some of these patterns of upcountry dissent. A number of them came from areas marked by Unionism and a strong northern Methodist presence. John Lakin Brasher and Mary Lee Cagle, who would distinguish themselves as popular holiness evangelists, were raised in Unionist strongholds in north Alabama. Brasher's association with the outnumbered Methodist Episcopal Church played a large role in his later identification with holiness at the turn of the century. Cagle, too, eschewed southern traditions and chose to become a traveling evangelist in a climate inhospitable to women preachers.[30] The dissenting spirit existed in many even before they encountered the holiness movement. The beliefs of some upcountry folk who would join ranks with holiness adherents were antagonistic to those of both their denominations and southern culture in general. B. F. Haynes, a southern Methodist minister and editor in Tennessee, was a populist critic of mainline denominationalism long before he adopted holiness. Haynes's widely circulated newspaper, the *Tennessee Methodist,* rose to prominence by scourging official Methodism for its many moral failings. Haynes and his writers fought for what they considered the "original landmarks of Wesley's Methodism." Accordingly, Haynes was a militant prohibitionist who championed denominational primitivism, freewheeling evangelism, and low-church worship.

Readers were warned against the denomination's moneyed power. Wealthy patrons, he argued, were intent on overcivilizing Methodism and reducing the church to an effete social club.[31] When Haynes first encountered holiness preaching in 1894, he rushed into the movement. It seemed to suit his populist religious temperament perfectly. Thus sanctified, he focused all his righteous rage on the southern Methodist hierarchy. In the late 1890s MECS officials sought funds to rebuild the denominational publishing house, which had suffered damage during the Civil War. Haynes disputed the denomination's claims and condemned what he considered a corrupt leadership. The Tennessee Landmark Baptist newspaper praised Haynes as a maverick. According to an editorial, the Tennessee holiness preacher was bravely challenging southern Methodism, or what the writer called "the great iron wheel." The paper asserted that Haynes had the same courageous, independent spirit commonly seen in members of the Populist Party.[32]

There were other features of southern perfectionism that made it a potent form of religious and social protest. Holiness achieved its initial success in the southern cities—including Charleston, Savannah, and Augusta—where northern leaders first conducted revivals.[33] But as evangelists and newspapers spread perfectionist doctrines into the far corners of the South, the movement took on a new shape. By the mid-1880s the majority of followers came from rural communities. The nostalgic, restorationist theology of holiness appealed to them in the face of a changing world. These rural believers raised a collective complaint against the emerging popular culture and urbanism of the New South. Although the late-nineteenth-century South remained predominately rural, men and women throughout the region felt the effects of urbanization and the commercial revolution.[34] Methodism made great strides in the major cities of the South. As a result, church leadership increasingly reflected the tastes and values of the middle and upper classes. Church architects built ornate Victorian Gothic edifices, and high-church worship services took root in urban settings as wealthy New South Methodists largely abandoned the austere, unadorned style that once defined their denomination. To the horror of holiness stalwarts, costly apparel as well as smoking and theater attendance seldom received a rebuke from the church's most respectable pulpits.[35]

In the late 1890s a north Georgia holiness supporter voiced the misgivings of many by condemning the new urban leadership as decadent and overindulgent. With a heavy dose of sarcasm the author wrote in a holiness paper, "The city churches are . . . nice gathering places for the rich and tony crowd who go to spend Sunday in a respectable place and keep up a reputation for general business." Worse yet, thought the disgruntled correspondent, "a large majority of our presiding elders live, move and have their being in the city of Atlanta," seldom venturing into the countryside to visit rural churches.[36] Cloistered in comfortable New South cities, Methodists leaders, it seemed, had lost sight of their plain-folk roots.

Rural holiness disciples' fears of urban culture resemble the typical anxieties of late-nineteenth-century America at large. During this period the city became the bête noire of agrarian mythology. For many late Victorians, urban comfort seemed the source of both bodily and spiritual enervation. The city appeared to be an abstraction, unreal and disconnected from traditional society and rural values. As Protestantism became more liberal, one historian notes, "it accommodated itself to secular habits of mind and lost much emotional power." Americans "yearned for a solid sense of self by recapturing the 'real life' of the premodern craftsman, soldier, or saint."[37]

Rural southern holiness advocates vigorously battled all they thought to be representative of such overcivilization and moral decay. Not only did they decry nearly all popular amusements, expensive clothing, the use of alcohol, tobacco, and Coca-Cola, but also they condemned church innovations such as oyster suppers, paid choirs, pew rentals, and plays. Some of the more radical believers even forbade the consumption of pork and coffee as well as the wearing of neckties.[38] Other southern evangelicals, of course, could be legalistic too.[39] But the amplitude of southern holiness enthusiasts' legalism—their myriad prohibitions and condemnations—was far greater than that of their contemporaries. Hence many southern evangelicals found holiness asceticism offensive in its humorlessness and severity. In the mid-1890s a Baptist minister in Natchez, Mississippi, reviled two Holy Ghost evangelists for upsetting his community with their excessive moral regulations. Unable to understand why these Kentucky preachers upheld such strict standards, the Baptist preacher suspected they had come to steal all the "rings, watches, ear-rings," and other accessories, which they persuaded their gullible audiences to shed. "What's the matter with the people to be so swindled," he wondered.[40]

Although holiness legalism dumbfounded quite a few evangelicals, the faithful certainly thought themselves justified. Believers felt particularly threatened by the cultural changes and what they perceived as signs of the moral laxness of their era. In response, they banned all the accouterments of refinement and leisure so readily accepted by their contemporaries. When radical disciples first denounced the wearing of neckties, one convert from Delma, Texas, balked. But then, through the exacting calculus of perfectionism, he asked himself and the readers of *The Way of Faith:* "Do you wear your ties for the glory of God? Would Jesus wear a tie if he were on earth now?"[41] To ask such questions was invariably to answer them with a resounding "no." Southern initiates knew too well that life was wasted on all manner of frivolity. Too many unsanctified Christians,

"Lost, Saved, Sanctified." A holiness allegory depicting the journey from wickedness and sin to entire sanctification.

lamented the evangelist and author L. L. Pickett, spent their free time "gambling, buying lottery tickets, reading Sunday newspapers, going to theaters, drinking whiskey, using tobacco, and riding Sunday trains."[42] It seemed to Pickett and others that there were ever-increasing opportunities for southerners to participate in such "sinful" activities. These pursuits were "sinful," so went the logic, since they hindered the propagation of the gospel. Worse still, diversions like these competed with traditional evangelicalism for the attention of sinners and churchgoers alike.[43]

Their fears were somewhat warranted. Toward the end of the century, town and country became less isolated from each other in the South. A few decades earlier, mass cultural amusements—such as the circus, traveling theater troupes, and large-scale sporting events—were less common.[44] Indeed, the emergence of a strong market economy and a mass entertainment industry offered turn-of-the-century southerners the chance to lose themselves in exotic spectacles and "escape for a few hours the moral standards that ruled their daily lives."[45]

Mainline churches offered similar diversions from everyday life through fundraisers and social events. Church entertainments, as they were called, first appeared after the Civil War in middle- and upper-class churches in the South's major cities. As these began to spread into the countryside, rural holiness people mounted a vigorous crusade against them. Such "abominations" deeply offended them and struck at the core of their plain-folk values.[46] Sanctified prophets preached jeremiads on the subject. Holiness evangelist Beverly Carradine raged over the infiltration of mass culture into the church: "The Church Entertainment fairly floods the sacred building with every conceivable kind of proceedings," he fumed, and "the house is often made a playground." To condemn popular secular entertainments and then allow them in the church smacked of hypocrisy.[47] H. C. Morrison offered the most vivid critique of urbane and "worldly" Methodism. In 1899 he published *From the Pulpit to Perdition,* a short moral tale concerning a wealthy congregation located in a large city. The parishioners of Morrison's fictitious "White Temple" were a picture of New South respectability and refinement. Well dressed and well mannered, members of the White Temple prided themselves on their cultural and social accomplishments. Judgment loomed. In the midst of one of their elaborate church plays, a cyclone struck the Temple and killed all those present. God had rained down judgment on the vain congregants. Morrison ended his revenge fantasy by portraying the once-proud parishioners being refused entry into paradise.[48]

A number of laypeople and most church officials, of course, were embarrassed by the priggishness of Morrison and his brethren. Holiness believers, it seemed, wanted to bring the church back to a distant, premodern past. Perfectionists were anachronistic, bigoted religious Neanderthals, claimed their many detractors. By the mid-1890s MECS bishop Atticus G. Haygood had become one of the movement's most vocal critics. His views resonated with like-minded urban Methodists and those who thought holiness a crude throwback to a bygone era. Haygood, like his opponent Morrison, crafted his own moral tale. His popular 1895 novel *The Monk and the Prince* depicted the fifteenth-century messianic monk Savonarola as an example of unchecked pious fanaticism. He paralleled Savonarola's life with that of contemporary evangelists, who "invent conditions of salvation out of their own poor heads" and "demand acceptance of their theories as a condition of being saved."[49] Haygood's story, and the pronouncements of official southern Methodism in general, were intended to discredit holiness people as half-crazed rustics. Regardless of such efforts, the holiness movement continued to succeed in the region wherever individuals felt threatened by the trappings of modern culture.

The legalistic attitudes of southern holiness advocates toward culture and church were undoubtedly provincial and rooted in rural southern values. Yet at the same time that they lashed out against New South city life and popular culture, they paradoxically also reached beyond their region, breaking with many of the traditions that most characterized the South of this era. Consequently, the southern movement resists easy regional categorization. Its very "southernness" is problematic. Moreover, holiness adherents' views on region, race, class, and gender put them at odds with southern hierarchal traditions and occasionally made them targets of aggression.

Even more important than the influence of rural southern folkways on holiness people was their dedication to a greater cause. Holiness commitments largely superseded local and regional loyalties. The movement was national and drew its followers into larger spheres of being. Some converts were adventurous enough to seek religious and social sustenance beyond their immediate surroundings. Others were dissatisfied with the limited possibilities offered by regional institutions. Joseph H. King, a young southern Methodist holiness stalwart in north Georgia, represented the latter type. King left the MECS in the mid-1890s after his conference voiced disapproval of his perfectionist theology. He later joined the northern Methodists, who approved of his views and sent him to receive his education at U. S. Grant University, a school established by the Freedman's Bureau in Chattanooga, Tennessee. King delighted in the interregional environment he encountered at the school. Two of his fondest memories of his time there, he later recalled, were an international Methodist conference held on campus and the dedication of the Chickamauga battlefield. Each event well symbolized his changing outlook. These mass meetings opened him up to a wider world. At the church conference he marveled at the sight of "the most eminent ministers and laymen of Methodism on the North American continent" delivering sermons on every conceivable topic. And at the battlefield dedication he stood in awe of the thousands of veterans, North and South, gathered to commemorate the conflict.[50] Holiness, as King and others understood it, held the power to unite men and women across social and geographic boundaries in much the same way.

There were greater contemporary forces at work which drew holiness folk into larger social spheres. At roughly the same time that perfectionism crossed over the Mason-Dixon line, communities throughout the country were in crisis as industrialization, new modes of transportation, consumer culture, urban growth, and political upheavals contributed to the breakdown of traditional society. Before the 1870s America had remained remarkably decentralized. Now, what one historian describes as island communities, insulated by geography and culture, were fast becoming connected in innumerable ways.[51] While many resisted the change to a translocal culture, some courageous souls embraced it wholeheartedly and began to identify "community" with something other than one's immediate surroundings and interests. Some even gravitated to organizations and social networks that were utterly independent of place.[52] Interest groups are perhaps the best example of this phenomenon. National organizations—including those in support of Populism, temperance, and women's rights—often undercut regional and local affiliations. When National Farmers Alliance delegates from the South and West met in Ocala, Florida, at their 1890 annual session, they declared their interests in translocal terms. "There shall be no sectional lines across Alliance territory," stated a resolution formulated at the meeting. Attendees from Kansas, Virginia, Pennsylvania, Texas, Michigan, and South Carolina arrayed themselves against plutocracy and "wicked sectional agitators."[53]

Holiness advocates across the United States also joined forces against common, even regional, enemies. Initiates came to think of themselves as part of a larger religious family that obliterated sectionalism.[54] In this regard the movement in the

South proved radically different from other southern religious traditions. Southern Baptists, restorationist sects, and antimission churches had little or no influence outside the region. Some of these, including Antimission Baptists, scorned national organizations and outsiders. Provincialism was a fundamental feature of many primitivist churches. Conversely, those who would convert to holiness eagerly read northern literature, attended meetings led by northerners and westerners, and traveled widely to participate in perfectionist conventions. Some even felt obliged to speak out against geographic chauvinism. "Before I was sanctified," wrote W. B. Godbey, "I was scarcely known outside of my Conference." After experiencing a second work of grace, though, he considered it his "duty to discriminate no longer between North, South, East, and West." The eccentric preacher was also fond of claiming that "sanctification makes you free of all the North and South and East and West. I am as free in Michigan as in Texas, and I go where the Lord leads me."[55] Godbey, like many other southern preachers and laypeople, became a peripatetic saint. He held revivals in all the states of the South and also in the West, the Northeast, and around the globe.[56] Laypeople journeyed far afield in search of rare holiness revivals. In the 1890s Watson Sorrow, a young seeker from central Georgia, traveled north with his father to attend a meeting in Abbeville, South Carolina. More than fifty years later Sorrow would remember that "to cross a state line was as foreign then as going to Europe now, especially for we people from the middle of Georgia to go into South Carolina."[57] Sorrow and his father were eager to experience what seemed an impossibility to many. The allure of perfection drew them and a number of others many miles away from their homes and communities. The movement found its chief advocates in such restless visionaries.

Frequently those in search of holiness looked beyond the

South or to independent groups in their spiritual quests. It was not until the late 1890s, though, that a significant portion of southern holiness folk came out of their mother churches, forming new denominations and independent fellowships. The vast majority, at least until then, remained in the MECS. Yet a few bold individuals affiliated early with northern denominations and sects which they thought more amicable to perfectionism. R. L. Harris, a west Texan dubbed "the cowboy evangelist," represented this type of dissent. When the wayfaring revivalist joined what had once been a northern abolitionist church, the Free Methodists, he bore the reproaches of mainline southerners who despised this typical Yankee sect.[58] Similarly, the northern-based Wesleyan Methodist Connection succeeded in some areas where traditional southern denominations failed. Roughly four hundred holiness folk in South Carolina left the MECS during the 1890s to join the Wesleyans. Most of these entered the northern denomination because they felt dissatisfied with the lack of zeal for perfection in their mother church.[59]

Free Methodists and Wesleyans were still far less successful in the South than the much larger and more influential New York–headquartered Methodist Episcopal Church. And when leading southern Baptists and Methodists began to scrutinize and rebuke their holiness members, MEC officials took full advantage of the situation. The northern church wooed a number of disenchanted enthusiasts into their fold. In Texas, Bud Robinson's MECS presiding elder warned him either to give up his second work theory of sanctification or to leave the southern Methodist church. Robinson withdrew and immediately contacted officials of northern Methodism in Texas. They welcomed him into their church and assured him that they had no quarrel with the doctrine of "full salvation."[60] Sensing the opportunities at hand, one official of the northern church, who had himself left the southern denomination over the issue of perfection, informed the members of a Texas holiness association in 1899 that northern "Methodism is the mother of holiness." He implored them to enter the denomination, which he promised would commission them to preach holiness and pay them handsomely. Quite a few were convinced by such appeals and joined the northern church.[61] Those who did affiliate with the MEC found that their new denomination won them few friends in the region. Ever-watchful southern Methodist officials took note of the exodus and any other forms of denominational mutiny. The *Alabama Christian Advocate* lashed out at holiness ministers for even the slightest signs of disloyalty. The author of an 1895 article accused MECS minister Beverly Carradine of having "no loyalty to his church," asserting, "We know of an instance in which [Carradine] held a meeting last winter, or spring, in a Northern Methodist church, during which time he made capital for his popularity by slight remarks about the struggling band of Southern Methodists and their pastor."[62] Far from inhibiting what was tantamount to religious treason, denunciations like this only increased followers' resolve.

African American holiness stalwarts also turned to non-southern agents in their search for religious fulfillment. Like white followers, they, too, represent a certain degree of trans-localism. Leading black advocates of perfection were mobile and in contact with northern individuals and ideas. C. P. Jones and C. H. Mason both encountered holiness in Arkansas under the influence of northern missionaries such as Joanna P. Moore. Sanctification, too, found its greatest champions in ministers like Jones and Mason, who traveled and itinerated much more widely than most other African Americans in the region.[63] Some black adherents clearly understood the transregional roots of the movement. In 1887 the South Carolina–based minister Irving E. Lowery reported in *The Christian Witness* that through the efforts of ministers in the North and the South, his

Founder of the Church of God in Christ, Charles
Harrison Mason.

state was becoming a black holiness stronghold. Scores of participants at a conference held in Kingstree, South Carolina, testified to "full salvation." "We imagined ourselves in a New York or Boston holiness meeting," Lowery reported ecstatically.[64]

Holiness people of both races found a number of reasons to align themselves with a movement that originated outside the South. Of course, if asked why they joined, most would likely have stressed the religious component. The Spirit moved them. But there were other less acknowledged factors at work, too, which often put them at odds with their contemporaries. Many perfectionists, for instance, remained aloof from the Lost Cause ideology so potent in the postwar South. They remembered the Civil War very differently than did mainline evangelicals in the region. It is not surprising that African American holiness leaders like C. P. Jones framed the Civil War as the white South's atonement for the sin of slavery. Former slaves throughout the South considered the war just punishment against the miscreant Confederacy.[65] By contrast, scores of white leaders in the late-century South praised the virtues of the prewar plantation, populated with loyal slaves and kindly masters. Slavery had served as a civilizing institution. The war, said such voices, had devastated the region and wreaked havoc on race relations. African American holiness folk provided a sharp rebuttal. A black MEC minister in Charleston offered his view to Boston's *Christian Witness,* declaring that slavery was "accursed of God and man." The South's peculiar institution "had no elements to draw out the best in any one, be he master or slave. It was calculated to bring out the worst in both, and develop it to an unlimited degree."[66]

What is truly striking is that many white holiness leaders held similar views. Some white adherents from the southern upcountry even represented the anti-Confederate, antislavery sentiments of the region. Unionism was well represented in the upcountry and border states. Upper South Unionists seldom came in contact with slavery and were instrumental in bringing about the Confederacy's defeat.[67] W. B. Godbey fit this pattern. A staunch Unionist, he was serving as president of Harmonia College in Perryville, Kentucky, at the outbreak of the war. He moved the school to Russellville, Indiana, to escape the ensuing conflict and any possible reprisals. Years later Godbey would employ the Civil War as an image in his sermons to illustrate the order of salvation for his southern audiences. "In this memorable crisis," he told them, "Ohio, with her sister free states, represents political sanctification." Kentucky, a Union state with thousands of secessionists living within its borders, symbolized the merely saved Christian, in whom sin still resided. At the bottom was the southern Confederacy, which stood for the unrepentant, rebellious soul. Years after the war both Godbey and Tennessean preacher B. F. Haynes still brandished their antislavery credentials. Godbey gloried in the fact that his grandfather in "old Virginia" had freed his slaves after being converted at one of Bishop Francis Asbury's revivals, and Haynes declared that although his family owned slaves, he detested the institution. Hearing "Aunt Nancy," one of his father's slaves, sing spirituals had affected him profoundly. He recalled that he "early imbibed abolition sentiments, and all through my childhood and maturer years I was an honest abolitionist though my parents were true to the Confederacy."[68]

If other holiness folk were not as antagonistic as Haynes and Godbey, most who looked back on the war were not comfortable with the Confederacy, slavery, or sectionalism. J. B. Culpepper was only in his teens when war raged in Georgia. Years later, as a well-known holiness preacher, he recollected that when he heard that his father was raising a Confederate company to "assist the 'southern cause,'" he "despised the very idea." Culpepper boasted, "I would have turned my back on home and all that a boy's heart held dear, and gone alone to the very jungles of Africa as a missionary," but he would not have marched off to fight in an ungodly rebellion, even if his age had permitted. Older holiness leaders such as Miller Willis and G. D. Watson, who served in the Army of Northern Virginia, looked back on their actions with regret and professed that God eradicated all their sectional hatred when they were sanctified.[69] Others who had fought for the Confederacy rarely if ever mentioned their war experiences.[70] Indeed, the silence on the subject is striking. In the hundreds of southern holiness newspapers printed in the 1880s and 1890s, rarely did the topic of the Civil War or glosses on the Lost Cause ever appear.

Among white southern Baptists and Methodists the situation was quite the opposite. In the last two decades of the nineteenth century they produced a steady stream of material commemorating and enshrining Confederate war efforts. The Confederacy's afterlife and the mythology of the Lost Cause served as a civil religion for much of the South. In this period church life and mass culture in the region were inseparable.[71] The Lost Cause did not unite all southerners, but it was a remarkably cohesive force among many mainline groups. The *Religious Herald* (Richmond, Virginia) and the *Christian Advocate* (Nashville, Tennessee), the two most influential denominational papers in the region, brimmed with exaltations of the soldier saints of Dixie.[72] These journals also defended sectionalism as natural, even patriotic. It was, wrote one southern Baptist editor, far better than the new antisectional cult, "whose chief tenet is the preference for other customs, institutions, and people than one's own." A flurry of postwar articles in these papers turned readers' attention to the Confederate pantheon. A Methodist writer in the *Christian Advocate* eulogized Jefferson Davis, a martyr to a sacred cause: "No stain of dishonor eve[r] attached to his name. . . . His courage was equal to any test." Davis, imagined the author, stood firm, undaunted by the "storms of denunciation and ridicule" that roiled around him in his final years.[73]

While mainline evangelicals valorized sectionalism and memorialized the Civil War, southern holiness people embraced translocalism and distanced themselves from the Lost Cause. Followers repeatedly called regional prejudice into question and aligned themselves with the national perfectionist movement. The former Confederate general C. A. Evans called for the 1885 national holiness meeting in Augusta, Georgia, "inviting a thousand Northern brethren" to invade the region. Participants in this and other large southern meetings reveled in intersectionalism. One enthusiast thought that such events could annihilate "all there is of 'Mason and Dixon line' prejudice." In baroque tones, another correspondent from Augusta wrote, "An invasion from the North, East, and West five thousand strong" would boldly challenge national prejudice, and promote "the unity of the spirit in the bonds of peace."[74] As the movement flourished and entered new areas of the South, the theme of regional reconciliation grew even stronger.

Unlike most other attempts at sectional reconciliation in the 1890s, holiness efforts did not resort to the degradation of African Americans.[75] Adherents attacked sectionalism much the same way they assailed other forms of prejudice. For instance, in 1901 a writer in the Nashville holiness newspaper *Zion's Outlook* challenged sectionalism along with several other matters he considered social sins. He asked his readers rhetorically, "Should not the church be as ready to surrender sectionalism in the interest of soul-saving as commerce is ready to surrender it in favor of money-getting, or education in the interest of knowledge-getting?" Like countless other believers, this writer insisted that holiness could cleanse individuals of all prejudice. Modifying a passage from scripture, he wrote that there was "no North, no South, no Jew, no Greek, no Barbarian to the sanctified."[76]

If the opinions of holiness disciples about sectionalism and the Civil War set them apart from many of their southern contemporaries, their openness to interracial dialogue and occasionally even fellowship proved even more remarkable in a region increasingly dominated by Jim Crow and intense racism. The holiness press and holiness gatherings in the South served as liminal spaces where blacks and whites could interact and freely share their ideas about Christian perfection. Martin Wells

Radical holiness minister and author W. B. Godbey, early
twentieth century. Godbey's work was popular with countless southerners in the holiness movement. He later had a
profound impact on pentecostals in the region.

Knapp's paper, *God's Revivalist,* frequently corresponded with
and supported black holiness leaders such as the African Methodist Episcopal Church evangelist Amanda Berry Smith. Occasionally the paper even included features hinting at an openness to integrated services. In 1901 a letter published in *The*

Revivalist asked whether blacks and whites had worshipped together in biblical times. Kentucky-based evangelist W. B. Godbey answered emphatically, yes. Thumbing his nose at Jim Crow conventions, Godbey proclaimed that "Philip, the evangelist, unhesitatingly got up on the chariot and rode along beside the black Ethiopian eunuch, and preached to him and baptized him." In the segregated South, where the color line reigned supreme in railway cars and public spaces, these were shocking words. Godbey offered several other proof texts to back up his position. Finally, he concluded that early Christians recognized no racial distinctions "but all work[ed] together in perfect equality and Christian affection."[77]

Godbey's forthright declarations did not prove the exception. Elsewhere in his home state a few practiced what Godbey preached. One of those was "Sister Roxy," a black evangelist in central Kentucky. At the turn of the century Sister Roxy acted as general overseer of the holiness Christian Faith Band's twenty-five churches. Described mockingly by newspapers as a "squat, fat," uneducated "ebon priestess," Roxy drew a devoted following of the poor of both races. "The white folks come to my meetin's everywhar I goes," she allegedly told a curious reporter. Whites came, exhorted, and testified "jes' the same as us." Yet her message of egalitarianism and spiritual empowerment upset genteel middle-class African Americans. Black detractors called her and her followers "those Power niggers."[78]

Like Godbey and Sister Roxy, W. A. Dodge, H. C. Morrison, Irving Lowery, and scores of other ministers preached to integrated crowds. The white preacher James Epps Jr., a former plantation owner in South Carolina, held integrated meetings in a church building he constructed near his home. Lowery noted, "the demon caste is never seen there."[79] Such gatherings often provoked outrage among whites. Richard Baxter Hayes, a radical evangelist who traveled the back roads of Georgia and South Carolina, encountered hostility wherever he challenged racial norms. After he asked a few African Americans to lead in song at an 1898 revival in Carlton, Georgia, "a man who weighed over two hundred pounds" confronted Hayes, brandishing a stick and accusing him of "showing Negro equality." For Hayes's breaches of racial, social, and religious norms, his meeting tents were burned down several times, he was punched in the face by a Baptist minister, he was shot at, and he regularly faced belligerent crowds. Much like Hayes, the northern-born white traveling revivalist and colporteur Frank Bartleman was routinely met by enraged southerners. Between 1897 and 1899 he claimed to have preached 150 sermons and traveled 2,500 miles over the region's dusty roads. White Baptists, he observed, were particularly suspicious of his work with blacks and derided the holiness movement. He sarcastically wondered if whites feared "that we might do the 'nigger' a kindness." The young minister preached and distributed books and tracts to thousands of African Americans in North Carolina, South Carolina, Florida, Alabama, Mississippi, Virginia, and Georgia. As he and his rotating cast of companions made their way through the former Confederacy, they engaged in graffiti evangelism, using brushes to paint biblical passages on fence posts, bridges, and rocks. Bartleman was impressed that "negroes looked upon us as friends." The injustice of the white South struck him deeply. "It was very easy to lay the blame on a black man" for "some white man's crime," he observed. Furthermore, "the white man robbed the negro systematically," noted Bartleman. "He considered him lawful prey. A whole town would turn out to lynch a negro."[80]

African American adherents in Mississippi met with similar, if not greater, retribution for their views and actions, as black ministers felt empowered to challenge the racism and excesses of white male culture. On one occasion Frank Palmer, a black holiness preacher from southern Mississippi, upbraided a group of white men for gambling by the side of the road on a Sunday morning. "You shouldn't be gambling," Palmer admonished them. "Come to prayer meeting." Incensed, these local toughs took Palmer by force to a nearby wooded area, laid him across a log, and whipped him severely. Palmer, fearing for his life, fled the region shortly after that terrifying incident.[81]

Encountering harsh opposition, both white and black ministers found it difficult to maintain integrated services. To avoid antagonizing local whites, evangelists would segregate their congregations or hold completely separate meetings for blacks and whites.[82] The integrationist and egalitarian strain of holiness remained strong, though, and certain stalwarts refused to conform to southern prejudice. A number of holiness authors denounced bigotry and promoted racial equality. Ohio-born prison evangelist "Mother" Elizabeth Wheaton refuted the Jim Crow South's answers to the purported "race problem." Touring the deadly stockades and prison camps in Alabama, Georgia, Texas, Florida, and the Carolinas in the 1890s, Wheaton was often "not allowed to stay with white people if I preached to negroes." The color line was closely drawn, observed the perfectionist reformer. Looking back on her experience in the South, Wheaton recalled with rhetorical flourish, "I was taught in the word of God that all nations were made of one blood and that God was the Father of us all."[83] Like Wheaton, the white southern evangelist J. Livesey considered scripture and holiness a balm for troubled race relations. "The colored people of the South are still universally regarded and treated as inferiors," wrote Livesey in 1886. This, he thought, made it necessary for white ministers to take "special pains to convey to them, and to indoctrinate them in, the Wesleyan teachings on the subject of holiness." Holiness would cleanse southern whites of their "undue assumption of superiority, the domineering insolence, the shameless imperiousness and haughtiness" toward blacks. More important for Livesey, holiness would dignify African Americans "as redeemed and sanctified MEN—as common heirs with all the saints." Another white minister in New Orleans, L. P. Cushman, urged holiness people to challenge the prejudices of mainline evangelicals. He called for the integration of MEC-operated colleges and challenged the notion that race was a biological fact. The church must lead the way on racial equality, Cushman insisted. Methodists in particular, he believed, had aligned themselves with Bourbons in a white supremacist campaign. He called upon his fellow believers to "not trample upon the ten commandments, the Lord's Sermon on the Mount, and every principle of the New Testament, to gratify the base, cowardly, and unholy sin of caste."[84] Cushman keenly exposed the moral contradictions and twisted logic of race prejudice.

Other white devotees noted the violence and unreason of southern racism. Tennessee native Amanda Cheek, who later joined the Church of God (Cleveland), was a mere teenager when she first witnessed the brutalities of white southerners' "great prejudice against the colored race" soon after moving with her family from the hill country near Dayton, Tennessee, to northwest Georgia in 1890. When three black men arrived in town by train, suspicion gripped her neighbors, who tried to arrest the men on trumped-up charges. The newcomers fled for their lives, only to be pursued by a seething mob. When the black men tried to defend themselves, the vigilante rabble murdered them in an "unmerciful scene" of rage. Cheek and her family never forgot the horrifying incident. They later moved back to Tennessee.[85]

Kentucky preacher H. C. Morrison used his newspaper to

denounce the savage inequities of the kind that Cheek and her family witnessed so vividly in north Georgia. Morrison excerpted a stinging moral tale about race relations in an 1889 issue of *The Old Methodist*. The story castigated racist white Christians blinded by wealth and mammonism. "Why did you take that nigger in your pew?" a white laymen in Maine asks a member of his congregation. Answering, the churchman explains that the man is a close friend and a prominent citizen from Haiti. "I don't care from what 'ti' he is, he is nothing but a nigger," inveighs the agitated white man. When finally told that the Haitian is a millionaire, the antagonist responds, "Is he? Introduce me."[86]

Some openly received the message of Livesey, Cushman, and Morrison and modified their beliefs accordingly. In South Carolina a white blacksmith named J. A. Williams repented of what he described as his wicked, racist ways when he adopted holiness. Those who had known Williams for years stood in awe of his conversion and sanctification. This once-violent man who used to terrorize local blacks now aligned himself with African Americans in the cause of holiness. In his autobiography Williams summed up his changed point of view with an excerpted hymn, "No Distinction." Written in black dialect and later popularized by the Carter Family, the song portrays a desegregated heaven as a place very unlike the late-century South:

> In de same kind of rai-ment, in de same kind of shoes,
> We'll all sit to-geth-er in the same kind of pews;
> De white folks and de cul-led folks, de gen-tile and de Jews,
> Case we'll all be so hap-py dat we das-n't re-fuse.
>
> Dar'll be no dis-tinc-tion dar, Dar'll be no dis-tinc-tion
>   dar . . .

To dine wid de white folks we'll not try in vain,
They'll neb-ber re-fuse us a-gain and a-gain;
We'll ride in Pull-man coach-es, wid none to com-plain,
Case dar'll be no jim-crow cars on de gos-pel train.

Dar'll be no dis-tinc-tion dar, Dar'll be no dis-tinc-tion dar.[87]

Holiness pronouncements on race, though, were not altogether otherworldly. A few courageous writers even cast their criticisms in political terms. Clement Cary, an influential north Georgia MECS holiness minister and author who challenged the Jim Crow politics of his state, took to task duplicitous leaders who demanded black disfranchisement or cautioned African Americans who did vote to cast their ballots for "decent" government. "Why is not that good advice for the white man?" asked Cary. "Why should not every good white citizen 'vote for good government, irrespective of party?'" Cary's very questions seemed to dispute the South's Democratic hegemony. Why should the blacks be chastened, he asked, "while the white man ties his vote to the apron strings of some political party, . . . [supporting] a man running for office simply because he is a nominee."[88] Cary and other disciples, though rarely political and not by any means radical, questioned hypocrisy in their papers and upheld holiness as the ultimate panacea for all social problems. Southern white holiness folk only occasionally pitted their perfectionism against social injustice, but in a region where rigid, systematic racism thrived, holiness views must have appeared all the more unusual. Like southern Populists, holiness adherents considered themselves part of a movement that, at least in some respects, transcended race.[89]

Holiness challenges to the shibboleths of southern racism stood in stark contrast to secular and denominational dictums. Southern literature did not just mirror much of the Jim Crow segregation that took hold of the region but often stoked the fires of intolerance and injustice. It is little wonder, then, that this was the era of rampant lynchings, the Wilmington race riot, and the landmark "separate but equal" doctrine formulated in *Plessy v. Ferguson*. Racist images and themes were ever present in the popular culture of the 1880s and 1890s South. These ranged from the banal reconciliation romances of New South novelists to virulent racist diatribes in major southern newspapers. Like many other dailies, the *Atlanta Constitution* regularly featured gruesome anti-black stories on its front page and gave space to editorials by white demagogues.[90]

Though much less sensational than its secular cognate, the denominational press proved to be just as bigoted. Leading southern Methodist papers such as the *Alabama Christian Advocate* denounced holiness in blatantly racist terms. Key detractors scorned the movement for breaching the racial divide. Writers recoiled at its interracial character and depicted it as a savage, ignorant farce. One critic labeled B. F. Haynes's populist-style paper the *Tennessee Methodist* vulgar and coarse: "Its language resembles too much the lingo of the negro cabin, or the dirty wit. . . . It is nasty slush, malodorous, mephitic." Elsewhere this same writer portrayed the southern holiness cause as racially deviant and fanatical, charging that "mystical ecstacy [*sic*], and negro foolry [*sic*] marks so many of these Sanctificationists."[91]

Such aspersions came naturally to southern Methodist leaders motivated by deep racial anxieties. The denomination's record on race in the last decade of the nineteenth century was certainly dismal by current standards but was sanctified in its own eyes. A writer in the Charleston, South Carolina–based *Southern Christian Advocate* offered one widely accepted solution to the much-discussed "negro problem." Claiming to be an expert on race relations, this alarmed southern Methodist warned, "If we fail to do something in the form of self-protection, amalgamation and social degeneracy will certainly be our fate." The education of African Americans, he thought, was to no avail and only overburdened white southerners. Black populations must be redistributed across the country, "scattering the race" and thereby curtailing their power as a group.[92] Most white denominational leaders' views on lynching were nearly as poisonous. Like many a secular journalist, one commentator in the official newspaper of the MECS condemned mob justice while condoning the outcome. He recounted the brutal execution of a black man accused of committing an "unspeakable outrage" against a well-to-do white woman. Undoubtedly, claimed the writer, "the negro deserved what he got. No penalty can be adequate for such fiendishness."[93]

Most white southern Baptists of the era also pursued a racist agenda, endorsing nearly all forms of Jim Crowism. White Baptists, like many other white Christians in the region, defended white supremacy in political and religious spheres with a deep urgency. Editors of southern Baptist newspapers embraced the "tragic era" school of Reconstruction history and aligned their denomination against all forms of northern radicalism. Leading southern Baptists in the 1890s warned readers of "Negro domination," which would necessarily follow social or religious integration.[94]

At the high point of such hysteria, black and white holiness advocates integrated their newspapers by featuring the work of both races in their pages. White-operated papers such as *The Christian Witness* and *Zion's Outlook* highlighted the work of African American evangelists and published editorials by leading black holiness ministers. Throughout the late 1880s *The Christian Witness* included pieces by prominent Methodist ministers both black and white, including L. P. Cushman and

Irving Lowery. In scores of articles for the paper, Lowery encouraged white holiness evangelists to take their message to African American congregations and called on black ministers to feature sanctification in their ministry. J. O. McClurkan, a former Cumberland Presbyterian minister in Nashville, Tennessee, gave space for African Americans to testify and announce upcoming conventions in the pages of his new journal, *Zion's Outlook*.[95]

Simultaneously, newly established black periodicals covered the work of leading white evangelists in the South. In 1896 C. P. Jones began publishing *Truth* in Jackson, Mississippi, as a holiness journal for African Americans. But he kept its pages open to the work of both races, reporting on white holiness activities in South Carolina, Georgia, and Tennessee. He lauded the efforts of well-known white southern revivalists such as George Watson, J. M. Pike, N. J. Holmes, and the popular hymn writer Charlie Tillman.[96] The same level of interaction took place in Georgia, where W. A. Dodge lent his support to black holiness ministers such as W. J. Adams. Moreover, there is evidence that Dodge's own paper, *The Way of Life,* maintained a significant black readership. Adams later recalled that quite a number of African Americans in Georgia "subscribed [to] this paper, and took it as long as [Dodge] published it," noting, "Dodge, also, sold holiness books and tracts, and a few of the [African American] preachers went to his home for these books and papers so often until we called it the 'Power House.'" Concerned with spreading holiness among African Americans, Dodge encouraged Adams to publish his own paper and helped name the new periodical *The Herald of Full Salvation.*[97]

There were several basic reasons for this surprising degree of openness. Holiness believers largely valued religious experience and spiritual power over traditional hierarchical authority, and the movement provided an equality of fellowship often lacking in mainline southern evangelicalism. Not only was there greater interaction between African Americans and whites, but also women achieved prominent positions of authority as evangelists and lay leaders. Following the examples of northerners like Phoebe Palmer and the black minister Amanda Berry Smith, southern holiness women assumed roles denied them in Baptist and Methodist churches.

Many southern evangelicals who shunned holiness thought repugnant the key roles women played in the movement. Since the antebellum period, most whites in the region had adhered to a conservative view of gender relations, an ideology shaped by slavery and biblical literalism. The subordination of women to men, the South's chief religious leaders maintained, rested on scripture and reason.[98] This patriarchal social order continued to thrive in the late nineteenth century. It is not surprising, then, that the agrarian movements, which drew women into positions of leadership in the West, looked very different in the South, which offered little precedent for women as political or social activists. An entrenched southern tradition of male authoritarianism made it difficult, if not impossible, for women to assume any meaningful positions of power.[99]

A number of southern holiness women, though, challenged that prevailing order.[100] Some enthusiasts were no doubt drawn to the movement precisely because it offered opportunities that were nonexistent elsewhere in the South. Women ministers, however, more often cited biblical precedents, holiness theology, or the work of perfectionist authors as the basis for their entrance into the fold. Certainly there was no shortage of apologists for women preachers. Men such as W. B. Godbey, W. A. Dodge, and J. B. Culpepper offered biblical and experiential arguments for women's right to preach and encouraged many women to enter the ministry. In 1891 Godbey authored a short pamphlet on the subject, describing women's ministry in rhapsodic terms as critical to the evangelization of the world: "Glory to God for this prophetic vision of hosts and armies of women going forth preaching the gospel to all nations." Culpepper contended that the new work of "Pentecost" bestowed the power of the Holy Ghost on both men and women. Moreover, he argued, scripture emancipated women: "Moses in the law and Jesus in the gospel, conferred on women the right to think, feel, to worship and to act." Southern mainliners battled perfectionists over the meaning of the Bible and the norms of gender. Texas evangelist R. M. Guy defended women preachers in *The Pentecostal Herald* and challenged the manly culture of the region: "Now that Christianity has emancipated woman and lifted her back to her place by man's side . . . where is the man who will boast of his superiority, and refuse her the God-given right to fulfill her part of the commission found in Gen. 1:27–29, and then refuse to grant her, her portion in the promise in Joel 2:28–29."[101] Similarly, Texas preacher Annie May Fisher developed a detailed defense of women in the ministry based on biblical proof texts and personal experience. She thought it absurd that women could be found in almost every profession except the ministry and noted scores of examples of godly women and prophetesses from the Old and New Testaments.[102] However logical such arguments appeared, women entered the ministry in the South at their great peril. The north Alabama native Mary Lee Cagle decided to become a preacher only after a long inner struggle. Following her sanctification under the ministry of R. L. Harris, Cagle felt the call to preach, even though "there was awful opposition to a woman preaching, both from the church and the world."[103]

Indeed, criticism and strident opposition from local adversaries and mainline denominational leaders dogged women holiness preachers all over the South. Postwar southern evangelical newspapers ardently defended their doctrine of "separate spheres" against the onslaughts of women's rights and northern liberalism. Southern churchmen cast blame on northern agitators. An 1895 editorial in the *Alabama Christian Advocate* fumed at a southern women's rights campaign: "We hope that Susan B. Anthony with her parasites and converts may soon go back across the [Mason-Dixon] line and stay there, for we want neither her nor her doctrines."[104] Southern Methodist writers portrayed women professionals, political activists, and preachers as "harpies" and "shrews." One church official expressed the sentiments of many when he declared in a leading denominational paper, "I don't think the Lord ever showed His common sense more than when he failed to call women to preach and take charge of churches." Another cynical observer from Hendersonville, Texas, wrote to the *Dallas Morning News* denouncing holiness fanatics and their "unhinged minds." There were never more than two or three sanctified souls on earth, he challenged. He concluded with a rhetorical question: Did it ever occur to so-called holiness people that those few perfect saints in the Bible "were men and not women?"[105] Undoubtedly most white southern Methodists did not appreciate the egalitarian message holiness doctrine espoused. Representative of this view, an editor of the *Christian Advocate* argued that radicals grossly misinterpreted Galatians 3:28: "There is neither Jew nor Greek, there is neither bond nor free, there is neither male or female: for ye are all one in Christ Jesus." This verse, the editor proclaimed, showed only that all could be saved, regardless of sex or race. There was not "a hint here of wider meaning." To read more into this text would lead to social anarchy: "Any effort to break down, set aside, or ignore the barriers and limitations which [God] has set up can result in nothing but disaster. In particular is it the case that the two sexes, representing as they do the opposite and supplementary sides of our humanity, are appointed to the discharge of widely

Left to right: Trena Platt, Rev. Mary Lee Cagle, and an unidentified woman in a holiness revival tent, late nineteenth century.

varying functions. The 'reform' that loses sight of this fact is a reform against nature and against God."[106] In short, women preachers ministered and evangelized in direct defiance of the southern Methodist party line.

Not only did women ministers meet with hostility at the highest levels of their denomination, but they faced the resentment and suspicion of southern laypeople as well. An elaborate antiholiness folklore developed in rural communities where antagonists maliciously represented women preachers as unladylike and unnatural. In the early 1890s holiness evangelist Amanda Coulson met with severe criticism while holding meetings near Harrison, Arkansas. Many locals were shocked at the evangelist's unorthodoxy. Rumors quickly spread that she had murdered her husband and abandoned her children. Elsewhere in the South some evangelicals refused to attend holiness revivals in which women presided.[107]

Not all those who heard women preachers reacted so negatively. In fact, some embraced wholeheartedly their message and ministry. These people tended to judge female evangelists not by the dictates of southern patriarchy but on the merits and power of the woman preacher's message. Hence J. H. King remembered a Miss Haskins from Athens, Tennessee, as an accomplished preacher who drew large audiences through her "sober, sound, and spiritual" exposition of scripture. Likewise, a reporter covering Mary Lee Harris's revival meetings in Milan, Tennessee, noted her skill as a preacher and the practical results of her work. "While the scripturalness of women preaching may not yet be settled," he proclaimed, "there are some points fully settled in the minds of hundreds of those who attend these services." Mrs. Harris knew how to preach as clearly and forcefully as any of the leading male ministers in the area, commented the reporter. More important, the masses who thronged her meetings seemed to prove her calling and her spiritual effectiveness. Mary McGee Snell experienced much the same reaction at her revival held in Columbus, Mississippi. Snell was a spectacle to those who had never seen a female preacher. Southerners descended on the town to witness her work for themselves. Many "sinners" who were "inaccessible," as one observer put it, converted as a result of Snell's campaign. Enthusiasts in attendance accused ministers who opposed Snell's work of jealousy. The effete unsanctified preacher, said the faithful, could not bear to be outshone by an anointed woman evangelist.[108]

Southern holiness folk developed pragmatic and populist criteria for judging everything. Their egalitarianism and alternative value systems were natural outgrowths of this. Anyone, they thought, could be a spiritual conduit. The Holy Ghost used persons apart from the normal patterns of social certification, ecclesiastical training, or ordination.[109] As a result of such openness, they were not affected by the same regional, racial, gender, and class prejudices which so shaped their mainline brethren. It did not matter to southern holiness advocates, for instance, that their movement originated north of the Mason-Dixon line. Rather, they gloried in the thought of the barriers that holiness broke down. An increasingly cantankerous W. B. Godbey best summed up the populist assumptions of the movement, chiding an overeducated, irreligious mainline: "An illiterate old negro, full of the Holy Ghost, has more Gospel in his soul ready to transmit to others through his great thick dictionary-and-grammar-butchering lips than a whole car-load of plug-hatted theologians without the dynamite of the Holy Ghost."[110] Although Godbey's statement sounds unbearably racist to twenty-first-century ears, at the time he penned it in the late nineteenth century it certainly ran counter to wider cultural assumptions about authority. Southern holiness people in the MECS would bear the brunt of their denomination's scorn for such wayward views. By the end of the century, holiness sectarians and mainline evangelicals were clashing heatedly over doctrine and authority. These internecine conflicts, erupting in pulpits and in print, would alter southern holiness considerably, setting in motion forces which would help radicalize the movement throughout the region.

THREE

The Words of God
Spread South

BY JUNE 1890, thirty-one-year-old L. L. Pickett had seen much of the South. Born in Mississippi on the eve of the Civil War, he later lived in Texas, Arkansas, and South Carolina, and had traveled all over the former Confederacy. By any reckoning he was ambitious. While still a young man, Pickett embraced holiness theology, became a controversial firebrand preacher, a staunch prohibitionist, and a composer of folksy, sentimental Victorian hymns. He promoted the holiness cause with a dire sense of urgency. "There is a great revival on the doctrine, experience, and literature of holiness," he proclaimed in 1890. Ecstatic with hope, Pickett wrote that the contentious doctrine of perfection was "firing the pulpit, energizing the pew," and revitalizing camp meetings across the South. Never one for subtlety, he marshaled an army of mixed metaphors to advance his cause: the holiness movement was "harassing the press to the car of a more spiritual and unctuous religious experience than has prevailed for many years." This "press" would carry the movement into every city, village, and hamlet in Dixie. "Books, papers, and tracts are opening many eyes to the beauties of holiness, and feeding the many hungry souls with this 'hidden manna' of the Lord."[1]

Roughly half a century before the southern holiness revival began in earnest, Alexis de Tocqueville observed, "Only a newspaper can put the same thought at the same time before a thousand readers." Periodicals, wrote Tocqueville, were the sine qua non of modern mass social movements. In a democracy an association could not be powerful unless it was numerous. For a group of widely dispersed people to become a large collective, they needed some way of communicating on a day-to-day basis without actually having to meet together. Newspapers allowed discrete individuals to feel themselves part of a community (be it national, religious, or social) that superseded local or provincial interests. Newspapers brought readers together and continued to hold them together over distance and time.[2]

Southern holiness folk would distinguish themselves as avid readers of religious newspapers, books, and pamphlets. They placed the distinctive literature of their movement second only to the Bible in importance. If the Bible was the Word of God, then believers' many publications were the Words of God. W. B. Godbey, one of the most influential southern holiness authors and evangelists, summed up his co-religionists' sentiments, writing in his autobiography, "Let us remember that there is magic in print, rendering it far more influential than words spoken." Spoken words faded away soon after they were uttered, but the printed word could last indefinitely and influence far more individuals as a result.[3] Godbey devoted himself completely to print evangelism. Though more prolific than most southern-born holiness leaders, he, like other evangelists, poured his energies into holiness newspapers, pamphlets, tracts, and books. By the end of his life, Godbey had published over 230 books and booklets and penned hundreds of editorials in holiness journals.

Oddly enough, many observers still describe holiness and later pentecostal religious culture as fundamentally oral. Preaching was, of course, instrumental to the development of the holiness movement. At revivals throughout the South, holiness ministers introduced audiences to new doctrines and persuaded scores of southern evangelicals to join the holiness ranks. But too great an emphasis on the orality of the movement overshadows other critical factors. From the beginning believers relied heavily on print culture and shrewdly manipulated modern technologies.[4] Followers were disparaged by their many detractors as ignorant and antimodern. Yet the faithful used the latest technologies and inventions to spread their old-time message. And printed materials were the primary agents through which the emerging holiness community first imagined itself.[5] Southern holiness print culture had strong antecedents in the South as well as the North. Evangelicals' astonishing prior success with print media proved instrumental to the later holiness movement.

The technological innovations and marketing strategies evangelicals employed earlier in the century laid the foundation for subsequent endeavors. By the 1820s and 1830s, mass production and the availability of relatively cheap materials enabled religious publishers to reach a much wider audience. Before then, book publishing in America was the province of a small number of desperately undercapitalized printers. Consequently, until the second quarter of the century, reading materials remained limited to a narrow range of economic and social groups. Advances in presses, typesetting, typecasting, papermaking, and bookbinding contributed to the change. The nation's economic growth and the revolution in transportation allowed centralized publishers to print specialized materials and reach far-off consumers.[6]

At the same time, wandering evangelists served as colporteurs, aggressively selling denominational newspapers, tracts, and books in city and countryside. Their success at marketing religious products achieved tangible results. By the 1830s, the Methodist weekly *Christian Advocate and Journal* had gained a circulation of 25,000, a much larger readership than any other serial in the country.[7] Of course, interest in religious periodical literature in the South did not rival that in the North. But by 1850 circulation figures for twenty-eight leading magazines and newspapers in the South Atlantic states reached approximately 50,000. Not surprisingly, evangelical publications made the greatest gains in the region.[8]

Evangelicals had long excelled at popular communications. Baptists and Methodists, not inhibited by the same cultural proprieties and theological rigors constraining high-church Protestants, created a torrent of pamphlet and newspaper copy. They also produced millions of hymnals, missionary journals, and devotional books.[9] As contentious and competitive as evangelical denominations were with one another, the content of their publications was much the same. After the 1820s writers and editors employed a populist discourse that challenged theological specialists. Authority flowed not from the learned elite but from those stalwart leaders whose personality and rhetoric grabbed the attention of the common folk.[10] Such leaders' populist style made it easy for them to adopt new techniques and ideas that other, more conservative Protestants deemed vulgar or unfitting agents of the gospel. The evangelical climate in the first half of the nineteenth century privileged religious insurgents who made use of new strategies that would gain the attention of average citizens. Such evangelicals were not bothered by the novelty of using modern means to promote old-time values and ideas. In fact, many embraced new media wholeheartedly. As a writer in an 1823 issue of the *Christian Herald* reasoned, "The kingdom of God is a kingdom of means." If gospel preaching "is a Divine institution," then "'printing' is no less so." Print evangelism for this observer was "to be regarded with a sacred veneration and supported with religious care."[11]

New developments in printing in the late nineteenth century and rising literacy rates accelerated an already booming print industry. Newspapers experienced extremely rapid growth in the post–Civil War period. Between 1870 and 1900 the number of religious and secular daily newspapers quadrupled, while the number of copies sold increased nearly sixfold. Technological advances—including the development of high-speed presses, the invention of the typewriter, and the shift from rag to wood-pulp paper—greatly contributed to an extensive popular print culture.[12] These postwar developments set the stage for the southern holiness revival.

Much like earlier revivals in America, the holiness revival would be invented by the press, which unified its discourse and oriented the movement along communal lines.[13] Little has been more crucial to the creation of movement cultures than literature.[14] Northern reform and evangelical unions in the antebellum period, the temperance cause in the postbellum era, and southern Populism in the late nineteenth century owed much of their success to print media. Without some basic regional or national communication network, these groups would have found it difficult, if not impossible, to unite behind a common cause. Holiness was no exception.

The carpetbag holiness missionary William Baker first introduced numbers of southerners to the holiness cause beginning in the 1870s through his paper, *The Way of Holiness,* published in Spartanburg, South Carolina. Baker and his co-editor, R. C. Oliver, excerpted the work of northern holiness authors in their journal and offered scores of Wesleyan holiness books for sale through their Southern Tract Association. One of Baker's basic goals was to introduce southerners to the language and style of holiness, which he did by applying plain-folk idioms and rudimentary analogies to perfectionism. It was not enough for Christians to be converted, Baker urged. Mature believers must experience a more complete salvation. "The unsanctified Christian," Baker contended, "is like the sickly child." This infantile half-Christian might grow slightly but would never be perfect or whole until he or she experienced full salvation.[15] The zealous editor encouraged readers to devalue their previous conversion experiences and to comprehend sanctification as having changed their lives more fundamentally than earlier experiences had.[16] At other times subtler tactics proved more effective. For instance, another writer in *The Way of Holiness* avoided deprecating conversion in his depiction of sanctification. Instead, using similes familiar to rural southern readers, the aptly named Sammy Hick identified sin in the merely justified, unsanctified Christian as something like a tree that had been cut down. The stump, representing the continued presence of evil, remains until its roots are torn out of the earth. In like manner, only when God ripped sin out of the believer would he or she be set free from earthly concerns and desires.[17]

Some southern readers still found this otherworldly perfectionism dumbfounding, even when illustrated by the plainest and earthiest of metaphors. A confused writer from South Carolina wondered what it really meant to be "entirely sanctified." The perplexed correspondent knew a woman who, during the grisly years of the Civil War, seemed to exemplify purity and holiness better than anyone else. Through poverty and sorrow she struggled to be a model Christian, recalled the writer. "Tell me," he asked Baker, "is this not sanctification?" Baker, ever cautious about how sanctification was described in his paper, answered no.[18] The entirely sanctified person uses a peculiar language that sets him or her apart from other Christians.[19] Persons who achieved the second work of grace used biblical imagery as they described the state of being without inner conflicts or strife. Their nomenclature, said Baker, distinguished them. Converts often depicted their spiritual pilgrimage as a journey from Egypt to Canaan or as finally arriving in Beulah Land, a spiritual geography readers learned from hymns, books, and newspapers like *The Way of Holiness*.[20]

New converts also had to testify to the experience in no uncertain terms. Those who rallied to Baker's message did just that. J. B. Stevenson, presiding elder of the North Alabama Conference of the Methodist Episcopal Church, South, presented his anguished testimony in *The Way of Holiness* in 1876. Stevenson recalled that he had nearly lost sight of the second blessing during the Civil War years, as carnage, poverty, and chaos occupied his thoughts. Obtaining copies of Baker's paper in the mid-1870s, he turned to holiness for answers. He modeled his experience after those described there. In particular, Baker's printed testimony influenced him deeply. While reading about how Baker had "entered in the Canaan of perfect love," Stevenson claimed, he too experienced entire sanctification.[21]

Others longed for similar experiences. But before the mid-1880s few southern evangelicals had actually ever heard a sermon devoted to this second-work holiness. Hence most of the scattered readers of Baker's journal were familiar with perfectionism only as it was described in books or magazines. J. W. Baker, a southern Methodist minister writing from Dawsonville, Georgia, expressed the yearnings of many. Though he had read William Baker's publication for years, he felt that his faith was somehow incomplete. "O! how can I preach what I only know from books when it is a matter of experience?"[22] As this letter indicates, *The Way of Holiness* only partially met the religious needs of its readers. During the years William Baker published his journal, there were few holiness preachers and virtually no organizations in the region that might have facilitated the growth of the movement.

These circumstances changed rapidly in the 1880s. With the growing circulation of *The Christian Witness,* a holiness newspaper based in Boston, thousands of evangelicals across the South became aware of the movement. It spread through the region much the same way the earlier revival of 1857–1858 had in the North. Newspapers played a vital role in that massive prewar awakening. Editors in New York printed arresting accounts of the urban religious excitement. In turn, periodicals in Boston, Philadelphia, and New Orleans emulated the writing styles of secular papers in New York, excerpting testimonies, anecdotes, and firsthand accounts. These journals, then, defined and disseminated the basic vocabulary of expression.[23] In like manner, *The Christian Witness* served as a model for southern readers roughly three decades later.

William McDonald and fellow National Camp Meeting leaders first printed the *Witness* in July 1870 with the primary purpose of spreading the doctrine of entire sanctification. Within ten years this holiness weekly was supporting a host of both southern and northern evangelists in the South and encouraging thousands to join the movement. *The Christian Witness* corresponded with southern-born evangelists such as R. C. Oliver in South Carolina, George Watson in Florida, A. J. Jarrell in Georgia, and former slave Irving Lowery in South Carolina. They all formed new ties with northern holiness people

South Carolina native, former slave, Methodist Episcopal Church minister, educator, and author Irving Lowery first heard holiness preached in the years after the Civil War, when northern Methodist divines entered the South. Lowery promoted holiness across the state and regularly wrote articles for the Boston-based perfectionist newspaper *The Christian Witness.*

through the pages of *The Christian Witness.* The paper thus bridged the regional divide and slowly chipped away at some of the cultural barriers that had separated northern and southern evangelicals for decades.

This was not an isolated phenomenon. In general, literature played a vital role in reuniting northern and southern interests. Books and magazines gained massive readerships by embracing the romance of the so-called Lost Cause. Writers north and south memorialized the war efforts of both regions while forgetting the horrors of sectionalism and slavery. The plantation romances of Joel Chandler Harris and Thomas Nelson Page and the racial moral tales of Thomas Dixon exploited increasingly popular myths of the Old South and Confederate defeat. Indeed, during the last two decades of the nineteenth century, sentimental reconciliationist literature rose to unsurpassed levels of popularity. Many Americans escaped the vicis-situdes of the postwar years by immersing themselves in quaint regional literature that promoted fairy tales of a pristine, idyllic past.[24]

The Christian Witness, however, owed its success to the missionary zeal of evangelists and to something much more mundane as well. Northern holiness evangelists used the paper to promote the salubrious atmosphere of the sunny South as a means of encouraging other missionaries, both northern and southern, to remake the region into a holiness Zion. These depictions corresponded with larger trends in the postbellum South. In the 1870s and 1880s northerners, no longer preoccu-pied with wartime anguish and devastation, came to think of the South as an ideal tourist destination, a region replete with romance and rural charm that was a relaxing, slow-paced re-spite from northern life.[25] Accordingly, correspondents of Bos-ton's *Christian Witness* recounted the glories of Dixie and held forth on the limitless possibilities for evangelism there. In July 1883 William McDonald extolled the virtues of the popular health resort of Summerville, South Carolina, informing the paper, "No better place can be found in the South for persons suffering with lung or throat troubles." At the end of his re-vival tour his health and that of his northern co-laborers had been much improved.[26] Similarly, George Watson promoted the advantages of his new community, Windsor, Florida (east of Gainesville), in *The Christian Witness,* describing it as an Edenic setting where holiness and industry might thrive. The small town had no whisky dealers and was free from malaria. The townspeople were eager to obtain copies of the popular holiness newspaper from Boston. For those Christians seek-ing physical and spiritual health, he declared, "I can say I know of no better place in this State than Windsor."[27] Others, too, used *The Christian Witness* to urge holiness converts on both sides of the Mason-Dixon line to enter the mission field. Heeding the call, two northern holiness women championed Grovetown, Georgia, as a healthful retreat ripe for holiness evangelism and temperance work. Cassie and Lois Smith, who preached holiness to black congregations and held Women's Christian Temperance Union meetings in the town, reported that their work obliterated sectionalism by uniting North and South in a common cause. Like the Smiths, the white evangelist F. W. Linton also preached and ministered to former slaves. Linton reported on his holiness and benevolent work among African American congregations in Florida, and northern readers responded by sending money and Bibles for black churches.[28]

With such enticements, the northern paper encouraged prospective missionaries to set up permanent work in the region. *The Christian Witness* persuaded J. M. Pike, a native of Newfoundland, Canada, to become a holiness apostle to the South in the 1880s. Responding to the paper's call for evangelists, Pike ventured to South Carolina. He acknowledged his indebtedness to the editor of *The Christian Witness* in a letter reprinted in the paper: "Humanly speaking, you are the means of my coming South, and your recommendation secured for me an immediate place in the confidence of the ministers."[29] Thus certified, he worked through the MECS as a holiness preacher and publisher. Pike proved instrumental to what would become the most influential holiness paper in the South, *The Way of Faith*. R. C. Oliver and the irascible L. L. Pickett began publishing the serial in 1891. Oliver died that same year, and Pike later assumed his duties as editor. He devoted the publication to disseminating holiness doctrine and literature and furthering the city mission work Oliver had initiated in Columbia, South

Carolina. Pike enlarged the readership tremendously. In 1896 he reported that his publication had a circulation of eight to ten thousand in South Carolina alone and reached nearly every state in the Union.[30]

In the 1880s and early 1890s several prominent southern-born holiness converts also began publishing papers that catered to southern readers. In those years north Georgia became a stronghold for the nascent southern holiness movement. Revivals in Charleston, Savannah, and Augusta, sponsored by John Inskip's National Camp Meeting Association, persuaded a number of young leaders in the MECS to adopt holiness views. Some of them—including W. A. Dodge, A. J. Jarrell, William C. Dunlap, and E. G. Murrah—felt that there was enough interest in holiness in the South to warrant the publication of additional perfectionist newspapers. With the support of these ministers and others, Dodge began editing and publishing *Tongue of Fire* in 1882. The following year Georgia disciples organized the Georgia Holiness Association and adopted Dodge's paper, which they renamed *The Way of Life,* as their official publication.[31]

Dodge's journal was a boon to the southern movement. Subscriptions came in from as far away as Texas, Mississippi, Kentucky, and North Carolina. During the peak of its influence, circulation reached over seven thousand. Yet Dodge struggled to keep the paper running. Perhaps too generous toward his readers, he barely gained enough revenue from subscriptions or advertising to cover the cost of printing and postage. After sinking much of his own savings into the paper, he finally decided to merge his publication with *The Methodist,* a new holiness periodical in Kentucky.[32]

In Kentucky, Henry Clay Morrison, the ambitious MECS minister who founded *The Methodist,* was motivated by a single-minded purpose. Shortly after Morrison's sanctification experience in the late 1880s he began to seek out new means of evangelism. Lying in bed one night in 1888, Morrison reflected that if he could multiply himself into a "score of men," he could propagate his holiness message throughout the country. At this point he hit on the idea of publishing a paper. It might do the work of hundreds of preachers, he reasoned. Morrison envisioned a journal that would inspire a return to plain-folk religion and the "old paths" of Methodism. *The Methodist* was soon renamed *The Pentecostal Herald,* reflecting its larger goal of restoring the early Christian church and reviving the faith of the apostles. Morrison's journal quickly gained a loyal readership. In 1893 the newspaper claimed a circulation of 15,000, which doubled in less than thirty years. In just one week in early 1898, the *Herald* gained 1,078 subscribers.[33] Surprisingly, before Morrison embarked on the venture, he had no experience in newspaper publishing. But that seemed immaterial to him.

Other holiness enthusiasts, sensing immense opportunities, overcame inexperience just as Morrison did. Before W. A. Dodge began publishing his newspaper, *The Way of Life,* in Georgia, he had no knowledge of publishing or editing a paper. Likewise, in the 1890s, Texas holiness minister Denis Rogers edited and published *True Holiness* though he "knew nothing about the printing business and had scarcely seen [the] inside of a printing office." Rogers made up for his deficiencies by taking courses in typesetting and editing at a printing office in McKinney, Texas. Dozens of men and women in the region did the same. In general, to edit and operate a weekly rural paper in the postwar South required only a rudimentary education. Few editors of such weeklies in this era had attended college, and many had failed to complete or even attend high school. All that was necessary was a keen interest in the subject matter and an ability to read and write. It was also possible to begin publishing a paper with little capital and scant technical knowledge of printing. The equipment might consist merely of a small stock of paper, four iron chases (where blocks of type would be set), a towel, a roller and an inking pan, and a Franklin or Washington hand press. Small presses cost as little as $125, and paper and supplies were also relatively inexpensive. Taking advantage of increasingly low-cost equipment and materials, holiness entrepreneurs established presses dedicated to perfectionism and radical religion.[34]

An avid young second work evangelist in Cincinnati began publishing a perfectionist serial, fittingly titled *The Revivalist.* The impassioned Martin Wells Knapp later renamed his paper *God's Revivalist,* claiming that it was under the sole proprietorship of God, published in "His" interests. Knapp made use of

A holiness print shop at Pilot Point, Texas, ca. 1908.

pentecostal language and imagery that captivated the imagination of his many southern readers. In apocalyptic tones, he presented accounts of "Revival Dynamite," "Revival Tornados," "Lightning Bolts from Pentecostal Skies," and "Revival Fire."[35] Southern holiness adherents were enthralled by Knapp's paper. Accordingly, it enjoyed one of the largest circulations of any such publication, North or South. By the late nineteenth century, Knapp was giving away or selling approximately twenty thousand copies monthly to a readership that included both blacks and whites.[36]

It was a promising time for popular religious publications. State expenditures on education rose rapidly in the South during the late 1880s, and as a result, illiteracy declined substantially. By the turn of the century, 85 to 90 percent of southern whites were literate. African Americans made the greatest strides during this period. Black illiteracy fell by as much as 30 percent or more. This was all the more remarkable in light of the fact that in 1865 barely 10 percent of former slaves could read.[37] African Americans, once deprived of reading, eagerly obtained books and newspapers and seized new educational opportunities. Black newspaper and religious journal production flourished in the period between 1890 and 1910. Most of those new publications were produced in large cities, but increasing numbers were now also printed in rural areas. In poverty-stricken rural Mississippi the growth rate was staggering. In that state after 1890 African Americans produced approximately 150 newspapers and journals across forty-four counties. Readers often passed them from house to house.[38] Religious literature was no less important for white evangelicals. The abundance of holiness periodicals, books, and pamphlets printed in this era, and holiness adherents' preoccupation with reading, attest to these new circumstances.[39]

Editors of holiness newspapers also established small pub-

Cincinnati-based author, editor, and evangelist Martin Wells Knapp ushered thousands of southerners into the radical holiness movement.

lishing houses to meet the growing demand for specialized religious literature. In 1888 there were no fewer than four publishing houses engaged exclusively in producing holiness materials in the United States. In the same period, twenty-seven holiness journals were being published, most issued on a monthly basis. Yet just four years later the number of periodicals had risen to forty-one, and an increasing number of them were now printed as weeklies. In the South alone, there were at least twenty holiness journals being published in the 1890s. Morrison, Knapp, Pike, and other editors established publishing houses and subscription book companies to supplement their newspaper work. They published thousands of books, which, if limited in content, still held wide appeal. Southern authors such as W. B. Godbey, Morrison, Watson, and Beverly Carradine cranked out works on Christian perfection, the failings of the Methodist Church, and the moral perils of popular entertainments.[40] Only a decade before, the cantankerous southern Methodist divine Lovick Pierce had complained, "I doubt if you can find a member in all our [southern Methodist] Church that has read a book on holy living in his or her life."[41] Had he lived much longer, Pierce would have seen sweeping changes in his denomination. Popular holiness literature soon helped spread the movement into areas where little or no interest had existed before.

Evangelists carried perfectionist papers and books into every southern state. In the late 1890s the wayfaring revivalist Frank Bartleman handed out hundreds of perfectionist newspapers, tracts, books, and hymnals throughout the former slave states. His best customers were often African Americans eager to read the material the northern preacher carried. Still, Bartleman was frequently destitute. On foot for most of the journey, he wore the soles of his shoes down to nothing and had to cut the pockets out of an old pair of pants to use as socks. Nonetheless, he was overjoyed by the possibilities of print evangelism. A holiness minister from Raleigh, North Carolina, also sensed the opportunities at hand. In J. M. Pike's *Way of Faith*, W. J. W. Crowder extolled the virtues of the newspaper and Pike's publishing company. "I have read and distributed many of your excellent tracts," he declared. Preaching and holding holiness meetings in the South, Crowder acted as a tireless distributor of the paper, scattering what he estimated to be over 150,000 pages of "printed truth in books, papers, and tracts."[42] For Crowder and others like him, the dissemination of holiness literature went hand in hand with evangelism. Armed with bundles of Wesleyan literature, Crowder and his brethren drew in thousands of new recruits. D. A. Futrell, a North Carolina minister and associate of Pike's, typified those who warmly received the Wesleyan message. Before reading John Wesley, Futrell felt that he "had an enemy [sin] within that had to be conquered or it would conquer me." In the midst of deep spiritual anguish he came upon Wesley's *Plain Account of Christian Perfection* as well as *Experimental Religion* (1854) by Leonidas Rosser, a Virginia Methodist. After reading them, Futrell saw clearly what had appeared so murky before. Summarizing his religious pilgrimage in 1895, Futrell rejoiced, "I could be made free from sin that remained in my heart."[43]

Before W. B. Godbey began his fecund writing career, he too circulated other writers' works at revivals and holiness conventions in Kentucky, Missouri, Tennessee, and Georgia. He was perhaps the most dedicated distributor of perfectionist literature in the former Confederacy. Godbey recounted in his autobiography purchasing thousands of copies of Wesley's *Plain Account* to sell at places where he preached. In the early 1880s he obtained a copy of southern-born author G. D. Watson's *Holiness Manual.* He devoured it cover to cover, he remembered years later, "and seeing that its plain teaching was the thing my people needed, I wrote [Watson] a postal card ordering a thousand copies." Godbey rapidly sold these and ordered another two thousand to give to his audiences.[44] Realizing how eager converts were to purchase holiness literature, he began churning out his own books and tracts on devotion, theology, and biblical exposition to meet the growing demand. Southern holiness presses published most of his widely read work—including *Sanctification* (1884), *Christian Perfection* (1886), *Commentary on the New Testament* (1887), and *Holiness or Hell?* (1893). The Pentecostal Publishing Company and Pickett Publishing House, both in Louisville, and Living Waters in Nashville printed tens of thousands of Godbey's works.

God's Revivalist Press, operated by Martin Wells Knapp in Cincinnati, acted as Godbey's chief publisher and helped make Godbey the most visible and influential minister in the southern movement.[45]

As early as 1873, northern holiness missionaries in Tennessee promoted the movement through books. At the National Camp Meeting held in Knoxville, local reporters noted the presence of a bookstore on-site, where "persons visiting the grounds can make valuable additions to their libraries."[46] In the years that followed, holiness bookselling flourished. Newspapers catalogued numerous works for sale at affordable prices. Both northern and southern holiness periodicals regularly featured full-page advertisements for holiness literature. Editors sold the works of authors from the Wesleyan canon—John Wesley, John Fletcher, Madam Guyon, and Adam Clarke—as well as texts by newer lights who were reshaping Wesleyanism, such as Phoebe Palmer, Daniel Steele, W. B. Godbey, S. A. Keen, and G. D. Watson. In November 1885 *The Christian Witness* advertised 211 books and tracts for sale from a wide range of holiness-affiliated authors and hymn writers. Similarly, W. A. Dodge's journal *The Way of Life* listed 157 books for purchase in one 1891 issue. These ranged in price from ten cents for Wesley's ever popular *Plain Account* to three dollars for a two-volume set of Frances R. Havergal's poetry.[47] Largely because of such incessant advertising, Knapp sold as many as 100,000 copies of the first edition of his and L. L. Pickett's popular, hypersentimental holiness hymnal, *Tears and Triumphs*.[48]

Sanctificationist editors felt certain that the literature and hymnals they circulated wrought deep changes in all who read and sang from them. J. M. Pike asserted that scores "had been saved, healed, or greatly helped in their experience" by reading S. B. Shaw's gushing Victorian holiness devotional

Touching Incidents and Remarkable Answers to Prayer (1893), advertised repeatedly in *The Way of Faith*. Pike offered several examples that he thought verified the near-magical power of print:

> A lady bought one of these books and laid it on her center table and two souls were converted by reading it. A man in Michigan was sent to jail for a great crime, and a friend sent him one of these books. He read it, wept over it, and gave his heart to God. . . . Just recently a Christian man in Nebraska who had entirely lost his speech and had been unable to make a sound for ten years read the book and was encouraged to ask God for healing. . . . God answered his prayer and restored his speech.[49]

These totems of grace seemed to hold a kind of power which dazzled believers. Holiness leaders became tireless promoters of their sacred literature. Many newspaper editors most heavily featured their own works or the books of their field agents. At times book revenues provided the basic financial support for their newspapers. E. E. Shelhamer, a Free Methodist author and publisher in Atlanta, sold over ten thousand copies of his *Popular and Radical Holiness, Contrasted* by incessantly plugging it in his monthly periodical, *The Repairer and Holiness Advocate*.[50]

Holiness editors, writers, and lay readers clearly understood the importance of their literature in disseminating doctrine and creating a vibrant movement culture. Followers of Populism, the cultural and political movement that roughly paralleled holiness, relied on literature for some of the same basic reasons that holiness folk did. That movement required a high order of cultural education and tactical accomplishment. Populists achieved their goals not only by sending out agents to

Advertisements like this for holiness titles regularly appeared in holiness newspapers, books, and tracts. The volumes listed here, published by the radical holiness leader Martin Wells Knapp, gained a wide readership in the South.

stump across the region but also through a myriad of papers and journals. By the 1890s their *National Economist* was educating thousands of farmers and laborers about currency theory and the iniquities of northern industrialism. In 1895, 195 papers in the South—including *Comrade, Toiler's Friend, Wool Hat,* and *People's Party Paper*—declared themselves Populist publications and championed the cause with righteous vigor.[51]

Movement journalism, as seen in Populism as well as holiness, helped create what some scholars call a counterpublic. Members of the holiness counterpublic defined themselves in opposition to the standards of society. In turn, mainline southern evangelicals thought perfectionists crass and undignified. Fringe perfectionist publications only widened the divide and imparted a sense of coherence to readers scattered from Texas to Virginia. Editors of such papers achieved success largely by pitting themselves against mainstream institutions and leaders. The resulting counterpublic maintained an awareness of its supposed subordinate status.[52] Initiates longed for a separate, unique religious identity. Hence, southern adherents would establish their own presses, journals, and tract societies mostly outside the authority and control of mainline denominations.[53] Enthusiasts devoted such publications to doctrines and practices that were often at odds with the more sedate mainline majority.

Editors and correspondents in newly established holiness papers wrote of their unwavering commitment to radical perfectionism. The Virginia-born evangelist G. D. Watson expressed the perfectionist sentiments of many in his periodical *Living Words* (Pittsburgh), arguing that anyone "born of God doth not commit sin." Other initiates believed that when they were entirely sanctified, God removed their carnal mind, cleansing them of all sin.[54] Soon readers mastered the terminology and practice of this doctrine.

Holiness newspapers advertised what converts needed. Simultaneously they met those needs and provided believers with a new and unusual expressive vocabulary. Not surprisingly, this process bears a striking resemblance to what was taking place in the late-nineteenth-century advertising culture. Circulation of religious journals in the United States peaked in the 1870s. At roughly this same time, advertisements increased markedly in religious publications, and revenues from these reached unparalleled levels. Advertisers saw the growing opportunities offered by popular denominational magazines. No less than ad agents, religious publishers readily employed advertising techniques to sell religious ideas and products to their readers.[55] Their new approach yielded tremendous gains. Consequently, as southern holiness converts pored over the pages of their newspapers and books, they began to speak the same language and to consider themselves part of a wider culture.[56]

Holiness periodicals and books introduced thousands to the movement. Within their pages leaders and laity first read and wrote about their perfectionist experiences, however sacred or mundane. Newspapers were also a democratic space, noted H. C. Morrison in his *Pentecostal Herald*. With the skills of an adman, he proclaimed, "The Pentecostal Herald is the people's paper; the people own it, run it, write for it, read it, love it, and scatter it broadcast over the land."[57] Though exaggerated, his claims were not far off the mark. Southern readers sent their testimonies to holiness newspapers and professed their indebtedness to holiness literature. G. T. Allen, a man from Gainesville, Georgia, wrote to *The Way of Life* about how holiness acquaintances had brought him into the movement. Before this Allen had never thought much about the possibility of perfection in this life. Moreover, in his childhood he had been taught that sanctification came to the believer only at death. But in the early 1880s friends from California wrote to him about the perfectionist movement and mailed holiness books and papers to him. "Through reading them," testified Allen, "I was brought to see my need of salvation." Under the influence of Phoebe Palmer and other popular northern writers, Allen sought out like-minded believers in Georgia and joined them in holiness work in the South.[58]

A decade after Allen came in contact with the movement, *Tennessee Methodist* editor B. F. Haynes began to read about perfectionism in books recommended to him by a colleague. Haynes was entranced by Wesley's *Plain Account* and J. A. Wood's *Perfect Love* (1860). While reading these works, Haynes vividly sensed "that there was a higher and sweeter realm of spiritual life to which I was privileged, and the reading of these books definitized [*sic*] and clarified my vision as to what that was." John B. Culpepper, a restless preacher from Georgia, experienced something very similar when he came to accept entire sanctification after reading a variety of perfectionist books and periodicals. Hearing of the second blessing controversy raging in his state, Culpepper ordered a large box of holiness literature. It cost him the hefty sum of $151. But, as he later recalled, it was well worth the exorbitant expense, since it brought him to the experience of a second work of grace.[59] Like countless other southerners, Haynes and Culpepper first adopted sanctificationist views while perusing holiness works. Indeed, they had rarely heard a perfectionist message preached from Methodist pulpits. Books and papers traversed the nation at greater speed and more broadly than holiness ministers could itinerate.

By 1890 initiates in the South had turned their attention to the work of dozens of southern holiness writers. Such new authors appealed to southern readers through their use of plain-folk idioms and radical evangelical imagery. These holiness leaders persuaded their reading audience to seek sanctification and schooled them on the ascetic life that holiness demanded. On a practical level, perfectionist commitments precluded participation in secular entertainments, such as theatergoing, sporting events, or social dancing. The faithful also frequently prohibited the consumption of alcohol, tobacco, coffee, Coca-Cola, or anything else that "'blunted' one's 'moral quality.'"[60] As editors broadcast their distinctive social beliefs in newspapers scattered throughout the region, southern stalwarts constructed a countercultural environment in opposition to what they described as the "sinful world."

This religious counterculturalism continued to spread through the influence of holiness writers. The southern-born preacher and author L. L. Pickett exerted a powerful influence on T. M. Elliott, an avid holiness reader in Young Harris, Georgia. One of Pickett's works, *The Book and Its Theme,* convinced Elliott that tobacco use inhibited holy living. After he read Pickett, Elliott's old "sinful" habits no longer gave him any pleasure. "I could not get my tobacco to taste right," he told *The Pentecostal Herald.* Elliott decided to abstain from tobacco and many other vices he now believed damaged his soul and wasted his time and resources. After reading Pickett, Elliott spent his hard-earned money exclusively on holiness literature, including books by Carradine, Godbey, Wesley, and Shaw.[61] A Texas correspondent in *The Way of Faith* read the same materials and gained much the same insights from them. The Bible, though, wrote E. M. Murrill, was the most important text for all Christians, and especially holiness adherents. He encouraged readers to mark up their Bibles, studying every passage with great attention to detail. Besides the Bible, "you need to read holiness books. I read certain holiness books over and over and always with great profit." But perhaps even more important, Murrill argued, was *The Way of Faith.* He strongly exhorted readers to subscribe to it and other holiness news-

A late-nineteenth-century portrait of holiness evangelist, publisher, songwriter, and controversial author L. L. Pickett.

papers. There were many important religious papers that served as sources of inspiration to Christians, he acknowledged. Yet none compared to holiness journals, in either religious depth or power.[62] It is little wonder, then, that so many holiness readers described studying their newspapers as if they were sacred texts, as one initiate put it.[63]

Perfectionist papers exercised immense power over converts' lives. Widely circulated periodicals such as *The Christian Alliance and Missionary Weekly* (New York), *The Gospel*

Trumpet (Anderson, Indiana), *The Way of Faith, Zion's Out-look, The Holiness Advocate* (Lumberton, North Carolina), *The Way of Life,* and *Live Coals* (Royston, Georgia) told adherents which books to read, whom and what to pray for, which doctrines to accept or reject, and which evangelists to follow and support.[64] These and other periodicals did much to help foster a robust sense of an integrated community.

In 1891 Dodge used *The Way of Life* to survey the new holiness community. "Will all the preachers in the South that are in the experience of 'Perfect Love', please drop us a card," he asked. Perhaps to discern between the true standard-bearers and the nominal, Dodge also requested the place and date each had become entirely sanctified, "and please say if you have it as a second, distinct and separate work of grace." Dodge thought his inquiry would show how the movement was progressing in the South. It also would give him important contacts with preachers, missionaries, and evangelists who could be called on to assist at revivals and conventions.[65]

Following Dodge's example, other holiness editors regularly printed directories of approved holiness evangelists, including contact information. Such lists promoted preachers deemed acceptable by leaders of the southern movement. In deference to the opinion of newspaper editors, readers invited these certified evangelists into their communities to conduct successful meetings.[66] Sanctificationist newspapers were also the leading advertisers of holiness conventions and revivals. Soon after the African American minister C. P. Jones began publishing his newspaper, *Truth,* in Mississippi, he used it to announce a holiness convention to be held in Jackson. The meeting, which owed much of its success to the paper, lasted two weeks. Attendees fervently studied the Bible and prayed night and day.[67] Eager subscribers read months in advance of holiness events like this one. The faithful even planned their work schedules to accommodate such protracted meetings.

Holiness literature was able to create a strong sense of fellowship where no physical community existed. Spread out across the South, many devotees could not actually attend the various revivals being reported throughout the region. But through the pages of their books and newspapers they entered an imagined community which united them even as they were apart. A Mobile, Alabama, judge named Price serves as a case in point. For years Judge Price had subscribed to northern holiness papers such as *The Christian Standard* (Philadelphia) and knew the names and read the editorials of a host of holiness leaders. Although he never met any of them in person, he felt strongly linked to them over space and time through a shared religious experience.[68]

Some holiness converts even thought of their periodicals and books as a kind of substitute for actual religious communities. Readers from the southern upcountry and the sparsely populated Texas plains found that holiness literature met their religious needs as well as, if not better than, their traditional Methodist, Baptist, and Cumberland Presbyterian churches. A letter to *The Way of Faith* in the early 1890s praised Beverly Carradine's book on sanctification for giving clear guidance on the subject. Moreover, the correspondent found rich spiritual nourishment in *The Way of Faith* itself. "I feel after reading it," claimed the elated Texan, "that I have been to a good class meeting. Don't see how I can do without it." Holiness literature served as the primary source of religious instruction for believers, especially those living in out-of-the-way circuits. Mary A. Murphy, a follower from Madisonville, Kentucky, was one such individual. In Dodge's paper she grieved that she and others like her in the backcountry were visited only infrequently by a handful of itinerant ministers. Murphy, like the majority of rural southerners at the time, could attend church only occasionally. But when she could not go to church, she read holiness literature, particularly *The Way of Faith,* which, she remarked, ably taught and guided her.[69]

The imagined community of holiness took shape in other ways as well. Readers of *The Way of Faith, The Pentecostal Herald,* and *God's Revivalist* found religious sustenance in the testimonies of other readers. The printed letters of laypeople and ministers often helped form readers' own religious experiences. Almost any text can determine a reader's response, however active the reader may be. Histories of reading must, therefore, take into account the ways that texts both constrain and liberate readers. Such a process was always at work among nineteenth-century American evangelicals. Although the content of the southern holiness movement was different from that of earlier awakenings, the means of transmission was much the same. In the early nineteenth century, evangelicals read thousands of stock testimonies in all manner of printed material as well as in personal letters from friends and relatives. Evangelical readers were intimately familiar with the steps of conversion and duplicated these in their own written and spoken testimonies.[70]

Disciples experienced sanctification in similar ways. In the pages of *The Way of Faith,* E. M. Pafford of Willacoohee, Georgia, recalled that a copy of the paper had serendipitously fallen into his hands. In this issue he came across the holiness "experience of a sister in Texas, which I read over and over for several weeks." Pafford found the account mesmerizing. He even read the selection to several members of his church. The woman's printed testimony described in detail the same spiritual turmoil he was experiencing. Consequently, he was determined to resolve his personal conflict much as the woman in the paper had. Under the influence of *The Way of Faith,* he attended a local revival (which may well have been advertised in the journal), where he underwent sanctification just as his female counterpart had experienced it. Subsequently, Pafford zealously lauded *The Way of Faith* and five other holiness periodicals—all of which he subscribed to—for ushering him into the movement. Converts all over the South felt similarly connected through their print community.[71] Indeed, they urgently shared their spiritual reading experiences in holiness papers and helped foster religious solidarity across the region. In an 1899 issue of *Live Coals of Fire,* one initiate from Hartwell, Georgia, wrote that after reading testimonies and reports of the "warfare of God," he had felt as if he were in the midst of a "red-hot testimony meeting." Furthermore, he believed that if he did not write to the paper to testify about his own experience, he would somehow lose the fullness of his faith.[72]

Holiness folk clearly considered their literature a principal agent for evangelism. Numbers of converts, eager that more should know about entire sanctification, circulated their older holiness newspapers and books among friends and neighbors. Some believed so wholeheartedly in print missions that they became ardent newspaper agents, selling or giving out copies at revivals, in local stores, and on street corners.[73] Miller Willis, an eccentric evangelist based in Georgia, even worked out a systematic plan of holiness print evangelism. He suggested to the readers of *The Christian Witness* that they start up holiness circulating libraries in their churches. Once holiness proponents won over their congregations, they should introduce a "good holiness paper" and "get it into as many homes as you can." Willis found, too, that reading extracts from holiness books and papers from the pulpit yielded tremendous results.[74] Yet Willis's zeal for literature was hardly exceptional. Sarah Bicknell, a preacher in South Carolina, wrote to *The Christian Witness* about a revival meeting she and others held in Charleston. As part of her afternoon services she read Wesley's *Plain Account of Christian Perfection* to her congregants. Many of the attendants were still unfamiliar with holiness, and Bicknell found that reading to them from that classic text proved most effective.[75]

Followers regularly lent out their journals and books and encouraged converts to subscribe to perfectionist periodicals. Believing in the usefulness of such an approach, a Virginia subscriber to *The Revivalist* offered her advice on print evangelism. "Mrs. Hendrick" gushed in a letter to the monthly, "The Revivalist is the best paper I ever read." After Hendrick carefully studied each issue, she usually passed it along to her neighbors. This publication was especially important, she found, because her local pastor did not believe in a second work of grace, and her community lacked strong holiness leadership. Some preferred merely to lend their papers out rather than give them away. In this way they could recirculate them in their communities to numbers of potential converts.[76] If borrowers liked what they read, then print evangelists would urge them to subscribe to the papers themselves. The South Carolina black preacher Irving E. Lowery aggressively pitched holiness newspapers. In the pages of *The Christian Witness* he urged black ministers of the South Carolina Conference to take this northern holiness journal. Once the paper gained a strong readership among African Americans in the state, he reasoned, the holiness movement would take hold of the church throughout the region. At a Kingstree, South Carolina, conference meeting in 1887, Lowery gave away 110 free copies of *The Christian Witness,* hoping to entice new subscribers. His plan worked. Southern blacks increasingly subscribed to the paper and a number of other sanctificationist periodicals.[77]

Holiness advocates' ardor for print evangelism was equally matched by their growing opposition to traditional denominations. By the 1890s their many books and papers were promoting a religious counterpublic identity antagonistic to much of southern Protestantism.[78] In fact, the faithful defined their movement by its resistance to mainline groups. Within the pages of their periodicals they held mainline churches accountable for any delinquency in doctrine or morality. Editors and correspondents lamented the growing indifference or outright opposition to perfectionism among established denominations. Speaking in the late nineteenth century, one fervid holiness evangelist charged: "Mr. John Wesley said when the Methodist church gave up the doctrine of holiness they would be a backslidden and fallen church. They have surely given it up for the people have quit getting their [sanctification] experience."[79]

Converts' disdain for traditional denominationalism did not go unnoticed by mainline church authorities. Already by the late 1880s southern Methodist officials were raising concerns over perfectionist zealotry. Methodist leaders clearly saw the power of the holiness press in generating enthusiasm and fostering community. Devotion to new second work periodicals ran high. Many readers announced that they would read only holiness works, leaving secular and denominational publications to "worldlings."

In turn, Methodist officials fumed at the exclusiveness of the new craze. Southern Methodist divines had reason for dismay. Denominational disloyalty, increasingly apparent in the sectarian press, seemed to threaten church strength on the local and regional level. In some areas church papers were even eclipsed by new holiness periodicals.[80] An alarmed southern Methodist official writing in the *Alabama Christian Advocate* observed the power of H. C. Morrison's periodical *The Methodist.* This newspaper, argued the appalled writer, exerted tremendous influence over holiness people, to the point where it was more authoritative than any of the individuals it represented and its followers advertised it to the exclusion of other publications.[81] Holiness periodicals commanded similar allegiance all over the South. One typical follower wrote to the journal of the South Carolina conference of the MECS to request the cancellation of his subscription. "Dear Brother: Please stop my ADVOCATE, as I take *The Christian Standard* and *Way of Life.*" The Methodist editor thought this gentleman's disloyalty outrageous and rebuked him and other enthusiasts who looked for spiritual fulfillment outside the confines of official southern Methodism. Wayward holiness folk, he declared, were obsessed with a religious hobby, a fad. Why not replace all Methodist Church hymnals and disciplines with holiness ones? he asked sarcastically. A farmer could replace his church periodical with an agricultural magazine, or a prohibitionist might subscribe to a temperance paper instead of his conference journal. The narrow logic of holiness infuriated him and appeared ridiculous in the extreme.[82] Another loyal southern Methodist, writing in the *Quarterly Review of the M.E. Church, South,* sensed the same dangers when "sanctificationists" rejected official church publications in favor of their own eccentric material. Their fervor, as he saw it, knew no bounds, for "they introduce their peculiar literature to the exclusion of all other." To counter the effects of perfectionist literature, church leaders furiously castigated holiness editors and readers. Holiness newspapers supported "insubordination" and "rebellion" against church authorities, wrote the Methodist minister J. W. Rush in the *Alabama Christian Advocate.* Rush advised watchfulness among Alabama Methodists and singled out B. F. Haynes's *Tennessee Methodist* as a chief culprit behind the denominational insurrection. Rush felt he was doing everything in his power "to save our church from the pernicious effects of such a weekly visitor."[83]

Leaders at the highest levels of southern Methodism ad-

Wagons in Kansas City loaded with issues of the perfectionist periodical *Herald of Holiness*, early twentieth century. The publication was shipped across the country to states such as Arkansas, Oklahoma, and Texas.

vised caution. In 1894 the General Conference of the MECS warned against the holiness menace. The bishops thought that perfectionism should still be preached. Yet holiness, they observed, was dividing the denomination: "There has sprung up among us a part with holiness as a watchword; they have holiness associations, holiness meetings, holiness preachers, holiness evangelists, and holiness property. . . . [W]e deplore their teaching and methods in so far as they claim a monopoly of the experience, practice, and advocacy of holiness, and separate themselves from the body of ministers and disciples."[84] The clannishness of the new sect, well demonstrated by its publishing ventures, only widened the gap between perfectionists and the mainline.

By the mid-1890s adherents were courting confrontation as if to prove their divine appointment. Holiness and denominational newspapers served as a virtual dueling ground where combatants hurled insults at each other with abandon. Soon after Indiana native A. J. Tomlinson began publishing a small holiness paper in Culberson, North Carolina, he encountered strong local opposition to his views.[85] Tomlinson would later distinguish himself as one of the principal founders of the pentecostal Church of God (Cleveland). But at around the turn of the century he was, like many other enthusiasts, a highly independent missionary who thrived on religious enmity. His newspaper, *Samson's Foxes,* often served as the chief weapon in his radical holiness arsenal. On one occasion Tomlinson was approached by a Baptist minister who was enraged by what he had read in Tomlinson's periodical. The minister believed that Tomlinson exaggerated the spiritual and material squalor of poor white southerners. Unable to take such criticisms lightly, and equipped with an enormous ego, Tomlinson surmised that his antagonist was unknowingly fighting against God. This and a series of other confrontations, including vandals firing bullets into Tomlinson's home at night, put the maverick preacher and his family in grave danger. For Tomlinson, recounting violent incidents like these in his paper affirmed the righteousness of his cause.

As the century came to a close, other fierce confrontations unfolded within the pages of the southern denominational press. Southern Baptists and Methodists could not bear holiness doctrinal hubris any more than they could tolerate initiates' ecstatic worship practices. Holiness people, mainline church leaders protested, disrupted congregations and communities and stirred up theological controversy wherever they ventured. In the *Christian Advocate,* one writer blasted the religious bigotry of believers. "This sort of medievaelism [*sic*]," railed the writer, "is a gross anachronism, out of place in the nineteenth century." Other southern Methodists recoiled at what they considered the pious pretensions of the movement. Of course, stalwarts did tend to describe the Spirit's leading as an intimate affair. On this account, one southern Methodist official satirized them on the front page of the *Christian Advocate.* It was as if they had a private wire running into the heavens, "along which they receive direct instructions from God concerning all the petty and trivial details of their daily conduct."[86]

Indeed, holiness people wrote to their conference and denominational papers to let readers know about all the minutiae of their entire sanctification experiences and their day-to-day communications with God. Such letters flooded the editorial office of the *Christian Advocate.* "In mercy to our readers," the editor of the journal declared, he refused to publish numbers of what he considered repetitive and unbearably dull testimonies.[87] Even worse than their dry religious bulletins, holiness people denigrated all who did not accept their unusual methods and doctrines, charged J. M. Boland, a southern Methodist preacher who published a searing critique of perfectionism in 1888 scorning "second blessingism." No man or woman who did not agree with entire sanctification could ever "get a hearing in the columns of their *bombproof* periodicals," he complained. He surmised that holiness writers thrived on religious chauvinism.[88] If nothing else, antiholiness commentators could dismiss the faithful for not living up to their supposed ideals. In *The Religious Herald* a Virginia Baptist described the failings of one adherent who was his neighbor. Although this "sanctified sister" claimed to be without sin, she did not offer any help when the man's wife became seriously ill. She did, however, send over a newspaper that advocated her strange new beliefs.[89]

It may seem peculiar, even inconsiderate, that this "sanctified sister" tried to meet the desperate needs of her neighbor by lending him holiness literature. Yet her act of questionable generosity reveals a basic truth about the new movement. This gesture expressed what most holiness folk took for granted. Printed matter was thought to be the very words of God by initiates. As such it was vital to the movement's success. It not only introduced southerners to doctrines and religious practices that they had seldom heard or read about before, but also linked them to one another in a vast network of like-minded readers. By the 1890s, as southern perfectionist newspapers began to dot the region, new adherents sent letters, announcements, and editorials to their cherished periodicals. Indeed, as many converts attested, print culture served as the basic medium for imagining southern holiness.

FOUR 🔥

Signs of
the Second Coming

BY THE MID-1890s the southern Methodist holiness preacher
B. F. Haynes was a beaten man. Looking back on that period
years later, he recalled the fierce battle he had fought with
church officials. "Mortal tongue or pen," Haynes lamented, "cannot portray the harrowing emotions of disappointment and
grief" he had suffered as his denomination "shamelessly" neglected the fundamental doctrine of holiness and waged war
against the foot soldiers of perfection. For five years Tennessee
Methodist authorities had moved Haynes from one small, se-
cluded, unsympathetic church to another in the hope that his
popularity as a writer and evangelist would diminish. To make
matters worse, Haynes saw his once handsome salary of $1,550
dwindle to a paltry $200 a year by 1899. The lesson was clear:
"I . . . lost place, position, money and all earthly prospects, in
my adherence to honest convictions." Distressed, Haynes could
barely support his growing family on his meager income. Elsewhere in the South the pattern proved much the same. Baptist
and Methodist officials from Texas to South Carolina routinely

disciplined holiness ministers or removed them from their pulpits, with similar results. Haynes, like so many others in the South, came to believe that Methodism could not be saved. He lost all hope in human progress, moral reform, and political activism. Turning to apocalyptic literature and the Bible, Haynes came to a simple conclusion: Jesus was coming to collect the saints. "Looking into this writhing, hopeless human vortex," he reflected, "and seeing that boasted Christendom was ecclesiastical, formal, worldly, proud, and fallen, my heart would have sunk in despair had I not caught sight of this 'Blessed Hope' of His glorious appearing."[1]

Within a ten-year span, 1896–1906, the southern holiness movement changed dramatically. Black and white adherents alike clashed with church officials over a host of issues concerning authority and power. Leading southern Protestants insisted that church law, the rulings of denominations, and biblical precedent validated clerical legitimacy. By contrast, holiness enthusiasts held that the Holy Spirit and apostolic Christianity, not human tradition or denominational ordinances, formed the basis of religious authority. For mainline church divines, the reckless holiness evangelist epitomized the movement. Itinerant ministers, it seemed to them, shunned the regular ministry and provoked controversy wherever they preached.

The theological and cultural skirmishes that surrounded these conflicts had profound consequences. Baptist, Methodist, and Presbyterian leaders forced a number of holiness zealots out of their churches. Other faithful left established churches of their own accord and formed new fellowships devoted solely to perfectionism. Even those who remained in their mother churches bore deep battle scars.

Jaded by their experience with antiholiness church officials and beset by social forces beyond their control, nearly all those

B. F. Haynes. Church officials demoted Haynes, a holiness preacher, from one small, low-paying parish to another. Haynes took solace in the thought that Jesus would soon return.

in the southern movement adopted a negative, apocalyptic, and otherworldly theology known as premillennialism. Converts believed that Christ would return before the millennium, as laid out in scripture, to carry the faithful into heaven. As a result, holiness folk like B. F. Haynes grew increasingly uninterested in social reform or politics of any kind. If anything made the southern movement unique, it was the nearly unanimous conversion to and wide acceptance of this fatalistic eschatology. Yet this new turn did not lead to spiritual defeatism. Quite to the contrary, a climate of expectancy prevailed among southern holiness folk by the early twentieth century. Adherents spent much of their time watching and waiting for signs of the fast-approaching apocalypse. Moreover, thousands of the faithful now focused not only on the postconversion experience of sanctification and theological perfection but also on spectacular works of the Spirit. Such divine manifestations, they believed, would follow the restoration of the true church in the last days. Southern stalwarts, disenchanted with evangelical orthodoxy, now looked to the heavens for their deliverance.

Certainly most alternative social movements encountered great obstacles in the late-nineteenth-century South.[2] The efforts of former slaves to better their lives met with defeat on a variety of levels. Those who did not escape the region by going to Kansas or northern cities faced increasingly vicious and demeaning conditions in the Jim Crow South. More successful was the agrarian revolt. For a brief period Populists challenged some of the basic economic and social inequalities of the region. Yet leading southern Democrats, industrialists, and religious leaders vigorously countered the uprising. Henry Grady, editor of the *Atlanta Constitution,* voiced the intense anxieties of his peers when he denounced agrarian insurgents as socialists and revolutionaries bent on altering "our entire system of government, shutting out all competition, placing the commerce, the producer and manufacturer in the hands of one man, [and] closing up all stores save their own."[3] Under the pressures of the one-party South, the Populists suffered a crippling defeat and fused with the Democratic Party. Its potential as a vibrant political and social protest movement faded completely.

Not surprisingly, holiness dissenters also encountered stiff opposition from mainline southern evangelicals. Church officials largely viewed the perfectionist movement much as Democratic Party leaders had viewed Populism, as a threat to religious order and denominational authority. By the mid-1890s southern Baptist officials throughout the South feared that the "holiness craze" was poisoning their congregations. In the pages of the Richmond-based *Religious Herald,* one Baptist author worried aloud about widespread "higher life" heresies.

To this writer, perfectionist enthusiasts seemed to denigrate conversion and underestimate the gravity of sin. Such fears of heterodoxy were much less threatening to church leaders than the very real possibility of churches splitting over religious speculations.[4]

The severest battles over the second work issue, however, were waged within the Methodist Episcopal Church, South. At least two factors made the conflict especially acrimonious in that denomination. First, southern Methodism contained the largest number of holiness believers. Second, and more important, denominational leaders were still reeling from the battles they had fought years before with northern Methodism. The southern church had lost both property and members to its northern brethren during the postwar years. Decades passed, but the humiliation lingered. Northern Methodist activity in the South, including the seizure of southern pulpits, was unparalleled. So bitter were the hostilities that quite a few southern Methodists came to see northern Methodism as just another wing of the Union Army. Southerners treated the agents of northern Methodism accordingly. Some missionaries to the region complained that they were pariahs, treated like "counterfeiters or horsethieves."[5] Vividly recalling the protracted war they had fought with the northern church, southern Methodist officials would brook no new challenges to their authority and maintained an overall defensive posture.

By the early 1890s Methodist leaders such as Warren A. Candler and A. G. Haygood in Georgia, J. M. Boland in Kentucky, and Wilbur F. Tillet in Tennessee were issuing a steady stream of condemnatory editorials and books in which they dissected the "sanctificationist" threat in all its menacing details. The pages of two of the denomination's key publications, the *Quarterly Review of the M. E. Church, South,* and the

Christian Advocate, ran grave warnings against the holiness movement as a "church-within-a-church."[6] Particularly vexing was what leading divines perceived as the clannishness of perfectionist associations. Most holiness opponents would have agreed with H. P. Bell, a prominent layman from Georgia, who lashed out against holiness adherents in the *Wesleyan Christian Advocate.* "They have changed the name of our meetings, substituting Holiness for Methodist," he charged. "They preach a different doctrine . . . ; they sing different songs, they patronize and circulate a different literature; they have adopted radically different words of worship."[7] Southern Methodists, Bell and other loyalists asserted, would never again allow their churches to be taken away.

Sanctificationist leaders and eminent southern Methodists even took their hostilities to the public through well-publicized and heavily attended debates. The holiness and Methodist press, as well as local newspapers, announced such events and reserved considerable space for their coverage. For example, from August 31 to September 3, 1896, the perfectionist evangelist L. L. Pickett matched wits with M. A. Smith, an antiholiness rival, in a debate held in Terrell, Texas. For several days the two ministers hurled epithets across the dais and came just short of condemning each other to hell. Smith accused Pickett and others like him of holding that the saved, regenerate Christian had the faith of a mere child and was in a state of "defilement." "God blesses many men who are not wholly sanctified," Pickett conceded, "but you cannot show one who has special power, and great success, who fights sanctification."[8] Three years before the Pickett-Smith debate, the roaming revivalist R. L. Harris held a similarly heated public exchange with J. N. Hall, a Kentucky Baptist minister, in Milan, Tennessee. A local reporter estimated that 1,500 people gathered for the momentous occasion. Despite the hopes of both Harris and Hall for converts, the *Milan Exchange* concluded that few in attendance changed their views as a result of the debate.[9]

African American Baptist officials also brought the holiness movement to the attention of that denomination's laity and clergy. They condemned perfectionism in much the same terms as their white counterparts. Beginning in the 1890s, writers in the National Baptist Convention's official publication, the *National Baptist Magazine* (Washington, D.C.), countered the black holiness movement by insisting that sanctification was a gradual process, not an instantaneous work. The Louisville minister and educator C. H. Parrish argued that there could be no sudden perfecting of believers. He considered the idea of "sinless perfection" an absurdity. Sinfulness, imperfection, and human weakness would always remain in believers.[10]

Across the South a myriad of conflicts erupted between mainline Protestants and the holiness faithful over style, theology, and territory. Itinerant preachers of the "second work," the shock troops of the revival, adopted more aggressive tactics during the 1890s. In turn, southern Methodist ministers felt particularly threatened by these freewheeling evangelists. Traveling "sanctified" revivalists paid little attention to conference and district boundaries and did not shy away from sermonizing about a cold, lifeless regular ministry. Unfettered evangelists preached holiness wherever they could gather a crowd of eager listeners. Angry clergymen complained in all the leading MECS newspapers about "unauthorized evangelists" who upset church life and split congregations into warring factions. An evangelist swaggered into town, erected his tent, and "assumed command of the entire forces," argued John A. Thompson in the *Southern Christian Advocate*. Worse still, the local pastor assumed a secondary role to the interloper, or was branded a betrayer if he opposed the evangelist's work.[11] A writer in the *Alabama Christian Advocate* accused holiness revivalists of preaching without church authority. Hence there was no way to regulate or control their work. "An evangelist," wrote the angry minister, "is a man, woman, or child, who with or without license to preach, itinerates from place to place, holding meetings and taking collections."[12]

Accordingly, denominational leaders moved against what they considered to be such "self-constituted," rootless ministers. When wandering "tramp evangelists," as their critics called them, did not respond to the many warnings appearing in the southern Methodist press, a number of southern conferences began to issue anti-evangelist measures to restrict or abolish the work of free-ranging prophets. In 1892 the South Georgia Conference refused to recognize the office of evangelist. In doing so it intended to blunt the ministry of "so-called evangelists, without warrant or authority of law," who "traveled under color of being local preachers." In 1893 the West Tennessee Conference responded to the revival campaigns of R. L. Harris and others by enacting similar measures. Conference leaders urged members to deny financial support as well as the use of church facilities to such ministers. In a state which had become a hotbed of holiness activity in the last decade of the century, the Northwest Texas Conference approved the antiholiness "Campbell Paper" in 1895. Authored by the Reverend James Campbell, the document called on presiding elders to report any individuals who attended or helped organize holiness meetings. Those found guilty of such involvement would face severe discipline.[13] Anti-evangelist measures were even drafted at the highest levels of the MECS. The bishops who met at the 1894 General Conference officially rejected the separate office of evangelist. The ruling struck out at all holiness itinerants: "We do not want an order of pastors to keep up a routine or a higher, freer, bolder order of prophets to bring down fire from heaven. The offering of the regular army is more important than any guerrilla warfare, however brilliant."[14]

Undoubtedly many southern Methodists were right to fear the encroachments of holiness enthusiasts. Local preachers had much to lose. Church members might quickly turn against their restrained pastors after attending the rousing revivals held night after night in a portable tabernacle. As the local minister's authority waned, church officials worried about the impact holiness would have on an otherwise well-ordered profession. Such fears were common throughout society in this era. Indeed, the professionalization of medicine, law, and teaching as well as the ministry developed as a way to meet the challenges posed by contemporary crises of cultural authority. The organization and rationalization of professions created order out of chaos. Individuals banded together to regulate their professions by requiring formal education, training, and licensing of new entrants and by distancing their professions from suspect practitioners. At roughly the same time that medical doctors began to guard their field against quackery and mass-marketed instant cures, many southern clergymen tried to ward off what they thought to be religious fanaticism or debilitating sectarianism. The traveling evangelist, then, seemed as threatening to southern Methodist ministers as allopaths, eclectics, homeopaths, and osteopaths were to licensed physicians.[15] One concerned southern Methodist, the Reverend B. M. Messick, even drew a direct link between the perils faced by the medical and clerical establishments, writing to the *Christian Advocate:*

> A man on a street corner with an all-potent patent medicine
> may attract more people, and seem to have more patients,
> and to be effecting more cures, than all the regular physicians
> in St. Louis. But alas for the bodies of men! So the patent
> medicine soul-curer may seem to be saving the gospel-

neglected masses, and may be tempted to point the finger of scorn at the regular ministry for inefficiency and failure. But alas for the souls of men! Salvation is too delicate and transcendent a matter to be committed to the hands of any but the most skillful and experienced practitioners of the soul-healing art. . . . Quackery is, or ought to be, at this day of marvelous progress of the medical art, under the ban; and surely spiritual quackery should be under the ban of an enlightened Church.

Messick's barbs were clearly aimed at wayfaring holiness preachers. These dangerous religious drifters seemed to dismiss the authority of both the regular ministry and church law.[16]

Messick's fears were well warranted. Holiness believers often renounced clerical professionalism as vain and harmful to spiritual advancement. Since many leading southern holiness preachers felt that in order for an individual to become sanctified, he or she must repudiate all worldly ambitions, holiness adherents developed an alternative set of values with regard to authority. At times they derided professionalism and the established church as vehemently as they condemned drunkenness and secret societies. Such holiness stalwarts as Beverly Carradine, W. B. Godbey, and C. P. Jones felt that to be holy, one had to give up his or her worldly reputation and be willing to be an outcast.[17] Carradine related that before he was sanctified, God had asked him, "Would I be willing to be misunderstood, all my life, and tread a path of human loneliness to the very portals of the tomb?" He unhesitatingly answered the call and accepted the role of social leper.[18]

Holiness and nonholiness southerners held very different notions of authority, power, and legitimacy. By the late nineteenth century, most ministers in the Methodist Episcopal Church, South, conceived of authority in terms of church hierarchy, tradition, and biblical precedent. The rulings and pronouncements of church elders, leading educators, and the bishops determined policy and set boundaries. By contrast, holiness adherents thought that authority and power rested in any individual who was filled with the Holy Ghost. Holiness was a prime example of popular, informal, plain-folk religion. Official or established religion is usually routinized and bureaucratic. Its practitioners view with suspicion disruptive religious expressions and anti-establishment movements, whereas popular religions tend to find signs of God in everyday experience.[19] Holiness, as a popular religion, brought about an equality of the Spirit and acted, even if unintentionally, as a social leveler. Believers imagined that anyone might be used by the Holy Ghost to interpret scripture, teach perfection, or preach.[20]

In lieu of traditional modes of power, some southern holiness people embraced the British Reformed or Keswick theory of Holy Spirit empowerment. Beginning in 1875, the town of Keswick in northern England became the site of an annual holiness conference. Participants focused on what they called the "higher Christian life" and the need for spiritual potency. Yet the roots of "higher life" went back even further. Phoebe Palmer, founding mother of the nineteenth-century holiness movement, saw no conflict between "power" on the one hand and "purity" on the other. Sanctification imparted both to the believer. The men and women who organized the Keswick Conventions embraced Palmer's message. One of them, G. Campbell Morgan, served as pastor of Westminster Chapel in London. In a sermon delivered at the convention, Morgan homed in on a passage from Ephesians 3:16, "That He would grant you, according to the riches of His glory, to be strengthened with might by His Spirit in the inner man."[21]

This quest for power was certainly not unique to perfectionists. Indeed, it preoccupied many late Victorians. Widespread fears of nervousness—and the related pseudoscientific disorder neurasthenia—gripped turn-of-the-century Americans as well. At one time or another Theodore Roosevelt, Thorstein Veblen, Charles Beard, and Edith Wharton believed they suffered from the devastating effects of neurasthenia. The afflicted described it as debilitating, both physically and spiritually. It now appears that this fin-de-siècle malady was a direct response to modernization, urbanization, and other sweeping changes of the era. Indeed, countless Americans sensed that as the nation grew, they had somehow become "oversophisticated" and "effete," in other words, powerless.[22] A. M. Hills, a leading holiness educator who taught in Kentucky and Texas, thought he knew the answer. "Truly something is needed besides church organization and machinery and culture and pulpit oratory," he claimed. "The only escape from our spiritual impotency, the only way out," was "a journey back to Pentecost" and Holy Ghost baptism. That alone would empower believers to meet the challenges of the day.[23]

Fittingly, southern holiness folk came to understand sanctification as not only a purifying work but also something that equipped them boldly to witness and minister to others. By the late nineteenth century, many affiliated with the national holiness movement had moved from a focus on soteriology (the doctrine of salvation) to an emphasis on pneumatology (the doctrine of the Spirit).[24] Holiness advocates all over the country had come to understand the workings of the Holy Ghost as supreme. Figuring out what exactly the Spirit accomplished in their lives became a nation-wide obsession. The popular holiness author Martin Wells Knapp described the "double cure" or sanctification as both a "purifying" and an "empowering" baptism. Dwight L. Moody, by far the most famous evangelist of the era, also focused on the baptism of the Spirit as an empowering work. Moody, in turn, profoundly influenced a number of holiness folk in the South. N. J. Holmes, a South Carolina Presbyterian minister, was drawn into holiness circles by Moody's work. Holmes read Moody's book *The Secret of Power* with rapt attention in the mid-1890s. Before reading it, Holmes remembered, "I was not satisfied with my own experience, and thought sometimes that my life was more of a theory than a real experience." Sanctification and the accompanying "enduement with power" relieved Holmes of many of his anxieties and gave him a clear sense of ministerial direction.[25] Proof of such power might be found in a fearless and effective preacher, or in a church that witnessed a string of successful revivals. In any case, Spirit baptism, initiates thought, pointed to evangelical zeal and religious vitality. Accordingly, white and black southern converts alike now looked beyond established churches for legitimacy and spiritual authority.

Some African American holiness believers also drew on a potent tradition of slave religion. The black holiness surge in Mississippi may even have represented a cultural renewal of slave religion. Years later the novelist and anthropologist Zora Neale Hurston described the black sanctified church as a "protest against the high-brow tendency in Negro Protestant congregations." New disciples challenged currents in the black Baptist Church just as a younger generation of progressives had attempted to suppress the influence of slave religion. In church periodicals ministers and educators warned against the religious superstitions and "African fetishes" of plantation days.[26] One outraged professor from Virginia decried the "ignorant masses" who found solace in the antics of old-style ministers. "Some are putting on all forms of gymnastic performances," W. E. Robinson remarked with disapproval, "while screams and bawls fill the air until three or four sisters become so excited that the services of twice so many of the most muscular brethren are called for to protect human life." African Methodist Episcopal bishop Daniel Alexander Payne also condemned what scholars now call African religious survivals. Payne witnessed the ring-shout, a ceremonial religious dance originating in Africa, on more than one occasion and judged it one of the "most ridiculous and heathenish" styles of worship he had ever witnessed.[27]

Yet despite such condemnations, some black holiness leaders looked back to slave religion as a vital source of spiritual power. As a youth, C. H. Mason prayed for a religion as invigorating as that practiced by his mother, Eliza Mason, and other ex-slaves in his community. He would later ardently defend the use of African survivals such as the ring-shout and the holy dance. "The people of God do not dance as the world dances," wrote Mason, "but as moved by the Spirit of God." In addition, dreams, visions, and signs played a special role for Mason and other African American initiates. Included in Mason's biography are photographs of various natural oddities such as strangely shaped roots. These he considered hallmarks of "God's Handiwork in Nature."[28] Gradually, black holiness fused a new understanding of Holy Ghost power with the ancient power of slave religion.

Both black and white holiness converts distanced themselves from the southern mainline by marrying intense restorationist beliefs with perfectionist theology. Southern followers pledged to "restore" a pristine biblical Christianity. Like the Disciples of Christ and Landmark Baptists before them, the holiness faithful relied heavily on the primitivist tradition.[29] They sought a return to what they considered to be the unadorned church of scripture, and dismissed all traditions and creeds they deemed antithetical to this goal.[30] W. B. Godbey and the Quaker turned holiness preacher Seth Cook Rees, known popularly as the "Earth Quaker," contended that they held absolutely no creed save the Bible. "The Bible's my creed.

Why certainly!" the two announced in a book they co-authored in 1898. Godbey dismissed the very idea of hermeneutics and argued that perfectionistic Methodism was not sectarian but rather was based solely on the "truth of God" contained in the Bible.[31]

Other preachers, heavily influenced by restorationist ideas, also disparaged the established church. In Mississippi, for instance, the African American minister C. P. Jones waged a restorationist war against the black Baptist Church. After Jones tried to change the name of his Baptist church to the "Church of Christ," concerned Baptist leaders in the state took Jones to court. In typically restorationist terms Jones acted the ventriloquist and spoke for the Spirit, declaiming: "You Baptists are liars. Nowhere in Holy Writ is the church called a Baptist Church. . . . I am robbed of My glory. . . . There is salvation in no other name but Mine."[32] Like Jones, the white holiness devotee R. G. Spurling mounted a primitivist crusade against what he denounced as an apostate church in eastern Tennessee. Between 1895 and 1900 Spurling wrote a short book, *The Lost Link,* in which he used church history and contemporary events to condemn a fallen institution. Spurling's "lost link" was the "great apostasy" of church history between the time of Constantine and the present. Existing denominations, Spurling contended, were so mired in human creeds and unbiblical doctrines that they were incapable of reformation.[33] Not surprisingly, such accusations only further enraged denominational officials. The *Southern Christian Advocate*'s response to radical primitivism represented the contempt of many other moderate evangelicals toward restorationists. They "look back to the radiant pages of the New Testament scriptures to find the saints," a writer in the paper observed. "But they seem to look for nothing very good or great in this their own day."[34]

In some instances the struggles turned violent. In 1899 van-

"On the Rock and on the Sand." This illustration, which appeared in one of Martin Wells Knapp's books, contrasts a corrupt mainline church with a true holiness fellowship.

dals burned a holiness revival tent to the ground in Pilot Point, Texas. Several holiness workers who were asleep in the tent managed to escape, hauling out an organ and a few chairs. Elsewhere in the state denominational loyalists squared off with perfectionist newcomers. A 1903 Paris, Texas, holiness revival divided that community into hostile factions. Sanctificationists had been holding their meeting next to a local schoolhouse, using the school's benches under their tent. Other churches in town demanded that the benches be put back for their own services in the schoolhouse. "A number of fights are alleged to have occurred," reported the *Dallas Morning News*. Police officers rounded up culprits, seven of whom pleaded "guilty to affray."[35]

Undoubtedly holiness proponents had become disenchanted with most organized churches in the South. Yet they were not without hope. Armed with alternative theories about the church, scripture, and authority, enthusiasts felt free to disregard church laws as they dismissed the disapproving opinions of clergymen. Perfectionist lay preachers and evangelists encouraged individuals to violate conference ordinances if necessary. Many in the movement believed that they had been called to keep a higher law. E. M. Murrill, an evangelist based in east Texas, offered his advice to conflicted readers of the holiness paper *The Way of Faith*. "You who are not licensed ministers are not under any obligations to be governed by any conference resolutions forbidding holiness meetings being held," Murrill counseled. He also suggested that lay men and women use vacant lots or rent out storehouses to hold holiness meetings right under the noses of scornful church officials.[36] He cared nothing for the decorum of the mother church. Scores of Methodists followed Murrill's advice, incurring the wrath of the regular ministry as a result.

While MECS leaders could only discipline or expel way-

Holiness believers reacted bitterly to lavish churches like Atlanta's neo-Gothic First M. E. Church South. Constructed in 1876, the structure cost roughly $60,000.

ward laypeople, they exercised much greater control and influence over ordained ministers. Conference elders, bishops, and professors moved against holiness preachers with full force beginning in the mid-1890s. The denomination sent a number of high-profile perfectionist ministers to isolated, low-paying antiholiness circuits. When that failed to achieve the intended result, the authorities might even revoke a minister's credentials. Some of the greatest clashes between holiness and non-holiness factions occurred in the North Georgia Conference. Warren A. Candler, Bishop A. G. Haygood, and other southern Methodist officials exerted their absolute ecclesiastical authority through conference appointments. This, more than anything else, curtailed the widespread influence of popular holiness preachers such as A. J. Jarrell, W. A. Dodge, and Clement C. Cary.

Dodge had filled the pulpits of the most prestigious churches in the conference in cities such as Atlanta, Gainesville, and Cartersville. North Georgia elders, though, quickly observed Dodge's pivotal role as founder, publisher, and key preacher of the movement. Fearing Dodge's popularity, the conference assigned him to a number of hardscrabble circuits. They hoped to silence him by destroying his morale. Dodge was successively demoted from presiding elder to junior preacher, circuit rider, and then colporteur.[37] The North Georgia Conference also disciplined A. J. Jarrell. They first transferred him to the South Georgia Conference. Eventually, however, church leaders removed him to St. Louis to serve in a church that Jarrell found "had views different from those I had cherished all my ministerial life."[38] The North Georgia Conference's strategy of suppression made a powerful impression on many younger men and women in that state. J. H. King, who would later help organize the Fire-Baptized Holiness Church and the Pentecostal Holiness Church, sadly recalled the systematic refilling of pulpits at churches he attended. When the conference appointed a stout antiholiness presiding elder to King's district, it nearly decimated the struggling movement.[39]

Across the South the story was much the same. Mainline church leaders tried to break the will of religious insurgents.

Even MEC officials entered the fray. J. D. Diggs, a well-respected black holiness minister of an MEC church in Winston-Salem, North Carolina, met the same fate as Dodge and Jarrell. Diggs had just completed a successful building program at the prominent Saint Paul Church when conference elders demoted him to Mount Airy, where there was no prospect for growth. Still, the greatest clashes occurred in the MECS. The southern Methodist Church in Texas mounted a tough campaign to discredit, muzzle, or expel influential holiness ministers. One of the most publicized controversies in Texas centered on the preaching activity of H. C. Morrison. In September 1896 organizers of a lay-sponsored revival in Dublin, Texas, invited Morrison to preach. Yet before the Kentucky-based evangelist even arrived, local ministers warned Morrison that they would regard his preaching at the meeting as a violation of church law. In typical fashion, Morrison did not heed their warning. He was brought up on charges, then was expelled from the church shortly after the Dublin revival. The Kentucky Conference reinstated Morrison the following year when the defrocked preacher won his case on a technicality.[40] Other ministers were not so fortunate. Within a relatively short period Texas Methodists ousted a number of key holiness ministers: the popular folk preacher Bud Robinson; R. L. Averill, who became a presiding elder in the Free Methodist Church; J. W. Lively, who joined the northern Methodists; and E. C. DeJernett, founder of Texas Holiness University in Greenville.[41] Stalwarts in the southern Methodist camp painfully referred to their experience as "put-outism." Although many of those who were "put out" of the church did not wish to leave, their perfectionist theology and strident evangelical commitments forced MECS officials to confront and expel them.

The plight of both black and white holiness Baptists was similar to that of Methodists, if not more desperate. Unlike

Methodism, southern Baptism had no perfectionist roots. The power of sin, said the church's leading divines, made the idea of perfection in this life a dangerous fantasy. Consequently, the holiness movement enraged Baptist leaders even more than Methodists. C. P. Jones's growing holiness fellowship in Mississippi was sharply rebuked by black Baptist officials in that state. According to Jones's enemies in the ministry, he had violated a number of Baptist principles when he adopted and disseminated sanctificationist views. In 1898 and 1899 church officials took action against the movement at the state and local levels. A Baptist council passed resolutions against Jones and his followers for questioning the orthodoxy of eternal security and gradual sanctification. Church spokesmen also condemned the group for renaming its church and for denying that the Baptist Church was the one "true Church." The ensuing legal battle over church property only widened the gap between the two factions.[42]

Dissenting white Baptists also threw their congregations into disarray. George W. Stanley, a young holiness convert from Silver City, North Carolina, conducted services in the homes of his Baptist neighbors after the local church refused to host his revivals. Stanley later recalled a subsequent confrontation with his congregation at a ruling session. "Turn him out. We can't have all kinds of doctrines in here," a deacon howled at Stanley in front of a packed house. Baffled and shamed, the irascible Stanley wondered why his perfectionist beliefs and actions had led to his expulsion while those who "drank whiskey" and "danced" remained.[43] At roughly the same time that Stanley was kicked out, a band of holiness followers from two small Baptist churches in the mountains of western North Carolina suffered the same fate. In the late 1890s W. F. Bryant, who would later help found the Church of God (Cleveland), and twenty-eight members of the Pleasant Hill and Old Liberty

Baptist churches came under the influence of several traveling holiness ministers. When Bryant and the other holiness converts from these congregations openly preached that they were "living free from sin," their congregations swiftly excommunicated them.[44]

Encountering direct opposition from clerical authorities, holiness followers faced a stark set of choices. They could alter or relax their views and remain in the church, they could align with another existing denomination that was not opposed to their theology, or they could form new independent churches or denominations based solely on perfectionist principles. A handful of enthusiasts joined the Methodist Episcopal Church, the Wesleyan Methodist Church, or the Free Methodist Church, all of which had northern headquarters. Yet the majority of southern dissenters did not affiliate with any of these. The more radical members of the movement considered these churches to be little different from existing denominations.[45] Why align with another formal, stuffy fellowship? they asked themselves.

A surprising number of older southern Methodists, many born before the Civil War, actually remained loyal to their denomination. These churchmen had spent their formative years in the orthodox enclosure and would continue to defend it in spite of the antiholiness upheaval. Most had come into contact with the holiness movement in the 1880s or earlier.[46] Among them were Beverly Carradine, Clement Cary, W. A. Dodge, W. B. Godbey, Irving Lowery, H. C. Morrison, L. L. Pickett, and J. M. Pike. Nearly all of these first-generation southern holiness leaders remained within the mainline church. A few were already well established and had less to fear than their younger brethren. Many even condemned the "come-outers" in the West who had recently left the Methodist Church and other established denominations over matters of theology and practice. Indeed, during the 1880s loosely organized holiness bands scattered throughout Arizona, Missouri, Illinois, Indiana, and Michigan formed separate holiness churches.[47] Their sectarian leaders espoused a radical restorationism and anathematized most denominations in the United States. But as far as Godbey, Jarrell, and Dodge were concerned, these groups represented "fanatical extremes that have brought the cause of holiness into . . . disrepute." A number of these older, loyal Methodists declared in a pamphlet addressed to the MECS, "We know no holiness that does not inspire devotion to the Church."[48] Others, forced out of the church by unsympathetic southern Methodists, would come to think differently.

Younger or more recent holiness converts, those who entered the movement amid a tumult of controversy, were much more likely to form or join new and independent fellowships. Within a ten-year span, dozens of sanctification churches and denominations emerged in the region. Many of the individuals who joined did not identify as strongly with mainline evangelicalism as their predecessors had. Moreover, a number of these were so disillusioned by their experiences with church hierarchies that they could not imagine going back into what they now considered inhospitable, even apostate denominations.

The experience of the holiness minister A. B. Crumpler was typical. In 1890 Crumpler was sanctified in Missouri under the ministry of Beverly Carradine. Throughout the decade Crumpler preached radical holiness to eager audiences all over his native state of North Carolina. He became an active, highly sought-after evangelist. In the summer of 1898 Crumpler scheduled holiness revivals in Elizabeth City, North Carolina. A local Methodist minister, however, invoked a new anti-evangelist ordinance against the traveling preacher. Rather than submit, Crumpler withdrew from the denomination and continued to hold his meetings.[49] Not long afterwards he decided to organize a new church. He envisioned it as a home for "those who had been saved and sanctified, many of whom belonged to no church, and many of whom had been turned out of their churches for professing Holiness."[50] In the spring of 1900 he and a group of believers in the state organized the Holiness Church in Fayetteville. The fledgling denomination united several independent perfectionist churches in North Carolina and provided a new sawdust trail for former Methodist evangelists.

Elsewhere in the South other enthusiasts organized similar breakaway churches. Groups in Tennessee and Texas bridged vast distances in the formation of their fellowships. R. L. Harris, his wife, Mary Lee Harris, and others established the New Testament Church of Christ in Milan, Tennessee, in 1894. Ten years later this church would join the Texas holiness preacher C. B. Jernigan's Independent Holiness Church to form the New Testament Church of Christ. The names of these churches—as well as the newly formed black Church of God in Christ in Mississippi, the white Church of God (Cleveland), and the white Church of God in Kentucky—reflected a powerful restorationist impulse. Each one desired to restore the true, unified holiness church.[51] Many, though, remained isolated sects, utterly incapable of reaching the lofty goals their founders had imagined. Perhaps no single fellowship united more independent southern holiness groups than the onetime Cumberland Presbyterian minister J. O. McClurkan's Pentecostal Alliance (renamed the Pentecostal Mission in 1901). McClurkan's Nashville-based organization and his holiness Bible school, orphanage, homeless shelter, and periodical *(Living Word)* drew together scores of ministers and laypeople from as far away as Texas, Mississippi, Alabama, Georgia, and the Carolinas. Those who journeyed to conventions and conferences held at McClurkan's mission were united in their dedication to unabashed holiness. They would also come to champion an un-

An early independent holiness church in Van Alstyne, Texas.

A holiness assembly at Rising Star, Texas, 1904.

usual view of the end of the world that was just beginning to gain wide acceptance among devotees.

Whether holiness folk remained in the southern Methodist Church, affiliated with other existing denominations, or joined the ranks of new sects, all believers were deeply affected by their contentious struggle with nonholiness factions. Southern adherents—scarred by theological battles over authority and challenged by the many social and cultural changes of their day—adopted a pessimistic worldview and an apocalyptic eschatology. Indeed, by the turn of the century the southern holiness movement had all but unanimously accepted a sober endtime theology known as premillennialism. It well suited their beleaguered self-conception. Writing in 1898 W. B. Godbey observed as a matter of fact that "you do not find one sanctified man in a thousand who is not looking for the speedy coming of the Lord."[52] This proved especially true in the South.

Since the early nineteenth century, a collection of English divines had been spreading premillennial doctrine in the British Isles and Europe through a number of journals, books, and prophecy conferences. The founder of the Plymouth Brethren, John Nelson Darby, the eccentric proto-pentecostal minister Edward Irving, and others who adopted this novel doctrine held that Jesus would return before the millennium to "rapture" the faithful into heaven. During the subsequent "tribulation" the devil would reign on earth until Christ returned with his saints to rule for a thousand years. Darby and others also helped spread the influential theory of dispensationalism. This view divided history into separate dispensations, or eras, all leading to the end of the world. Prophecy assumed a key place in determining the signs and other details of the last days. Unlike postmillennialists, who dominated the nineteenth-century Protestant establishment, premillennialists did not believe that reform, missionary activity, or any other human endeavor would bring about God's kingdom on earth. Thus, a fatalistic, hyper-Calvinist streak ran through this theology. All premillennialists thought the world was growing worse by the day and moving ever closer to cataclysm. The Bible, when rightly interpreted, revealed a clear story of decline.[53]

This end-time view at first gained few adherents in America. The Baptist lay preacher William Miller nearly doomed the doctrine after his widely publicized failed predictions of the end in 1843 and 1844. Immediately following the Millerite debacle, northerners and southerners alike kept a safe distance from any form of premillennialism. Only after the Civil War did British premillennial theologians, many of them affiliated with the Keswick "higher life" movement, begin to influence leading American evangelicals through mass-circulated literature and Bible conferences held in the Northeast. By the mid-1870s a number of conservative American clergymen were attending the Niagara Conferences (so called because the first meeting convened at Niagara-on-the-Lake, Ontario). Bible conference participants formed ties with British theologians and wholeheartedly adopted dispensational premillennialism. Among these new American converts were the Baptist minister A. J. Gordon, the Presbyterian writer and minister A. T. Pierson, the Methodist theologian W. E. Blackstone, and the enormously popular evangelist Dwight L. Moody. All agreed with their British brethren that the end was nigh. For American adherents, the post–Civil War onslaughts of modernism, industrialism, European immigration, and mass culture seemed to threaten the very fabric of Christian civilization. They likened salvation to being "rescued" from a dying and irredeemable world. "I look on this world as a wrecked vessel," Moody argued. "God has given me a life-boat, and said to me, 'Moody, save all you can.'"[54]

A late-nineteenth-century print of Dwight Moody preaching at one of his Northfield, Massachusetts, Bible conferences. Holiness, and to a lesser extent premillennialism, were common themes at the meetings. Eager participants from around the country attended, including some southern holiness folk.

Just as the holiness movement first originated in the urban North and later moved into the rural South, premillennialism followed a similar path. A few southern stalwarts came into direct contact with the doctrine early on, while attending Bible conferences in the North. The South Carolina Presbyterian holiness minister N. J. Holmes encountered premillennialism at one of Moody's Northfield, Massachusetts, Bible conferences in 1891. Here he met Moody and listened intently to A. J. Gordon and others as they revealed the secrets of an increasingly popular doctrine. Most other holiness folk, though, stumbled upon this new eschatology in the writings of first-generation American premillennialists. By the mid-1890s scores of southern holiness leaders were reading the works of Blackstone, the Lutheran author and minister J. A. Seiss, and Moody.[55] Like many others the Tennessee holiness preacher B. F. Haynes eagerly read Blackstone's books and experienced something of an epiphany as a result. The Bible, Haynes now came to see, was filled with dire predictions, warnings, and signs concerning the end of history.[56]

Premillennialism never gained as large a following among African American holiness believers. It certainly was not as great an influence on C. H. Mason and C. P. Jones as it was on their white brethren. Mason and Jones only occasionally referred to the premillennial return of Jesus in their writings. For instance, in one of Mason's printed sermons he predicted that the true holiness church would escape the "evil" that would "come at the end of the age shown to us."[57] This was undoubtedly a cryptic reference to the rapture and tribulation of the second coming. Yet such views did not represent the kind of dogmatic dispensationalism prevalent among whites.

There are some plausible reasons for the difference in emphasis. What remained most important to African American Christians was correct praxis, not correct doctrine or vague theories of the world's end.[58] Still, a number of blacks who identified with the radical holiness wing accepted premillennialism. W. E. Fuller, who joined the interracial Fire-Baptized Holiness Church, regularly exhorted readers of one holiness paper to remain vigilant until the return of Jesus. Although premillennialism was not Fuller's primary concern, it nonetheless suffused his radical rhetoric and gave urgency to his message. Other African Americans—such as the North Carolina preacher G. A. Mials—most likely taught and preached an imminent second advent. Indeed, by the late 1890s Mials had affiliated with a northern fellowship of premillennial militants led by a prominent white preacher, A. B. Simpson.[59]

Simpson was by far the most influential premillennial exponent for the majority of southern holiness people, black and white. This former Presbyterian minister founded the New York–based interdenominational Christian and Missionary Alliance (CMA) in the 1880s and drew thousands of clergy and laypeople into his circle. Southerners looked for guidance and insight on premillennialism in both Simpson's periodical, *Alliance Witness,* and his many books, which championed a fourfold gospel of Jesus as savior, sanctifier, healer, and coming king.[60] In fact, by the late nineteenth century, Simpson had gained enough of a following in the South to conduct a large-scale CMA camp meeting in Atlanta. That event, held at Exposition Park in August 1899, attracted perfectionists from across the South—including N. J. Holmes, J. M. Pike, Mattie Perry, J. O. McClurkan, and S. C. Todd. Drawn by Simpson's message, participants converged on the city to attend meetings held from 5:30 AM until well after 9:00 PM. On the final day of the gathering, the *Atlanta Constitution* estimated a total attendance of eight to ten thousand, all of whom endured the sweltering heat to listen to exhilarating lectures on "the second coming of Christ and other parts of the Bible that are prophetic in their nature."[61]

At least one holiness minister in the city scorned the heavily attended spectacle. Clement Cary, a lone southern holiness critic of premillennialism, grimly noted that the doctrine had fast become a hardened orthodoxy among the saints. At meetings like those hosted by Simpson, the theology "began to be unwisely introduced into this once promising movement." Worse yet, Cary noted with despair, the more radical southern premillennialists classed "all those of contrary opinion as heretics of the first water."[62] Cary may have wondered why premillennialism had taken hold of the southern fold so quickly, but there were clear reasons for the doctrine's appeal. The end-time theology

Scenes on the Opening Day of the Christian and Missionary Alliance Convention at Exposition Park.

In late summer 1899 the northern-based Christian and Missionary Alliance held a large camp meeting in Atlanta. Southern holiness leaders joined eight to ten thousand other participants and listened to speakers discuss the second coming of Christ and Bible prophecy.

of Blackstone, Seiss, Moody, and Simpson suited southern holiness believers' predispositions. Premillennialism helped them make sense of their embattled existence.[63] In an era of vast social and cultural change, this new belief was particularly cathartic.

Of course, like many other late-century Victorians, holiness people felt beset by a host of threats. The Panic of 1893 and the parallel political upheaval disrupted the lives of millions. Moreover, the eventual failure of Populism and the waning of reform efforts such as prohibition and women's suffrage dashed the hopes of those who looked to the amelioration of society for relief. Others felt the real or imagined hazards of industrialism and mass immigration. One correspondent who wrote to H. C. Morrison's Kentucky-based newspaper registered the fears of many. Catholics, Jews, and Buddhists, as well as anarchists and socialists, complained the distressed writer, were washing onto American shores at an alarming rate. Rehashing a well-worn theme, the writer remarked, "There is a vast inferiority between the immigrants of the present day and those of the past." These newcomers imperiled Christian civilization. Not just in the South, but all over the United States, anxieties mounted, reaching a high point as the century drew to a close.[64]

Not surprisingly, by 1896 most within the southern holiness movement considered the optimistic postmillennialism of their evangelical predecessors to be hopelessly out of date and completely irrelevant. The world was not being won to Christ as postmillennialists believed. Quite the reverse. The southern holiness faithful saw infidelity and decline all around them. The widespread acceptance of biblical criticism and Darwinian evolution only added to their disillusionment with American Protestantism. Like thousands of others in the South, B. F. Haynes had been taught from childhood that the "Church was gradually to overspread the earth with salvation until all mankind were saved, and that then the millennium would come." Yet by the late 1890s he "plainly saw that such was not being done."[65] Others came to the same conclusion. In 1896 the leading figures of the movement—including Beverly Carradine, G. D. Watson, L. L. Pickett, and Martin Wells Knapp—embraced the controversial premillennial doctrine.[66] All were quick to find fault with competing views of the end. Knapp offered a stinging critique of postmillennialism in the pages of his paper, *The Revivalist*. This "unscriptural dogma," as he called it, had deluded the church for centuries. The world was not getting better, Knapp contended. He cited the rising tide of murders, lynchings, divorces, and rapes as clear evidence of degeneration. He also charged that statistics claiming that church membership was on the rise were "bloated big with the gas of counterfeit censuses." Many who had entered the church gave no evidence of regeneration, not to mention sanctification. It was clear to Knapp and others like him that legions of false Christians had "the form of godliness but den[ied] the power thereof." The ubiquity of such apostates was "the fulfillment of the prophecy of these very days."[67]

The strained relationship of holiness adherents with the official church proved to be critical to their premillennial conversion. Enthusiasts repeatedly cited their contempt for mainline religion and their disgust with the "fallen church" as prime reasons for turning to this grim eschatology. For most, the church that so fiercely persecuted them was hopelessly lost. Premillennial writers from the North described precisely what southern holiness folk had come to believe about most established denominations. The popular premillennial author W. E. Blackstone claimed that the "true church" was a "persecuted, suffering, cross-bearing" fellowship.[68] But in fact the church was filled with doubters who cared little about the last days. Premillennialists found 2 Peter 3:3–4 to be a clear prophecy on this point: "Knowing this first, that there shall come in the last days scoffers, walking after their own lusts, And saying, Where is the promise of his coming?" All the leading southern holiness newspapers now contrasted the true premillennial church with the effete, even false postmillennial one. From the mid-1890s forward, *The Way of Faith, God's Revivalist, Zion's Outlook,* and the *Pentecostal Herald* included regular columns titled "Behold, He Cometh," "The Second Coming of Jesus," and "Watchman, What of the Night?" Southern holiness editors argued that the holiness movement itself was "God's last call to the world."[69] These papers now regularly included selections from the writings of Simpson, Seiss, Blackstone, and other champions of premillennialism.

Holiness publications began to interpret current events as startling signs of the "last days." Beginning in 1896 J. M. Pike's weekly, *The Way of Faith,* included a "Current Notes" feature which depicted world conflicts, natural disasters, and social turmoil as telling evidence of the fast-approaching second advent.[70] Similarly, C. H. Mason, drawing on African folk tradition, cited freaks of nature such as oddly shaped roots and sticks to teach his flock about the workings of the Spirit in the "latter days." In one such message, Mason deciphered meaning from the trunks of two saplings shaped like a hand and a foot. "God's way is a rebuke to men," Mason concluded from these strange specimens. God would soon judge "the world with His understanding, making the earth acknowledge His coming."[71]

For the majority within the southern movement, the greatest and perhaps most personal sign of the approaching end was the apostate church. H. C. Morrison's *Pentecostal Herald* presented scenes of the end which graphically illustrated the plight of the southern holiness movement vis-à-vis southern Methodism. Morrison, who had himself been turned out of the church for a period, drew clear lessons. The end would come in an instant and would reveal the immorality and decadence of the church: "The Quarterly Conference will just be reading the verdict on some holiness evangelist, 'Expelled from the ministry, and turned out of the Church.' And, behold! The man has disappeared," swept into heaven by God at just the right moment. W. B. Godbey and the radical Tennessee preacher R. L.

Harris also perceived the church as a kind of barometer of the end. As early as 1894 Harris concluded that 2 Timothy 3 prophesied the struggle that would take place between holiness and southern Methodism: "In the last days perilous times shall come." Perfectionists, Harris determined, must leave this sinful church. Although Godbey remained within the southern Methodist fold, he too read scripture through the dark lens of contemporary events. "Do you not know," he remarked in one of his books, "that Jesus said just before his coming that [church officials] would put you out of . . . the church?"[72]

Obsessed with the events that would precede the apocalypse, premillennialists tended to push aside other concerns. By the calculus of apocalypse, politics, reform, or any "worldly ambitions" became anathema. Of course, the holiness faithful had little interest in politics even before they adopted this doctrine, though a few—including Beverly Carradine and A. J. Tomlinson, a founder of the Church of God (Cleveland)—did flirt with politics in the 1880s and early 1890s. Occupying prestigious southern pulpits, Carradine promoted a host of causes ranging from anti-lottery activism to children's rights, and Tomlinson also entered the political sphere, even running for local office on the 1892 Populist ticket in Indiana.[73] Yet they would abandon politics entirely by the close of the century. Most rejected political activity altogether as a waste of time, or worse yet, a sinful diversion.

Certainly their postmillennial antecedents in the North had hoped to reform society and zealously entered the political fray.[74] The southern movement's new negative appraisal of the world, however, cut short such optimism. Indeed, Clement Cary accused premillennialists of promoting a dangerous otherworldliness. "Listening to premillennialists," said Cary, "we would be compelled to believe that the kingdom of God now has no influence on the earth, neither has it any dominion whatever."[75]

Cary's assessment was apt. After 1896 southern perfectionist writers seldom if ever took up matters such as labor, voting rights, economic distress, or lynching in their publications—unless, of course, these issues supported their view of the looming last days. Southern adherents were obsessed with exposing duplicitous Methodist and Baptist ministers and denouncing the pleasures of the flesh, but they had nothing to say about the robber barons or the unfair treatment of workers. There were a few exceptions. In the late nineteenth and early twentieth centuries, certain holiness periodicals such as *The Pentecostal Herald* and *The Battle Axe* (Danville, Virginia) championed the prohibitionist cause. Their zeal for prohibition was equally matched by fervent anti-tobacco crusading. Such specific moral interests seldom developed into larger political concerns. The premillennial faithful did sponsor missions to orphans, the poor, and the destitute, but, like Dwight Moody, they did so with a clear understanding that their efforts could not bring about qualitative societal change. A poem titled "For Whom Will You Vote" printed in an issue of *The Revivalist* illustrates the attitudes of holiness and later pentecostal believers toward politics. *"I am one of God's electioneering agents,"* the poet declared. "In this contest men, women, and children can vote. Then vote for Jesus! Vote for Jesus!! Vote for Jesus!!!"[76] Many heeded this advice and left politics to their "worldly" inferiors. L. L. Pickett and Martin Wells Knapp—the latter enshrined by the movement after his untimely death in late 1901—conveyed the otherworldly hopes of many through one of their popular hymns, "The Rapture":

Soon the darkness will be over
And the morning light appear
For the Master has declared it
And His coming draweth near.

Yes, our Saviour, as He promised
Soon shall come to earth again
And receive his own with rapture
With him evermore to reign.[77]

Undoubtedly southern perfectionists were uninterested in, even contemptuous of, politics. They had better things to do, like watch and wait for Jesus' swift return.

At the time, these views distanced southern holiness people from much of the national holiness movement. Likewise, it set southern believers apart from most other evangelicals in the region. Indeed, surprisingly few evangelicals in the nineteenth-century South championed premillennialism. The Tennessee Landmark Baptist James R. Graves was perhaps the only significant late-century southerner to adopt this brand of Darbyite dispensationalism.[78] Elsewhere in the South, implicit or explicit postmillennialism reigned among most Baptists and Methodists. At century's end a cheerful optimism, which went hand in hand with the New South creed, dominated most commentators' views. Whereas southern holiness believers saw religious and social decline all around them and imminent doom on the horizon, other southern Protestants noted the steady advance of learning, religion, and civilization. "Is the World Growing Worse?" asked a writer in Nashville's *Christian Advocate*. He answered with an emphatic no, and offered a host of secular and religious examples to prove his point. Another observer in the journal defended southern Methodism against the attacks of naysaying premillennialists, remarking, "How unlike Christ is the preacher who fastens on everything bad and crude and ridiculous about the age, the church, the individual." Far from recognizing the march of southern progress, these pessimists made out "man's great feelings for himself to be shame and contempt!"[79] Other leading southern evangelicals cited the spread of Christianity and social reform, the end of slavery, and advances in science as clear evidence of human achievement. In 1901 a black Baptist minister named W. W. Gaines heralded "Signs of the Times" in the *National Baptist Magazine*. The nineteenth century had passed with a "galaxy of inventions and discoveries in science and philosophy," he declared, and Christianity had spread across the globe. For Gaines, African American advances best exemplified this unmitigated progress. Echoing Booker T. Washington, Gaines catalogued the growth of black "churches, colleges, seminaries, insurance companies, factories, stores, farms, banks, and national conventions" as "marvelous signs of the times."[80]

In 1899 the Atlanta-based Baptist *Christian Index* offered a scathing critique of premillennialism, presenting it as an aberrant novelty, unheard of in orthodox southern Baptist churches. An Atlanta pastor spoke for many southern evangelicals when he contemptuously described the theology as "a 'crazy-quilt' style of handling the word of God . . . too common with many Sunday school teachers, evangelists, and highly emotional and spiritualizing preachers."[81]

The National Holiness Association and many holiness leaders in the North and West were also alarmed by the growth and popularity of premillennialism in the South. Northern divines such as Daniel Steele of Massachusetts and George W. Wilson of Illinois issued strong statements opposing the doctrine, which they considered to be a Wesleyan heresy. In particular, critics lashed out against premillennialists' negative appraisal of the world and their fixation on the last days. They argued that John Wesley had held an optimistic view of grace that was incompatible with the more Calvinistic teachings of premillennialism. The issue also proved divisive as holiness people around the country attempted to merge into a single church. Individuals who would organize the Church of the

Nazarene fought mightily over theology. Officials in the North and Far West, who espoused postmillennialism, faced off against their southern brethren. In the early twentieth century the evangelist J. O. McClurkan had considered uniting his Nashville-based mission with the Nazarenes. Yet McClurkan and his followers ultimately thought that the Nazarenes were not sufficiently committed to premillennialism to justify the merger. Elsewhere in the South, union proved nearly impossible. Factions were able to merge only as northern and western ministers downplayed their eschatology.[82]

Other postmillennialists would not be so irenic. As premillennialism gained more followers in the Midwest, Isaiah Reid, president of the Iowa Holiness Association, denounced the doctrine vehemently. In 1900 he even suggested that ministerial credentials be withheld from those who embraced both premillennialism and another menacing force sweeping the Midwest and South, the doctrine of divine healing. The National Holiness Association (NHA) also countered these controversial issues by banning the discussion of either at all NHA-sponsored revivals.[83] Southerners who were committed to both theories now charged that the national holiness movement had lost its way just as the mainline church had before it. L. L. Pickett railed against the NHA for striking a compromise. He, like other believers in the South, worried that the NHA would eliminate "a large part of God's Word . . . from our teaching."[84]

Divine healing captivated the attention of the southern movement in much the same way premillennialism had. Certainly, some adherents already accepted the role of healing long before their conversion to premillennialism. Southern devotees came under the influence of northern faith healers such as the medical doctor Charles Cullis, as well as A. B. Simpson, R. Kelso Carter, and the self-proclaimed Elijah of Chicago, John Alexander Dowie. Those guiding lights published hundreds of books on the subject and established healing homes and training schools around the country in the 1880s and 1890s where seekers hoped to find both physical relief and spiritual guidance. Following the lead of popular faith healers, a growing number of southern perfectionists came to believe that Christ's sanctifying work freed the individual of sickness as well as sin. The body, in other words, was perfectible much like the soul. An early southern proponent of faith healing, writing in *The Christian Witness,* declared that "sickness and sins are both represented as being nailed to the cross" in scripture. But "an unbelieving church declares that the days of healing are past." Mattie Perry, a holiness missionary in North Carolina, followed the same logic. "What makes man sick?" she asked in *The Way of Faith.* "It must be sin, for we have no account of Adam and Eve ever being sick before they sinned."[85]

In the late century southern disciples found direct links between the miracle of healing and the premillennial return of Jesus. Godbey and countless others now thought that "greater miracles will attend the second coming of Christ (for which we are constantly on the lookout) than bygone generations have ever witnessed."[86] Southern perfectionist newspapers printed articles on divine healing alongside others that featured the premillennial coming of Jesus. Newspaper editors also sold hundreds of inexpensive books and pamphlets that dealt with divine healing. The end of the world, so anxious readers believed, would be attended by all manner of signs and wonders. A similar spiritual vigilance had existed among seventeenth-century New Englanders, to whom wonders betokened the supernatural and demonstrated God's power over the laws of nature. Signs also linked the present age with the miraculous age of the Bible.[87] Holiness believers thought that the modern-day revival of sanctification literally restored the power of the apostolic church. Followers both black and white asserted as much when they defended contemporary miracles, including, but certainly not limited to, healing.[88]

A number of holiness people in the South became more radical and sectarian after adopting the doctrines of healing and premillennialism. The Book of Acts served as their handbook. They lived mimetic lives, reenacting the signs and wonders of scripture on a daily basis. Again and again they came back to Joel 2:28, their guide to the second coming: "I will pour out my spirit upon all flesh; and your sons and your daughters shall prophesy, your old men shall dream dreams, your young men shall see visions." Maria Woodworth-Etter, a popular national preacher dubbed the "trance-evangelist" by her many detractors in the media, summed up believers' hopes when she proclaimed that innumerable signs and wonders would precede the second advent: "The sick shall be healed, devils cast out, people shall speak in tongues—just before He comes."[89] Those in attendance at Woodworth-Etter's revivals frequently experienced trances, "holy dancing," and other spiritual exercises. All over the South, radical manifestations of the "Spirit" were ubiquitous at turn-of-the-century revivals. In newspapers, biographies, and religious texts, believers recounted supernatural occurrences taking place in what they believed to be these "latter days" and accepted unprecedented works of the Spirit as commonplace.

At holiness revivals held in small southern towns, attendees felt themselves to be at the center of a divine end-time drama. Congregants created a vibrant holiness lore which helped them make sense of the chaotic world around them. They repeatedly described how sinners were thrown into convulsions or struck to the ground by God. The Texas minister C. B. Jernigan recollected an incident that occurred at an eastern Texas camp meeting held in 1898. A young man, known to be a flagrant sinner by those present, fell into an agonizing trance for forty-eight hours. When he awoke, he preached to the assembly concerning the awful vision of hell he had seen. Jernigan proclaimed that the event seemed to be taken right out of the Book of Acts. Movement newspapers regularly featured similar visions and dreams as conveyed by latter-day holiness seers.[90]

Divine retribution was one of the most commonly reported supernatural acts. As late as the 1920s the perceptive journalist Duncan Aikman ironically noted this phenomenon in the *American Mercury.* "Holy Rollers," Aikman declared, were fond of recounting tales of profligate adolescents who were killed in gruesome train wrecks just minutes after rejecting salvation.[91] To the faithful it seemed that God had struck down their enemies just as he had smitten the deceitful Ananias and Sapphira in the New Testament. At one of the Georgia evangelist Miller Willis's unbridled services a man who came to mock believers was seized by epileptic fits. Doctors, Willis recounted in morbid tones, could not relieve him. Only after submitting to the prayers of Willis and another minister did the young man recover.[92] Other doubters, it seemed, were not so fortunate. George W. Stanley, a traveling preacher from North Carolina, proudly declared that everyone "who tried to lay hands on me met with destruction." Shortly after the local Baptist church expelled Stanley, several of its leading members died inexplicably. For Stanley, God had visibly judged these enemies of holiness. Others who opposed his ministry met a similar fate. "Some said I should be lynched for causing so many to die," Stanley boasted.[93] This was a kind of divine power few holiness people had experienced before, and it was intoxicating.

In Texas, adherents often gloried in reports about the swift hand of God's judgment. At a meeting held in Paris, Texas, a Disciples of Christ minister publicly denounced the perfectionists who had invaded his community. When this college-educated minister of an influential congregation died shortly after the episode, C. B. Jernigan and other holiness followers who witnessed his demise were certain that it was God who had brought an end to the unbelieving clergyman.[94] No one who willfully opposed perfection escaped God's wrath. When a community shut its churches to holiness meetings, some revivalists even called on God to mete out punishment. Such was the case when local Wesleyan evangelists petitioned God to awaken the people of Gainesville, Georgia, even "if He had to send coffins to do it." But Gainesville's Protestants wanted nothing to do with the rabble-rousing preachers. In January 1903 a tornado swept through the city, killing over one hundred residents and causing $700,000 worth of damage. The Baptist minister's house had stood directly in the path of destruction. The catastrophe was no mere coincidence to the Wesleyan preachers who observed it. In her biography of her husband, C. H. Mason, Mary Mason mentioned several individuals who had tried to hinder his work. God, she wrote, dealt severely with each. For instance, for opposing Mason, an antiholiness black Baptist deacon from Hazelhurst, Mississippi, suffered an affliction which left him bedridden. According to Mary Mason, the deacon's house later "caught on fire one night, and he and his dog were burned alive." Perfectionist apostles read such calamities not only as wonders foretelling the end but also as evidence of their anointing.[95] After losing their battle with mainline evangelicalism, beleaguered initiates took comfort in the fact that God regularly came to their aid, vanquishing their many foes.

Perfectionist evangelists and lay preachers struck fear in the hearts of their congregants. By 1900 holiness lore had become an effective tool of self-promotion. So prevalent were stories of divine retribution and power that a number of southerners trembled at the mere thought of bands of sanctificationists entering their town or village. Rumors spread that adherents dusted crowds at their revivals with a powder that caused trances and paralysis. Southern stalwarts were occasionally accused of being mesmerists or psychic tricksters. Some holiness ministers found that local people would not even shake hands with the saints, fearing that "power might be transmitted to them through the hand."[96] Girded with a sense of their immense spiritual potency and election, and watching for signs of the impending end, southern holiness folk came to expect ever greater spiritual manifestations. The most widely read authors of the movement certainly helped create an atmosphere of anticipation. For instance, W. B. Godbey, Martin Wells Knapp, and G. D. Watson encouraged believers to seek all the spiritual gifts described in the New Testament. They held that the Bible offered an abundance of blessings not available to nominal, unsanctified Christians.[97] Indeed, Godbey charged that the fallen church had hidden this knowledge for at least 1,500 years. Yet with the renewal of the church in the last days, legions of enthusiasts might claim the gifts of healing, miracles, prophecy, discernment of spirits, and tongues—by which Godbey meant an aptitude for foreign languages.[98]

One former Baptist itinerant preacher in the Midwest took the notion of spiritual gifts even further than his holiness predecessors. B. H. Irwin, born in Mercer County, Missouri, and based in Iowa, accepted the Wesleyan holiness message in the early 1890s. Following his conversion he began preaching sanctification in Methodist Episcopal churches throughout Iowa, Nebraska, Kansas, the Oklahoma Territory, and Colorado. Yet Irwin was not entirely satisfied with his religious experience and yearned for something more. He found answers in the Wesleyan-holiness canon. By the mid-1890s he was intently reading G. D. Watson's books, Thomas Upham's biography of the quietist mystic Madame Guyon, and the writings of the eighteenth-century Methodist John Fletcher. In particular, Irwin found that all these authors spoke of a "fire baptism," or a purging work of the Spirit foretold by John the Baptist in Matthew 3:11: "I indeed baptize you with water unto repentance: but he that cometh after me is mightier than I, whose shoes I am not worthy to bear: he shall baptize you with the Holy Ghost, and with fire." This baptism, Irwin believed, would take place after sanctification.[99] Fervently seeking the experience, Irwin received what he called his "baptism of fire" at Enid in the Oklahoma Territory in October 1895. The following month, submitting his mystical testimony to the South Carolina–based paper *The Way of Faith,* Irwin reported that he had seen a cross of transparent fire and literally felt burned to the core. "The whole room seemed to be all luminous," and Irwin had vividly sensed that he was in the "midst of a fiery presence."[100]

Isaiah Reid, president of the Iowa Holiness Association, moved swiftly against the radical preacher. Reid, fearing what he and other moderate leaders called the "third blessing heresy," severed all official ties with the mystical renegade Irwin. Thus shunned by the Iowa Holiness Association, Irwin mounted a preaching tour throughout the Midwest and organized a number of independent Fire-Baptized Holiness Associations. In October 1899 he also established his own paper, *Live Coals of Fire,* which he operated from his new home in Lincoln, Nebraska. The ambitious preacher sent back regular reports of his feverish revivals to his publication and to *The Way of Faith,* claiming that hundreds were undergoing their "fiery baptisms" in his meetings, though the "devil" fought him in every town where he took his message. Rowdies cut down and burned revival tents and physically abused some converts. *The Way of Faith* recounted one such instance in which "masked murderers" broke up Irwin's meeting by firing revolvers and throwing chairs at congregants. Local toughs thrashed Irwin and his flock, who night after night condemned the "vices" of the age:

alcohol, fine clothes, Sunday newspapers, and Coca-Cola. Unmoved, Irwin assured his readers that God would soon strike dead those who opposed his ministry.[101]

Southern subscribers to *The Way of Faith* and *Live Coals of Fire* were awestruck by Irwin's reports and the events unfolding on the pages before them. Some southerners soon began to seek the powerful baptism Irwin so provocatively described. J. M. Pike, editor of *The Way of Faith,* declared that his paper received scores of letters inquiring about this mysterious baptism of fire. For Pike and the paper's anxious readers, this new religious experience seemed to prefigure the return of Jesus. Writing in *Live Coals of Fire,* J. H. King agreed. Scripture clearly prophesied the collection of "fire-baptized saints" into one "true church" before the last days. By the logic of this argument, it was not enough to be sanctified. One must attain higher works of grace in order to meet the tests of the end. King thus began to question and eventually move beyond sanctification in search of fuller spiritual equipment. Others similarly changed their views. A woman from Cleveland, Tennessee, presented her testimony in *Live Coals of Fire:* "I read B. H. Irwin's experience on the fire, and I at once became hungry for it." The South Carolina African American minister W. E. Fuller also came to the same conclusion, seeking his fire baptism shortly after reading Irwin's reports.[102] In fact, Irwin generated enough interest in the South that he mounted a preaching and church organization tour there late in 1896. After a series of stunningly successful meetings in South Carolina, Georgia, and Florida, Irwin formed associations in each state. In late July and early August 1898 he convened a national meeting in Anderson, South Carolina, to establish a more structured denomination.

Although the Fire-Baptized movement did not win over the majority of southern holiness folk, the fledgling church did claim seventy-five ordained ministers in the region, both black and white, male and female, by March 1900. This accounted for 58 percent of the church's total clergy in the United States and Canada. Another 30 percent of Fire-Baptized ministers resided in the Midwest, while roughly 11 percent lived elsewhere in the United States and Canada.[103] Certainly, then, quite a number of the southern faithful identified with the exciting new sect. Most believed that it offered more potent works of the Spirit which their sedate holiness brethren ignored or opposed. In these perilous end times, according to Fire-Baptized southerners, an unfettered radical holiness was necessary. "If there be not progress toward these higher attainments," J. M. Pike declared in *The Way of Faith,* "there is danger of retrogression."[104]

Fire-Baptized believers possessed a hyperbolic religious imagination. Their spiritual experience exceeded the well-defined boundaries of organized religion and the rational, ordered worship of the era.[105] The sober religiosity of both moderate holiness practice and southern mainline Christianity could not satisfy these seekers. Not surprisingly, Irwin and his southern followers soon advocated further baptisms or effusions of the Holy Ghost. Influenced by W. B. Godbey's translation of the New Testament Greek word for "power" as "dynamite," Irwin began to promote a "baptism of dynamite" as early as 1898.[106] The radical apostle employed such theatrical imagery with panache. Irwin proclaimed that this extra baptism would "tear things up" and make "people feel that they never had any religion at all." Fire-Baptized converts marveled at the power of this "dynamite" to uproot religious moderates and stir the devil. It is no coincidence that devotees employed the kinds of spectacularly violent metaphors the American public tended to associate with radical bomb throwers. One champion of the baptism of dynamite described the experience in terms that a mid-1880s Chicago anarchist might have approved. The baptism was "explosive" and "would create havoc and destruction" in much the same way that nitroglycerin did. Irwin later preached more extravagant and opaque baptisms of "lyddite" and "oxidite."[107]

Of course, only a small fraction of holiness people adopted such bizarre, extremist rhetoric. Many thought it patently absurd. Still, the wide acceptance in the South of premillennialism and healing coupled with the emergence of fire baptism altered the movement considerably. Only the latter, though, deeply divided the southern movement. Heated debates and confrontations racked the movement from the late 1890s forward as evangelists and laypeople took sides on the "third blessing" issue. Moderates found it especially difficult to curb the influence of radicals. In South Carolina and Georgia, Irwin drew a number of Wesleyan Methodists into the Fire-Baptized fold. In response, the South Carolina Wesleyan Methodist Conference prohibited the teaching or preaching of the "third blessing" from their pulpits.[108] Moderate southern holiness leaders— including H. C. Morrison, C. B. Jernigan, and the influential Texas minister and author A. M. Hills—not only worried about the soundness of the new sect's doctrines but also feared the reproach that these zealots would bring on the entire movement. Fire baptism and late-century extremism certainly drew the scorn of outsiders. Commenting on an emotional revival in Texas, the *Waco Telephone* newspaper accused participants of wild enthusiasm and ridiculous emotionalism. The *Nashville Christian Advocate* blamed Irwin and papers like *The Way of Life* for giving rise to such fanaticism. Irwin's many works of grace, wrote a southern Methodist editor, were unbiblical and devoid of meaning: "Fanciful language of this sort is without any definite signification." Defenders of fire baptism shot back. An Oklahoma minister penned a combative hymn directed at the movement's many enemies: "The carnal heart opposes light. . . . It hates the fire and dynamite." Deluded Methodists and Campbellites despise that "which makes men laugh and shout and dance / And puts them in a holy trance."[109]

Concerned holiness disciples, who had much more at stake than those outside the movement, lined up to combat what they called "Irwinism." In South Carolina the Methodist holiness minister and former editor of *The Way of Faith,* J. A. Porter, argued that northerners rightfully objected to the extremist language of fire baptism, and that when radicals used the term "third blessing" they not only weakened the case for sanctification but also turned other holiness adherents into second-class Christians. Camp meetings in Texas and Georgia reflected the striking divisions rending the movement. Warring factions held separate services on the same grounds. In an ironic turn, moderates now found the smug prudishness of radicals particularly repugnant. Fire-Baptized believers slandered Wesleyans and mainline holiness people as "twice-dead" followers of "moonshine holiness." These were fighting words to those who battled "demon rum." Radicals also further distanced themselves from the rest of the movement by adopting Old Testament dietary laws forbidding the consumption of oysters, "swine flesh," and coffee. A. M. Hills, a leading critic of the new sectarians, sarcastically shunned these brethren as "little infallible male and female popes" who seemed to glory in their otherworldly "boorishness."[110]

None of these barbs, however, hurt the radical wing more than Irwin's public fall from grace in the spring of 1900. Rumors circulated—largely through H. C. Morrison's *Pentecostal Herald*—that Irwin had walked the streets of Omaha drunk and smoking a cigar. *The Christian Witness* picked up the story and spoofed the fallen "Whisky Baptized" preacher.[111] Only through the determined efforts of J. H. King, the new general overseer of the Fire-Baptized Holiness Association, did the denomination avert a massive loss of membership. This turn of events, however, did not mark a significant victory for advocates of the moderate cause. The Fire-Baptized Holiness Association had gained its greatest following in the South. And though its influence waned after Irwin's professional demise, the radical sect's impact on the region was profound. Swept away by speculations about the latter days and entranced by the possibility of further works of the Spirit, numbers of southern holiness people, even those who did not join the Fire-Baptized fold, were now more than ever predisposed to radicalism. Between 1896 and 1906 thousands of initiates in the region took as indisputable facts the failure of most organized churches and the imminent return of Jesus. Accordingly, many eagerly awaited the signs and wonders of the "Pentecostal Age." A climate of expectancy reigned in the early years of the twentieth century. As one historian describes it, the movement at this time was a "pre-Pentecostal tinderbox awaiting the spark that would set it off." It certainly seemed an auspicious age to southern enthusiasts. A popular turn-of-the-century Fire-Baptized hymn expressed their sense of anticipation:

Oh! ye saints, the Lord is coming for His own
From the kingdom of his father upon high
Soon His glory will be streaming from his throne
Yes, the Bridegroom is coming by and by

Trim your lamps and be ready, ready, ready
Trim your lamps and be ready
For the Bridegroom comes.[112]

FIVE

The Emergence of
Southern Pentecostalism

IN APRIL 1907 the North Carolina holiness preacher G. B. Cashwell reflected on the startling changes that were redirecting the perfectionist revival: "Pentecost has come to the South. The Power is falling from the Atlantic to the Mississippi river. The cities and country are filled with the glory of God, healing, working of miracles, divers kind of tongues, [and] interpretation of tongues. . . . [Jesus] is coming soon, and the bride must be dressed and ready."[1] Similar exhortations filled perfectionist newspapers in the region from 1906 to 1910. In those years a West Coast revival would come to dominate the beliefs and practices of southern stalwarts. Led by a southern-born African American minister, William J. Seymour, the Azusa Street revival in Los Angeles enchanted thousands. Seekers in the South adopted the doctrine of tongues speech, so central at Azusa, and eagerly attended revivals modeled after the Los Angeles meeting.

The "tongues movement," so called by its detractors, matched what radical perfectionists in the South recognized as authentic Holy Ghost religion. For legions of adherents, tongues speech was the ultimate evidence of both Spirit empowerment and the coming of Jesus. Divinely equipped with foreign tongues, so they believed, they would preach the gospel to the nations and hasten the second coming. Nearly all the members of the largely southern Fire-Baptized Holiness Church, the Holiness Church of North Carolina, and the Church of God (Cleveland) rushed into the movement. Other denominations in the South—including the Church of God in Christ, the Free Will Baptists, the Pentecostal Church of the Nazarene, and the Wesleyan Methodist Church—saw thousands of their members turn to pentecostalism.

Converts were drawn largely from holiness fellowships.[2] Consequently, battles between pentecostals and their nonpentecostal holiness foes became commonplace. As before, conflict and strife shaped the southern movement to a considerable degree. Southern pentecostals' numerous adversaries—nontongues-speaking perfectionists, mainline evangelicals, and others—offered proof to initiates that they were God's oppressed chosen people. The faithful even purposefully provoked their opponents, whom they viewed as misguided at best and demonic at worst. Devotees also drew criticism for embracing pentecostalism's egalitarian message. Anyone, regardless of age, sex, or race, might receive the "gift of tongues," as described in the Book of Acts. Most saints, however, did not join the movement because it brought some measure of equality. Southern converts instead found speaking in tongues, and ecstatic worship in general, to be liberating and fulfilling. They claimed to have direct contact with the divine. This, thought many, was surely the most convincing sign of the approaching apocalypse.

This new eschatological and Spirit-centered southern tradition actually had deep roots. As the holiness movement had once entered the South from the North, other new doctrines and worship styles would also come from outside the former Confederacy. The roots of the new pentecostal movement lay in the Midwest, a region that once again proved fertile ground for the religion of the Spirit. Radical holiness in the heartland and in Dixie had, of course, suffered a tremendous blow with the apostasy of the controversial Fire-Baptized Holiness leader Benjamin Hardin Irwin. The movement lost its guiding light and its principal organizer. But a slight, frail former Kansas Methodist soon captured the attention and loyalty of devotees in the Midwest, thus filling the void left by the publicly humiliated Irwin.

Charles Fox Parham was born in Muscatine, Iowa, in 1873. For much of his childhood, spent in Kansas, Parham suffered from a number of health problems. Not surprisingly, he embraced holiness and divine healing after a severe bout with rheumatic fever while in college. He subsequently entered the Methodist ministry. But the structure and formalism of mainline Protestantism was far too constricting for the fiercely independent preacher. By the mid-1890s Parham, like thousands of other adherents across the United States, abandoned the established church and set off on an independent ministry of healing and radical holiness.[3]

He was a religious adventurer, always looking for new signs of the Spirit. Irwin's Fire-Baptized saints in Kansas inspired awe in Parham, who adopted their "third work" doctrine. Premillennial eschatology assumed an equally prominent place in the young preacher's ministry. In the late 1890s Parham promoted a host of ultra-perfectionist views from his Bethel Healing Home in Topeka, Kansas. Here, too, he produced a bimonthly journal, *The Apostolic Faith*. Parham regularly featured Irwin's fire baptism theory in the pages of his paper. Yet Parham thought that Irwin's theory lacked hard evidence.

How might believers know for certain that they had experienced a third work of grace?[4]

By the turn of the century Parham was spending much of his time searching for that proof. What would be the physical sign, he wondered, of Holy Ghost baptism? Throughout the summer of 1900 he traveled across the country in search of tangible evidence. Parham visited the maverick minister Frank W. Sandford's holiness commune in Shiloh, Maine. He also passed through both A. B. Simpson's Christian and Missionary Alliance school in Nyack, New York, and a Chicago outpost of Zion City's self-proclaimed Elijah, John Alexander Dowie. All these leaders placed great emphasis on healing and the imminent return of Jesus. Yet it was Sandford, in particular, who captivated the peripatetic Kansan. Most important, at Shiloh, Parham heard reports that after Spirit baptism some of Sandford's flock spoke in foreign tongues (xenoglossy), just as the apostles had in the second chapter of Acts. Parham was exultant.

Returning to Topeka, he organized a Bible school in a garish Victorian mansion on the outskirts of town. (The pretentious structure was dubbed Stone's Folly by locals when its indebted builder abandoned the costly project.) Parham encouraged his roughly thirty-five students to search the Book of Acts for the true sign of Spirit empowerment. Chapter 2 served as their inspiration: "And they were all filled with the Holy Ghost, and began to speak with other tongues, as the Spirit gave them utterance."[5] Using the Pentecost account, the teacher and his disciples concluded that speaking in tongues was the sure sign they so eagerly sought. By early January 1901 they were certain that the Spirit had come, and they were speaking in what they believed to be dozens of foreign languages.

Within a matter of days curious local and regional reporters descended on the towering mansion to witness the spectacle. Scripture, Parham told these visitors, clearly indicated that before the second coming of Jesus the faithful would receive miraculous powers that would enable them to evangelize the nations. "It is Parham's intention to send forth students into the world," wrote one skeptical reporter, to show other Christians how useless it was to prepare "for foreign missionary work in the usual way," that is, by laboriously studying other languages, when they could be imparted by the Spirit in an instant. Indeed, Parham told the swarming journalists that he and his students, with no education in foreign languages at all, spoke and even wrote in French, German, Swedish, Bohemian, Chinese, Bulgarian, Russian, Italian, Spanish, and Norwegian. Theological subtleties were lost on the secular press, which blared, "Parham's New Religion," "New Sect in Kansas Speaks with Strange Tongues," "A Queer Faith," and "Strange Gibberish, 'Students' Talk but No One Understands Them."[6] The Topeka saints, like other mission-centered evangelicals of the era, were always looking outside the United States for potential converts. Yet in other ways they were unique. No other Protestants championed the miraculous gifts that Parham and his followers claimed to possess. To these modern-day apostles, scripture foretold the gift of tongues in the last days. "In the close of the age," Parham wrote in a treatise on the subject, "God proposed to send forth men and women preaching in languages they know not a word of." The believers hoped to fulfill the "great commission" and convert the world in a generation (Acts 1:8, Matthew 28:20, Mark 13:10).[7]

Unfortunately for Parham and his followers, such lofty goals met with defeat. After an initial flurry of reportage, the public soon lost interest in the strange scenes taking place at Stone's Folly. Parham's school disbanded later in the year, and new lodgers converted the healing home into a roadhouse. Not long afterwards it burned to the ground. Meanwhile, Parham and his wife, along with a few other initiates, refocused their energies on healing evangelism, drifting through Kansas, southwest Missouri, and Texas. Parham's own paper, *The Apostolic Faith,* never spread the news of the Topeka revival as thoroughly as did the secular press. Hence the first wave of what would become known as pentecostalism remained limited primarily to Kansas, Missouri, Texas, and Arkansas.[8] The vast majority of southern holiness folk had not heard of Charles Parham or his work.

By late 1905 Parham's Apostolic Faith movement achieved some success in the suburbs surrounding Houston. Building on a network of newly established churches, Parham settled there and organized a new Bible school. The themes were much the same as those at Topeka: healing, tongues speech as evidence of Holy Ghost baptism, and the second coming of Christ. One of his pupils, an African American by the name of William J. Seymour, was allowed to participate only if he sat outside the classroom in a hallway. Although Seymour's experience was limited by the restrictions of Jim Crow, he nonetheless eagerly absorbed Parham's theology. He ventured into the city, preaching alongside his mentor and other students. The thirty-five-year-old Seymour, born to former slave parents in Louisiana, would eventually supersede his teacher as the unofficial leader of the new pentecostal movement. Moreover, he would prove instrumental in the spread of pentecostalism into the South.

Seymour was much like other radical southern holiness folk, black and white. Always a restless soul, he traveled widely in search of ever greater religious insight. He disregarded regional boundaries just as he shrugged off theological orthodoxy. As he moved about the country, he drew inspiration from the various new lights he encountered. Accordingly, his theology was an amalgamation of Wesleyan perfectionism and Holy Ghost empowerment. Before studying under Parham, Seymour spent some years in Indianapolis, where he worked several service jobs. There he affiliated with the Evening Light Saints, an integrated perfectionist sect in that city. By the turn of the century he had moved to Cincinnati, where, according to oral tradition, he attended God's Bible School, founded by Martin Wells Knapp. It certainly seems that Knapp's premillennial theology and radical holiness theories had a strong impact on the wayfaring Seymour. Also while in Cincinnati he contracted smallpox and lost sight in one eye. It was, he thought, God's punishment for his not having entered the ministry sooner. As a result, he left Cincinnati for Houston early in the new century to gain further ministerial training and to reconnect with family members who had been lost during slavery. But before Seymour entered Parham's Bible school, he made one last pilgrimage to Jackson, Mississippi. There he sought advice and guidance from C. P. Jones, the most prominent African American holiness figure in the South. Jones's unwavering commitment to Wesleyan perfectionism and his abilities as a leader impressed Seymour deeply.[9]

Thus equipped, Seymour enrolled in Parham's school with the encouragement of Lucy Farrow, a native of Norfolk, Virginia, and a niece of the renowned abolitionist and black intellectual Frederick Douglass. Seymour had shared a holiness pulpit with Farrow and, more important, first learned about the "Bible evidence" of speaking in tongues from her. Seymour attended Parham's school for roughly five weeks, long enough to adopt Parham's premillennial view of tongues as a preparation for world missions.

Word of Seymour's preaching abilities reached a black holiness church in Los Angeles, which invited the minister to assume leadership of the congregation. Shortly after his arrival in

February 1906, his doctrine of tongues as evidence met with sharp resistance from his new flock. His adversaries promptly locked him out of their church. He then held services emphasizing the tenets of pentecostalism in the homes of his supporters. Seymour and these seekers of "Pentecost" finally secured a building at 312 Azusa Street in the city's industrial district. The rundown structure had previously served as an African Methodist Episcopal church before being converted into a tenement house and livery stable.

Soon after the revival began in April 1906, the interracial, multiethnic gathering attracted the attention of *Los Angeles Times* reporters, who lampooned the congregants for their wild religious excesses. The spiritual acrobatics performed at the Azusa Mission—jumping, dancing, falling prostrate on the floor, shouting, speaking in tongues, and prophesying—made the participants easy targets of ridicule. One reporter mocked the meeting as a "Weird Babel of Tongues" and mercilessly caricatured Seymour: "An old colored exhort, blind in one eye, is the major-domo of the company. With his stony optic fixed on some luckless unbeliever, the old man yells his defiance and challenges an answer." The press, whether positive or negative, helped disseminate pentecostalism far beyond the confines of Los Angeles. Frank Bartleman, a widely traveled leader at Azusa, later claimed that the *Los Angeles Times* gave "us much free advertising" and made thousands aware of the revival who otherwise would never have come in contact with it. Indeed, the revival at the Azusa Street Mission would spread across the country and around the globe. Although it was Parham who first made the connection between tongues and Spirit baptism, the revival that Seymour inaugurated would dwarf his teacher's earlier efforts.[10]

Speaking in tongues was not a new phenomenon, of course. Throughout history devotees of ecstatic religious movements,

Leaders of the Azusa Street mission. W. J. Seymour is seated in the front row, second from right.

usually associated with a revival or religious awakening, practiced tongues speech. In America the manifestation of such spiritual gifts was at least as old as the First Great Awakening. More recently a group of southern holiness people who would later help form the Church of God (Cleveland) claimed to have spoken in tongues at an 1896 revival held in Cherokee County, North Carolina. Yet the tongues movement that Parham inaugurated and Seymour brought to the attention of thousands was in many ways unparalleled. Earlier believers certainly did not think tongues speech to be the sign of Spirit baptism. In previous revivals signs such as speaking in tongues and healing were occasional, even accidental manifestations, often dissipating with a revival's termination. Interestingly, when Parham and his acolytes searched the annals of church history for other tongues speakers, they found dozens of what they considered forerunners of the modern movement. The Welsh revival of 1904–1905, which received extensive press coverage in the United States and Britain, seemed an especially fitting precursor. But Parham and later pentecostals came to believe that these manifestations of the Spirit were necessary for a full Christian experience.[11]

Tongues speech assumed a variety of meanings for different adherents. To some initiates it represented unmediated divine contact. To others it proved a saintly status. But to all early pentecostals it foreshadowed the last days. The interpretation of speaking in tongues as both certain evidence of Spirit baptism and the ultimate sign of the world's end defined this new movement.[12] And just as tongues speech heralded the last days for Parham, Seymour likewise focused on the eschatological significance of the gift. Consequently, certainty of the fast approaching second coming of Christ was central to first-generation adherents.[13] Contemporary critics surely thought as much. One University of Southern California graduate student who interviewed dozens of the Azusa's faithful argued that tongues speaking and millennialism were inseparable. C. W. Shumway had yet to meet a tongues speaker, he wrote in his thesis, who was not a "premillennial second adventist through and through." Shumway also observed that the most commonly interpreted tongues message was "Jesus is Coming!"[14]

Seymour's Azusa Street Mission newspaper, *The Apostolic Faith,* which he began publishing in September 1906, brimmed with warnings of the second coming and discussions of tongues as preparation for world evangelism. *The Apostolic Faith* reached thousands of anxious holiness enthusiasts, many in the American South, who pored over its pages in anticipation of the baptism of the Holy Ghost. The first issue ran five thousand copies, but by May 1908 the Azusa Street Mission was publishing fifty thousand copies every month.[15] Most of the paper's radical holiness readers embraced the tongues messages coming from the movement's latter-day seers that "Jesus is coming again, coming again soon and we shall meet him then." Prophecies similar to this tongues interpretation appeared repeatedly in the widely read paper. Seymour also printed a number of premillennial hymns in the first year of the paper's publication—with titles such as "Jesus Is Coming," "A Message Concerning Christ's Coming," "When Jesus Comes," "The Signs of the Times," and "The Warfare, the Rapture, and Afterwards"—further stressing the movement's apocalyptic theme.[16] Converts used the image of the "former" and "latter rain" (Joel 2:28) to explain the California "Pentecost." In Palestine, rainfall came in the spring planting season and again in the fall to ripen crops for harvest. The outpouring of the Spirit, so reasoned devotees, was this "latter rain" before the great spiritual harvest of the last days. Hence, Seymour wrote in the second issue of *The Apostolic Faith,* "latter rain" missionaries, divinely equipped with foreign languages, were setting out from Azusa to reap a world harvest. "Awake! Awake!" he urged. "There is but time to dress and be ready for the cry will soon go forth. 'The Bridegroom cometh.'"[17]

Missionaries from Azusa were not the first to spread this message to southerners, or at least not in person. In fact, most radical perfectionists in the region initially encountered the new movement through familiar media: holiness newspapers, pamphlets, and books. It is not surprising that the West Coast revival would also enter the South in this fashion. The southern movement already had a substantial print culture. Since the mid-1890s the southern faithful had read news of revivals across the country, followed the lives of beloved evangelists, and received notice of sanctification conventions in widely circulated journals. Pentecostal Holiness Church leaders in the South recognized the all-important role of literature. "There is

"The Rapture." Martin Wells Knapp included this image in his 1898 work *Lightning Bolts from Pentecostal Skies, or Devices of the Devil Unmasked.* By 1900 nearly all southern holiness folk believed Christ would soon return to carry the saints into heaven.

perhaps no agency among us greater than the printing press," they reported at a 1915 convention. "Hence, we are admonished by the Word of the Lord to give attendance to reading." Others, too, knew well how instrumental the press would be in spreading the message. Several years after Azusa, A. J. Tomlinson continued to believe that newspapers would propagate the revival far and wide. "Thousands will believe and say good by [*sic*] to old forms and creeds, and will be stanch [*sic*] followers of Christ," he wrote.[18] Although his spelling was horrific, Tomlinson could not have put things more succinctly. Seymour's *Apostolic Faith* was soon reaching many hundreds of southerners. Some of the paper's eager readers would request bundled copies to distribute to relatives, neighbors, even strangers. The strategy worked well. Seymour's Azusa office was flooded with as many as fifty letters of inquiry a day from around the country. Frank Bartleman, a tireless promoter of the revival and a writer for *The Apostolic Faith*, was also inundated with over five hundred letters from those who read his editorials and wanted to know more about the work in the West. He gladly obliged.[19]

Many of the curious were southerners. Hundreds of "sanctificationists" in the region had obtained the first copy of the Azusa Mission's newspaper. As a result, prominent southerners would soon persuade other sympathetic souls to accept the new tenets. The Fire-Baptized Holiness leader J. H. King in Georgia and the independent minister and educator N. J. Holmes in South Carolina read *The Apostolic Faith* with rapt attention. In it, they and others like them found what they had long been lacking: concrete evidence of their anointing and a startling sign of the end. At first King had some reservations concerning the gift of tongues. Was it real? he wondered. Yet within months after he first read about the California revival, he embraced the new message. He then transformed his Royston, Georgia, newspaper, *Live Coals,* into a pentecostal bulwark. The newly dubbed *Apostolic Evangel,* King reported in the Azusa Mission paper, would proclaim "that Pentecost is evidenced by speaking in tongues" and would publish nothing to the contrary. He envisioned his journal as a kind of southern disseminator of apostolic orthodoxy. N. J. Holmes, too, became engrossed by the new message. He believed that the saints in Los Angeles had been praying for the same thing his southern brethren had. But those in California "seemed to be more definite in their petition, for Pentecost with the manifestations of Pentecost," or speaking in tongues.[20] In Louisville, the prominent Baptist healing evangelist and author A. S. Worrell also lent his support to Azusa. He lauded Seymour and the West Coast disciples in the pages of his periodical, *The Gospel Witness,* and eventually made the long trip to the Azusa Street Mission.[21] Experiencing similar epiphanies, dozens of other perfectionist editors and educators in the South altered their theology according to the new light.

Along with Seymour's *Apostolic Faith,* the southern radical holiness press proved crucial to the transmission of the Azusa message.[22] Leaders like Frank Bartleman eagerly promoted tongues speech in cheaply priced pamphlets and in southern holiness and pentecostal papers. In particular, Bartleman wrote stirring editorials. He provocatively recounted the miracles occurring at Asuza in *The Way of Faith, The Apostolic Faith, God's Revivalist,* and a number of other periodicals. At the same time, Seymour advertised southern newspapers that were "on the apostolic line," and encouraged his subscribers to lend their support to them.[23] The circulation rates of these southern papers rose dramatically. The radical holiness press in the South would convince many holiness adherents that the more zealous pentecostals were the rightful bearers of gospel truth. As editors tantalizingly described the strange new "gifts of the Spirit" manifested at Azusa, they also provided space for elaborate testimonies. Men and women, some barely literate, from Tennessee, South Carolina, Georgia, Florida, Alabama, and Mississippi penned letters that expressed their hunger for experiences equal to those occurring in the West.[24]

Consequently, pentecostal papers assumed a kind of sacred aura. Certain papers, including *The Apostolic Faith,* were so revered, in fact, that they were thought to have curative powers. Some adherents even believed that their newspapers would bring relief to the infirm if applied like a balm.[25] Not long after southern seekers began reading Seymour's newspaper in the fall of 1906, *The Holiness Advocate,* published in Clinton, North Carolina, featured the revival in its pages. The paper's editor, A. B. Crumpler of the Holiness Church of North Carolina, reprinted an article that had appeared in *The Way of Faith,* which read, "We have written scores of letters of inquiry to persons who have been in touch with the work [at Azusa] from the beginning." The writer was "profoundly convinced that God is in the movement."[26] Like hundreds of others, a woman representing a small band of holiness people in New Orleans wrote to the Azusa Street paper to offer her elated testimony. "As soon as we received those Apostolic Faith papers," she reported, "we began praying, and fasted . . . and Glory to His name, He made Himself known in our midst."[27] The experience of a holiness minister from southern Florida was also typical. The moment he read of the California revival, he told his wife and anyone else who would listen that it came from God. In a flash he "became an earnest seeker of the baptism with the Holy Ghost" and the gift of tongues.[28] Because of the extensive press coverage of Azusa, some could describe in detail what they sought. A letter from one M. H. Alexander illustrates this pattern: "In the Fall of 1906 I began to read how the power was falling in California and people were speaking in tongues and the sick were being healed. . . . My heart began to leap within me; I realized that this was what I needed; so I began to see how clear the word of God taught it [and] I began to ask the dear Lord to give me this wonderful blessing."[29] With the possibilities of the latter rain laid out before them, readers soon came to view everything through a pentecostal lens. Some who read of the outpouring even stopped attending any meeting that did not espouse tongues and other end-time signs. Pentecostal editors lent their support, of course, and told readers which revivals were authentic and which were bogus.[30]

J. M. Pike's South Carolina–based journal *The Way of Faith* quickly became the key southern disseminator of the Los Angeles movement. Reports of the revival filled its pages beginning in 1906. The paper reprinted startling accounts of men and women speaking in tongues and performing miracles at Azusa. The editor convinced hundreds, if not thousands, of holiness people that they had somehow been denied the full gospel until now. A North Carolina holiness preacher, Gaston Barnabas Cashwell, wrote in to *The Apostolic Faith* with his testimonial: "I began to read in the Way of Faith the reports of meetings in [the] Azusa Mission, Los Angeles. I had been preaching holiness for nine years, but my soul began to hunger and thirst for the fullness of God. . . . After praying and weeping before God for many days, [Jesus] put it into my heart to go to Los Angeles to seek the baptism with the Holy Ghost."[31] Cashwell made the long journey west in November 1906. At first he recoiled from the interracial fellowship he found there. But soon he overcame his prejudice and asked Seymour and other African American ministers in attendance to pray that he might receive the baptism. Subsequently, Cashwell spoke in tongues and felt empowered to go back to the South as a self-proclaimed pentecostal apostle.[32]

Cashwell was an imposing figure, tipping the scales at roughly 250 to 300 pounds. Contemporaries described him as red-faced, blond, tall, and strong. Years before Azusa, working as a traveling tobacco agent, he roamed throughout Georgia, demonstrating the crop's ability to take to soil in unlikely places. But that was all before he became saved and sanctified. As a new convert, he fulminated against tobacco, drink, and "loose living" just as furiously as his holiness co-laborers did. Those who attended his revivals were astounded by the preacher's booming voice and powerful presence. Following the trip west, he channeled his energies into promoting Pentecost.[33]

After returning from Azusa, Cashwell went to Dunn, North Carolina, where he rented a tobacco warehouse to hold a revival in December and January. He may have known the owners of the facility from his previous career. Cashwell intended Dunn to become a southern re-creation of Azusa. Soon it was. Congregants witnessed healings, tongues speech, interracial fellowship, and a host of mystical religious experiences. The southern perfectionist press printed glowing reports of the Dunn revival and helped encourage the uninitiated to seek their "Pentecost." Not long afterwards, Cashwell mounted a barnstorming tour of the South. He preached his new message in Memphis, Tennessee; High Point, North Carolina; Danville, Virginia; West Union, Clinton, and Lake City, South Carolina; Toccoa, Royston, and Valdosta, Georgia; and Birmingham, Alabama. So intriguing were Cashwell's high-energy 1907 meetings that the *Atlanta Constitution* took note. The North Carolina preacher's Azusa connection made such an impression on one reporter that he inaccurately identified Cashwell as a Los Angeles native. Just as at that West Coast revival, initiates in Georgia claimed strange powers. "The fortunate one to receive" the Holy Ghost under Cashwell, wrote the journalist, "falls in a trance and remains so for some time, but on recovering from the trance at once begins to speak in the particular tongue given him." Whether or not it was all a fraud, it made for a stunning display. "An interpreter is called forth to explain to this fortunate one in what country or nation this language is used and if possible to go to that country and begin work for the Fire Baptized Holiness church." But perhaps Cashwell's most effective tool was his new paper, aptly called *The Bridegroom's Messenger*, published in Atlanta. In the October 1, 1907, inaugural issue he forthrightly summarized its singular purpose: "We believe that . . . the South [should] have a paper in which nothing contrary to this great Pentecostal truth is allowed to enter."[34]

At first Cashwell printed four thousand monthly issues, but by September 1908 he was publishing eight thousand copies per month. Half of these were sent out for free, the other half by subscription. *The Bridegroom's Messenger* became the mouthpiece for pentecostalism in the Southeast. A group of regional editors covered most of the former Confederacy. These correspondents reported announcements for revivals, and the paper allotted considerable space for testimonies from those who attended such meetings. It also ran features that cultivated the nascent movement's theology. Consequently, Cashwell's paper and his ceaseless evangelism helped guide the Church of God (Cleveland), the Fire-Baptized Holiness Church, and the Holiness Church of North Carolina into the pentecostal fold.[35]

Cashwell was certainly not the only evangelist to carry the Azusa message back to the South. It seemed to Frank Bartleman that "everyone had to go to 'Azusa.'" No fewer than fourteen key southern holiness leaders made the trek. (Undoubtedly scores of other anonymous disciples were also drawn there.) By 1908 hundreds of energetic evangelists were crisscrossing the South, preaching tongues and converting thousands.

At roughly the same time Cashwell ventured west, an African American minister from Alabama experienced Spirit baptism under Seymour's ministry. F. W. Williams quickly returned south, preaching throughout Mississippi and Alabama. In Mobile he established the Apostolic Faith Mission as an outpost of Azusa. Others followed Williams's lead. Charles Harrison Mason, a leader of the Memphis-based African American Church of God in Christ, also made the pilgrimage to California. Writing to *The Apostolic Faith* in 1907 he declared: "I had a great desire to come to Los Angeles. I had preached the Pentecost to my people and they were hungry for it." The outbreak on the West Coast, Mason concluded, was prophecy fulfilled. On arriving at Azusa, Mason recounted, he "surrendered perfectly to [Christ] and consented to Him." Next he began to sing a song in "unknown tongues" and received what he described as an agonizing vision of Christ's crucifixion. After this mystical experience, he felt confirmed that the Church of God in Christ must adopt the new message. Following a disagreement with the nonpentecostal wing of his denomination, Mason led his camp into the movement. Like many of his contemporaries, he began publishing his own pentecostal paper, *The Whole Truth,* which served to unify the otherwise loosely organized new church.[36]

Such converts devoted all their energies to the new movement and traveled thousands of miles in order to spread their gospel of the Spirit. But why did southerners like Mason, Williams, and Cashwell embrace pentecostalism so zealously? Surely southern stalwarts, steeped in premillennial eschatology, were well prepared for the new message reported in such detail in the perfectionist press. As a result, the majority of southern holiness people came to see the tongues revival as the answer to their many questions. G. F. Taylor, an emerging leader of southern pentecostalism, was the first author in the region to formulate a systematic pentecostal eschatology. In his 1907 book, *The Spirit and the Bride,* he quoted liberally from W. B. Godbey, G. D. Watson, and other leading lights of southern holiness. But unlike them he laid out an apocalyptic theology which culminated in pentecostalism. Taylor argued that the doctrines of sanctification, divine healing, and the premillennial coming of Jesus were precursors to the baptism of the Spirit and tongues speech.[37] For Taylor and other southern adherents, speaking in tongues proved the most conspicuous sign of the times.

This notion was remarkably commonplace among first-generation believers. Correspondents to southern papers were fond of quoting Acts 2:17–19: "And it shall come to pass in the last days, saith God, I will pour out of my Spirit upon all flesh. . . . And I will shew wonders in heaven above, and signs in the earth beneath." Latter-day apostles fanned out across the South. When "Rev. Kinne," a "Pentecostal preacher," held a revival in Texarkana, Texas, the *Dallas Morning News* noted that men and women at Kinne's meeting received what they described as a Holy Ghost baptism and spoke in tongues, "in the ancient apostolic way." The Book of Acts assumed an even greater place for southern pentecostals than it had for holiness enthusiasts. "We speak in new tongues here in Atlanta," wrote one female initiate, just like, she said, the disciples in Acts, Chapter 2. She concluded that the message received was the same everywhere: "Jesus is coming soon."[38]

Outside observers in the region also perceived the link between tongues and premillennialism. When pentecostals converged on north Birmingham in June 1907, reporters quickly arrived on the scene. One account in the *Birmingham Age-Herald* described the "religious fervor" and "strange antics" occurring at the revival. Yet such exercises, the journal noted with heavy sarcasm, were not without meaning to the self-proclaimed prophets. Devotees interpreted the languages they purported to speak as "a warning to the world to prepare for the millennium."[39]

G. B. Cashwell exemplified the sense of urgency within the

holiness movement. He told those who attended his revivals that Jesus could return at any given moment. And Cashwell firmly believed in Charles Parham's and William J. Seymour's pragmatic theory of tongues speech. "If Jesus tarries until we have to learn all the languages of the world," Cashwell argued in the first issue of *The Bridegroom's Messenger,* then the rapture would surely be delayed. The gift of tongues and the subsequent evangelization of the world would speed up the process considerably, he reasoned. Perhaps hoping that some foreign reader would be converted, Cashwell even printed a tongues message in the same issue: "Nutula oca seta oca, duta e miloo ackile iro." At Dunn as well, tongues and the second coming dominated all thoughts. One seeker at that meeting, Florence Goff, even voiced her fear that she would not make it to the revival in time. "Oh, I hope Jesus will not come until I get the Holy Ghost," she fretted.[40]

Yet belief in an inevitable apocalypse was certainly not the only reason why southern holiness folk turned to the new movement. A number of cultural, personal, and communal factors led the curious to join the Holy Ghost ranks. Some of these factors are lost in the silences of the historical record, but others remain detectable.

A few contemporary critics and later historians contended that pentecostalism was the religious product of social dispossession, poverty, and ignorance. One early commentator found that the movement thrived only among "people in a low state of culture," who were vulnerable to the power of suggestion.[41] Later historians developed similar analyses, according to which pentecostals were largely rural, uneducated, and besieged by a host of troubles—including ill health and declining social status. Yet, as with holiness folk before them, a few followers enjoyed upper-middle-class standing, and many others were situated solidly in the middle class. Converts were representative of Americans in general with regard to financial worth, employment, and education.[42]

In other ways, though, southern pentecostals were unusual in at least one regard. Most adherents were extremely mobile, even restless. They seemed to be on a constant quest for new spiritual insights. Fiercely independent, they leaped from one religious fellowship to another, often on a whim. An outside observer familiar with dozens of southern devotees described them as "the unsettled, the 'floaters,' the eccentric and the discontented." Another harsh critic found enthusiasts to be "adventurers, renegades, discounted men and women" who were "without religious anchorage."[43] Pentecostals in the South represented the same type of translocalism that was so apparent among their holiness predecessors. Much like W. B. Godbey, G. D. Watson, and Mary Lee Cagle, pentecostals paid little attention to geographic and cultural boundaries. That is why, at least in the early years, pentecostalism was largely a movement of itinerants.

The wayfaring life of the radical holiness preacher Daniel P. Awrey, though extreme, was not all that unusual. A native of Momosa, Ontario, Awrey ventured to eastern Tennessee in the 1890s, where he worked as an evangelist and set up a holiness school in a remote mountain village. At the end of the century he affiliated with Benjamin Hardin Irwin's Fire-Baptized Holiness fellowship. He then toured through thirteen states and Canada, preaching "fire and dynamite." After Irwin's disgrace, Awrey, undaunted, moved to Arizona and then on to Los Angeles once the Azusa revival erupted. He would go on to conduct short-term pentecostal schools in the United States and around the world until his death in 1913.[44] Such individuals were driven by a single-minded purpose. Their primary goals of spreading "Pentecost" crowded out many allegiances—to region, to denomination, to family—that other Americans adhered to so closely.

Believers immersed themselves in the new crusade. Holy Ghost religion sustained them as nothing else could. Pentecostal experience also served as a great social leveler. Although it was not the main reason why southerners adopted pentecostalism, this movement toward equality must have drawn many into the fold. Eager southerners read that at Azusa no distinctions were made to differentiate who could receive the gifts of the Spirit. "No instrument that God can use is rejected on account of color or dress or lack of education," declared one eyewitness.

Indeed, southern initiates deliberately challenged social rank and cultural distinctions, just as their co-laborers in Los Angeles did. A journalist for a Birmingham, Alabama, newspaper noted the phenomenon when he attended a boisterous revival in that city. The power of the Spirit, he reported with amazement, "is no respecter of class or color—men, women, children and negro servants having come under its influence."[45] The gift of "foreign" tongues, so it appeared, could be claimed by anyone. A letter sent to *The Holiness Advocate* (Clinton, North Carolina) in 1907 illustrates this point. It reads in full: "Dear Advocate, I praise God for saving, sanctifying, and filling me with His blessed Holy Ghost. I am a little boy of eight years old." Other youngsters wrote to the paper's "Children's Corner," one closing with, "I want God's children to pray that I may hold out until Jesus comes." It was a faith that required no formal education or cultural experience. Initiates relished pointing this out to supposedly superior doubters. At a revival in Southern Pines, North Carolina, discussed in the June 1906 issue of *The Holiness Advocate,* Anna Kelly described how a "sister McLaughlin" received the gift of language. In confirmation of this experience she reported, "A highly educated doctor of Southern Pines told me he could understand what [McLaughlin] said except one word, and that she spoke the purest Latin." Kelly added, God "is just as able to give [people] languages as He is to confound them."[46] It was like the Old Testament story of Babel reversed. An *Atlanta Constitution* reporter noted a similar phenomenon while attending a Gate City, Georgia, meeting. Shouting and crying "'Glory, glory, glory,' over and over again, as fast as possible," disciples encouraged all in attendance to get the Holy Ghost. "'Praise the Lord,' 'Push your claim, sister,'" they yelled. When the observer frankly asked what it all meant, one apostle remarked that seekers were getting the gift of languages, just as on the day of "pentecost." "Why, a woman just now who had never read or known what a Greek word was, shouted forth a Greek phrase." The untutored were now on a par with the brainiest Oxford dons.[47]

Racial and gender divisions among converts were also not as clearly demarcated as they were in society at large and in the mainline churches. The holiness movement had certainly set the tone, offering women and African Americans opportunities that were largely unavailable elsewhere.[48] In the earliest years, female holiness evangelists such as Maria Woodworth-Etter were extremely popular among both whites and African Americans in the South. She frequently preached to racially integrated crowds in the region.[49] Similarly, many who became pentecostals believed that the Spirit favored men and women equally. Writing in *The Holiness Advocate*, one female convert argued that when a believer received the baptism with the Holy Ghost, she would come to see that scripture did not prohibit women from preaching. For her it was clear: "God don't call all women to preach neither does He call all men to preach. But if He does call and they fail to obey—woe is pronounced upon them."[50] At Azusa this tradition thrived and became even more pronounced. *The Apostolic Faith* published testimonials from men and women, African Americans and whites. In theory and in practice the Spirit was said not to discriminate by color or sex. Anyone could potentially be a spiritual conduit. It is doubtful, however, that Azusa's egalitarian message was received with the same enthusiasm in the Southeast.[51]

Southern pentecostals only occasionally broached the subject of race. Indeed, even periodicals edited by African Americans, including *Whole Truth* and *Voice in the Wilderness,* showed remarkable inattention to matters of racial justice. Yet it is amazing that southern adherents grappled with issues of race at all.[52] Southern churches were among the most racially segregated institutions in the country. William Archer, an English observer of the early-twentieth-century South, found the region to be the most "sincerely religious" place he had ever visited. Still, he noted, most white southern Christians "would scarce be at ease in heaven unless they enter it, like a southern railway station, through a gate marked 'for whites.'"[53]

The testimony of A. A. Boddy, another Englishman and an Azusa participant, provides a sharp contrast to Archer's remarks. In his newspaper, *Confidence* (Sunderland, England), Boddy recalled witnessing an astounding interracialism among southerners at Azusa. Elizabeth A. Sexton, the new editor of *The Bridegroom's Messenger,* subsequently reprinted Boddy's observations. Her inclusion of his testimony in her Atlanta-based paper was all the more remarkable in light of the fact that the nadir of New South race relations had been reached not long before in the Atlanta race riot of 1906:

One of the remarkable things [at Azusa] was that preachers of the Southern States were willing and eager to go over to those negro people at Los Angeles and have fellowship with them, and through their prayers receive the same blessing. The most wonderful thing was that, when those white preachers came back to the Southern States, they were not ashamed to say before their own congregations that they had been worshiping with negroes, and had received some of the same wonderful blessings that had been poured out on them.

W. J. Seymour considered this breakdown of racial prejudice at Azusa to be a sign of "the Lord's coming." It seemed far too extraordinary to be attributed to a human cause. The biracialism at Azusa inspired Bartleman to note that "the 'color line' was washed away in the blood."[54]

In many ways both black and white southern pentecostals appear to have agreed. They attended tent revivals together, shared pulpits, and wrote in each other's newspapers. On occasion a white man would minister to a mixed congregation, and at other times a black woman would do the same. Lucy Farrow (the African American preacher who first encouraged Seymour to pray for Spirit baptism) traveled from the Azusa Street Mission back to Houston in August 1906. Once there she conducted a heavily attended, convulsive interracial camp meeting. She preached and laid hands on both black and white seekers who desired the "baptism of the Holy Ghost." A white minister who witnessed what he considered Farrow's miraculous display remarked that although the woman preacher was "a Negro, she was received as a messenger of the Lord to us, even in the deep South of Texas."[55] Pentecostals in both the South and the West delighted in upsetting what many thought to be the natural order of race, class, and sex. Azusa set a strong precedent. A puzzled reporter for the *Los Angles Times* wondered why the message of "Pentecost" came so frequently

HOLY ROLLERS WORSHIP
IN THE POLICE COURT

The Holy Rollers Do a Turn in the Police Court.

The *Atlanta Constitution* published this crude caricature of African American "holy rollers" in 1908. The artist depicted them worshipping in a local courtroom after their arrest for disturbing the peace.

"through ignorant negroes." "Because," answered one less than enlightened white initiate, "God has always chosen the simple, trustful minds to do His work."[56]

The egalitarian ethos and instances of "race mixing" attracted the attention, and sometimes the anger, of insiders as well as outsiders. Some of Seymour's fiercest critics disparaged him in clearly racist terms, perhaps none with more venom than Charles Parham. When the Azusa movement rejected

Parham, he turned against his former pupil, blasting Seymour and the interracial pentecostals. Whites "were imitating unintelligent, crude negroisms of the Southland," Parham fumed. Worse still, black and white men and women at pentecostal meetings knelt together or fell across one another in what Parham bitterly described as orgiastic frenzies.[57] Shortly after the feud broke out between Parham and Seymour, Parham was accused of committing sodomy with a younger man in Texas. Consequently, his authority as a leader of the movement waned considerably, and he posed no further threat.

Yet Parham's fall did not put an end to racist attacks on pentecostals. In fact, the fiercest and most violent opposition came from angry white southerners determined to enforce Jim Crow justice. Two confrontations in particular serve as illustrations. Burt McCafferty, a pentecostal evangelist who preached at lumber camps up and down the Texas-Louisiana border, upset local toughs by ministering to interracial crowds. In one village a white preacher and a band of armed white men faced off against McCafferty, whom they accused of stating that "a negro was as good as a white man." The unconventional pentecostal evangelist had gained an impressive reputation for shooting at such opponents. This standoff, however, ended without incident.

Other pentecostal itinerants in the South were not so fortunate. When F. F. Bosworth preached at an interracial Holy Ghost camp meeting at Hearne, Texas, he enraged a number of whites in the area. After the services Bosworth was met by a group of white ruffians—"extreme nigger-haters," as he described them. They threatened to shoot him on the spot unless he left town at once. Heeding their advice, he was again met by a vigilante mob at the train station. They demanded punishment for his breach of segregation and beat him unmercifully with boat oars until they broke his wrist, leaving him cut and bruised.[58] Satisfied, they abandoned him on the train tracks. Bosworth's only consolation was that he later discovered that two of his attackers suffered violent deaths. One was hit by a train on the same tracks where Bosworth had been pummeled.[59] God had avenged him.

Bosworth tried to plead with his assailants. He had come to preach only to the whites, he told them. Blacks just happened to be in attendance as well. There were certainly limits to the degree of black-white interaction. When necessary, southern pentecostals evaded reprisals for race mixing by segregating their tent meetings, or by having blacks and whites meet at separate times. Of course, the extent of gender and racial equality in the South should not be exaggerated. Social equity was never pentecostals' primary concern.[60] And like the holiness people with whom they were once associated, pentecostals were overwhelmingly uninterested in, if not contemptuous of, politics. Few thought of lending their support to racial uplift, political parties, or labor organizations. The political sphere, they thought, did not concern them. Even voting in "worldly" elections was often scorned. The pentecostal revival emanating from Azusa offered a type of spiritual liberation that its converts believed transcended more immediate forms of social liberation.[61]

When initiates rhapsodized about the revival, they seldom referred to the fact that it brought some form of gender, racial, or political equality. Instead they recounted its spiritually transformative possibilities. They also adopted pentecostalism because it affirmed so much of what they had come to believe about the New Testament church and Christian history. In part, the more radical sects in the South favorably received pentecostalism because of the movement's sharp restorationist vision. One enthusiast wrote to *The Bridegroom's Messenger:* "Many are being saved, sanctified, filled with the Holy Ghost, and speaking in tongues. . . . Pentecost is the same today as it was 1900 years ago." The restorationist trope infused accounts of revivals in Florida, Tennessee, Georgia, the Carolinas, and Alabama. In their published testimonies, converts occupied an anachronistic space, proclaiming freedom from nineteen hundred years of church history and dogma. Writing from Birmingham, Alabama, the Reverend M. M. Pinson claimed: "Those who get the baptism of the Spirit in my meeting speak and sing in other tongues . . . as on the day of Pentecost, and at the house of Cornelius. It surely works as of old, for Jesus is the same yesterday, today, and forever."[62] Accordingly, for those wanting assurance that their experience was in fact a restoration of the apostolic faith, southern pentecostals offered the most literal version as well as a faith free from the taint of the past.

That same electrifying Spirit that overwhelmed Cornelius and the apostles in Acts was again available to all. Fittingly, then, pentecostal worship might overwhelm human emotions, washing away despair through the hope of spiritual euphoria. Moreover, converts experienced what they believed to be unmediated divine contact. A woman at a North Carolina revival who sang a song in tongues describing the Lord's return exclaimed, "Oh, is it not wonderful for God Himself to speak and sing through us!"[63] Southern believers described speaking in tongues as being taken over by the Spirit. Their jaws were moved by some "unseen hand," their throat and vocal cords were possessed by the Holy Ghost. Occasionally initiates who claimed to have no musical talent pounded away on pianos, furiously strummed guitars, or sang "in the Spirit." The first time the South Carolina leader N. J. Holmes spoke in tongues he was sure that it was not by his own power. His teeth chattered "without my effort or control," he claimed. He seemed to speak effortlessly in another language.[64]

Yet to their disappointment, when many first-generation pentecostals entered the mission field, they discovered that they were mistaken. From 1906 to 1909, over a dozen freshly installed pentecostal missionaries traveled abroad, armed, so they thought, with the gift of foreign languages. One of them, A. G. Garr, a native of Kentucky, felt certain that when he and his wife reached India in 1907, he would present the good news eloquently in Bengali. A missionary who spoke Hindi pointed out to the Garrs that his words were nothing but gibberish. After several unsuccessful evangelistic outings, Garr reluctantly acknowledged his shortcomings. The Garrs moved on to Hong Kong, where they studied Chinese.

Oddly enough, the embarrassment over foreign tongues mattered little. Enthusiasts like Garr adopted a view that would accommodate this frustrating realization. Subsequently they interpreted the gift as speaking in unknown or unintelligible tongues (glossolalia). Most important, the faithful still believed that their ecstasy was of divine origin and that they were not the agent or cause of their experience. When they sang in tongues, prophesied, or performed miracles, it was through the direct working of God. With this new revelation in view, pentecostals perceived themselves at the center of God's restored order.[65]

For those southerners who became pentecostal, neither the holiness movement nor mainline denominations could generate this kind of excitement. Indeed, holiness fellowships which rebuked tongues speakers actually came under suspicion for being inadequate in pentecostals' eyes. So too did numerous independent sects and denominations, including southern Methodists, southern Baptists, and Free-Will Baptists. Posturing against "dead religion" and "cold formalism" became a full-time calling for southern pentecostals. The movement clearly did not take shape in a vacuum. Fierce confrontation with local authorities and other religious bodies in the region proved formative. And those who were attracted to Holy Ghost religion thrived on acrimonious conflicts.

The saints read the abuse regularly heaped on them by outsiders as a clear indication of divine anointing. Persecution thus meant far more to southern pentecostals than it did to their holiness predecessors. Followers saw themselves as lone warriors battling the forces of darkness all around them. It was, as one historian describes it, a kind of "reverse conceit." Rejected by scoffers, they viewed themselves as a spiritual elite. In the 1920s an observant writer in H. L. Mencken's *American Mercury* ridiculed this self-perception. Pentecostals, wrote Duncan Aikmen, were united in their belief that the "infernal kingdom" was arrayed against them because of their "success in enlarging on earth the power of the arch foe, Jehovah." Indeed, some young southern evangelists doubted their calling when local adversaries failed to persecute them. Texas Apostolic Faith leader H. A. Goss recalled one preacher who hoped to have "at least a few stones, tomatoes, or rotten oranges thrown at him or his tent (for Jesus' sake)."[66]

Usually, though, the faithful did manage to draw hostile attention from their southern neighbors. Community members were troubled by their odd beliefs and wild services held night after night. Pentecostals regularly faced attacks for upsetting life in mill towns. In 1910 a tumultuous pentecostal tent meeting in Alabama City, Alabama, kept workers up late, infuriating mill bosses and local residents. Leaders of the community stepped in to counter the work of the rambunctious holiness-turned-pentecostal preacher J. W. Buckalew. Owners of a nearby cotton mill continued to operate late into the night, hoping to keep employees away from the meetings. The *Gadsen Evening Journal* and *Gadsen Daily News* satirized the revival in reporting on the "Divine Hypnotism" and religious mania breaking out in revival tents. Buckalew retaliated, hurling epithets at the editors. Town officials in return accused the pentecostals of disturbing the peace and attempted to enforce a 9:00 PM curfew on the gathering. When that failed, police arrested the revival's leaders while vigilantes burned meeting tents and chairs.[67] Pentecostal preachers denounced ministers and townsfolk from their makeshift pulpits. As in Alabama, violence typically broke out as a result of such challenges. In 1908 the *Atlanta Constitution* reported that a "Holy Roller" preacher in Florence, Alabama, was assaulted after he repeatedly condemned one local man: "James Powers hit him with his fist in the face. He was about to follow up the blow when the preacher escaped by calling on the Lord and police, the latter responding."[68]

These struggles, vividly narrated in the local press, meant genuinely different things to pentecostal believers on the one hand and their southern rivals on the other. For the former they represented a cosmic battle between God's elect and the forces of hell. For the latter they represented the imposition of order against religious frenzy, communal breakdown, and chaos. Local leaders were rightly troubled. Pentecostal converts felt an overwhelming sense of religious and social superiority. Local opposition, always diabolical, only confirmed them in their spiritual pursuits. Moreover, it substantiated their claims that the end was close at hand. The scripture, as W. B. Godbey once pointed out, foretold the persecutions that believers would face in the latter days.

For this reason, pentecostals often played the antagonist. Editors of the new southern pentecostal press abused local officials and mainline Protestants regularly in their pages. They seized on the tensions between established churches and newer sects and printed up accounts of religious dissatisfaction in their papers. *The Evening Light and Church of God Evangel*

(Cleveland, Tennessee) published a provocative letter from a Baptist preacher to his wife in which the clergyman described his heightened attraction to the freewheeling pentecostals. After explaining how devotees spoke in tongues, performed healings, and seemingly cast out devils at their tent meetings, he noted that in comparison, "any meeting of Baptists is as the silence of death." Similarly, G. G. Miller, a pentecostal minister, concluded that traditional churches had become ineffective or spiritually moribund. In July 1908 he wrote to *The Way of Faith,* describing revival services he held in Berrydale, Florida. Shortly after pitching his tent between a Methodist and a Mormon church, he denounced the Methodists and asked the local minister to "show five conversions in ten years." The preacher could not, wrote the exultant Holy Ghost evangelist, reporting that by contrast, after two weeks of meetings he had seen "thirty-six professions [at] the altar; three reclaimed, sixteen converted, eleven sanctified and six Baptized with the Holy Ghost."[69] For preachers and laypeople alike, the sedate forms of conventional evangelicalism could not compete with the liberating emotionalism of the new denomination.

Southern Methodist and Baptist leaders were, of course, outraged. They resented pentecostals' arrogance and their claims to the sole truth. Mainline opponents soon assumed the defensive and warned laypeople to guard against the fanaticism of "tonguers." Public conflicts replicated some of the same tensions that once existed between mainline groups and the holiness movement. The stakes, however, were even higher now. In the summer of 1907 a Methodist minister near Tampa who once battled local independent holiness bands encountered a new nemesis, pentecostalism. In the pages of *The Florida Christian Advocate* he cautioned local Methodists to beware of the "tongue crowd" and "fanaticism gone to seed." Responding to the same revival, a Presbyterian minister warned his flock against the "hallucinations and delusions of cranks who with pharisaic pride thank God that 'they are not as other men.'" This zealous new sect threatened to draw many away from both churches while challenging regular ministerial authority.[70] The holiness movement seemed tame by comparison.

Other southern Methodists denounced the new "holy rollers" as just another example of perfectionist extremism. When G. B. Cashwell stormed through Toccoa, Georgia, the Methodist minister in that town waged a war of words against him in the local newspaper. The "tongues" people who had invaded John G. Logan's community were promoting a "deadly farce." They were far more menacing than either the sanctificationists or the "Baptism of Fire" crowd who had come before them, he proclaimed. Logan understood that some of the townspeople attended pentecostal revivals for sheer amusement, just to see the "Linguo-Dynamiters," who "jabbered like 'barnyard fowls.'" But he pleaded with Methodists to take no interest in such "fanatics," as he called them. "These people hate your churches," he railed. Their stock in trade was abuse. One preacher, Logan furiously reported, went so far as to condemn all nonpentecostals in town as adulterers and prostitutes. Still, the Methodist minister announced his confidence that the movement "was now on its last legs." He could not have been more wrong. Toccoa city officials nevertheless did their best to slow the progress of the zealots. In the same *Toccoa Record* in which Logan admonished citizens to stay clear of tongues speakers, the city council published an ordinance prohibiting disorderly conduct on the city's streets. Guilty parties would pay a fine of up to $100 or serve a prison term of as much as sixty days. The measure seems to have been crafted to blunt the influence of apostolic street preachers and roaming Holy Ghost prophets.[71]

Southern Baptists also mounted an attack. Much like their

Methodist counterparts, North Carolina Baptists traced pentecostalism to the excesses of previous perfectionist schemes and predicted the movement's inevitable demise. A critic in the *Biblical Recorder* noted that just a few years before "in certain quarters one's standing was not good unless he claimed to have been endued with power." A little later, some held that true believers must be "perfect and sinless." It seemed only fitting, then, that this new sect would add one more superfluous demand, tongues speech. Other Baptist adversaries were more systematic in their criticism. An article which appeared in a 1908 issue of the *Baptist Argus* (Louisville) is characteristic of this posture. Following an investigation of tongues speech, the *Argus* published its findings. Nonpentecostal missionaries from India, China, and Japan were cited in order to disprove the validity of the gift. One missionary described what he had heard spoken by pentecostals as unintelligible, little resembling any actual language.[72] The *Argus* concluded that the false claims of speaking in foreign tongues discredited the entire movement. In the competitive sphere of foreign missions, allegiance was critical.

Yet the battle for adherents that erupted between southern holiness and pentecostal factions was even more turbulent. The tumult between non-tongues-speaking holiness people and pentecostals recalls what Sigmund Freud called "the narcissism of minor differences."[73] But despite the similarities between the two groups, the conflict took the form of outright warfare. The success of pentecostalism in the South often depended on the competitive drive against holiness fellowships. Contemporary outside observers knew of this progression from more established churches to unencumbered sects. Thus, in the 1920s the *New York Times* editor Grover C. Loud observed that the religion born of holiness demanded "an even stronger revival for its own perpetuation."[74] Pentecostals were soon defining themselves as the spiritual successors of perfectionists. And the new pentecostal message compelled converts to attest that their former religious experience was not just incomplete but inauthentic. It was not the *Whole Truth* (as the Church of God in Christ named its newspaper). J. H. King declared that holiness made a false claim of completeness. The sanctificationists only brought seekers into the "vestibule of Pentecostal power," as King put it. Holiness enthusiasts, regardless of their saintliness, did not have the gift of tongues, or what a South Carolina initiate called "heaven's trademark." From this vantage point the newly converted pentecostal H. H. Goff saw "the holiness people as I never saw them before. They are the foolish virgins without the oil."[75]

Such challenges were ubiquitous. This undoubtedly infuriated those who stayed within the holiness movement.[76] Consequently, the antipentecostal offensive from the second blessing camp was particularly brutal. Holiness leaders issued a steady stream of vitriol against "tongues people," accusing them of "masquerading" as true believers. The movement was "An Open Door for Heresy," "A Confusion of the Devil," full of "BORDER LAND HOLINESS PEOPLE" and backsliders.[77] Several perfectionist denominations also singled out pentecostalism for special rebuke. The Wesleyan Methodists led a two-year charge. With most of their southern congregations in South Carolina and Georgia, the Wesleyans felt particularly threatened by pentecostals. Church leaders feared a loss in membership and cautioned laypeople to remain alert. One northern observer from the denomination believed that pentecostalism was the work of the devil. Only Satan, he argued, could lead sanctified saints to conclude that they were not Spirit baptized unless they spoke in tongues. Other Wesleyans blamed the controversy on Fire-Baptized Holiness and other radical movements. "The 'third-work-of-grace' heresy," wrote one angry minister, "is a veritable hot-bed in which any vile religious thing may be hatched." Pentecostalism thrived among those who sought the latest novelty or religious fad, he charged.[78]

Holiness people also disdained the unfettered worship style and the intense emotionalism of pentecostal meetings. By the time of the tongues revival (1906–1908) emotionalism among older holiness groups was declining. Hence some southern perfectionists viewed pentecostals as menacing extremists. These fanatics lacked self-control, their detractors remarked. Southern holiness folk also frequently decried pentecostal meetings for creating "religious frenzy," "excitement and delirium."[79] At least by comparison, pentecostal meetings were less predictable and more freeform than holiness ones. The pentecostal preacher H. A. Goss remembered the fast-paced spirituals he sang at camp meetings in Texas. The songs were nothing like evangelical hymns. They were plain, lacking in poetry or composition, Goss recalled. Yet these "breakneck speed" songs, which others deemed "too worldly," stirred the soul and threw believers off guard. Such scenes of pandemonium shocked some holiness folk. Rumors spread in holiness circles that tongues meetings were carefully planned charades. From Texas the evangelist C. B. Jernigan reported that leaders of the tongues movement taught converts to repeat the same word over and over until they received the "gift." They would say "glory, glory" all through the night until they "would break into a strange tongue." To Jernigan, these contrived outbursts of the Spirit surely discredited new sectarians. There were basic reasons why Jernigan and others expended so much energy denouncing pentecostals. Perhaps above all else the holiness faithful feared guilt by association with the pentecostals, whom they certainly perceived as their inferiors.[80]

A few high-profile southern preachers also joined the antipentecostal crusade. The Kentucky evangelist W. B. Godbey, the widest-read and most influential perfectionist in the South, would become pentecostalism's harshest critic. It was an ironic twist. Godbey was revered by many first-generation pentecostals, and tongues speakers cherished his books. Yet he penned several venomous diatribes against the movement in which he described the newcomers as a demonic threat. They were deceiving "millions" of sanctified folk. The well-known evangelist even visited Azusa. Once there, the ever eccentric dilettante Godbey rebuked the congregants in Latin. "I had a language," Godbey crowed, "but they did not, as the demons who imparted the counterfeit . . . cannot give a language."[81]

Perfectionist leaders like Godbey never acknowledged that they were, in many ways, responsible for the "tongues movement." But Godbey, Martin Wells Knapp, and G. D. Watson focused much attention on the fourfold gospel—Jesus as savior, sanctifier, healer, and coming king—and contributed significantly to the rise of pentecostalism.[82] Pentecostals also received their first basic instruction on premillennialism and the gifts of the Spirit from such leading southern authors. Certainly, non-tongues-speaking perfectionist denominations with a presence in the South also held premillennialism to be an essential doctrine. For instance, the Wesleyan Methodist Church defended this end-time view against all critics. Yet Wesleyan Methodists were baffled by the premillennial logic of pentecostalism. Other holiness representatives knew that the debate hinged on a matter of emphasis. The Nazarene evangelist C. W. Ruth was doubtless a staunch premillennialist. He toured the South as an evangelist in the late nineteenth and early twentieth centuries and was well aware of some of the changes taking place in the region. Ruth believed that pentecostals overemphasized the fourfold gospel. Those who claimed the gift of tongues, he surmised, placed far too much stress on divine healing and the second coming.[83] Indeed, the majority of south-

In the early twentieth century, Elizabeth A. Sexton edited the Atlanta pentecostal newspaper *The Bridegroom's Messenger,* which helped spread the new movement throughout the South. Sexton, like many others after 1906, focused much of her attention on the second coming of Jesus.

ern sanctificationists concentrated almost exclusively on premillennialism and Spirit empowerment. It is hardly surprising, then, that the new faction would sweep through Dixie as it did.

From 1907 to 1910 thousands of initiates broke their ties with their former brethren. For some, such as the North Carolina evangelist H. H. Goff, this proved no easy task. He respected and admired holiness preachers and authors such as A. B. Crumpler and G. D. Watson. Yet Goff's newfound faith made it impossible for him to associate with those who scorned glossolalia. Similarly, dozens of pentecostal preachers and teachers who had affiliated with J. O. McClurkan's Nashville Pentecostal Mission were now at odds with their mentor. McClurkan helped convert scores to premillennialism, but he wanted nothing to do with "tonguers." McClurkan disfellowshipped all those who adopted the new doctrine, including N. J. Holmes,

M. M. Pinson, and H. G. Rodgers.[84] Although McClurkan's mission maintained a strong presence in the region, other holiness endeavors would not weather the storm of controversy. When A. B. Crumpler turned against the new movement, he used his North Carolina newspaper, *The Holiness Advocate*, to denounce tongues forthrightly. He quickly lost his loyal readership. In 1908 Crumpler, beset by debts, ceased publishing the paper.[85]

Throughout the South, second work disciples felt besieged by recently converted pentecostals. Sanctification churches and fellowships lost members by the thousands to the enthusiastic newcomers. In Mississippi, C. H. Mason and C. P. Jones split over Mason's new pentecostal beliefs. The break was far from amicable. Both parties fought an intense legal battle for sole rights to the name Church of God in Christ. Mason won, forcing Jones to organize another church.[86] Disgruntled second work adherents both black and white wrote to their newspapers to voice their many grievances against the rapidly growing tongues movement. The recently founded Pentecostal Church of the Nazarene—which later dropped "Pentecostal" from its name to avoid being confused with the new movement—lost congregations to pentecostals in Florida, Arkansas, and Texas. "The Tongues Movement has destroyed three of our churches," a jaded Nazarene pastor in Arkansas reported. After a popular camp meeting was held in Durant, Florida, hundreds of converts left their Nazarene congregations or pentecostalized existing ones. Accordingly, the Texas Conference of the Nazarene Church issued a resolution forbidding pentecostals from preaching to their flocks. It could not stem the tide, though. To this day, the Church of the Nazarene has little strength in the South.[87]

The Wesleyan Methodists suffered some of the greatest losses as a result of the new movement. Traveling southern evangelists reported massive attrition in *The Wesleyan Methodist,* the official organ of the denomination. Churches in north Florida, Georgia, and the Carolinas divided along holiness and pentecostal lines. "Fanaticism" was ubiquitous in North Carolina, wrote the Wesleyan evangelist B. L. Padgett. Pentecostals, he continued, seemed intent on converting Wesleyans to their cause. Not surprisingly, pentecostalism was quite alluring to the devoutly premillennial Wesleyans. Pentecostals ably convinced many Wesleyans that tongues speech was the Holy Ghost evidence so many had sought but not found. Delegates at the South Carolina Wesleyan Methodist Conference debated the fate of those pentecostals who remained in their churches. A number at the conference considered pentecostals little better than the average sinner. One participant noted that some members of his church "were tangled up in dancing." Even worse, though, others were involved "in the tongues movement." Still, he felt assured that God would give "us back good members in their place." Such optimism belied a grimmer reality. From 1908 to 1912 the Wesleyan Methodist Church of South Carolina lost more than one-third of its members. A large portion of those who left doubtless became pentecostal. Moreover, the denomination in South Carolina would not regain its pre-1908 numbers until 1933.[88]

Southern pentecostals considered the growth of the movement a sure sign of God's favor. The revival that began under the southern-born William J. Seymour in California spread rapidly into the South, prompting A. J. Tomlinson, the first general overseer of the Church of God (Cleveland), to apply the well-worn incendiary metaphor: "The Fire is spreading for miles and miles in every direction."[89] But few contemporary observers could have predicted the phenomenal growth rate in the South. In 1914 Arthur S. Booth-Clibborn, the son-in-law of the Salvation Army's founders, estimated that tongues speakers throughout the world numbered seventy thousand.[90] The 1916 census of religious bodies grossly underestimated the number of believers in the United States. (Some significant denominations, including the Church of God in Christ, were not represented at all.) The total membership of those fellowships that were included numbered approximately 32,000. These partial figures indicate that as many as 81 percent of the faithful resided in the South.[91]

What accounted for this remarkable growth below the Mason-Dixon line? Radical holiness followers in the South were well prepared for the tongues message preached first by Charles Fox Parham and later, more successfully, by William J. Seymour. The overwhelming majority of southern perfectionists had long embraced the pessimistic end-time view of premillennialism. Many of these became seekers of ever greater spiritual gifts, which they thought would flow abundantly from heaven in the "last days." The word of Seymour's revival needed only some means of reaching the South. The emerging pentecostal press ably accomplished that purpose. Following the Azusa revival, the radical holiness and pentecostal press enabled southern enthusiasts to reimagine their religious community in accord with pentecostalism. The reporting of the Azusa revival allowed discrete individuals in the region to reconstruct their religious experience along pentecostal lines. Once in attendance at revivals, southern converts began to have firsthand experience of what they had only read and heard about before. The massive press coverage and the roaming evangelists who spread the revival's message linked together believers throughout the United States. Pentecostalism seemed to have no geographic boundaries. The transregional revival appealed to a host of southerners who jeered at social propriety and scorned the many proscriptions on life in the region.

Moreover, although the message was new, converts found it strikingly familiar. They were enthralled by it. Anyone, so it seemed, could become a medium of the Spirit or the voice of God. This was all the more extraordinary for those in the South who came of age at the nadir of race relations. Men and women, black and white, old and young might be filled with the Spirit and speak some divine truth, even if it was incomprehensible. Those who mocked and abused them only offered pentecostals more proof of their righteousness. Indeed, devotees deliberately sought out confrontations with holiness people, mainline believers, and local authorities. But in the end, it mattered little what outsiders thought. For as many of the tongues messages foretold when translated, the end was near: "Jesus is coming soon!"

SIX

The Eagle Soars

JESUS DID NOT RETURN. Regardless, throughout the twentieth century, southern pentecostals continued to watch and hope for his arrival. The end-time revival initiated by the Azusa Street meeting spread so far and wide by the 1910s that a staunch critic estimated "there is not a town of three thousand population in the United States where the movement is not represented." Indeed, by 1936 pentecostalism claimed at least 350,000 followers in the United States, many of them in the South. Never leery of the latest technology, stalwarts continued to produce mountains of printed matter and later branched out into radio and television. In the last decades of the twentieth century, pentecostal television pitchmen—Jimmy Swaggart, Oral Roberts, and Jim Bakker—were operating from the South. In those years, too, American pentecostalism soared in numbers, reaching nearly 11 million by 2000. (This was only a fraction of the worldwide total, which was estimated to hover at around half a billion.) Of the 81 percent of Americans who identified themselves as Christian, 14 percent claimed to be pentecostal.[1]

For all that remained the same in the South—the use of

new technology, the baroque theologies of the Spirit, millennial-ism, tongues speech, and freewheeling evangelists—the move-ment had changed dramatically over the course of the twenti-eth century. As the faith grew, many adherents adopted the lifestyles and tastes of the middle class. In such cases the ex-travagant religious exercises and heterodox views of earlier years softened or faded. Controversy still remained central, as internal divisions rent the movement. Devotees continued to part company over theology, worship styles (which for a few in-cluded serpent handling), and a range of nettlesome social is-sues. Outside threats seemed as menacing as ever, too. Since the 1920s, and increasingly after the 1960s, pentecostals took aim at a host of enemies: evolutionary biologists, liberal Protes-tants, feminists, and alleged communists. Over time, the once apolitical, egalitarian fringe faith came to look very different in certain quarters.

Already by the late 1950s observers of the American reli-gious scene took notice of pentecostalism's rising profile. In 1958 *Life* magazine published a photo essay on what it called the "Third Force in Christendom." This group consisted of "'fringe sects'—those marked, in the extreme, by shouting re-vivalists, puritanical preachers of doomsday, faith healers, jazzy gospel singers." *Life's* relatively fair treatment of the movement contrasted sharply with earlier appraisals.[2] A little more than two decades before, a critic writing in the scholarly journal *So-cial Forces* described "holy roller" religion as an "escape from reality," distinguished by worshippers' hypnotic frenzies and epileptic-like fits. The author, a professor at Tuskegee Institute in Alabama, observed, "Psychologically, the communicants of sanctification fall into two general classes: neurotics, and [the] mentally retarded." Their churches harbored "childminded types."[3] Old stereotypes continued to linger. In 1955 the scholar of American religion Will Herberg portrayed holiness and pentecostal "outsiders" as poor, apolitical, and inconsequential. Believers, he wrote, gathered in "very minor denominations, hardly affecting the total picture" of American religion. Such assessments did nothing to halt the growth of pentecostalism or its actual influence. From the 1940s to the 1950s membership in the third force jumped as much as 600 percent.[4] Though once shunned, depicted as ignorant rubes or miscreants, followers were in fact a diverse lot. By mid-century, believers in the South varied more widely than ever. They included wealthy businessmen in Atlanta, sharecroppers in Alabama, street preachers in Nashville, and well-known television healers.

Still restless, thousands of them emigrated from the South, carrying their religious beliefs with them. In the 1930s pentecostal Okies, Arkies, and Texans trekked to the Far West along Route 66. Some of them joined Assemblies of God and Holiness Pentecostal churches in the Golden State and came to make up the rank and file of the new religious right.[5] Millions of African Americans left the South as well. Black pentecostals headed north in the Great Migration and set up storefront churches and urban temples in dozens of cities. Southern-born sanctified churches dotted the streets of Chicago, New York, Boston, and Philadelphia. James Baldwin's stunning first novel, *Go Tell It on the Mountain*, recounted the lives of new southern arrivals in Harlem in the 1930s. "Their church was called the Temple of the Fire Baptized," he wrote. "It was not the biggest church in Harlem, nor yet the smallest, but John had been brought up to believe it was the holiest." With keen insight, Baldwin portrayed the emotional church services, tongues speaking, strict moralism, and millennial fervor of the migrants' transplanted religion. The young protagonist, John, wakes one morning shaken by the silence of his house. Could it be, he wonders, that the saints "had risen to meet Jesus in the clouds, and that

Detail from a photograph of the International Religious Congress of Triumph, the Church and Kingdom of God in Christ, Elder E. D. Smith, Apostle, Chicago, 1919. This denomination, like the much larger Church of God in Christ, aided thousands of African American pentecostals as they moved to northern cities during the Great Migration.

he was left, with his sinful body, to be bound in hell a thousand years"?[6]

Although certain religious themes and cultural patterns persisted even as southern pentecostals climbed the social ladder and ventured into other parts of the country, in essential ways, second- and third-generation believers charted a new course. By the end of the twentieth century, pentecostals in the South, like believers elsewhere, had become comfortable with the values and ideals of an affluent society. Many white and black adherents in the region had adopted a prosperity gospel that contrasted sharply with the antimaterialistic views of early followers. Others embraced conservative politics and aligned themselves with militant Christian fundamentalists and super-patriots.

Ironically, early enthusiasts were drawn to the movement in part because it contrasted so sharply with both mainline Protestantism and bourgeois culture. This is one of the reasons why pentecostalism resonated especially with southern holiness folk. The new faith would largely eclipse the more restrained holiness movement in the South by the 1920s. In that decade one writer in the Church of God (Cleveland) journal, *The Faithful Standard,* recognized the older movement's demise, noting, "The great leaders of the holiness movement turned down the Baptism with the Holy Ghost . . . and urged their people against it." As a result, all such adversaries sank into oblivion and lost whatever influence they had over the elect. Though exaggerated, his observation was astute.[7] In the South, the astounding growth of pentecostalism often came at the expense of non-tongues-speaking holiness fellowships. The novel movement seemed to offer seekers a more faithful version of Holy Ghost religion and to embody the most startling sign of the world's imminent end.

Most southern adherents continued to think that the second coming could occur at any moment. They perceived more and more evidence of "His coming" as the century progressed—World Wars I and II, modernism, theological liberalism, and a cast of possible Antichrists that included the pope, Adolf Hitler, Henry Kissinger, Mikhail Gorbachev, and Saddam Hussein. The chief publication of the Assemblies of God served as a barometer of eschatological concern. *The Pentecostal Evangel* dealt with the topic with increased intensity as world crises mounted: during World War I, following the establishment of the state of Israel in 1948, and as the year 2000 approached. In the mid-1940s that church's general council even looked into "requirements for the rapture." Could a believer be whisked to heaven if he or she was not a tongues speaker baptized with the

Holy Spirit? In that case the council ruled yes.[8] In 2006 an extensive survey found that 90 percent of American pentecostals believed that the faithful would be raptured before the end of the world. Only 53 percent of nonpentecostal Christians thought the same. Belief in the premillennial coming of Jesus remained a major tenet of faith for most pentecostals in the South and elsewhere. In the new century, however, the doctrine was no longer as central as it once had been.[9]

Even though the message of Christ's return continued to unite many southern pentecostals, other issues divided them sharply. They would come to disagree over countless matters: the nature of God, interpretation of scripture, the place of Holy Ghost baptism, the role of tongues, racial integration, and women in the ministry. Early believers organized new churches as controversies rent the movement. The nearly all-white Assemblies of God formed following a 1914 conference in Hot Springs, Arkansas. Black leader C. H. Mason was present, but his Church of God in Christ (COGIC) would seldom interact with the new white denomination. Many ministers who joined the Assemblies of God had once aligned themselves with the Church of God in Christ, which had been one of the only holiness or pentecostal churches in the region with official state recognition. The Assemblies gathered adherents largely from Texas, Arkansas, Missouri, and parts of the Midwest and West. Meanwhile, rifts over doctrine and church policy as well as personality clashes split older groups in the South. In 1921 the Congregational Holiness Church broke from the Pentecostal Holiness Church, pulling hundreds away from that southern denomination. The new denomination's members disagreed with Pentecostal Holiness officials on the matter of church government and healing. In particular, the Congregational Holiness Church permitted the use of medicine to fight off sickness.

Several African American fellowships broke away from C. H. Mason's Church of God in Christ, some of which promoted an incipient sanctified Afro-centrism.[10]

The southern movement, always characterized by bitter arguments, continued to be enveloped in fierce theological and personal struggles. Breaches quickly developed between the movement's powerful, headstrong leaders. For instance, many in the South considered the key founder of the Church of God (Cleveland), A. J. Tomlinson, to be an authoritarian tyrant. In 1923 a COG government committee impeached Tomlinson for misappropriating $14,000. Ousted from the organization he had helped build, Tomlinson gathered his followers into another Church of God. The factions battled for exclusive legal use of the name. Tomlinson lost. The new fellowship later called itself the Church of God of Prophecy. After Tomlinson's death, his two sons fought for control of the new body.[11] Others broke away from the movement altogether. Egos clashed repeatedly. G. B. Cashwell, one of the most significant evangelists in the early years, abandoned pentecostalism entirely by 1910 and returned to the Methodist Episcopal Church, South. His exodus was most likely provoked when the Pentecostal Holiness Church failed to install him as its leader. At the same time, in the period after 1910 denominations began to stake out new territory. Evangelists vied for converts in Florida, Georgia, Alabama, and Tennessee. It was not uncommon for revivalists to scorn their fellow laborers as overly competitive, even devious. One prominent revivalist described a minister he frequently shared a pulpit with as "a very smart man" who could "preach like an angel and live like the devil."[12]

Early-twentieth-century pentecostalism in the South was thus anything but stable and unified. The movement was already undergoing considerable change as early as the 1910s. Thousands of pentecostals remained open to further revelations, embracing new theories with little trepidation. Two extremely controversial theological developments at the time altered pentecostalism significantly and divided believers across the country. Tensions resulting from these ruptures still exist today. The "finished work" movement (so called because of the "finished work" of Christ on Calvary) would largely supplant Wesleyan perfectionism among the faithful. William H. Durham, a leading exponent, persuaded thousands of devotees to abandon second work theories of sanctification for a more Calvinistic soteriology. Disciples debated over the deadly serious new issue. The ever cantankerous Charles Fox Parham reemerged to challenge Durham on the matter. In 1912 Parham prayed that God would strike dead whichever preacher had erred on the issue. There was no doubt in Parham's mind of the outcome, so when Durham perished suddenly six months later, Parham was jubilant.[13] His victory was short-lived. Parham could do nothing to stem the tide of Durham's theology. The Assemblies of God, soon the largest pentecostal denomination in the country, early adopted "finished work" theology, and by 1936 the overwhelming majority of adherents nationwide had accepted this view.

Soon after, another even more divisive issue arose in the West. At a 1913 camp meeting outside Los Angeles, the leading Canadian evangelist R. E. McAlister emphatically declared that the formula for true biblical baptism was through the name of Jesus and not "the Father, Son, and Holy Spirit." Several enthusiastic ministers in attendance agreed and sought to restore what they considered the original, non-trinitarian faith. What would come to be known as "Jesus Only" or "Oneness" pentecostalism rapidly swept through the United States, sparking intense debates and bitter rivalries from coast to coast. By the mid-1930s nearly 10 percent of all pentecostals had become "Oneness" believers.

Interestingly enough, both "finished work" and "Oneness" gained remarkably few converts south of the Mason-Dixon line. While three out of every five pentecostals nationally accepted the "finished work" view by the 1920s, fewer than one in four embraced it in the South. Similarly, "Oneness" remained limited largely to the Midwest, where it claimed nine out of ten pentecostals. But in the South of the 1930s only 3.1 percent had joined the "Jesus Only" camp. The new issues did not affect southerners to the same extent because many believers in the South came out of the holiness movement and still held strongly to the Wesleyan second work position.[14] Indeed, southern pentecostalism appeared strikingly homogeneous when compared to the faith in other parts of the country.

Yet other controversies unrelated to doctrine would divide adherents in the region. The fragile racial alliance between black and white disciples began to break down not long after Azusa. Mixed-race worship did not lead to institutionalized biracialism. When early pentecostals crossed the color line, they did so in the liminal space of revival tents, street meetings, and makeshift tabernacles. Still, even that much was astonishing in the Jim Crow South. When black and white tongues speakers worshipped together in 1912 in the West End of Atlanta, the *Atlanta Constitution* headlined, "'Rollers' Have No Color Line." White residents were scandalized to learn that "white women mingled nightly until midnight with negroes in 'Holy Roller' meetings" and "joined the negroes in their wild demonstrations of 'religious intoxication.'" An observer complained of "white women in the embrace of a negress, dancing and shouting in the center of the congregation." Law enforcement officials ordered participants to cease their shocking displays or move elsewhere. The leaders of the "cult," however, refused to cave in to pressure. One convert told an *Atlanta Constitution* reporter that "Holy Rollers" frequently bridged the racial divide and worshipped together, "as the religion knew no color boundary, and . . . all classes possessed souls alike."[15]

A decade later, followers were still defending themselves against charges of racial egalitarianism and "mongrelization." A violent struggle near Kingston, Georgia, illustrates the ongoing dilemma. In 1922 three men tried to break up a tent meeting held by the white evangelist Horace Van Metre. The toughs had become enraged after hearing that the pentecostal minister was "conducting among negroes religious meetings in which he preached in favor of equal rights for blacks and whites." Van Metre denied the charge, but that mattered little to his antagonists. Horton McMaree, a one-armed man, wrestled the preacher to the ground in the middle of a service and pummeled him for challenging white supremacy. Van Metre's flock squared off against the rabble-rousers in a bloody row. One of the minister's followers fired a shotgun at McMaree, blowing a gaping hole in his stomach and killing him almost instantly.[16] The circumstances surrounding the riot are sketchy, but they do reveal the outside perception that the pentecostal view on race was unacceptable in a closed society. Such incidents, however, were largely limited to the early twentieth century, when the movement was not yet institutionalized.

Whether because of the pressures of the segregated social order or the challenges of denominational conformity, African American and white pentecostals largely parted company. In 1908 the members of the Fire-Baptized Holiness Church, both blacks and whites, mutually agreed on separation. Although the split was amicable, it represented one of the first southern failures of the sanctified interracialism championed by W. B. Godbey, L. P. Cushman, and William J. Seymour, among others. Meanwhile, by 1911 Seymour's integrated Apostolic Faith fellowship in Los Angeles had divided over the finished work issue. After white adherents left the Azusa Mission, Seymour continued to pastor a small congregation of devoted African Americans. In the decade that followed, the Church of God (Cleveland) drew the color line as well. Even Oneness pentecostals, the more biracial segment of the movement, broke into separate white and black congregations by the late 1930s.[17]

A minority of churches remained undivided. The relatively small Church of God of Prophecy maintained its biracialism throughout the twentieth century. Members of that organization, though by no means interested in politics or social reform, even rebuked white southern racists. A 1965 article in the denomination's Cleveland, Tennessee, newspaper warned: "To have racial distinction would be against the will of God or the purpose of the Church. . . . The speckled bird has many different colored feathers, and so is [sic] the Church of the last days."[18] Black churches such as the Bible Way Church of Our Lord Jesus Christ also championed racial equality. A series of articles in the pages of its Washington, D.C., paper, *The Bible Way News Voice,* reported on gains made in the desegregation of schools and challenged the shibboleths of white power in the early 1950s. "All races are essentially alike," one writer noted with regard to a recent scientific study. Black subscribers in Virginia and the Carolinas read that "no biological harm comes from mixed marriages." The head of the church, Smallwood E. Williams, who worked with the Washington, D.C., branch of the Congress of Racial Equality, spoke out sharply against the vicious racism still present throughout the former Confederacy. When the arch-racist Mississippi senator Theodore G. Bilbo died in 1947, Williams proclaimed that he had prophesied the demagogue's demise. In a sermon delivered to a packed church, Williams envisioned Adolf Hitler and Benito Mussolini commiserating with Bilbo in hell.[19] Few African American pentecostals in the South could afford to be so bold. In states like Mississippi and Alabama, where white political leaders considered such statements punishable offenses, opportunities for social protest remained limited.

For the most part, the views of the Church of God of Prophecy and the Bible Way Church were exceptional. Through much of the twentieth century, members of the largest black denomination, the Church of God in Christ, concerned themselves with personal morality and right living. C. H. Mason, the founder of the denomination, opposed the racial fracturing of the faith but stopped short of political protest. James L. Delk, one of the church's few white ministers, did lash out against prejudice in the region and called for an end to racial oppression. In 1944 the Kentucky-based evangelist challenged race hatred in the "Southland," proclaiming that "neither Brother Mason nor myself believe in segregation or Jim Crow." Delk framed his protest in evangelical terms: "When we get Jesus in our hearts, nicknaming people, segregation and Jim Crow vanish away like the smoke of the hour."[20] Mason, however, appears to have been more cautious. He, like most others, did not openly fight the segregated order.

A minority of African American pentecostals in the region did back the civil rights movement and campaigned for racial justice, though black pentecostals were typically more timid than their black Methodist and Baptist brethren when it came to overt political activity.[21] For white supremacists in the region, that distinction mattered little. In 1965, as Klan-sponsored violence swept throughout the Deep South, whites burned a Louisiana Church of God in Christ sanctuary even though, as FBI agents reported, there was "no record of civil rights or voter registration activities connected therewith."[22] Some black pentecostals did eventually voice their concern on matters of social and economic injustice. Martin Luther King Jr.'s final campaign in 1968, the Memphis sanitation workers' strike, was aided by the local Church of God in Christ. The church's massive Mason Hall served as headquarters for strikers, and it was from its pulpit that King delivered his stirring final speech to a crowd of two thousand. Since then, black pentecostals in the South have been more willing to challenge the prevailing order. They have done so with a clear sense of divine purpose. Hence, while the denomination's 1973 discipline manual called for the prohibition of alcohol and a ban on legalized gambling, it also supported the abolition of capital punishment and promoted social equality for all, regardless of "race, creed, or national origins."[23]

Fairly representative of the white southern segment of pentecostalism was the Assemblies of God. From its founding until the 1950s, the matter of race and racial prejudice was seldom considered or debated by laity or leaders. Occasionally, though, a southern official would take up the issue. In 1915 W. F. Carothers, a Texas Methodist who converted to pentecostalism, wrote to *The Weekly Evangel* on the subject. Racial separation was natural and in accord with biblical principles, he asserted. God did not intend for "men to have one color." Neither did he want whites and blacks to worship in the same churches.[24] Carothers assured his northern brethren that southern mores would not compromise the faith. Northern white mainline denominations generally supported civil rights, fair employment practices, and residential integration far in advance of their southern counterparts.[25]

At mid-century, church leaders considered establishing a separate "Colored Branch" of the Assemblies of God. Such efforts stalled, however, as church officials pondered the negative southern response. Instead the denomination charted an exclusionary and gradualist course. In the mid-1950s South African missionary Nicholas Bhengu wrote to Ralph M. Riggs, the general superintendent of the church, to offer his support and propose himself for leadership of a separate black group.

Riggs was uncertain. It would be "a revolutionary move in connection with our work here," he told Bhengu. "You are aware of the race prejudice which exists, especially in our Southland." The majority of the church's members resided south of the Mason-Dixon line. On the one hand, southern hostility might hinder eventual integration, Riggs feared. On the other, if the denomination set up a colored wing, the recent Supreme Court decision in *Brown v. Board of Education* would make it appear that the Assemblies encouraged segregation. In the end, the church decided against the proposal.[26]

Until the 1960s the Assemblies did not officially ordain blacks. A handful of African Americans did assume leadership positions before mid-century, but not in the South. As with the issue of establishing a colored branch, the church rejected ordination of blacks on the grounds that it would upset southern congregants. As one African American who was in contact with the denomination in the 1930s put it, church officials feared that "if we put black preachers in our white churches in the South, we're in for a lot of trouble." Instead, ministers encouraged African Americans to seek ordination in the Assemblies' "sister organization," the Church of God in Christ. Robert E. Harrison, a young black member of the Assemblies of God, found that out when he applied for ordination in the northern California district in 1951. A minister told Harrison, "I'm sorry, my brother, but it is not the policy of our denomination to grant credentials to Negroes." Crushed, Harrison almost lost his faith. He later wrote of his experience: "The black Christian (with token exceptions) is told by the white believer: 'You can't study the Bible in our schools.' 'You can't go to the camps where white kids are challenged to give their hearts to Christ, to enter the ministry, and to go to the mission fields of the world.'" Harrison later became a leading black evangelist and worked with the Billy Graham crusade around the world.

After he received that honor, the denomination decided to ordain him.[27]

Through the 1960s a number of whites in the Assemblies of God, like many other conservative white Protestants, disapproved of the civil rights movement. For the most part, they did not overtly oppose equal rights and opportunities for African Americans. Instead they disagreed with Martin Luther King Jr.'s program of civil disobedience. An Assemblies minister in Atlanta put the matter succinctly as he reflected in 1968 on the recent assassination of King. Protesters violated the scriptural injunction "to submit to our rulers," the minister wrote in the denomination's paper. "Civil rights legislation and government spending cannot meet the basic needs of the ghettos, but the gospel can." Many black preachers, he charged, "are now preaching social revolution instead of the Gospel of Christ's saving power." His conservative, antigovernment message resonated with churchgoers.[28] In the early 1990s the white bishop of the Pentecostal Holiness Church, B. E. Underwood, reflected on his church's response to the social crises of 1950s and 1960s. "White Pentecostals have been fairly inactive socially," he lamented. "We were more or less invisible during the civil rights movement." Yet from the mid-1960s on, white adherents slowly adopted a clearer policy on civil rights and racial tolerance. For instance, in 1965 the general council of the Assemblies of God affirmed "our belief in the teachings of Christ including His emphasis upon the inherent worth and intrinsic value of every man, regardless of race, class, creed, or color."[29]

In recent years, white and black pentecostals in the South and throughout the nation have moved toward racial reconciliation. They looked to the early movement for a usable past. An October 1994 gathering in Memphis serves as a powerful example. Heads of the nation's largest pentecostal denominations, both black and white—including the Church of God in

Christ, the Church of God (Cleveland), the Assemblies of God, and the International Pentecostal Holiness Church—convened to bridge what they referred to as an eighty-year racial rift. Organizers promoted the event as the "Memphis Miracle." Planners and participants self-consciously looked to the racial egalitarianism that seemed possible following the Azusa revival. One white Pentecostal Holiness official in attendance exulted, "We are going back to our roots." Indeed, the Memphis *Commercial Appeal* newspaper published a lead article on the event headlined "Pentecostals Prepare to Heal Rift. Interracial Reconciliation Would Mirror 1906 Move." Vinson Synan, a Virginia native, Pentecostal Holiness Church executive, and historian, discussed the work of the gathering in light of his predominantly white denomination. "I grew up in the Old South and have personal knowledge of the awful racist attitudes of Pentecostal pastors, evangelists and bishops," he remarked. It was time, Synan declared, for blacks and whites to unite. Those present agreed. They decided to abolish the Pentecostal Fellowship of North America. Founded in 1948, that interdenominational group excluded African American churches. In its place the Memphis assembly established the Pentecostal/Charismatic Churches of North America, which included the Church of God in Christ and other black denominations. COGIC bishop Ithiel Clemmons became the fellowship's first chairman.[30] One of the chief accomplishments of the gathering was the creation of a "Racial Reconciliation Manifesto" that acknowledged past injustices and called for change with the words "I pledge in concert with my brothers and sisters of many hues to oppose racism prophetically in all its various manifestations within and without the body of Christ."[31]

The 2006 centenary of the Azusa Street revival carried the theme of reconciliation into the new millennium. The event was a massive gathering. Approximately 31,000 pentecostal

Assemblies of God general superintendent Thomas E. Trask embraces Bishop Ithiel Clemmons of the Church of God in Christ at the "Memphis Miracle" in October 1994. The event gathered black and white pentecostals from around the world in an effort to confront racism.

and charismatic Christians from around the world joined together in Los Angeles in April 2006 to mark the advent of the modern movement. Participants packed the Los Angeles Convention Center and heard performance groups such as Voice of Africa sing, shout, and "confuse the devil" by loudly stomping their feet. African Americans and whites worshipped together and listened to a collection of pentecostal superstars, including faith healer Benny Hinn, self-help guru Kenneth Copeland, and gospel singer, preacher, and author T. D. Jakes.

Whereas press reports of the 1906 revival had been sensationalist and condemnatory, coverage of the centenary was marked by fascination with the movement's tremendous growth. Most noted the biracialism of the assembly and alluded to the origins of the movement.[32] Of course, those who gathered in Memphis and later in Los Angeles still disagreed on just how to meet the challenges of racism. Yet participants at both events forthrightly acknowledged discrimination and intolerance and looked to the movement's early years for direction. A reporter for the *Washington Post* noted that theme: "One hundred years ago, a series of boisterous revival meetings in a converted stable on Azusa Street launched a global movement that overcame differences in class, gender and race to unite around the belief that the Holy Spirit still works miracles."[33] In 1994 the faithful in Memphis considered the issue of gender as well, though it remained secondary to race. Still, questions about the status of women and the official and unofficial roles they would play continued to shape the ever-changing southern movement.

For the most part, the gender equality that seemed within reach after Azusa did not materialize. In much the same way that occasional biracial services did not lead to church-sponsored integration, women served as unofficial evangelists and preachers but were seldom recognized by the newly formed, male-dominated institutions. Scholars have long debated whether or not holiness and pentecostal adherents were ever particularly progressive on the issue.[34] But in the South at least, it appears that in many cases they were.

Some large pentecostal denominations refused to grant full ordination to women, citing biblical passages and tradition for support. For instance, the Church of God (Cleveland) denied women ordination, though it allowed them to act as evangelists. In the 1920s, an era marked by new social roles for women, the denomination's leaders equivocated. While they recognized that female teachers and evangelists were instrumental in spreading pentecostalism, they also warned that the apostle Paul's "instructions should be followed to the letter." If woman were to "usurp the authority of those that have the rule over her," the church admonished, "it's goodbye, sister."[35] In pentecostal and holiness churches, many of the dress codes and warnings against frivolity targeted women. Church manuals and sermons condemned as modern-day harlots women who wore makeup and jewelry, cut their hair short, or rose above their proper station in life. As late as 1973, the Church of God (Cleveland) specified that women evangelists could not have "bobbed hair." If a woman cropped her hair too short, "she should not be allowed to be active as a minister until her hair grows out again."[36]

Throughout the century the Church of God in Christ also opposed the ordination of women. They could serve as evangelists but not as pastors or church officials. Still, the tradition of consecrating "Church Mothers" gave women active leadership roles. Derived from African American kinship networks, the office of Church Mother had no white analogue. She was often an older woman, acknowledged by her congregation as a religious and social authority. Apart from this, the church manual sums up the official position clearly: "The Church of God in Christ recognizes that there are thousands of talented, spirit-filled . . . and devout women. . . . But nowhere can we find a mandate to ordain women to be an Elder, Bishop, or Pastor."[37]

Many first-generation southern pentecostal males believed that women would become gospel co-laborers in the last days before Jesus returned. Women might prophesy and teach, but that provisional equality did not always lead to ministerial authority. Women, insisted some, must remain subordinate to men. A few denominations did find a biblical mandate for ordaining women. The Assemblies of God early acknowledged the important roles women would play in the movement, though some prominent officials, such as the one-time southern Baptist Eudorus N. Bell, clearly placed limits on female authority. Men were best suited for church leadership, Bell asserted. In the absence of a suitable man, however, a woman might fill in. The denomination finally admitted women to full ministry in 1935. Later in the century, as the Assemblies of God inched toward mainstream evangelicalism, the dictates of domesticity further hemmed women in.[38]

Other holiness and pentecostal denominations such as the Pentecostal Assemblies of the World and the Pentecostal Holiness Church ordained women early, and were far in advance of many other religious bodies both in and outside the South. Of mainline groups in the region, the African Methodist Episcopal Church led the way, ordaining women in 1948. In 1956 the United Methodist Church and the Presbyterian Church in the United States did so as well. The latter's southern compatriots followed suit in 1964. The Episcopal Church granted women the priesthood in 1976. The Southern Baptist Convention (SBC), by contrast, lagged far behind. With roughly 15 million members in the United States, the denomination counted only 1,300 clergywomen in 1998, and only 50 of those served as pastors. In 2000 the Southern Baptist Convention ruled definitively on the subject. Women could not be ordained as pastors, the denomination's governing body declared from Orlando, Florida. Two years before, the increasingly conservative SBC had called on women to submit to their husbands and tacitly blamed women, and Eve in particular, for humanity's fall from grace.[39] Remarkably, however, some holiness and pentecostal fellowships in the South actually led liberal northern denominations in the ordination of women through much of the twentieth century. Even in Cambridge, Massachusetts, women would be excluded from ecclesiastical positions for most of the century. In 1921 the first woman preached at Harvard's Divinity School, but women would not gain full admittance for another thirty-five years.[40]

At a 1983 meeting in Cleveland, Tennessee, of scholars who studied pentecostalism, the California Presbyterian minister and educator Paul K. Jewett compared his tradition with that of pentecostals. Speaking to a group largely composed of pentecostals, Jewett observed that the two had followed opposite trajectories. The Presbyterian Church, U.S.A., had been ordaining women as elders and preachers for several years, he noted, but "beginning with relative openness to women in ministry, you have moved in the direction of narrowing the definition of their ministry so as to exclude them from the ministerial office," he told his audience. Women held prominent positions in many churches, but few denominations would ordain them. In such cases, women's "Spirit baptism" did not impute full authority to them.[41]

In response to such observations and to a decline in the number of ordained women ministers, a few within the holiness and pentecostal tradition turned to history as a guide, much as theologians, pastors, and laypeople had done with regard to race matters. Reformers pointed to the once critical role women played in the early movement and expressed the wish that they would again assume positions of power. In 1976 Donald W. Dayton and Lucille Sider Dayton, both Wesleyans, surveyed the history of holiness and its "feminist theme" in the hope that their study might spark renewed interest in the topic. By late century there was evidence of some increase in the number of women evangelists, teachers, and ministers. In the 1990s, 15.3 percent of Assemblies of God ministers were women, while women made up 17 percent of the clergy in the International Pentecostal Holiness Church.[42]

As the egalitarian vision faded somewhat, a few southern believers channeled their creative religious energies into other areas. New revelations captured their attention, often provoking public outrage. A handful of literalists in the South came to interpret Mark 16:18—"They shall take up serpents; and if they drink any deadly thing, it shall not hurt them"—as a divine injunction. As early as 1914 a reporter for the *Washington Post* observed that snake handlers in the Tennessee hills cited the scriptural passage as justification. "Snakes are the latest proselytizing asset employed by a large class of fervid religionists in Bradley County," the article noted. Thomas McLain, a local leader, freely discussed his beliefs with the reporter. How did it start? he was asked. "Well," McLain answered, "you see what the Bible says, that was quoted, and sinners got to bringing snakes to meeting to test us. They keep on bringing them. So you see the sinners are simply helping along the church of God." McLain and other upcountry initiates also drank poison, usually strychnine, to prove their saintliness and refused medical treatment as one of the "signs following" their power. McLain declared that he had never given his young son "a drop of medicine, [the boy] having been cured of various deadly ills by praying alone."[43]

George W. Hensley, an illiterate moonshiner from the hills of Tennessee, began handling serpents in the Church of God (Cleveland) around 1910. Hensley, who had received his "Spirit baptism" in that church, came to the attention of the group's founder, A. J. Tomlinson, and his son Homer A. Tomlinson. Homer recalled that the practice began much the way that Thomas McLain recounted. Hensley's old "moonshine and gambling cronies," wishing to "make a mockery of Hensley's religion," brought deadly rattlesnakes, water moccasins, and copperheads to the minister's church and turned them loose in front of the pulpit. The congregation fled in horror, but Hensley, filled with Holy Ghost power, gathered the snakes "like a boy would gather stovewood in his arms to carry to the house." Members of Hensley's flock described him as a small man who was a powerful preacher. Pacing while he exhorted, he sawed the air with his arms. He danced "in the spirit" and "spoke in tongues" during his services. His wife, Manda, would stand next to him, reading aloud biblical passages he shouted out. His dramatic meetings helped spread "signs-following" churches from Tennessee to Alabama, Georgia, Kentucky, Virginia, and North Carolina. These serpent-handling fellowships were largely composed of poor white hill folk, though at times African Americans took part in integrated services. In the late 1950s and early 1960s the anthropologist Weston La Barre, for one, observed an occasional black presence. Worshippers he studied in North Carolina were relatively tolerant, and many of them worked with African Americans in machinery companies and local mills. For some, he speculated, interracial services were a matter of pride.[44]

Snake handling, even more than the once controversial fire baptism revival, was largely limited to the South. It thrived in Appalachia. The number of believers was always small. One scholar estimates that by the late twentieth century there were fewer than 2,500 followers, and perhaps only 10 percent of them handled snakes.[45] Yet the very existence of such an extraordinary religious phenomenon bears scrutiny. Signs-following churches reveal a powerful literalist strain within southern pentecostalism. The Bible required, according to initiates, that disciples handle snakes. A. J. Tomlinson lent his support to the practice on those grounds. The successful handling of serpents, as well as taking up hot coals and drinking deadly poisons, proved both the faith of saints and the awesome power of God.

It mattered little to Tomlinson and others like him that the critical text in the Gospel of Mark was not found in the earliest manuscripts that scholars studied. "The verses are there," insisted Tomlinson, "and all the higher (?) criticism and lower criticism . . . have never been able to force Bible houses to stop printing them." The true church, he proclaimed, stood for the "whole Bible."[46]

Serpent handlers were, of course, denounced by local authorities for endangering lives. Throughout the century, as many as one hundred worshippers died from snakebites. In 1919 the *Washington Post* reported one such fatality on its front page. Cleveland Harrison, a thirty-two-year-old man from northwest Alabama, died "after two days of intense suffering from bites of a rattlesnake at a meeting of the so-called 'Holy Rollers.'" Harrison thought that he, like Saint Paul, would be immune from the venom. He was bitten five times. Southern devotees who jeopardized the lives of their children came under even more intense public scrutiny. In 1920 Alabama hill folk were ready to lynch a father whose baby died from a rattlesnake bite "during a séance" at a signs-following church. The authorities occasionally fined, jailed, and otherwise punished initiates. Whenever the press did cover snake handlers, it depicted believers as dangerous, ignorant rustics or degenerates. Buddy Simmons, a tenant farmer in Alabama, wanted to prove his faith at a "Holy Roller" meeting, wrote a reporter in a 1924 issue of the *Atlanta Constitution*. The rattlesnake thwarted his plans by biting him twice on his fingers. Simmons's arm ballooned in reaction to the toxins and would likely need amputation. Another in the crowd at the meeting "fared better than Simmons," the reporter joked. "He picked up the reptile, handled it at will, and was not bitten, but it was claimed that he was well 'saturated with wildcat liquor'—so much so that no fastidious snake would care to bite him."[47] By the 1920s, George Hensley had lapsed and returned to bootlegging liquor for a time. Yet the new sect continued to grow in the hills and "hollers" of the upcountry.

With so much negative publicity and controversy surrounding the devotion, many southern pentecostals repudiated the offshoot sect. The Pentecostal Holiness Church condemned Hensley and those who followed his lead as "fanatics." By the 1920s, Church of God (Cleveland) officials were cautioning members about the practice. The church's general assembly minutes included a question-and-answer item on the controversy: "Q. Shall our ministers teach that handling serpents is the evidence or test of salvation? A. No, that kind of doctrine will not stand." In 1928 the church officially renounced such life-threatening acts of faith.[48] For black pentecostal denominations—the Church of God in Christ, the United Holy Church, and the Fire-Baptized Holiness Church of God of the Americas—the matter was so remote that it did not deserve comment. By the end of the twentieth century, only a small fraction of white southern pentecostals, isolated in the Appalachian Mountains and their foothills, kept the tradition alive.

Southern pentecostals were innovators. Unlike mainline Protestants, they were without the accouterments of tradition. It is therefore not entirely surprising that something as new and scandalous as snake handling would originate in their churches. The saints had long used the latest technologies to distribute tracts and newspapers; they sang new, up-tempo hymns; and they worshipped in ways that made other Protestants shudder with disgust. They would go on to pioneer radio and television ministry. In the 1920s radio preacher Aimee Semple McPherson's programs entered millions of homes around the United States. Decades later TV ministers like Oral Roberts in the 1950s and Jim and Tammy Faye Bakker in the 1980s preached to worldwide audiences. By the twenty-first century, the largest religious network on American television was the pentecostal and charismatic Trinity Broadcasting Network. TBN rhapsodized about its use of technology. The company's "Devil Bustin' Satellite" aired programs around the globe. The African American preacher, author, and singer T. D. Jakes became one of TBN's most popular personalities. Jakes is a stunning example of religious entrepreneurship and business acumen. He pastored a Dallas megachurch boasting over seventeen thousand members, wrote best-selling books that counseled Christian women and promoted personal empowerment, and oversaw an unparalleled media empire. Jakes and many other pentecostal celebrities have been well aware of the power of technology. A 2006 Pew Forum study revealed that 74 percent of pentecostals surveyed in the United States claimed that they watched or listened to religious programming at least once a week. Only 35 percent of other Christians polled did the same.

Enthusiasts were innovators in other ways as well. Wild, unconventional revivals were long their hallmark. Pentecostal music for both black and white listeners broke many boundaries. In the early twentieth century, Sister Arizona Dranes, Eddie Head, and other black sanctified performers employed the instruments and musical styles of the secular scene, broadening sacred music as a result. Sister Rosetta Tharpe, a native of Arkansas, became so well known in the late 1930s for her guitar-accompanied gospel singing that she performed at New York's storied Cotton Club and landed a record deal with Decca. Tharpe and other black artists helped commercialize the new genre. In the 1920s and 1930s Okeh records issued a flurry of releases by energetic black pentecostal musicians and shouting preachers. Jazz trumpeters, boogie-woogie pianists, and jug bands led worship in Church of God in Christ churches across the South, while flat-picking white guitarists, washboard players, and fiddlers did the same in Church of God (Cleveland) congregations. The influence of such mavericks extended well beyond the confines of churches. A host of first-generation rock 'n' rollers who grew up in pentecostal denominations later gave much credit to church music. They would also claim that the unrestrained style of the sanctified, tongues-speaking faith had a lasting impact on them.[49]

As a boy in the 1930s Johnny Cash attended Church of God (Cleveland) services in Dyess, Arkansas, where local initiates held unfettered meetings in an old schoolhouse. Years later the "man in black" recalled scenes of religious mayhem. The "writhing on the floor, the moaning, the trembling, and the jerks" left a deep impression, and the fire and brimstone sermons and surrounding frenzy terrorized Cash. "My knuckles would be white as I held onto the seat in front of me," he remembered. Still, Cash loved the uninhibited music, the improvisation, and the variety of instruments played. It was a powerful experience. So it was, too, for Tammy Wynette, a future country music celebrity, who as a youth frequented the Oak Grove Church of God in northeastern Mississippi. She attended a Baptist church as well, but it could not compete with exciting pentecostal services. She would bang away on the piano, playing hymns and spirituals. Unlike the stodgy Baptist ministers, Wynette wrote in her autobiography, the Church of God preacher "would let you bring in guitars and play rockin' gospel more like black gospel music," as worshippers shouted in the Spirit and hollered in unknown tongues. Other southern-born rockers recalled similar experiences. Little Richard and B. B. King, who attended black pentecostal services, and Jerry Lee Lewis, a onetime member of the Assemblies of God, loved the lively preaching, the fast-paced music, and the antics of ecstatic worshippers. Little Richard summed it up best: "Of all the churches, I used to like going to the Pentecostal Church because of the music."[50]

Certainly the most famous performer to be attached to a

tongues-speaking fellowship was Elvis Presley. Born in Tupelo, Mississippi, he moved with his family to Memphis in 1948. His mother, a devout Christian, looked for a local church the family might attend. The burgeoning First Assembly of God originally met in a tent, then moved to a storefront, and finally settled in a permanent structure. Membership climbed to two thousand. One Sunday shortly after the Presleys arrived in town, a First Assembly bus swung through their rundown neighborhood. They climbed aboard and became regulars of Pastor James Hamill's congregation. As a teenager Elvis was quiet, shy, and awkward. The country boy's hair was too long and his trousers were too short, Hamill remembered, but he was a courteous, respectful youth. He attended Sunday school and witnessed the gospel stylings of the Blackwood Brothers and the Stamps Quartet, two groups that pioneered white southern gospel music. Members of each attended First Assembly. Elvis was exposed there to the best in pentecostal music, Hamill recalled. In a series of 1956 interviews, after he achieved international acclaim, Elvis always mentioned to reporters that he and his family belonged to Memphis's First Assembly of God. Speaking to an Associated Press reporter about pentecostal music, Presley said: "We used to go to these religious singins all the time. There were these singers, perfectly fine singers, but nobody responded to 'em. Then there were these other singers—the leader wuz a preacher—and they cut up all over the place, jumpin' on the piano, movin' every which way. The audience liked 'em. I guess I learned from them singers." Uninhibited pentecostalism gave young Elvis ideas about music and performance. He was sometimes called the "evangelist" by his inner circle of friends.[51]

Nevertheless, Presley's southern brethren did not see eye to eye with him about borrowing from sacred music for secular ends. This was an abomination as far as they were concerned.

Angry letters flooded the Assemblies of God headquarters after reports of Elvis's faith appeared in the papers. "I am sure you agree," a churchgoer from Richmond wrote to Assemblies general superintendent Ralph Riggs, "that this boy certainly should not be allowed to be a member of any 'Bible believing' church." A Sunday school teacher from Macon, Georgia, was "stunned over this thing they call 'Rock & Roll Music.'" She had tried to clear up the matter of Elvis's comments with neighbors and friends, "but what about the hundreds that don't understand?" she asked. Elvis's former pastor assured the church that the star had long stopped attending and had never been a formal member. Few cared. Even a hint about the rocker's connection to the church was shameful. White supremacist groups such as the White Citizens' Council called rock and roll "jungle music," "congo rhythms," "animalistic." Allegations of racial improprieties could not have been far from the minds of upwardly mobile southern white believers.[52]

A few pentecostals also sensed that the frenzy and sheer noise of rock concerts looked a little too much like Holy Ghost revivals. Pentecostal youth minister David Wilkerson saw the link clearly enough. In 1959 he described the new genre as a godless cult. For every Youth for Christ rally "Satan is now staging a rock and roll rally!" Wilkerson charged. Even worse, "Satan has used rock and roll to imitate the work of God at Pentecost! In these last days Satan has come down to baptize with an *unholy ghost* and *unholy fire!*" The enraged minister stretched the analogy further: "the shaking, the prostration" of worship "are imitated by this unholy baptism—as far even to speaking in vile tongues!" Tennessee native and self-described "King of the World" Homer A. Tomlinson dismissed the phenomenon. Presley was only a "guitarist and singer from one of our churches in Mississippi," and his gyrations were "just a vulgar adaptation of our dancing and rejoicing in the Spirit of

God in our Church of God services." Offering a mild defense, Elvis told a reporter, "It ain't vulgah."[53]

While some of the faithful fretted over horrifying innovations—salacious music, snake handling, unorthodox theology—other matters received scant notice. Pentecostal and holiness folk in the South long remained suspicious of politics. As future attorney general John Ashcroft first charted his political career in the late 1960s, he knew of only one other member of the Assemblies of God who had run for public office, J. Roswell Flower, and he had served only as a Springfield, Missouri, city councilman. In a 1988 interview Ashcroft pondered adherents' opposition to "government—almost as a worldly thing—in the same way that we shunned formal education for a long time."[54] At least until the 1960s, many of the faithful believed that political activity of any kind would unwisely divert their attention away from the church and their religious goals. So unimportant were social, political, and economic issues to some that they seldom considered them at all.

Many southern enthusiasts, whites as well as blacks, worked in mills and railroad yards or as field hands on large farms, occupations that would seem to draw them naturally to unions. But that was not the case. The renowned sociologist of religion Liston Pope studied the mill towns and churches of Gaston County, North Carolina, in the 1930s and found that preachers in the newer pentecostal and holiness groups were even less interested "in the social sphere than ministers of older denominations." Although members of the Pentecostal Holiness Church, the Church of God, and the Wesleyan Methodist Church prohibited all manner of "worldly amusements," Pope observed that none of "their proscriptions has extensive economic implications." He could not see that some of their many prohibitions did represent a protest, however veiled, to the cultural order of the day. When southern holiness and pentecostal folk condemned movies, the circus, soft drinks, and fancy attire, they were challenging conspicuous consumption. But as far as organized political activity went, Pope was right.[55]

The Pentecostal Holiness Church allowed members to join unions but not to take part in strikes or other forms of "agitation." This position was similar to that set out by the predominantly African American Pentecostal Assemblies of the World. In 1963 that denomination allowed members to join unions, but it prohibited them from assuming leadership roles. It also forbade picketing and striking. A number of pentecostal organizations opposed labor unions as unholy cooperatives that might overshadow the church. Such staunch convictions could lead to trouble. In 1913 a group of believers infuriated the 2,500 union men of the Chesapeake and Ohio Railroad in Huntington, West Virginia, by shunning union membership. A perplexed reporter covered the incident: "All men have agreed to quit work unless 14 men, who recently aligned themselves with the Holy Roller religious sect, join the union." The dissenters held their ground, claiming their religious affiliation prohibited them from joining. The issue was clear enough to members of the Church of God (Cleveland), which dealt with the subject in its 1913 general assembly minutes. The saints were forbidden to belong to lodges and secret societies as well as the United Coal Miners' Association. "The time will come," church officials warned, "when we cannot buy or sell unless we have the mark of the beast." As Pope put it, adherents favored "organization to await the Second Coming of Christ rather than to secure immediate economic benefits." With the arrival of Christ so near, compromise with "worldly" groups was out of the question. At a later meeting of the church assembly, general overseer A. J. Tomlinson cast doubt on the authority of monarchies and democracies alike. Only one form of government produced "absolute satisfaction," he proclaimed, the government of God. That logic bewildered Pope. According to him, only in their extreme pacifism did believers challenge the prevailing political order of the day.[56]

Indeed, throughout the early twentieth century, countless stalwarts remained resolute pacifists. Their gradual move away from that stance reveals much about adherents' changing outlook. Like many Quakers, Mennonites, and members of the Industrial Workers of the World, they first opposed the draft and fiercely renounced America's involvement in World War I. Members of the Church of God (Cleveland) were unhesitating. Their battle was with the forces of darkness and evil, not the German Kaiser. Worse still, the war, they argued, was a sign of the end, or the "last great conflict." The country was being drawn into the European conflagration because of America's "national sins." Fittingly, southern pentecostal draft resisters were often antinationalistic. So seriously was the matter taken that the Church of God (Cleveland) required its members to comply with the church's position; none could advocate war or try to persuade the saints to enlist. The Assemblies of God held similar views. That church issued a resolution in April 1918 declaring that it could not "conscientiously participate in war and armed resistance which involves the actual destruction of human life, since this is contrary to our view of the clear teachings of the inspired Word of God." One of the church's white ministers in Texas thought that disciples' divine citizenship required them to oppose war.[57] In 1917 Lamar County, Texas, police made their first arrest of an African American adherent, Robert Russell. "He claimed to belong to the religious sect known as 'holy rollers,'" reported the *Dallas Morning News*. Citing the biblical mandate "Thou shalt not kill," Russell declared that he would "follow the laws of God rather than man." Another dissident, a white minister in Tennessee, went even further. He was convicted in federal court in 1918 after advising his flock "not to report for military service if called, and to resist to death, if necessary." Conservative and mainline groups lined up against the pentecostals' "treasonable" outrages. One fundamentalist leader, the southern-born "Fighting Bob" Shuler, went on the attack. From his base in Los Angeles, Shuler labeled A. J. Tomlinson a "deceiver," a "traitor to country and a traitor to God." The superpatriot fundamentalist Billy Sunday declared in absolute terms that "Christianity and Patriotism are synonymous terms and hell and traitors are synonymous."[58]

Across the South, both white and black pentecostals stood their ground against their detractors as well as draft boards and law enforcement officials. Adherents paid dearly for their intransigence. They were jailed, harassed, and beaten. In northern Alabama policemen bloodied and then killed one Church of God (Cleveland) minister after he refused to register for the draft. Although this was an extreme case, he was not alone in bearing the brunt of the establishment's outrage. Church of God members also drew the attention of federal agents. The U.S. Post Office declared several issues of *The Evangel,* the official paper of the denomination, unmailable under the Espionage and Sedition Acts. The FBI investigated church members and reviewed the *Evangel*'s mailing list.[59] Federal officials similarly targeted the Church of God in Christ. Agents scrutinized the sermons and writings of C. H. Mason for signs of disloyalty. Fearing Mason's sway over "southern Negroes," the FBI arrested the leader and kept tabs on the denomination's ministers. Agents worried that Mason had as much influence over blacks in the region as the revivalist Billy Sunday had over whites.[60]

By World War II the beliefs of southern pentecostals had undergone considerable alteration. Even toward the end of World War I, some denominations revised their earlier, adamantly antiwar views. By late summer 1918, for example, key officials in the Church of God (Cleveland) and the Assemblies of God had considerably modified their pacifism. One leader even encouraged the faithful to destroy a popular pentecostal antiwar tract that had circulated widely. In the last days of the war, some in the movement, perhaps pressured by the stigma of disloyalty, encouraged followers to buy Liberty Bonds and support America's doughboys. Hence, by the time of the Second World War it was not unusual to find pentecostal soldiers proudly serving their country. By then only a few remained self-identified pacifists. The opinions of one white Kentucky-based Church of God in Christ evangelist were certainly unusual. In 1944 James Delk announced that his denomination believed "in the Constitution of the United States, and the American Flag, and believes in our President, but our church does not believe in war." He did not know how long the conflict in Europe and the Pacific would last, "but it will continue up to the War of Armageddon," he ventured.[61]

As some scholars have suggested, this slow transition may have occurred as enthusiasts increasingly became less certain about the second coming. In addition, by mid-century pentecostals were weary of being the targets of persecution as their predecessors had been. In 1941 the Pentecostal Holiness Church decided to permit both combatant and noncombatant service. The Church of God (Cleveland) did the same in 1945. During the cold war era many pentecostals responded to the real and imagined threats of communism by lending their support to the Korean War and the war in Vietnam. Oddly enough, for fifty years the Assemblies of God remained a pacifist church, at least according to its official documents. Finally, in 1967 the denomination ruled that members could make their own choice regarding military service. The church's general assembly insisted that the revision simply exemplified its long-standing position. One critic later ridiculed that amnesia: "A change in the

A/G position it was, and an unacknowledged banishment of pentecostal heritage it remains."[62]

Throughout these decades southern pentecostals desired the kind of respect, status, and citizenship that their forerunners tended to shun. As a result, enthusiasts had become more like their culturally conservative middle-class religious peers. The movement, however, is not monolithic. Followers are black and white, urban and rural, impoverished and well off. There has been some degree of diversity in political outlook as well. Although white believers, and a few of their black brethren, did become active social and political conservatives in the last decades of the twentieth century, it is likely that the majority of African Americans joined or identified with the Democratic Party. In recent years several black pentecostals in the South have served as state senators, all Democrats. A few white critics who sensed the rightward political shift in their tradition expressed concern. In 1980 one writer questioned those who "argued the necessity for [Ronald] Reagan's election in something approaching apocalyptic tones," as though they believed that "[if] the one-time actor and state governor were not elected . . . the nation would either collapse from inner moral decay or become immediately hostage to a superior Soviet military power."[63]

In any event, while many devotees remained apolitical, still considering politics a distraction from their religious concerns, a vocal segment within the movement soon aligned with other conservative Protestants and forged a new coalition. Union with nonpentecostal conservative Christians came slowly. Early in the century, fundamentalists and conservative evangelicals were, much like holiness organizations before, hostile to tongues speakers. The World's Christian Fundamentals Association once declared the "tongues movement" a frightening menace to the church. In 1928 that organization officially renounced the new faith as unscriptural fanaticism. Nonetheless, many pentecostals identified with the theology and social outlook of ultraconservative Protestants. Despite having been ostracized, they saw fundamentalists as natural allies. Several years after the Scopes trial, a North Carolina pentecostal magazine lauded the efforts of conservative crusaders. Their fight against evolution and modernism is ours, exclaimed a writer. He also noted that both traditions defended the inerrancy of scripture, the virgin birth of Jesus, and the premillennial second coming.[64]

Hostility slowly faded through the 1940s and 1950s as the two groups found common ground. In the last half of the century, the staggering growth rate of pentecostalism in the South and elsewhere made it a religious force to be reckoned with. In the 1990s alone the International Pentecostal Holiness Church, which had moved its headquarters to Oklahoma City, registered a 53 percent increase in membership. Black and white denominations alike experienced similar increases in the United States and abroad.[65]

There are many other reasons why pentecostals drew closer to conservative Protestants and entered the political arena after World War II. Fundamentalists and evangelicals, like many pentecostals, were intensely anticommunist, often anti-Catholic, and were opponents of theological liberalism. In 1960 Thomas Zimmerman, the general superintendent of the Assemblies of God church, became head of the National Association of Evangelicals. Once shunned by such organizations, white pentecostals were now welcomed into the conservative Protestant fold, though other interfaith alliances never materialized. In this same period, the Assemblies and the Church of God (Cleveland) denounced liberal ecumenical movements as "a sign of the times." Such organizations, said Assemblies officials, would become the basis for "a World Super Church," culminating "in the scarlet woman or religious Babylon of Revelation."[66]

Beleaguered by a host of threats, a growing number of holiness adherents and pentecostals turned to political solutions. Quite a few viewed communism in particular as a "godless" force that might sweep over the planet were it not for the vigorous efforts of American Christians. Following the Soviet launch of the Sputnik satellite in 1957, the Texas-based healing evangelist Gordon Lindsay declared, "There is a sinister significance to Russia's triumph." It would surely lead to World War III and Armageddon, he warned. The Soviet Union was doing Satan's bidding. Some thought the devil was enlisting others, too.[67] In the 1960s one of Martin Luther King's most vocal critics was the black holiness minister Solomon Lightfoot Michaux. The sanctified preacher had broken from C. P. Jones's Church of God (Holiness) and made a name for himself in the 1930s with his Washington, D.C., radio show. At its peak Michaux's program aired on fifty stations reaching 25 million homes. His upbeat broadcasts won him a personal friend in Franklin D. Roosevelt. Michaux supported the New Deal and helped usher thousands of blacks into the Democratic camp. Two decades later he was lauding what he called President Dwight Eisenhower's "Heaven-Born Deal." By the 1960s, his celebrity status diminished, he had become an ardent anticommunist. Martin Luther King, claimed Michaux, had played into the hands of the Reds. In 1965 Michaux and one hundred followers picketed King's voter registration conference in Baltimore. The holiness preacher corresponded with FBI director J. Edgar Hoover concerning King's activities. He also wrote to King asking the civil rights leader to apologize for recent disparaging remarks he had made about Hoover. "If Communists and their sympathizers manage to exploit the differences between Dr. King and Hoover," Michaux told a reporter, "this thing can cause the Negro in America to be put back 100 years." That was an argument made by both the John Birch Society and *Christianity Today*, the flagship publication of evangelicalism.[68]

By 1960 white southern pentecostals had already begun to scorn the Democratic Party and the liberal establishment. The Assemblies of God, the Pentecostal Holiness Church, and the Church of God (Cleveland) opposed John F. Kennedy's run for the presidency. His politics may have unsettled them, but they were more concerned about his faith. They thought that a Catholic was inherently unsuitable for the role of chief executive. Kennedy's loyalty, they argued, would be to the Vatican, not to the United States. Alluding to the frightening specter of communism, an Assemblies of God educator asked, "Haven't the American people enough 'security risks' as it is without placing another in the President's office?" In the months before the election, thousands of churchgoers sent letters to the Church of God's headquarters asking how they should vote. The denomination's general overseer warned the flock that if Protestants sat idly by, no one could complain if a Roman Catholic assumed the nation's highest office. Although it would have been unthinkable in 1960, just over a decade later conservative Catholics and pentecostals would forge new political alliances on issues such as human sexuality, tax laws, evolution, and prayer in schools.[69]

Scores of holiness and pentecostal followers issued a collective complaint against the perceived hedonism and moral relativism of the 1960s and 1970s. They hoped to reverse what they considered the country's downward moral spiral. The 1962 Supreme Court decision in *Engel v. Vitale,* forbidding prayer in public schools, outraged conservative believers in the South. Roughly a decade later the *Roe v. Wade* decision legalizing abortion added urgency to their cause. Great Society liberals, critics contended, wasted the nation's fortune on the undeserving poor and turned a blind eye toward soaring crime rates. Pentecostal and nonpentecostal conservatives alike now championed Christian civilization and public virtue. For newly politicized conservative Christians, the job of government was to ensure national morality. The religious right represented an activist evangelicalism that made establishment conservatives such as William Safire and Barry Goldwater quite uncomfortable. Among other enemies, the new movement targeted so-called secular humanists, "limousine liberals," evolutionary scientists, and feminists.[70]

From the 1970s forward, a collection of powerful, media-savvy conservative Protestants rallied the faithful. Their life and work, perhaps more than any other single factor, politicized southern pentecostals. Right-wing Christian television personality and politician Pat Robertson gained his largest following among pentecostal and charismatic evangelicals. A Virginia native, graduate of Yale Law School, and ordained Southern Baptist minister, Robertson emphasized the gifts of the Spirit and the centrality of prayer. Charismatics—those who adopted the intense worship styles and some of the theology of pentecostals yet could be found in Baptist, Methodist, and Episcopal fellowships—understood Robertson's language of the Spirit. So did pentecostals. His hard-line, moralistic stance on communism and his fusion of patriotism and biblical literalism drew millions to his side. In the 1970s and 1980s Robertson's *700 Club* television program and Christian Broadcasting Network built a political base of like-minded believers. Direct mailing campaigns and telethons contributed to his growing religious empire. He was a polarizing personality. Followers revered him, while his critics despised him. Few of Robertson's supporters thought it odd when in 1985 he claimed to have diverted Hurricane Gloria from the Virginia coast through the

Pat Robertson (left), presidential candidate and founder of
the Christian Broadcasting Network, with Raphael Farber,
Israel's consul and tourism commissioner for North America, July 1991.

power of prayer. "If I couldn't move a hurricane, I could hardly
move a nation," he told one journalist. "I know that's a strange
thing for somebody to say, and there's hardly anybody else who
would feel the same way, but it was very important to the faith
of many people."[71]

Robertson guided multitudes. His jeremiads against homosexuality, divorce, legalized abortion, secularization, and big

government catered to the interests of newly politicized constituents. Because of Robertson's charismatic and populist style, the television preacher exerted a more powerful influence than Jerry Falwell or Paul Weyrich, architects of the new Christian right. Pentecostal televangelists Jim Bakker in Charlotte, North Carolina, and Jimmy Swaggart in Baton Rouge, Louisiana, pledged their support to Robertson's 1988 presidential campaign. Both believed their viewers would back him as well. He also gained a small African American pentecostal following. The head of the Church of God in Christ, J. O. Patterson, supported him in the mid-1980s. When Robertson explained his vision of politics as a moral imperative, numerous other pentecostals in the South, steeped in premillennialism, joined the Virginia crusader.

His tone was urgent. From Robertson's Virginia Beach headquarters he assured TV audiences that the last days were nigh. Like pentecostals, he read history as a trail of anti-Christian conspiracy, from the time of the emperor Constantine to the formation of the United Nations. The new secular world order would banish the true faith. That was the theme of the celebrity preacher's 1995 novel, *The End of the Age*. The apocalyptic fantasy told of a demonic former campus radical who assumed the presidency and packed his cabinet with a Buddhist, a Lebanese Shiite Muslim, and a Harvard professor of Eastern religion. It represented the perils of pluralism that would mark the last days. Long before Robertson arrived on the scene, pentecostals had been speculating about the earth's final hours. Now more than ever, the political and the apocalyptic merged.[72]

In the early twenty-first century John Hagee, a San Antonio, Texas, pentecostal televangelist, rallied the faithful with a similar message of Christ's imminent return. Hagee pastored a twenty-thousand-member megachurch, and hosted a television program that aired twice a day on the Trinity Broadcasting Network. TBN also featured politically conservative talk shows, healing revivals, and children's programming. Hagee became one of the network's southern pentecostal celebrities and by any account a highly visible, influential leader. According to a 2005 survey conducted by a religious polling firm, the Barna Group, Hagee ranked among the top ten Christian spokesmen for both black and white pentecostal ministers, alongside James Dobson, T. D. Jakes, Jerry Falwell, and Billy Graham.

Hagee's call to arms against Israel's enemies and his message of America's moral failings won him an avid following. Christian Zionism, the minister argued, is a biblical imperative. Israel is "the only nation that God ever created," he told a National Public Radio reporter in 2006. "It's the only nation that Christians are told to pray for, and therefore, because the Bible is the compass of our faith, we do what it says." *Jerusalem Countdown,* his best-selling millennial warning, sold approximately half a million copies by the summer of 2006. At the same time, Hagee organized a mass meeting in the nation's capital, the Washington/Israel Summit, demanding that President George W. Bush and American lawmakers pledge greater support for Israel. In attendance were Republican National Committee chairman Ken Mehlman, Republican senators Sam Brownback and Rick Santorum, and Christian spokesmen Gary Bauer and Jerry Falwell. Hagee also organized his supporters in a campaign for a preemptive war on Iran, called Persia in his latter-day scenario. On the one hand Hagee justified such a move as the way to thwart Iranian terrorism, while on the other he relished the prospect that the ensuing conflagration would lead to Armageddon. As one journalist noted, "His endtimes theology is nothing new." Yet "TBN's relentless fund raising—along with advances in digital and satellite broadcasting technology—has permitted worldwide dissemination of his ominous predictions." As a result, Hagee was able to amass a fortune, using the money to further his millennial agenda and aid his allies in the cause.[73]

Israel's foes are not the only enemies of Christian civilization, according to such figures. Hagee, Pat Robertson, and a few leading African American pentcostals in the South have anathematized homosexuality and abortion and decried the separation of church and state. In the run-up to the 2004 presidential election Hagee spelled out his emphatic position to supporters. "In this upcoming election," he intoned, "the world wants to legislate into laws issues such as homosexual marriage, partial birth abortions, all the while making every effort to erase Christianity from the face of American politics and society as a whole." Said the Texas pastor, "Liberal lawmakers and activist judges are trying to convince the nation that religion has no place in the political arena." Hagee also argued that abortion, even in the case of rape or incest, violated God's law. Others in the region felt it necessary to voice their political opinions as well. African American pentecostal megachurch ministers Creflo Dollar in Atlanta and T. D. Jakes in Dallas targeted homosexuality in interviews and sermons.[74] Yet their position sounded mild compared with that of others.

The Memphis-based black pentecostal apostle Alton R. Williams preached a premillennial moralism that struck a chord with his twelve thousand congregants. His church bought full-page advertisements in local papers condemning the "sin of homosexuality" and sponsored enormous publicity campaigns. On July 4, 2006, his church unveiled a seventy-two-foot-tall "Statue of the Liberation through Christ," which Williams hoped would turn the attention of observers to the Christian foundations of America. Instead of holding a torch, like the Statue of Liberty, the figure holds a cross. A teardrop running down the face of the statue, said Williams, symbolizes God's displeasure with the nation's ills: legalized abortion, the absence of school prayer, and the "promotion of expressions of New Age, Wicca, secularism, and humanism." When questioned about the behemoth's $260,000 price tag, Williams retorted that the church gave millions to the needy.[75]

For a time John Ashcroft, former U.S. senator, two-term governor of Missouri, and former U.S. attorney general, was one of the most visible southern pentecostals in the nation. Ashcroft grew up in an Assemblies of God church in Springfield, a large town on the edge of southern Missouri's Ozark hills. His Irish immigrant grandfather was a roaming evangelist who toured America in a Chevrolet emblazoned with handmade signs reading, "Where Will You Spend Eternity?" and "Jesus Is Coming Soon!" Ashcroft's father, J. Robert, encouraged his precocious son to attend Yale. He subsequently went on to the University of Chicago Law School. At neither university did he mix well with his classmates. As he recalled years later, he felt like an "odd duck" in New Haven. As far as he knew, there were no fellow Yalie pentecostals. Like others of his religious tradition, Ashcroft was a teetotaler and was firmly opposed to dancing and gambling. (As governor of Missouri he banned alcohol from the governor's residence and refused to dance at his own inaugural ball.) While Ashcroft was in school, J. Robert, a fiery minister like his father before him, advised his son on his future. Unlike his father and grandfather, John Ashcroft chose to enter politics. Nonetheless, he entered the field with an evangelist's zeal.[76]

God's chosen servant, the Old Testament King David, served as Ashcroft's biblical role model. On the night before he was sworn in as a U.S. senator in 1995, his father arranged for fifteen to twenty friends and family members to come together to pray for him. They sang a hymn, "We Are Standing on Holy

Ground." John played piano. The next morning they gathered again in a house outside the capital and listened to Ashcroft's ailing father's exhortation. "It's too bad we don't have some oil," Ashcroft lamented to those gathered, recalling that "the ancient kings of Israel, David and Saul, were anointed as they undertook their administrative duties," and the Assemblies of God also anointed ministers and church officials. His father suggested they look in the kitchen.[77] He then blessed his son with cooking oil, an act that won the future attorney general the nickname "Crisco Kid."[78]

Biblical images and tropes filled Ashcroft's writing, speeches, and advice to colleagues. In 1999 he gave an address and received an honorary degree at Bob Jones University in Greenville, South Carolina, a conservative fundamentalist school that, at the time, still banned interracial dating. The United States was unique among nations, Ashcroft told his audience. Americans "recognized the source of our character as being godly and eternal, not being civic and temporal. And because we have understood that our source is eternal, America has been different: We have no king but Jesus."[79] Bob Jones III, president of the university, supported Ashcroft's 2000 presidential bid, as did conservative religious broadcaster Pat Robertson and Tim LaHaye, author of popular end-time novels.

Controversy dogged the ultraconservative Ashcroft. He was unfazed. J. Robert Ashcroft had long warned his son about the impieties of media elites and Beltway politicians swarming the nation's capital. "The spirit of Washington is arrogance," he told his son.[80] But when John Ashcroft became George W. Bush's attorney general in 2001, attacks on the pentecostal politician reached a new high. Detractors pointed to Ashcroft's conservative stance against abortion, even in cases of rape or incest, and his strident resistance to affirmative action. They denounced his opposition as senator to nearly all forms of gun control, including a ban on assault rifles. The attorney general's use of wiretapping and surveillance in the administration's war against terrorism angered civil libertarians. Others alleged that Ashcroft was a racist because in 1998 he had given an interview to the *Southern Partisan,* a neo-Confederate magazine that had defended slavery, lauded the Ku Klux Klan, and championed the Lost Cause. Ashcroft offered his views on states' rights and southern history. "Your magazine . . . helps set the record straight," he told his interviewer:

> You've got a heritage of doing that, of defending Southern patriots like Lee, Jackson, and Davis. Traditionalists must do more. I've got to do more. We've all got to stand up and speak in this respect, or else we'll be taught that these people were giving their lives, subscribing their sacred fortunes and their honor to some perverted agenda. . . . The right of individuals to respect our history is a right that the politically correct crowd wants to eliminate, and this is not acceptable.

Missouri governor John Ashcroft addresses a gathering of the National Religious Broadcasters in the mid-1980s.

After the article appeared, an editorialist in the *Boston Globe* charged that "the nation's top law enforcer cannot be someone who vacillates between civil rights and Civil War fantasies."[81] Some were even more acerbic. Julian Bond, chairman of the NAACP, lambasted Ashcroft, who, he claimed, "knew something about the Taliban, coming as he does from that wing of American politics."[82]

Ashcroft does not represent all southern pentecostals, let alone all pentecostals in America, though many white adherents may share his views. He does, however, serve as an interesting contrast to early followers in the South. Ashcroft's cultural outlook and political career would have been unimaginable to countless first-generation believers, who denounced politics and had no truck with Dixie's defenders. Ashcroft committed himself to God *and* country. That fusion of faith and intense patriotism would have been equally unthinkable to earlier followers.

In February 2002 the attorney general spoke to a gathering at the Charlotte, NC, campus of Gordon-Conwell Theological Seminary, a small evangelical school. Before he wrapped up his comments, he treated the crowd to a performance of a song he had composed called "Let the Eagle Soar." He belted out the tune accompanied by a karaoke-style CD. That rendition, and another on the Capitol steps at President Bush's second inaugural, became legendary. Comedians and left-leaning commentators had a field day. The song became a regular feature on late night television. Documentary filmmaker Michael Moore included footage of Ashcroft's bizarre performance in his blockbuster *Fahrenheit 9/11,* and television talk show host Jon Stewart aired it to viewers who were at once amused and horrified. Ashcroft's song was a curious mix of Lawrence Welk–style crooning and theocratic jingoism:

Let the eagle soar,
Like she's never soared before.
From rocky coast to golden shore,
Let the mighty eagle soar.
Soar with healing in her wings,
As the land beneath her sings:
"Only God, no other kings."
Let the mighty eagle soar.[83]

The overwrought anthem even embarrassed some of his staffers. When Ashcroft tried to get employees at the Justice Department to sing "Let the Eagle Soar" before starting their workday, they balked. "Have you heard the song?" one asked a BBC reporter. "It really sucks."[84] Heady patriotism had got the better of him. After that he was more careful not to let other views that might be considered even more peculiar or controversial come under public scrutiny. While in office he did not speak publicly about tongues speech and long remained silent on millennialism. Perhaps he had learned from the mistakes of predecessors who revealed far too much about their beliefs.

James G. Watt, also a member of the Assemblies of God, served as secretary of the interior under President Ronald Reagan. In 1981 Watt casually remarked to a congressional committee that the health of the environment was not terribly important, since no one knew "how many future generations we can count on until the Lord returns." Although Watt explained that the comment was a kind of tongue-in-cheek joke, the media aired his words without that disclaimer. Watt eventually had to step down from office after making other inflammatory remarks. In 1982 an administration colleague of Watt's, Secretary of Defense Caspar Weinberger, was asked about the "last days." He similarly remarked, "I have read the Book of Revelation and yes, I believe the world is going to end—by an act of God, I hope—but every day I think time is running out."[85]

In these years even Reagan openly speculated about prophecy and the end of the world. In October 1983 he commented to Thomas Dine, executive director of the American-Israeli Public Affairs Committee, "I turn back to your ancient prophets in the Old Testament and the signs foretelling Armageddon, and I find myself wondering if we're the generation that's going to see that come about."[86] When the president later wondered aloud whether "Armageddon is a thousand years away or [the] day after tomorrow" during a televised 1984 election debate with Walter F. Mondale, it shocked commentators and moderate religious officials alike. The reaction from critics was swift. Over a hundred public radio stations across the United States aired an alarmist ninety-minute special, *Ronald Reagan and the Prophecy of Armageddon.* In addition, roughly one hundred mainstream Protestant, Catholic, and Jewish leaders signed a well-publicized statement of concern, denouncing what they considered Reagan's misguided apocalypticism. White pentecostals in the South, who turned out in large numbers to vote for Reagan, understood the president's remark perfectly well. They found nothing objectionable about it. More than a decade before Reagan made his offhand comment about the world's inevitable demise before a national audience, he had devoured Hal Lindsey's best-selling end of the world drama, *The Late Great Planet Earth,* a book that was also popular with many pentecostals in the South.[87] Lindsey depicted a fearsome struggle between the forces of evil and the powers of heaven. The world was reduced to a panic of violence and holy terror. That book informed some of Reagan's basic views of the last days.

These developments at the highest levels of the American establishment revealed that premillennialism had become an unparalleled popular theology. A 2002 survey cited by the

Christian Science Monitor showed that 59 percent of Americans believed that the events described in the Book of Revelation would occur in the future. Even more telling, Jerry Jenkins and Tim LaHaye's apocalyptic adventure novel series, *Left Behind,* is a sure sign of the ascendancy of premillennialism. By 2006 the books had sold over 63 million copies and spawned a movie series, a video game, comic books, audiotapes, and numerous Internet fan sites. The series begins with the rapture of the saints. Bedlam ensues. Pilotless planes crash, cities devolve into chaos, and families search for raptured kin. The archvillain throughout is Nicolae Carpathia, secretary general of the United Nations. It is clear which side he is on. As one reviewer in the *Washington Post* noted, he sponsors causes such as "peace, disarmament, global cooperation, aid to Third World countries, interfaith dialogue and environmental treaties."[88]

In addition to the diffusion of premillennialism, the widespread growth of pentecostalism and the rise of its leaders to powerful political and cultural positions was a remarkable development. By 2007, a century after the faith first entered the American South, charismatic worship styles and premillennial beliefs were no longer only the province of disaffected sectarians on the margins of society.

At least in part, southern pentecostals who identified with cultural and political conservatism had become, like Baptists and Methodists before them, more affluent. Changes in believers' socioeconomic status were well under way after World War II. Yet more important, attitudes toward wealth, education, and society had changed considerably. By the second half of the century, leading denominations in the South championed their Bible schools and liberal arts institutions alike. The ever-expanding Assemblies of God geared its schools and churches toward a new suburban clientele. In the mid-1960s James S. Tinney, an African American author writing in *Christianity*

Today, noted these and other transformations. This "new Pentecostalism," he remarked "has little in common with the Holy Roller image." Pentecostals were now demanding more training of their ministers, playing down certain distinctions that set them apart from fellow Christians, and building lavish churches and recreation centers.[89] Assemblies of God TV personalities Jim and Tammy Faye Bakker would later celebrate prosperity on their *Praise the Lord* program. Before sexual and financial scandals destroyed their empire of the Spirit, the Bakkers' extravagant headquarters in Charlotte, North Carolina, boasted a Christian amusement park, luxury condos, and a high-tech television studio. At the height of the Bakkers' success, a white pentecostal minister summed up the transformation of the saints: "Rhetorically denying that it wanted, in any way, to be part of this world, the church showed an amazing ability to adapt to prevailing currents. For a group that was supposed to be 'outsiders' in the culture, there was an astounding adaptation to 'insider' fashions, music, promotional techniques, and institutional/bureaucratic structures as the movement experienced social and economic mobility."[90] The pentecostal-charismatic Trinity Broadcasting Network glorifies wealth and opulence. TBN's sets combine rococo flourishes with garish religious architecture, and ministers who appear on its programs wear loud, expensive suits and laud financial success as a sign of God's blessing. Such sanctified mammonism has entered the theology of the movement as well. John Hagee, T. D. Jakes, scandal-addled televangelist Robert Tilton, and a host of other prominent ministers embrace "word of faith" theology, which is much like the prosperity gospel of an earlier era, yet its charismatic-pentecostal origins gain it a wider hearing. Hagee describes the doctrine succinctly: "Investing in God's kingdom pays great dividends! If we give sparingly, we will reap sparingly, the Bible says; but if we sow generously, we will reap God's abundance (2 Cor. 9:6)." This more recent view contrasts sharply with the position of first-generation disciples. Early initiates took pride in the humble origins of the movement, the plain-folk element that typified turn-of-the-century preachers such as Uncle Bud Robinson and Watson Sorrow. Like them, A. J. Tomlinson pointed to the lowly birth of Jesus. The savior did not enter the world surrounded by luxuries, Tomlinson preached. He was born in a "lonely stable among the cattle and probably other animals."[91]

In so many ways, first-generation pentecostals were religious mavericks. They paid little heed to the many proscriptions on life in the South and thrived on the radical fringe of Protestantism. Gradually, however, southern pentecostals shed many of their characteristic beliefs and traits and moved slowly into the mainstream of American evangelicalism. Once apolitical and radically at odds with southern Baptists and Methodists, pentecostals in the region came in some respects to look more and more like their perennial enemies. Ironically, the majority of white followers, and some blacks, eventually identified with the same kind of social and political conservatism they had once shunned or even openly condemned. They had gone from being challengers of the social order to becoming its most ardent defenders. By the end of the twentieth century, according to Grant Wacker, most "worshiped in carpeted, climate-controlled buildings indistinguishable from the local Southern Baptist church."[92]

Indeed, pentecostals came to look more like other conservative Protestants. Even their fundamental doctrine of premillennialism would become commonplace among the South's evangelical Christians. It is hard to imagine that the same movement which produced preachers like G. B. Cashwell, C. H. Mason, and Elizabeth A. Sexton would later elevate such figures as

Jimmy Swaggart, John Ashcroft, T. D. Jakes, and John Hagee to public prominence.

Nevertheless, though leaning to the political and cultural right, pentecostals have still retained much of the unconventional, even contrarian spirit of their predecessors. Old and new themes merge in modern southern pentecostalism. Robert Duvall's now classic film *The Apostle* (1997), about a fiery Texas holiness-pentecostal minister, captures much of the tension in the contemporary faith. Sprinkled with allusions to the work of Flannery O'Connor, the movie portrays a dark, grotesque side of pentecostalism. Yet *The Apostle* is not entirely fantastic. The protagonist, "Sonny" Dewey, is both a rogue and a saint. His volcanic zeal is palpable. But his passion leads him into morally suspect and even criminal behavior. Revered by his followers, he is viewed as either foolish or diabolical by his opponents. Sonny is quarrelsome and unconventional. He calls himself "the Apostle," speaks directly to God, shouts his sermons on the radio, builds a Holy Ghost temple from an abandoned church, and leads interracial services that are anything but decorous.[93]

In other ways as well, some of the basic underlying themes of southern pentecostalism have remained the same. Seekers are still drawn by the promise of direct communion with God. Adherents find comfort in the assurance that tongues speech is a divine language. Charismatic services attract legions of followers who find formal religious worship constricting or lifeless. Moreover, devotees still watch and wait for the coming of Christ.

NOTES

ILLUSTRATION CREDITS

INDEX

Notes

INTRODUCTION

1. G. B. Cashwell, "Came 3,000 Miles for His Pentecost," *The Apostolic Faith*, 6 December 1907, 3. "Weird Babel of Tongues," *Los Angeles Daily Times,* 18 April 1906, sec. 2, 1.

2. 1 John 3:6. All biblical citations are from the King James Version.

3. J. Wofford White quoted in Irving E. Lowery, *Life on the Old Plantation in Ante-Bellum Slavery Days, Or a Story Based on Facts* (Columbia, S.C.: State Company Printers, 1911), 25. Thomas C. Oden, ed., *Phoebe Palmer: Selected Writings* (New York: Paulist Press, 1988), 188.

4. H. H. Goff, *The Apostolic Faith* (February–March 1907): 8.

5. C. W. Shumway, "A Study of 'The Gift of Tongues'" (A.B. thesis, University of Southern California, 1914), 192.

6. Grant Wacker, *Heaven Below: Early Pentecostals and American Culture* (Cambridge, Mass.: Harvard University Press, 2001), 271. Of these southern denominations only forty-one provide U.S. membership figures, totaling more than 6,549,278, still a conservative estimate. J. Gordon Melton, ed., *The Encyclopedia of American Religions,* vol. 1 (Tarrytown, N.Y.: Triumph Books, 1991), 231–291. Robert William Fogel, *The Fourth Great Awakening and the Future of Egalitarianism* (Chicago: University of Chicago Press, 2002), 15–19. Walter Russell Mead, "God's Country," foreignaffairs.org (September–October 2006) (accessed 9/8/06). Christian Smith, *Christian America? What Evangelicals Really Want* (Berkeley: University of California Press, 2000), 1–6.

7. Duncan Aikman, "Holy Rollers," *American Mercury* 15 (October 1928): 183. Liston Pope, *Millhands and Preachers: A Study of Gastonia* (New Haven: Yale University Press, 1942), 134.

8. See Richard Hofstadter, *Anti-Intellectualism in American Life* (New York: Vintage Books, 1963); Robert Mapes Anderson, *Vision of the Disinherited: The Making of American Pentecostalism* (New York: Oxford University Press, 1979); and R. Laurence Moore, *Religious Outsiders and the Making of Americans* (New York: Oxford University Press, 1986). These appraisals also misconstrue the faithful as mere ciphers, when in fact, as anthropologist Clifford Geertz suggests, believers do not merely interpret social and psychological processes in cosmic terms—which would be philosophical, not religious—but also shape them. Clifford Geertz, *The Interpretation of Cultures: Selected Essays* (New York: Basic Books, 1973), 93, 119, 124.

9. See, for example, Melvin Easterday Dieter, *The Holiness Revival of the Nineteenth Century* (Lanham, Md.: Scarecrow Press, 1996); Briane K. Turley, *A Wheel within a Wheel: Southern Methodism and the Georgia Holiness Association* (Macon, Ga.: Mercer University Press, 1999); Mickey Crews, *The Church of God: A Social History* (Knoxville: University of Tennessee Press, 1990); David G. Roebuck, "Limiting Liberty: The Church of God and Women Ministers, 1886–1996" (Ph.D. diss., Vanderbilt University, 1997); Vinson Synan, *Old Time Power: A Centennial History of the International Pentecostal Holiness Church* (Franklin Springs, Ga.: LifeSprings Resources, 1998); Daniel Glenn Woods, "Living in the Presence of God: Enthusiasm, Authority, and Negotiation in the Practice of Pentecostal Holiness" (Ph.D. diss., University of Mississippi, 1997); Edith Blumhofer, *Restoring the Faith: The Assemblies of God, Pentecostalism, and American Culture* (Urbana: University of Illinois Press, 1993); and R. G. Robins, *A. J. Tomlinson: Plainfolk Modernist* (New York: Oxford University Press, 2004).

10. Wacker treats pentecostalism as a "cultural whole" and pays little attention to "regional, ethnic, and gender differences." Wacker, *Heaven Below,* 16. In his study of the first wave of fundamentalism in the American South, William R. Glass makes an argument similar to mine. George Marsden, Joel Carpenter, and Margaret Bendroth, according to Glass, failed to discuss the movement's regional variations and lost sight of an important part of that tradition. Glass, *Strangers in Zion: Fundamentalism in the South, 1900–1950* (Macon, Ga.: Mercer University Press, 2001), viii, ix.

11. Rev. J. R. Fowler, Springfield, Mo., to M. M. Pinson, Oildale, Calif., 4 January 1950, Flower Pentecostal Heritage Center, Springfield, Mo. Frank Bartleman, *Azusa Street* (1925; reprint, South Plainfield, N.J.: Bridge Publishing, 1980), 153.

12. Stephen R. Tucker, "Pentecostalism and Popular Culture in the South: A Study of Four Musicians," *Journal of Popular Culture* 16 (Winter 1982): 68.

13. Those works that deal best with the regional element include Turley, *Wheel within a Wheel;* Robins, *A. J. Tomlinson;* J. Lawrence Brasher, *The Sanctified South: John Lakin Brasher and the Holiness Movement* (Urbana: University of Illinois Press, 1994); and Robert Stanley Ingersol, "Burden of Dissent: Mary Lee Cagle and the Southern Holiness Movement" (Ph.D. diss., Duke University, 1989).

14. John Leland Peters, *Christian Perfection and American Methodism* (New York: Abingdon Press, 1956), 131–132. C. B. Jernigan, *From the Prairie Schooner to a City Flat* (Brooklyn, N.Y.: C. B. Jernigan, 1926), 51.

15. Anna Kelly, "More about Women Preaching," *The Holiness Advocate,* 1 March 1906, 5.

16. "John Dull's Letter," *Live Coals of Fire,* 15 December 1899, 7.

17. Aikman, "Holy Rollers," 183.

18. "History of Pentecost: The Shout Heard Round the World," *The Faithful Standard* (October 1922): 9. Historian Deborah McCauley argues that Appalachian pentecostals were more tied to an indigenous plain-folk camp meeting religion of the upcountry, but she offers little solid evidence to support her claims. By all appearances, most believers were deeply rooted in the late-nineteenth-century holiness revival which originated in the North. Deborah Vansau McCauley, *Appalachian Mountain Religion: A History* (Urbana: University of Illinois Press, 1995), 257, 259–260, 262, 265, 267, 271, 304.

19. *Gastonia Gazette,* 15 April and 6 December 1910, quoted in Pope, *Millhands and Preachers,* 129.

1. ANGELS FROM THE NORTH

1. George D. Watson, *Fruit of Canaan: Notes of Personal Experiences* (Boston: McDonald and Gill, n.d.), 10.

2. "National Camp Meeting," *Knoxville Daily Chronicle,* 24 September 1872, 1.

3. Gordon B. McKinney, *Southern Mountain Republicans, 1865–1900* (Chapel Hill: University of North Carolina Press, 1978), 36–37. *Knoxville Daily Chronicle,* 25 September 1872, 1.

4. W. McDonald and John E. Sears, *The Life of Rev. John S. Inskip: President of the National Association for the Promotion of Holiness* (Boston: McDonald and Gill, 1885), 285.

5. *Knoxville Daily Chronicle,* 22 September 1872; 1 October 1872, 4; and 24 September 1872, 1.

6. *Knoxville Daily Chronicle,* 27 September 1872, 1. Peter Cartwright, *Autobiography of Peter Cartwright* (New York: Abingdon Press, 1986), 334–337, 45.

7. Donald G. Mathews, *Religion in the Old South* (Chicago: University of Chicago Press, 1977), 82, 101. John B. Boles, *The Great Revival, 1787–1805* (Lexington: University Press of Kentucky, 1972), 90, 96, 99. Nathan O. Hatch, *The Democratization of American Christianity* (New Haven: Yale University Press, 1989), 93, 194, 195.

8. *Journal of the General Conference of the Methodist Episcopal Church, South, 1870* (Nashville: Publishing House of the Methodist Episcopal Church, South, 1870), 164–165. *Journal of the General Conference of the Methodist Episcopal Church, South, 1878* (Nashville: Southern Methodist Publishing House, 1878), 33.

9. L. Pierce, *A Miscellaneous Essay on Entire Sanctification: Showing How It was Lost from the Church and How It May and Must Be Regained* (Nashville: Publishing House of the M. E. Church, South, 1897), 3, 4, 15, 56–57. L. Pierce, "Experience of Rev. L. Pierce," *The Way of Holiness* (May 1876): 18.

10. Pierce, *Essay on Entire Sanctification,* 63. Reverend Leonidas Rosser of the Virginia Conference was another promoter of entire sanctification in the antebellum period. See his *Experimental Religion: Embracing Justification, Regeneration, Sanctification, and the Witness of the Spirit* (Richmond: by the author, 1856).

11. O. P. Fitzgerald, *Eminent Methodists: Lovick Pierce, D.D.* (Nashville: Barbee and Smith, 1895), 15–16.

12. Thomas L. Boswell, "Salvation and Its Individual Relations," in *The Methodist Pulpit South,* ed. William T. Smithson (Washington, D.C.: William T. Smithson, 1859), 224. Briane K. Turley, *A Wheel within a Wheel: Southern Methodism and the Georgia Holiness Association* (Macon, Ga.: Mercer University Press, 1999), 78. Anne C. Loveland, *South-*

ern Evangelicals and the Social Order, 1800–1860 (Baton Rouge: Louisiana State University Press, 1980), 13.

13. See Allan Coppedge on William Williams's discussion of sanctification, "Entire Sanctification in Early Methodism: 1813–1835," *Wesleyan Theological Journal* 13 (Spring 1978): 39. See Loveland's account of the second blessing experience of William Capers, *Southern Evangelicals and the Social Order,* 19. Coppedge argues that Wesleyan perfectionism was much more prevalent in early-nineteenth-century America than most historians would admit. His examples, however, are drawn primarily from northern and western Methodists. Coppedge, "Entire Sanctification in Early Methodism," 34–46. John Leland Peters, *Christian Perfection and American Methodism* (New York: Abingdon Press, 1956), 92–95.

14. Peters, *Christian Perfection and American Methodism,* 100. Turley, *Wheel within a Wheel,* 37, 77. Boles, *The Great Revival,* 65–66. Samuel S. Hill Jr., *Southern Churches in Crisis* (New York: Holt Rinehart and Winston, 1966), 25, 61, 65.

15. Henry E. Partridge, "A Mississippi Letter," *The Way of Faith,* 27 November 1895, 2.

16. John B. Boles observes that the Great Awakening in the early nineteenth century "set into motion the diverse forces that by the decade of the 1830s had created an orthodox South, a South resistant to change and criticism in every form." Boles, *The Great Revival,* 183, 191.

17. George M. Smith, *The Life and Times of George Foster Pierce* (Sparta, Ga.: Hancock Publishing Company, 1888), 11. Ted Ownby, *Subduing Satan: Religion, Recreation, and Manhood in the Rural South, 1865–1920* (Chapel Hill: University of North Carolina Press, 1990), 162.

18. David Douglas Daniels, "Cultural Renewal of Slave Religion: Charles Price Jones and the Emergence of the Holiness Movement in Mississippi" (Ph.D. diss., Union Theological Seminary, 1992), 63. On the unity of evangelicals, see Christine Leigh Heyrman, *Southern Cross: The Beginning of the Bible Belt* (Chapel Hill: University of North Carolina Press, 1997), 4. Loveland, *Evangelicals and the Social Order,* 4, 7. Dickson Bruce, *And They All Sang Hallelujah: Plain-Folk Camp-Meeting Religion, 1800–1845* (Knoxville: University of Tennessee Press, 1974), 42. Eugene D. Genovese, "Religion in the Collapse of the American Union," in *Religion and the American Civil War,* ed. Randall M. Miller, Harry S. Stout, and Charles Reagan Wilson (New York: Oxford University Press, 1998), 80. See also Paul K. Conkin, *The Uneasy Center: Reformed Christianity in Ante-*

bellum America (Chapel Hill: University of North Carolina Press, 1995), 87–88.

19. W. J. Cash, *The Mind of the South* (New York: Vintage Books, 1991), 81, 132, 350–351. For critiques of Cash, see C. Vann Woodward, *American Counterpoint: Slavery and Racism in the North-South Dialogue* (Boston: Little, Brown, 1971), 261–283. Michael O'Brien, *Rethinking the South: Essays in Intellectual History* (Baltimore: Johns Hopkins University Press, 1988), 179–189. John H. Leith, "Calvinism," in *Encyclopedia of Southern Culture,* ed. Charles Reagan Wilson and William Ferris (Chapel Hill: University of North Carolina Press, 1989), 1281. Harold J. Douglas and Robert Daniel, "Faulkner's Southern Puritanism," in *Religious Perspectives in Faulkner's Fiction,* ed. J. Robert Barth (Notre Dame: University of Notre Dame Press, 1972), 39–40.

20. Loveland, *Evangelicals and the Social Order,* 74, 79, 83. Deborah Vansau McCauley, *Appalachian Mountain Religion: A History* (Urbana: University of Illinois Press, 1995), 6, 128, 158. Bertram Wyatt-Brown, "The Antimission Movement in the Jacksonian South: A Study in Regional Folk Culture," *Journal of Southern History* 36 (November 1970): 511. See also James R. Mathis, "'Can Two Walk Together Unless They Be Agreed?' The Origins of the Primitive Baptists" (Ph.D. diss, University of Florida, 1997), 12–13.

21. Mathews, *Religion in the Old South,* 163–164.

22. James Henry Thornwell to James Gillespie, 13 June 1835, quoted in James Oscar Farmer Jr., *The Metaphysical Confederacy: James Henry Thornwell and the Synthesis of Southern Values* (Macon, Ga.: Mercer University Press), 6, 53, 129, 155.

23. Donald G. Mathews, "'We have left undone those things which we ought to have done': Southern Religious History in Retrospect and Prospect," *Church History* 67 (June 1998): 320–321. Edward L. Ayers, *Vengeance and Justice: Crime and Punishment in the Nineteenth-Century American South* (New York: Oxford University Press, 1984), 122.

24. C. Vann Woodward, *The Burden of Southern History* (Baton Rouge: Louisiana State University Press, 1960), 21. See also Bertram Wyatt-Brown, *Yankee Saints and Southern Sinners* (Baton Rouge: Louisiana State University Press, 1985), 214–215, 217, and *Southern Honor: Ethics and Behavior in the Old South* (Oxford: Oxford University Press, 1982), 29.

25. Turley, *Wheel within a Wheel,* 61–67. For the definitive treatment

of honor culture in the Old South, see Wyatt-Brown, *Southern Honor.* I do not think that honor culture was as detrimental to holiness as Turley suggests. The white South's theological and ideological systems, especially in opposition to the North's, I deem far more critical.

26. Heyrman, *Southern Cross,* 232–248. Conkin, *The Uneasy Center,* 135.

27. On Wesley's influences, see R. Newton Flew, *The Idea of Perfection in Christian Theology: An Historical Study of the Christian Ideal for the Present Life* (London: Oxford University Press, 1934), 314–315. For Wesley's changing view of sanctification, see Peters, *Christian Perfection and American Methodism,* 29–31. John Wesley, *A Plain Account of Christian Perfection* (Kansas City, Mo.: Beacon Hill Press, 1966), 38, 61. Flew, *The Idea of Perfection in Christian Theology,* 325.

28. Timothy Smith emphasized the strong "utilitarian impulse" of the holiness revival in the North. Key leaders hungered "for an experience that would 'make Christianity work.'" Timothy L. Smith, *Revivalism and Social Reform: American Protestantism on the Eve of the Civil War* (Gloucester, Mass.: Peter Smith, 1976), 145, 149. See also Melvin Easterday Dieter, *The Holiness Revival of the Nineteenth Century* (Lanham, Md.: Scarecrow Press, 1996), 4–5. For an excellent analysis of Palmer's pragmatism, see Turley, *Wheel within a Wheel,* 51–59, 58. Harold E. Raser, *Phoebe Palmer: Her Life and Thought* (Lewiston, N.Y.: Edwin Mellen Press, 1987), 149–226.

29. James H. Moorhead, "The Erosion of Postmillennialism in American Thought, 1865–1925," *Church History* 53 (March 1984): 62.

30. *The Higher Christian Life* sold approximately 200,000 copies in the United States and England. Timothy L. Smith, *Called unto Holiness: The Story of the Nazarenes, the Formative Years* (Kansas City, Mo.: Nazarene Publishing House, 1962), 11.

31. Flew, *The Idea of Perfection in Christian Theology,* 338.

32. Palmer's most popular book, *The Way of Holiness,* sold 24,000 copies by 1851 and went through thirty-six editions before the Civil War. Although she had written for *The Guide to Holiness* for years, in 1864 she and her husband, Dr. Walter Palmer, acquired the journal and quickly developed it into a major enterprise. By 1870 the paper's circulation had reached 37,000. Smith, *Revivalism and Social Reform,* 116–117. Dieter, *The Holiness Revival of the Nineteenth Century,* 42.

33. William C. Kostlevy, intro. to *Historical Dictionary of the Holiness*

Movement, ed. William C. Kostlevy (Lanham, Md.: Scarecrow Press, 2001), 1–2.

34. Lucille Sider Dayton and Donald Dayton, "'Your Daughters Shall Prophesy': Feminism in the Holiness Movement," in *Modern American Protestantism and Its World: Historical Articles on Protestantism in American Religious Life,* vol. 12, ed. Martin E. Marty (Munich: K. G. Saur, 1993), 243–250.

35. George G. Smith, *The History of Georgia Methodism from 1786 to 1866* (Atlanta: A. R. Caldwell, 1913), 267.

36. "Editors Table: Wesley and Christian Perfection," *Quarterly Review of the M. E. Church, South* (January 1893): 396, 397.

37. Lovick Pierce accepted Palmer's views, as did three of his colleagues—Russell Reneau, J. A. Evans, and Samuel Anthony—in the North Georgia Conference of the MECS. Turley, *Wheel within a Wheel,* 76. Evans, one of the oldest preachers in the North Georgia Conference, became a convert of Palmer's in 1854 and opposed the election of George Pierce to bishop on the grounds that Pierce denied the second blessing. Harold W. Mann, *Atticus Greene Haygood: Methodist Bishop, Editor, and Educator* (Athens: University of Georgia Press, 1965), 161. Rev. John F. Tillet of North Carolina also accepted Palmer's theology in the years before the Civil War. Robert Stanley Ingersol, "Burden of Dissent: Mary Lee Cagle and the Southern Holiness Movement" (Ph.D. diss., Duke University, 1989), 38.

38. See "Sanctification—Another Letter," *Weekly Message,* 6 November 1851, 1; "Entire Sanctification—Another Letter," *Weekly Message,* 29 November 1851, 2; quote from "Holiness," *Weekly Message,* 12 February 1852, 1; and "A Sad Mistake," *The Message,* 29 March 1861, 1.

39. On the holiness revival's northern urban origins, see Smith, *Revivalism and Social Reform,* 9–10, 23, 62. J. Lawrence Brasher, *The Sanctified South: John Lakin Brasher and the Holiness Movement* (Urbana: University of Illinois Press, 1994), 34.

40. *The Guide to Holiness* 30 (1856): 158, quoted in Smith, *Revivalism and Social Reform,* 144.

41. *The Way of Holiness* (May 1876): 16. Historian Charles Edward White points out that five hundred subscribers in Mississippi could no longer receive the magazine after the outbreak of war. Charles Edward White, *The Beauty of Holiness: Phoebe Palmer as Theologian, Revivalist,*

Feminist, and Humanitarian (Grand Rapids: Zondervan Publishing House, 1986), 93.

42. Writing at the same time as W. J. Cash, Clement Eaton noted, "At a period when the rest of the United States was effervescing with experiments of utopias and efforts to eradicate 'the evils' of society, the South was strikingly free from reformers." Against their northern foes, "the Southern people set up an intellectual blockade, a *cordon sanitaire.*" Clement Eaton, *Freedom of Thought in the Old South* (New York: Peter Smith, 1951), 315–317. For a counterargument to Eaton's, see O'Brien, *Rethinking the South.*

43. Peters, *Christian Perfection and American Methodism,* 131–132.

44. Bertram Wyatt-Brown, *Hearts of Darkness: Wellsprings of a Southern Literary Tradition* (Baton Rouge: Louisiana State University Press, 2003), 66. On the defensive posture of the white South, see Elizabeth Fox Genovese and Eugene Genovese, "The Divine Sanction of the Social Order: Religious Foundations of the Southern Slaveholders' World View," *Journal of the American Academy of Religion* 55 (Summer 1987): 215.

45. Douglas Strong, *Perfectionist Politics: Abolitionism and the Religious Tensions of American Democracy* (Syracuse: Syracuse University Press, 1999), 4, 7–8, 2. Mitchell Snay, *Gospel of Disunion: Religion and Separatism in the Antebellum South* (Cambridge: Cambridge University Press, 1993), 13. John R. McKivigan, "The Sectional Division of the Methodist and Baptist Denominations as Measures of Northern Anti-Slavery Sentiment," in *Religion and the Antebellum Debate over Slavery,* ed. John R. McKivigan and Mitchell Snay (Athens: University of Georgia Press, 1998), 344.

46. Strong, *Perfectionist Politics,* 93. The Wesleyan Methodists and the Free Methodists, both reform sects, though established some years apart, early identified themselves as holiness churches. Smith, *Revivalism and Social Reform,* 129–131, 116–117. Timothy Smith and John L. Peters contended that denominational disunion was not the result of differing theologies. At a fundamental level, however, theological disparities were implicit causes. Smith, *Revivalism and Social Reform,* 25. Peters, *Christian Perfection and American Methodism,* 124, 126.

47. Lee M. Haines, "Radical Reform and Living Piety," in *Reformers and Revivalists: The History of the Wesleyan Church,* ed. Wayne E. Caldwell (Indianapolis: Wesley Press, 1992), 41–42.

48. Orange Scott, *An Appeal to the Methodist Episcopal Church*

(Boston, 1838), 138, quoted in Donald G. Mathews, *Slavery and Methodism: A Chapter in American Morality, 1780–1845* (Princeton: Princeton University Press, 1965), 208. Stanley Harrold, *The Abolitionists and the South, 1831–1861* (Lexington: University Press of Kentucky, 1995), 27.

49. In the late 1840s the Wesleyan Methodists claimed 386 members in Virginia and North Carolina. Roy S. Nicholson, *Wesleyan Methodism in the South* (Syracuse: Wesleyan Methodist Publishing House, 1933), 29, 31, 40.

50. On northern efforts to distribute abolitionist literature, see Bertram Wyatt-Brown, "The Abolitionists' Postal Campaign of 1835," *Journal of Negro History* 50 (October 1965): 227–238. For the southern response, see Snay, *Gospel of Disunion*, 19–20, 33.

51. Nicholson, *Wesleyan Methodism in the South*, 29–30, 39, 37, 42, 82, 98.

52. The *Richmond Times*, the *National Era*, the *Greensboro Patriot*, and other newspapers inflamed public outrage with articles condemning the missionaries. Nicholson, *Wesleyan Methodism in the South*, 73, 74.

53. Mathews, *Religion in the Old South*, 175. Loveland, *Southern Evangelicals and the Social Order*, 259.

54. On the lack of guilt over slavery among white southerners, see Eugene D. Genovese, *Roll, Jordan, Roll: The World the Slaveholders Made* (New York: Vintage Books, 1976), 120. Loveland, *Southern Evangelicals and the Social Order*, 192, 217. Farmer, *The Metaphysical Confederacy*, 199. Donald Mathews suggests that through a slaveholding ethic and missions to the slaves, southern evangelicals developed a practical religious defense against outside criticism. Mathews, *Religion in the Old South*, 136–137, 149–150. In his study of the holiness movement in Georgia, Briane Turley argues that the pervasiveness of guilt impeded the progress of perfectionism. It is unlikely that uneasiness over slavery played a large role. Nevertheless, a broader theological preoccupation with guilt, sin, and human depravity surely proved critical. Turley, *Wheel within a Wheel*, 79–86. In his study of religious division in antebellum America, Mitchell Snay examines the biblical defense of slavery. "Slavery, in the minds of southern clergymen, was clearly and unequivocally sanctioned in the Bible," he writes. Any attack on slavery was thus an assault on God's moral order. "Abolitionism then became a dangerous form of religious infidelity that threatened not only slavery but the basic fabric of Western civilization." Snay, *Gospel of Disunion*, 60. For analyses of the development of

proslavery thought, see Larry E. Tise, *Proslavery: A History of the Defense of Slavery in America, 1701–1840* (Athens: University of Georgia Press, 1987); Drew Gilpin Faust, *A Sacred Circle: The Dilemma of the Intellectual in the Old South, 1840–1860* (Baltimore: Johns Hopkins University Press, 1977); and Genovese and Genovese, "The Divine Sanction of the Social Order."

55. Quoted in David Brown, *The Planter: Or, Thirteen Years in the South* (Philadelphia: H. Hooker, 1853), 16. George Foster Pierce considered the abolitionist much more than a misguided philanthropist: "He was a wild fanatic, an insane anarchist, a law-breaker, a wicked intermeddler in other men's matters, who was disloyal to the laws of God and of man." Pierce's father, Lovick Pierce, lamented the division of the Methodist Church and was ill at ease with secession. The younger Pierce, less disposed to perfectionism than his father, may represent a new generation of sectionalists who came of age in the period of greatest political strife. Smith, *Life and Times of George Foster Pierce,* 435, 437. Mann, *Atticus Greene Haygood,* 43. Turley, *Wheel within a Wheel,* 78.

56. "The New Catechism," *Macon Daily Telegraph,* 3 May 1860, 2.

57. Robert W. Delp, "The Southern Press and the Rise of American Spiritualism, 1847–1860," *Journal of American Culture* 7 (Fall 1984): 94, 91.

58. Ibid., 88.

59. Hunter Dickson Farish, *The Circuit Rider Dismounts: A Social History of Southern Methodism, 1865–1900* (Richmond: Dietz Press, 1938), 28–29, 21, 30, 31. Daniel Stowell, *Rebuilding Zion: The Religious Reconstruction of the South, 1863–1877* (New York: Oxford University Press, 1998), 18–19, 21.

60. Stowell, *Rebuilding Zion,* 33–48, 49–64.

61. Farish, *The Circuit Rider Dismounts,* 45–50. When Union forces captured Charleston, South Carolina, in 1865, northern denominations seized church properties and installed ministers in six of the principal pulpits of the city. Francis Butler Simkins and Robert Hilliard Woody, *South Carolina during Reconstruction* (Chapel Hill: University of North Carolina Press, 1932), 376. For more on northern Methodism and the postwar South, see Ralph E. Morrow, *Northern Methodism and Reconstruction* (East Lansing: Michigan State University Press, 1956), 20–25.

62. Donald G. Jones, *The Sectional Crisis and Northern Methodism: A Study in Piety, Political Ethics, and Civil Religion* (Metuchen, N.J.: Scarecrow Press, 1979), 247–301.

63. Farish, *The Circuit Rider Dismounts*, 52. Nearly a century after northern Methodists descended on the South, the historian Ralph E. Morrow noted that "no other church in Christendom more earnestly tried to release the Negro from the shackles of ignorance." Morrow, *Northern Methodism and Reconstruction*, 248.

64. Farish, *The Circuit Rider Dismounts*, 212. *Advocate*, 24 June 1869, quoted ibid., 59. Farish thought that the aggressive policies of northern Methodists retarded reform in the South. Loyalists denounced individuals influenced by northern reform ideas as monomaniacs and "negrophiles," and accused them of "Yankee fanaticism." Farish, *The Circuit Rider Dismounts*, 161. As late as 1895 the editor of the premier Methodist journal in the South bitterly complained of northern encroachments. When the *Northwestern Christian Advocate* chided white southerners for their abuse and neglect of African Americans and called for missionaries to take the gospel to the South, the southern editor scorned northern benevolence. African Americans, he wrote, received numerous benefits and opportunities from paternalistic southern whites. "Fraternal Sweetness," *Christian Advocate*, 10 January 1895, 1.

65. Stowell, *Rebuilding Zion*, 130, 28, 133. According to the religious historian Paul Harvey, "Just as carpetbaggers had 'stolen' the reins of politics, so northern missionaries would seize control of the ecclesiastical government and religious customs of the South." Paul Harvey, *Redeeming the South: Religious Cultures and Racial Identities among Southern Baptists, 1865–1925* (Chapel Hill: University of North Carolina Press, 1997), 23. See also Simkins and Woody, *South Carolina during Reconstruction*, 374–375. Eric Foner, *A Short History of Reconstruction, 1863–1877* (New York: Harper and Row, 1990), 129–130. For a discussion of the Puritan and Yankee values of religious carpetbaggers, see James M. McPherson, *The Abolitionist Legacy: From Reconstruction to the NAACP* (Princeton: Princeton University Press, 1975), 161–183.

66. William R. Glass, *Strangers in Zion: Fundamentalism in the South, 1900–1950* (Macon, Ga.: Mercer University Press, 2001), 34, 276.

67. George Hughes, *Days of Power in the Forest Temple: A Review of the Wonderful Work of God at Fourteen National Camp-Meetings from 1867 to 1872* (Boston: John Bent and Company, 1873), 10–17.

68. Dieter, *The Holiness Revival of the Nineteenth Century*, 86–89. Although the NCMAPH was interdenominational, Methodist divines dominated the organization's membership and top ranks.

69. Brasher, *Sanctified South*, 35. Ingersol, "Burden of Dissent," 39.

70. Wm. Baker, *A Concise Description of Middle Tennessee* (McMinnville, Tenn.: Wm. Baker and Son Printers, 1868), 5.

71. Foner, *A Short History of Reconstruction*, 130.

72. "My Own Experience," *The Way of Holiness* (February 1876): 8.

73. *The Way of Holiness* (April 1876): 25, and (August 1879): 141. Baker and Oliver also planned to publish a weekly holiness paper, *The Southern Methodist*. There is no evidence that they ever succeeded in this endeavor. Baker intended the weekly to be "devoted exclusively to religious reading of a higher type in point of spirituality than the weekly press of the church affords, pointing the reader to a higher attainment in religious experience than is commonly enjoyed by Christians." *The Way of Holiness* (May 1876): 1.

74. L. Pierce, "Experience of Rev. L. Pierce," *The Way of Holiness* (May 1876): 18.

75. Daniel Steele, "Five Years with the Indwelling Christ," *The Way of Holiness* (February 1876): 21, 22. Briane Turley proposes that in the late 1870s "southerners came to terms with defeat and began reordering their ambitions." Accordingly, "the antebellum rejection of the doctrine of instantaneous perfection gave way to acceptance among a growing number of Methodists." Turley, *Wheel within a Wheel*, 7, 87.

76. "A Word of Admonition," *The Way of Holiness* (August 1879): 141.

77. Helen Arnold, *Under Southern Skies: Reminiscences in the Life of Mrs. Adelia Arnold* (Atlanta: Repairer Publishing Company, 1924), 15. Evelyn Brooks Higginbotham, *Righteous Discontent: The Women's Movement in the Black Baptist Church, 1880–1920* (Cambridge, Mass.: Harvard University Press, 1993), 98. By the early twentieth century, *Hope* claimed a circulation of sixteen thousand. "Joanna P. Moore—1832–1916," *Crisis* 12 (August 1916): 178.

78. Joanna P. Moore, *"In Christ's Stead": Autobiographical Sketches* (Chicago: Women's Baptist Home Mission Society,), 229.

79. Daniels, "Cultural Renewal of Slave Religion," 153, 154, 163. Mary Mason, *The History and Life Work of Elder C. H. Mason, Chief Apostle, and His Co-Laborers* (n.p., 1924), 113. In her holiness work among African Americans, Moore was joined by Harrison Woodsmall, a white Baptist missionary from Indiana. Woodsmall, who had served as an Indiana delegate to the 1868 Republican National Convention, introduced scores of African Americans to sanctification doctrine through his writings, at black

Baptist conventions, and as president and teacher at black colleges in Alabama. Daniels, "Cultural Renewal of Slave Religion," 155–156. C. P. Jones met Joanna P. Moore in 1891. By all accounts she gave him a great deal of guidance on holiness. Yet according to a short biography of Jones, it was Elder A. N. Kelly, another northern evangelist, who ushered Jones into "Holy Ghost" baptism. J. H. Green, intro. to Charles P. Jones, *An Appeal to the Sons of Africa* (Jackson, Miss.: Truth Publishing Company, 1902), xi.

80. Quoted in Higginbotham, *Righteous Discontent,* 101.

81. A coalition of Wesleyan reformers from upstate New York and northern Illinois established the Free Methodist Church in 1860. Its founders were expelled from the Methodist Episcopal Church for their radical neo-Puritan beliefs. Free Methodists championed abolitionism and anti-Masonry. Sternly ascetic, they condemned church pew rental (a sign of the growing embourgeoisement of Methodism) and prohibited tobacco use, consumption of alcohol, costly attire, secular amusements, and instrumental church music. Leslie R. Marston, *From Age to Age a Living Witness: A Historical Interpretation of Free Methodism's First Century* (Winona Lake, Ind.: Light and Life Press, 1960).

82. Arnold, *Under Southern Skies,* 67.

83. Henry L. Fisher, *History of the United Holy Church of America, Inc.* (n.p., n.d.), 5. One of Lowney's key converts to holiness was H. L. Fisher. Fisher later helped found the United Holy Church of America, which became a leading holiness-pentecostal denomination in North Carolina.

84. Little is known of Whittier's wider work. Irving E. Lowery, *Life on the Old Plantation in Ante-Bellum Slavery Days, Or a Story Based on Facts* (Columbia, S.C.: State Company Printers, 1911), 24, 21. Daniels, "Cultural Renewal of Slave Religion," 157–158.

85. Smith, *Called unto Holiness,* 30–31. John A. McKinney, a Texas minister who avidly read Phoebe Palmer's *Guide to Holiness,* experienced sanctification under Wallace at Clavert, Texas. Afterwards, McKinney invited Wallace to hold a revival at Ennis, Texas. This meeting, according to firsthand accounts, proved to be Wallace's most influential revival. George McCulloch, *History of the Holiness Movement in Texas, and the Fanaticism which Followed* (Aquilla, Tex.: J. H. Padgett, 1886), 1.

86. Wealthy southern Methodists in towns where Wallace held his revivals thought *The Banner of Holiness* boorish and puritanical. The austere paper denounced all pleasures and excesses deemed self-indulgent or

sinful. Among these were tobacco, alcohol, costly churches, and church festivals or fundraising suppers. Smith, *Called unto Holiness,* 29, 31. C. B. Jernigan, *Pioneer Days of the Holiness Movement in the Southwest* (Kansas City, Mo.: Pentecostal Publishing House, 1919), 87–90.

87. "Corsicana Enthusiasts," *Texas Christian Advocate,* 22 November 1879, 2. William Miller, a Baptist lay preacher from New York, gained a large following in the early 1840s by predicting and preparing for the second coming of Christ. The "Corsicana Enthusiasts," like the Irvingites, can accurately be termed proto-pentecostal. Their eschatology and emphasis on spiritual gifts closely parallel the doctrines of later pentecostals. See Barry W. Hamilton, *William Baxter Godbey: Itinerant Apostle of the Holiness Movement* (Lewiston, N.Y.: Edwin Mellen Press, 2000), 76–77; and Larry Christenson, "Pentecostalism's Forgotten Forerunner," in *Aspects of Pentecostal-Charismatic Origins,* ed. Vinson Synan (Plainfield, N.J.: Logos International, 1975), 17–37.

88. "Too Much Preaching," *Texas Christian Advocate,* 20 December 1879, 6. Jernigan, *Pioneer Days of the Holiness Movement in the Southwest,* 150–151.

89. H. S. P. Ashby, "Sanctification—So-called," *Texas Christian Advocate,* 29 November 1879, 2. The gendered critique of antiholiness writers closely parallels northern and southern newspapermen's repudiation of Populism. Rebecca Edwards observes that Populist women, according to mainline critics, "were aggressive and threatening 'harpies' and 'shrews' whose power destabilized politics." Rebecca Edwards, *Angels in the Machinery: Gender in American Party Politics from the Civil War to the Progressive Era* (New York: Oxford University Press, 1997), 113.

90. Walter N. Vernon, Robert W. Sledge, Robert C. Monk, and Norman Spellman, *The Methodist Excitement in Texas: A History* (Dallas: Texas United Methodist Historical Society, 1984), 127–128.

91. Dennis Rogers, *Holiness Pioneering in the Southland* (Hemet, Calif., 1944), 16.

92. "The Theology of the Plymouth Brethren," *Southern Review* 42 (April 1877): 254, 256.

93. Warren A. Candler to A. J. Jarrell, 7 November 1885, quoted in Turley, *Wheel within a Wheel,* 109–110. A decade later Candler expressed similar reservations about the mostly northern-controlled Women's Christian Temperance Union. He denounced it with equal vehemence as a front for the women's suffrage movement. Mann, *Atticus Greene Haygood,* 155.

M. L. Haney, *The Story of My Life: An Autobiography* (Normal, Ill.: by the author, 1904), 385.

94. *The Christian Index* quoted in "The 'Holiness' Matter," *Atlanta Constitution,* 9 January 1883, 4.

95. "New and Old Reforms," *Atlanta Constitution,* 20 February 1890, 4.

96. Paul M. Gaston, *The New South Creed: A Study in Southern Mythmaking* (New York: Alfred A. Knopf, 1970), 48, 54.

97. Eva M. Watson, *George D. Watson, Fearless for the Truth* (1929; reprint, Salem, Ohio: Schmul Publishing Company, 2001), 13, 25.

98. Turley, *Wheel within a Wheel,* 90.

99. Smith, *History of Georgia Methodism from 1786 to 1866,* 401.

100. J. Wm. Garbutt, *William Asbury Dodge: Southern Holiness Pioneer,* ed. Kenneth O. Brown (1906; reprint, Hazelton, Pa.: Holiness Archives, 2001), 16.

101. F. W. Henck, "From Tennessee," *The Christian Witness and Advocate of Bible Holiness,* 27 October 1887, 5. At the end of the century most southern-born holiness adherents were either unaware of William Baker's contributions or thought them too insignificant to warrant attention. The north Georgia minister W. O. Butler considered William Asbury Dodge's paper *The Way of Life,* begun in 1882, to be the first southern holiness periodical. Garbutt, *William Asbury Dodge,* 43. G. W. Mathews also failed to note Baker's earlier efforts in a short history of the southern holiness movement. G. W. Mathews, "The Holiness Movement in the Southeast," *Pentecostal Herald,* 25 March 1908, 4.

102. Bud Robinson, *Sunshine and Smiles: Life Story, Flash Lights, Sayings, and Sermons* (Chicago: Christian Witness Company, 1903), 66. B. Carradine, *Sanctification* (Nashville: Publishing House of the M. E. Church, South, 1892), 11.

103. Irving E. Lowery, "The Need of Holiness Evangelists among the Colored People," *The Christian Witness and Advocate of Bible Holiness,* 19 November 1885, 1. For other personal testimonies to the paucity of holiness in southern communities before the mid-1880s, see C. B. Jernigan, *From the Prairie Schooner to a City Flat* (Brooklyn, N.Y.: C. B. Jernigan, 1926), 51; *The Old Methodist* (November 1889): 4; Joseph H. King, *Yet Speaketh: Memoirs of the Late Bishop Joseph H. King* (Franklin Springs, Ga.: Publishing House of the Pentecostal Holiness Church, 1949), 19, 27. Isaac

Gamble, "Memoir of Isaac Gamble, Colored Evangelist," *Live Coals of Fire,* 1 June 1900, 5.

2. HOLINESS STRANGERS IN A SOUTHERN ZION

1. Bud Robinson, *Sunshine and Smiles: Life Story, Flash Lights, Sayings, and Sermons* (Chicago: Christian Witness Company, 1903), 26.

2. Roger Glenn Robins, "Plainfolk Modernist: The Radical Holiness World of A. J. Tomlinson" (Ph.D. diss., Duke University, 1999), 53.

3. "A Church within a Church," *Southern Christian Advocate,* 9 June 1887, 4. "Holiness," *Southern Christian Advocate,* 16 June 1887, 4. "Letter from Natchez, Miss.," *Baptist and Reflector,* 25 June 1896, 4.

4. Merrill Elmer Gaddis, "Christian Perfectionism in America" (Ph.D. diss., University of Chicago, 1929), 457, 458. W. J. Cash, *The Mind of the South* (New York: Vintage Books, 1991), 289, 290. Later scholars—Richard Hofstadter, Robert Mapes Anderson, and David Edwin Harrell among them—employed the materialist model and assumed that the movement owed its beginnings and continued existence to the poverty and dispossession of rural southerners. H. Richard Niebuhr's work influenced such interpretations considerably. He maintained that religion "is so interwoven with social circumstances that the formulation of theology is necessarily conditioned by these." H. Richard Niebuhr, *The Social Sources of Denominationalism* (Cleveland: World Publishing Company, 1957), 17, 75–76. In the 1940s sociologists Liston Pope and John Holt argued that holiness found most of its adherents among society's dispossessed rural poor. For Holt and Pope, a believer's response to social crises was a natural byproduct of social disorganization. Holt posited that "migration and concomitant urbanization of an intensely rural, and religiously fundamentalist population" led to the creation of holiness sects, which yearned to "recapture their sense of security." John Holt, "Holiness Religion: Cultural Shock and Social Reorganization," *American Sociological Review* 5 (October 1940): 740–741. Liston Pope, *Millhands and Preachers: A Study of Gastonia* (New Haven: Yale University Press, 1942), 84–91, 126–140. For sociologists such as Charles Y. Glock and Howard Ellinson, religion served as an escape mechanism for the deprived who were unable to alter their social status. Charles Y. Glock, "The Role of Deprivation in the Origin and Evolution of Religious Groups," in *Religion and Social Conflict,* ed. Robert

Lee and Martin E. Marty (New York: Oxford University Press, 1964), 27, 29. For more recent yet similar views, see David Edwin Harrell Jr., "The Evolution of Plain-Folk Religion in the South," in *Varieties of Southern Religious Experience,* ed. Samuel S. Hill (Baton Rouge: Louisiana State University Press, 1988); David Edwin Harrell Jr., "Religious Pluralism: Catholics, Jews, and Sectarians," in *Religion in the South,* ed. Charles Reagan Wilson (Jackson: University of Mississippi Press, 1985); and selections from Robert Mapes Anderson, *Vision of the Disinherited: The Making of American Pentecostalism* (New York: Oxford University Press, 1979).

5. Robinson, *Sunshine and Smiles,* 10, 12, 27–29, 46.

6. Joseph H. King, *Yet Speaketh: Memoirs of the Late Bishop Joseph H. King* (Franklin Springs, Ga.: Publishing House of the Pentecostal Holiness Church, 1949), 13, 14, 17–18. For other examples of the lower-class roots of individuals who came of age in the postwar period, see W. B. Godbey, *Autobiography of Rev. W. B. Godbey, A. M.* (Cincinnati: God's Revivalist Office, 1909), 6, 23–24; M. M. Pinson, "Sketch of the Life and Ministry of Mack M. Pinson," 6 September 1949, Flower Pentecostal Heritage Center, Springfield, Mo., 1; Watson Sorrow, *Some of My Experiences* (Franklin Springs, Ga.: Publishing House of the Pentecostal Holiness Church, 1954), 8–9, 10; and George W. Stanley, *My Life's Experiences with God* (Franklin Springs, Ga.: Publishing House of the Pentecostal Holiness Church, n.d.), 9.

7. "Robert C. Oliver," *Southern Christian Advocate,* 10 December 1891, 1.

8. H. V. Synan, "Holmes, Nickels John," in *The New International Dictionary of Pentecostal and Charismatic Movements,* ed. Stanley M. Burgess and Eduard M. Van Der Maas (Grand Rapids: Zondervan, 2002), 730. N. J. Holmes and Wife, *Life Sketches and Sermons* (Royston, Ga.: Press of the Pentecostal Holiness Church, 1920).

9. Beverly Carradine, *Graphic Scenes* (1911; reprint, Salem, Ohio: Schmul Publishing Company, 1990), 8, 109–110. See also selections from Beverly Carradine, *Mississippi Stories* (1904; reprint, Salem, Ohio: Schmul Publishing Company, 1989).

10. J. Lawrence Brasher describes his grandfather, John Lakin Brasher, as a member of "the southern middle-class majority of self-sufficient farmers" described as "plain folk." J. Lawrence Brasher, *The Sanctified South: John Lakin Brasher and the Holiness Movement* (Urbana: University of Illinois Press, 1994), 4, 56. Ted Ownby, *Subduing Sa-*

tan: Religion, Recreation, and Manhood in the Rural South, 1865–1920 (Chapel Hill: University of North Carolina Press, 1990), 17.

11. Briane K. Turley, *A Wheel within a Wheel: Southern Methodism and the Georgia Holiness Association* (Macon, Ga.: Mercer University Press, 1999), 7–8, 18, 93–95. Turley may be faulted for focusing too heavily on the middle-class makeup of the movement and failing to recognize its predominance among the lower classes as well. For a similar revision of southern holiness, see Brasher, *The Sanctified South*, x, 173.

12. C. H. Mason and C. P. Jones both attended Arkansas Baptist College in the early 1890s. Historian Ithiel C. Clemmons characterizes Jones and others at the college as leaders of the black middle class in Mississippi, Tennessee, Arkansas, and Alabama who struggled "to convince whites of blacks' intellectual and social equality." Ithiel C. Clemmons, *Bishop C. H. Mason and the Roots of the Church of God in Christ* (Bakersfield, Calif.: Pneuma Life Publishing, 1996), 17. See the entry on Elder E. M. Page in Mary Mason, *The History and Life Work of Elder C. H. Mason, Chief Apostle, and His Co-Laborers* (n.p., 1924), 103–104. See also the short biographies of Church of Christ (Holiness) leaders in Otho B. Cobbins, *History of the Church of Christ (Holiness) U.S.A., 1895–1965* (New York: Vantage Press, 1966), 45–58. David Daniels argues that the black holiness movement in Mississippi emerged as a struggle within the new educated African American religious community: "These were the young progressive ministers dedicated to sound religion and racial uplift." Although black holiness believers differed from black mainliners, both intended to reform slave religion in the South. David Douglas Daniels, "The Cultural Renewal of Slave Religion: Charles Price Jones and the Emergence of the Holiness Movement in Mississippi" (Ph.D. diss., Union Theological Seminary, 1992), 7, 11, 12.

13. William Clair Turner, "The United Holy Church of America: A Study in Black Holiness-Pentecostalism" (Ph.D. diss., Duke University, 1984), 52–53.

14. J. Wm. Garbutt, *William Asbury Dodge: Southern Holiness Pioneer*, ed. Kenneth O. Brown (1906; reprint, Hazelton, Pa.: Holiness Archives, 2001), 51–52.

15. Robinson, *Sunshine and Smiles*, 74, 73.

16. Godbey, *Autobiography*, 281, 282, 283.

17. C. B. Jernigan, *Pioneer Days of the Holiness Movement in the Southwest* (Kansas City, Mo.: Pentecostal Publishing House, 1919), 111.

18. Timothy L. Smith, *Called unto Holiness: The Story of the Nazarenes, the Formative Years* (Kansas City, Mo.: Nazarene Publishing House, 1962), 47–53. Jernigan, *Pioneer Days,* 138.

19. Briane Turley, Stanley Ingersol, and J. Lawrence Brasher grapple, to some extent, with the regional aspect of the movement. Robert Stanley Ingersol, "Burden of Dissent: Mary Lee Cagle and the Southern Holiness Movement" (Ph.D. diss., Duke University, 1989); Turley, *Wheel within a Wheel;* Brasher, *The Sanctified South.* Yet most other historians deal primarily with the holiness movement as a national phenomenon, neglecting regional differentiation as a result. See, for example, Vinson Synan, *The Holiness-Pentecostal Tradition: Charismatic Movements in the Twentieth Century* (Grand Rapids: William B. Eerdmans, 1997); Charles Edwin Jones, *Perfectionist Persuasion: The Holiness Movement and American Methodism* (Metuchen, N.J.: Scarecrow Press, 1974); Melvin Easterday Dieter, *The Holiness Revival of the Nineteenth Century* (Lanham, Md.: Scarecrow Press, 1996); and Donald W. Dayton, *Theological Roots of Pentecostalism* (Metuchen, N.J.: Scarecrow Press, 1987).

20. Steven Hahn, *The Roots of Southern Populism: Yeoman Farmers and the Transformation of the Southern Upcountry, 1850–1890* (New York: Oxford University Press, 1983), 6, 10.

21. Bertram Wyatt-Brown, "The Antimission Movement in the Jacksonian South: A Study in Regional Folk Culture," *Journal of Southern History* 36 (November 1970): 501–529.

22. C. Vann Woodward, *Tom Watson: Agrarian Rebel* (New York: Oxford University Press, 1963), 68, 69.

23. Edward L. Ayers, *The Promise of the New South: Life after Reconstruction* (New York: Oxford University Press, 1992), 37, 38.

24. Michael R. Hyman, *The Anti-Redeemers: Hill-Country Political Dissenters in the Lower South from Redemption to Populism* (Baton Rouge: Louisiana State University Press, 1990), 13, 16, 17.

25. See David Edwin Harrell, "The South: Seedbed of Sectarianism," in *Varieties of Southern Evangelicalism,* ed. David Edwin Harrell (Macon, Ga.: Mercer University Press, 1981), 45–57.

26. Hunter Dickson Farish, *The Circuit Rider Dismounts: A Social History of Southern Methodism, 1865–1900* (Richmond, Va.: Dietz Press, 1938), 79, 80.

27. On the need for a broader understanding of southern religious culture, see Beth Barton Schweiger, "The Captivity of Southern Religious

History," paper delivered at a meeting of the Southern Intellectual History Circle, Birmingham, Ala., 21 February 1997. Among other things, Schweiger maintains that historians' notion of a Baptist-Methodist hegemony unduly overshadows profound religious differences in the region.

28. On the distribution of slaves and the production of cotton in the South, see Andrew K. Frank, *The Historical Atlas of the American South* (New York: Routledge, 1999), 40–41, 42–43.

29. On the failure of the holiness movement in southern Alabama, see G. D. Watson, "Holiness on the Gulf," *The Christian Witness and Advocate of Bible Holiness,* 20 December 1883, 5.

30. Brasher, *The Sanctified South,* 12, 16. Ingersol, "Burden of Dissent," 3, 61.

31. T. P. Crutcher, "The Future of Methodism," *Tennessee Methodist,* 25 June 1895, 2.

32. B. F. Haynes, *Tempest-Tossed on Methodist Seas; Or, A Sketch of My Life* (Louisville: Pentecostal Publishing Company, 1921), 205. "The Spirit of Independentism," *Baptist and Reflector,* 5 November 1896, 8. On the connection between holiness and Populism, see Joe Creech, *Righteous Indignation: Religion and the Populist Revolution* (Urbana: University of Illinois Press, 2006), 143–146.

33. Smith, *Called unto Holiness,* 26. Harold W. Mann, *Atticus Greene Haygood: Methodist Bishop, Editor, and Educator* (Athens: University of Georgia Press, 1965), 162.

34. On the widening gap between urban and rural Methodists, see Dieter, *Holiness Revival,* 172–173. On the growth of towns and cities, see Ayers, *Promise of the New South,* 55, 58–59, 62, 79. C. Vann Woodward noted that the urban population of the South Atlantic states climbed only 1 percent from 1890 to 1900. C. Vann Woodward, *Origins of the New South, 1877–1913* (Baton Rouge: Louisiana State University Press, 1951), 139–140. Of the 24,500 white southern Baptist churches in the region in the 1910s, 20,000 were rural and 18,000 of these heard preaching only once a month. For the same period, 16,500 of the 19,800 white southern Methodist churches were rural. Of these rural churches, 15,000 had once-a-month preaching. Victor I. Masters, *Country Church in the South* (Atlanta: Southern Baptist Convention, 1916), 119.

35. Social historian Hunter Dickson Farish noted that "from 1880 to 1888, the rate of increase in membership in the larger urban centers surpassed that in the Church at large." Farish, *The Circuit Rider Dismounts,*

68, 67, 69, 76–77. Membership growth in cites was accompanied by an increase in church wealth and elaborate accommodations.

36. "The Future of Methodism," *The American Outlook,* 15 July 1897, 2. For other examples of antiurban sentiment, see Smith, *Called unto Holiness,* 165, and Brasher, *The Sanctified South,* 150.

37. T. J. Jackson Lears, *No Place of Grace: Antimodernism and the Transformation of American Culture, 1880–1920* (New York: Pantheon Books, 1981), 28, 29, 30, 6. On rising standards of refinement and class stratification in Victorian-era urban America, see John F. Kasson, *Rudeness and Civility: Manners in Nineteenth-Century Urban America* (New York: Hill and Wang, 1990), 6–7.

38. Vinson Synan, *Old Time Power: A Centennial History of the International Pentecostal Holiness Church* (Franklin Springs, Ga.: LifeSprings Resources, 1998), 56. Synan, *The Holiness-Pentecostal Tradition,* 58.

39. H. C. Morrison, like countless others, considered tobacco use not only unhealthy and ungodly but also an inexcusable waste of money. Percival A. Wesche, *Henry Clay Morrison: Crusader Saint* (Berne, Ind.: Herald Press, 1963), 39. Ayers, *The Promise of the New South,* 168.

40. "Letter from Natchez, Miss.," *Baptist and Reflector,* 25 June 1896, 4.

41. W. D. McGraw, "A Testimony from Texas," *The Way of Faith,* 21 October 1896, 5.

42. L. L. Pickett and M. A. Smith, *The Pickett-Smith Debate on Entire Sanctification, a Second Blessing* (Louisville: Pickett Publishing Company, 1897), 101. In this sense holiness groups resembled earlier evangelicals, whose asceticism distanced them from conventional society. Donald G. Mathews, *Religion in the Old South* (Chicago: University of Chicago Press, 1977), 20. Stanley Ingersol finds that the legalism of perfectionist preachers like R. L. Harris owed much to the northern Free Methodist sect of which Harris was a member. Ingersol, "Burden of Dissent," 147, 296. Yet this case cannot be made for the majority of holiness people, who were not affiliated with such northern denominations. It is more likely, then, that the legalism of the southern movement was a more organic response to the social and cultural milieu of the late-century South.

43. Clement C. Cary, *The Evils of Theater-Going: A Sermon Preached at St. John's Methodist Church, Atlanta, Ga., February 19, 1893* (Atlanta: by the author, 1893), 5.

44. R. Laurence Moore, *Selling God: American Religion in the Market-*

place of Ideas (New York: Oxford University Press, 1994), 164–165. Ownby, *Subduing Satan,* 66. The historian Charles E. Jones argues that holiness religion aided rural Americans' adjustment to new urban settings. Jones, *Perfectionist Persuasion,* xii, 70, 81, 85. In the South, however, most holiness folk remained in the countryside. For them the new movement provided refuge against the onslaught of popular culture and urban values moving into the hinterlands.

45. Ownby, *Subduing Satan,* 57.

46. Turley, *Wheel within a Wheel,* 10, 11, 12.

47. B. Carradine, *Church Entertainments: Twenty Objections* (Syracuse, N.Y.: A. W. Hall, 1898), 8, 24, 65, 72, 16. Pickett and Smith, *The Pickett-Smith Debate,* 233.

48. H. C. Morrison, *From the Pulpit to Perdition: A Strange Story* (Louisville: Pentecostal Publishing Company, 1899).

49. Atticus G. Haygood Sr., *The Monk and the Prince* (Nashville: Publishing House of the M. E. Church, South, 1895), 239.

50. King, *Yet Speaketh,* 49, 66–67, 70–71. The northern Alabama evangelist John Lakin Brasher also graduated from U. S. Grant University. Brasher, *The Sanctified South,* 54.

51. Robert H. Wiebe, *The Search for Order, 1877–1920* (New York: Hill and Wang, 1967), 47, xiii, 12.

52. Thomas Bender, *Community and Social Change in America* (New Brunswick, N.J.: Rutgers University Press, 1978), 89, 111, 113, 119, 108.

53. "Sectionalism," in *Proceedings of the Annual Session of the Supreme Council of the National Farmers Alliance and Industrial Union, at Ocala, Florida, December 2–8, 1890* (Washington, D.C.: National Economist, 1891), 11.

54. Historian Roger Glenn Robins finds radical holiness to be representative of a growing late-nineteenth-century transregional culture. Believers scorned "local importance" and moved in "larger spheres of life." Robins, "Plainfolk Modernist," 47, 48, 103–105.

55. Godbey, *Autobiography,* 154–155, 105. Godbey appears to have gloried in his many travels and his connection with individuals and movements all over the world. W. B. Godbey and Seth Cook Rees, *The Return of Jesus* (Cincinnati: God's Revivalist Office, 1898), 105.

56. Barry W. Hamilton, *William Baxter Godbey: Itinerant Apostle of the Holiness Movement* (Lewiston, N.Y.: Edwin Mellen Press, 2000), 104. George D. Watson mounted preaching tours in Canada, England, Japan,

Australia, and New Zealand. Eva M. Watson, *George D. Watson, Fearless for the Truth* (1929; reprint, Salem, Ohio: Schmul Publishing Company, 2001), 87. See also Pinson, "Sketch of the Life and Ministry of Mack M. Pinson," 5, 6.

57. Sorrow, *Some of My Experiences,* 7.

58. Ingersol, "Burden of Dissent," 69, 73. The restless Harris even served briefly as a missionary in Africa.

59. James Benjamin Hilson, *History of the South Carolina Conference of the Wesleyan Methodist Church of America: Fifty Years of Wesleyan Methodism in South Carolina* (Winona Lake, Ind.: Light and Life Press, 1950), 25.

60. Robinson, *Sunshine and Smiles,* 75.

61. Jernigan, *Pioneer Days,* 101–102. Examples of MEC attempts to attract southern holiness folk can be found in Smith, *Called unto Holiness,* 146, 160, 162; Wesche, *Henry Clay Morrison,* 86–87; and Brasher, *The Sanctified South,* 50–51.

62. "Religious Intelligence," *Alabama Christian Advocate,* 12 September 1895, 2.

63. Karen Lynell Kossie, "The Move Is On: African American Pentecostal-Charismatics in the Southwest" (Ph.D. diss., Rice University, 1998), xii–xiii.

64. Irving E. Lowery, "Holiness among the Colored People of Kingstree, S.C.," *The Christian Witness and Advocate of Bible Holiness,* 28 April 1887, 2.

65. Charles Price Jones, *An Appeal to the Sons of Africa* (Jackson, Miss.: Truth, 1902), 7. Daniel Stowell, *Rebuilding Zion: The Religious Reconstruction of the South, 1863–1877* (New York: Oxford University Press, 1998), 65, 69, 70.

66. J. Wofford White quoted in Irving E. Lowery, *Life on the Old Plantation in Ante-Bellum Slavery Days, Or a Story Based on Facts* (Columbia, S.C.: State Company Printers, 1911), 16.

67. William W. Freehling, *The South vs. the South: How Anti-Confederate Southerners Shaped the Course of the Civil War* (New York: Oxford University Press, 2001), xii, xiii, 22, 24, 61, 66. See also Daniel E. Sutherland, "Introduction: The Desperate Side of War," in *Guerrillas, Unionists, and Violence on the Confederate Home Front,* ed. Daniel E. Sutherland (Fayetteville: University of Arkansas Press, 1999), 3–15; and Hahn, *The Roots of Southern Populism,* 130–131.

68. Godbey, *Autobiography,* 90, 13–14. William B. Godbey, *Psychology and Pneumatology* (Cincinnati: God's Revivalist Press, n.d.), 25, quoted in Hamilton, *William Baxter Godbey,* 270, note 93. Haynes, *Tempest-Tossed,* 16–17.

69. J. B. Culpepper, *Some Women I Have Known* (Louisville: Pentecostal Publishing House, 1902), 12, 15, 16. W. C. Dunlap, *Life of S. Miller Willis: The Fire Baptized Lay Evangelist* (Atlanta: Constitution Publishing Company, 1892), 26. Watson, *George D. Watson,* 13.

70. Although Beverly Carradine's autobiography and W. A. Dodge's biography briefly mention the war, both are silent on their years in the Confederacy. Carradine, *Graphic Scenes,* 51. Garbutt, *William Asbury Dodge,* xi, 80, 120.

71. Charles Reagan Wilson, *Baptized in Blood: The Religion of the Lost Cause, 1865–1920* (Athens: University of Georgia Press, 1980), 1. See also Gaines M. Foster, *Ghosts of the Confederacy: Defeat, the Lost Cause, and the Emergence of the New South, 1865 to 1913* (New York: Oxford University Press, 1987).

72. "Gen. John B. Hood," *Christian Advocate,* 6 September 1879, 1. "Jefferson Davis," *Christian Advocate,* 12 December 1889, 8. "Robert E. Lee," *Christian Advocate,* 28 March 1895, 1. Lewis H. Foster, "A Veteran of Two Wars," *The Religious Herald,* 3 May 1906, 2.

73. "Is Sectionalism a Sin?" *The Religious Herald* quoted in *Christian Advocate,* 30 May 1895, 4. "Two Kinds of Sectionalism," *Christian Advocate,* 9 May 1895, 1. "Jefferson Davis," *Christian Advocate,* 12 December 1889, 8.

74. "National Campmeeting South," *The Christian Witness and Advocate of Bible Holiness,* 3 September 1885. "National Camp-Meeting in Georgia," *Zion's Herald,* 14 October 1885, 5. See also Watson, *George D. Watson,* 51–53, and later Nazarene reconciliationist efforts in Smith, *Called unto Holiness,* 178, 222–223.

75. C. Vann Woodward, *The Strange Career of Jim Crow* (New York: Oxford University Press, 2002), 70. David W. Blight, *Race and Reunion: The Civil War in American Memory* (Cambridge, Mass.: Harvard University Press, 2001), 9, 10.

76. "That They May Be One," *Zion's Outlook,* 7 February 1901, 8.

77. *The Revivalist* (June 1897): 6. W. B. Godbey, "Question Drawer," *God's Revivalist,* 31 January 1901, 12. Hamilton, *William Baxter Godbey,* 42–43. It is true, however, that holiness groups' equality of fellowship only

occasionally generated institutional equality. Donald G. Mathews, "'Christianizing the South'—Sketching a Synthesis," in *New Directions in American Religious History,* ed. Harry S. Stout and D. G. Hart (New York: Oxford University Press, 1997), 103.

78. "Ebon Priestess of Queer Sect," *Dallas Morning News,* 16 December 1900, 19.

79. Stowell, *Rebuilding Zion,* 182. Dodge encouraged other white evangelists to preach to black congregations, including Mrs. S. S. Garbutt. Garbutt, *William Asbury Dodge,* 111. For other examples of interracial revivals, see Geo. D. Watson, "The Work in Macon, Ga.," *The Christian Witness and Advocate of Bible Holiness,* 17 January 1884; "Letter from Natchez, Miss.," *Baptist and Reflector,* 25 June 1896, 4; and Mattie Perry, "Sister Mattie's Letter," *The Way of Faith,* 16 September 1896, 1. Lowery, "Holiness among the Colored People of Kingstree, S.C.," 2. The white holiness evangelist A. B. Crumpler regularly held integrated meetings in North Carolina. In 1896 the *Goldsboro Daily Argus* took notice of one such revival, reporting on a "colored service" Crumpler held in a building "filled with both races." Unlike at other mixed-race events, however, the African Americans in attendance, the reporter noted as a matter of fact, were "given the right of way" and treated with utmost respect. "The Crumpler Meeting," *Goldsboro Argus,* 24 June 1896, 5.

80. Frank Bartleman, *From Plow to Pulpit, From Maine to California* (Los Angeles: by the author, 1924), 41–42, 46, 48, 52, 59, 62, 42.

81. Cobbins, *History of the Church of Christ,* 49, 53, 128, 135, 136, 401, 416. "Our Weekly Sermon," *Truth,* 3 December 1903, 1.

82. "The Holiness Convention at Warrenton, Ga.," *The Christian Witness and Advocate of Bible Holiness,* 6 December 1883, 5. "From South Carolina," *The Christian Witness and Advocate of Bible Holiness,* 7 May 1885, 8. J. Livesey, "National Camp-Meeting in Georgia," *Zion's Herald,* 28 October 1885, 2. Turley, *Wheel within a Wheel,* 169–171. Bemused, Bartleman saw that whites in Florida "rode in separate cars here, and called for their mail at separate post office windows." Bartleman, *From Plow to Pulpit,* 51, 46.

83. Elizabeth R. Wheaton, *Prisons and Prayer: Or a Labor of Love* (Tabor, Iowa: Chas M. Kelley, 1906), 187.

84. L. P. Cushman, "Caste in the Methodist Episcopal Church," *The Christian Witness and Advocate of Bible Holiness,* 6 January 1887, 6. See

also L. P. Cushman, "Color-Line Holiness," *The Christian Witness and Advocate of Bible Holiness,* 17 December 1885, 1.

85. Mrs. James Cheek, *Cherished Memories: Or the Life of a Tennessee Girl* (Los Angeles: Bedrock Press, ca. 1945), 25, 34.

86. J. Livesey, "The Need of Holiness Evangelists among the Colored People," *The Christian Witness and Advocate of Bible Holiness,* 21 January 1886, 2. *Chautauqua Camp and Fireside* quoted in *The Old Methodist* (November 1889): 6.

87. J. A. Williams and Charlie D. Tillman, *Experience of J. A. Williams and His Favorite Songs* (Columbia, S.C.: Way of Faith, 191?), unpaginated.

88. Clement C. Cary, "From North Georgia," *The Pentecostal Herald,* 20 September 1899, 3.

89. On Populism and race, see Woodward, *Tom Watson;* Herbert Shapiro, "The Populist and the Negro: A Reconsideration," in *The Making of Black America,* ed. August Meier (New York: Atheneum, 1969), 32; and Gerald Gaither, *Blacks and the Populist Revolt: Ballots and Bigotry in the "New South"* (Tuscaloosa: University of Alabama Press, 1977).

90. On the rise of segregation and disfranchisement, see Woodward, *The Strange Career of Jim Crow,* and Ayers, *The Promise of the New South,* 156–159, 301–304. On the political and social motivations for lynching, see Terrence Finnegan, "Lynching and Political Power in Mississippi and South Carolina," in *Under Sentence of Death: Lynching in the South,* ed. W. Fitzhugh Brundage (Chapel Hill: University of North Carolina Press, 1997), 189–218. Blight, *Race and Reunion,* 221–230.

91. J. W. Rush, "'Fair Play,'" *Alabama Christian Advocate,* 17 January 1895, 1. J. W. Rush, "Shut Out," *Alabama Christian Advocate,* 11 July 1895, 1.

92. "The Other Side of the Negro Problem," *Southern Christian Advocate,* 25 March 1885, 2. For another, more detailed version of the redistribution plan written by a British traveler in the South, see William Archer, *An English Reading of the Race Problem* (New York: E. P. Dutton, 1910), 237–243. Archer imagined that a program of black redistribution would free the South of its ancestral crime of slavery. Archer rosily predicted that the region would "awaken, as from a nightmare, to the realization of its splendid destiny" (243).

93. "Another Lynching," *Christian Advocate,* 17 October, 1895, 1. Hunter Dickson Farish gives several examples of southern Methodist

newspapers clearly encouraging the staunch racial order of the day. Farish, *The Circuit Rider Dismounts,* 217–222. On the religious, sacrificial element of lynching, see Donald G. Mathews, "The Southern Rite of Human Sacrifice," *Journal of Southern Religion,* jsr.fsu.edu 3 (accessed 8/28/02).

94. Paul Harvey, *Redeeming the South: Religious Cultures and Racial Identities among Southern Baptists, 1865–1925* (Chapel Hill: University of North Carolina Press, 1997), 43, 42, 188–194, 232–233.

95. Irving E. Lowery, "The Need of Holiness Evangelists among the Colored People," *The Christian Witness and Advocate of Bible Holiness,* 19 November 1885, 1. Lowery, "A Wonderful Colored Man," *The Christian Witness and Advocate of Bible Holiness,* 7 April 1887, 2. J. T. Brown, a black evangelist writing to the white paper *Zion's Outlook,* described his successful work at a Columbia, Tennessee, African American holiness convention. "More than a score of people were swept into the experience of full salvation," he reported. *Zion's Outlook,* 10 October 1901, 12. In the late 1890s William E. Fuller, who established the Colored Fire-Baptized Holiness Church, read and was strongly influenced by J. M. Pike's *The Way of Faith.* Patrick L. Frazier Jr., *Introducing the Fire Baptized Holiness Church of God of the Americas* (Wilmington, N.C.: by the author, 1990), 9.

96. Daniels, "The Cultural Renewal of Slave Religion," 247, 248, 250. "Spreading among the White Baptists: The Holiness Work in South Carolina," *Truth,* 3 December 1903, 10. In addition, Jones covered the work of the white holiness minister L. P. Adams. In December 1903 Jones advertised Adams's Memphis Sunday school for whites, but noted that "all may drop in and learn." Jones also promoted Adams's eight-page monthly, *The Bible Witness.*

97. "Rev. W. A. Dodge's Work among the Colored People," *The Pentecostal Herald,* 24 February 1904, 4. Turley, *Wheel within a Wheel,* 170. For a discussion of other black periodicals, see Daniels, "The Cultural Renewal of Slave Religion," 247–248. The African American preacher G. A. Mials also operated a holiness paper which served a black readership in North Carolina. Mials, who helped found what would become the United Holy Church of America, published his *Holiness Review* between 1896 and 1898. G. A. Mail [sic], "Holiness among the Colored People in North Carolina," *The Way of Faith,* 14 March 1900, 1.

98. Elizabeth Fox-Genovese, "Social Order and the Female Self: The Conservatism of Southern Women in Comparative Perspective," in *What Made the South Different?* ed. Kees Gispen (Jackson: University Press of

Mississippi, 1990), 50. Stephanie McCurry argues that plain-folk whites developed patriarchal social relations as well, which aligned them with the plantocracy in the sectional crisis. Stephanie McCurry, *Masters of Small Worlds: Yeoman Households, Gender Relations, and the Political Culture of the Antebellum South Carolina Low Country* (New York: Oxford University Press, 1995). See also Jean E. Friedman, *The Enclosed Garden: Women and Community in the Evangelical South, 1830–1900* (Chapel Hill: University of North Carolina Press, 1985), 128–130.

99. Rebecca Edwards, *Angels in the Machinery: Gender in American Party Politics from the Civil War to the Progressive Era* (New York: Oxford University Press, 1997), 91–92, 100, 102.

100. Turley, *Wheel within a Wheel,* 133–142.

101. Garbutt, *William Asbury Dodge,* 100. William B. Godbey, *Woman Preacher* (Louisville: Kentucky Methodist Publishing, 1891), quoted in Ingersol, "Burden of Dissent," 152. Culpepper, *Some Women I Have Known,* 160–166. R. M. Guy, "Woman's Place under the Gospel," *The Pentecostal Herald,* 9 August 1899, 3, 4.

102. Annie May Fisher, *Woman's Right to Preach: A Sermon Reported as Delivered at Chilton, Texas* (San Antonio: by the author, n.d. [1904]), 3–8. See also Fannie McDowell Hunter, *Women Preachers* (Dallas: Berachab Press, 1905).

103. Mary Lee Cagle, *Life and Work of Mary Lee Cagle: An Autobiography* (Kansas City, Mo.: Nazarene Publishing House, 1928), 21–22.

104. *Nashville Christian Advocate,* quoted in the *New York Christian Advocate,* 26 September 1872, 306. W. A. McCarty, "Emancipated Woman," *New York Christian Advocate,* 30 May 1895, 3. "Are Women Better Than Men?" *Christian Advocate,* 23 January 1896, 1. On the conservative reaction to women's rights in the Southern Baptist Church, see Harvey, *Redeeming the South,* 211. "Woman Suffragist," *Alabama Christian Advocate,* 7 February 1895, 1. In August 1895 southern Methodist minister J. C. Morris delivered a sermon from his pulpit in Birmingham, Alabama, which outlined woman's proper place. "Her sphere is in the home," he insisted. "Physiology has plainly said that woman's sphere is at home as it has said that man is for the street and stores and workshop." "Woman's Rights," *Alabama Christian Advocate,* 1 August 1895, 1.

105. G. G. Smith, "Georgia Letter," *Southern Christian Advocate,* 9 August 1888, 1. "The State Press," *Dallas Morning News,* 13 August 1902, 6.

106. "Misreading the Scriptures," *Christian Advocate,* 11 June 1896, 1.

107. Jernigan, *Pioneer Days,* 33. Ingersol, "Burden of Dissent," 235.

108. Ingersol, "Burden of Dissent," 170. Henry E. Partridge, "Mississippi Letter," *The Way of Faith,* 27 November 1895, 2.

109. Lucille Sider Dayton and Donald Dayton, "'Your Daughters Shall Prophesy': Feminism in the Holiness Movement," in *Modern American Protestantism and Its World: Historical Articles on Protestantism in American Religious Life,* vol. 12, ed. Martin E. Marty (Munich: K. G. Saur, 1993), 260.

110. William B. Godbey, *Commentary on the New Testament,* vol. 5 (Cincinnati: Revivalist Office, 1896–1900), 18, quoted in Hamilton, *William Baxter Godbey,* 61.

3. The Words of God Spread South

1. L. L. Pickett, "Prefatory Introduction," in B. Carradine, *Sanctification* (Nashville: Publishing House of the M. E. Church, South, 1892), 3. Pickett would run as a Prohibition Party candidate in the 1907 Kentucky gubernatorial race. William C. Kostlevy, "Pickett, L(eander) L(ycurgus)," in *Historical Dictionary of the Holiness Movement,* ed. William C. Kostlevy (Lanham, Md.: Scarecrow Press, 2001), 205.

2. Alexis de Tocqueville, *Democracy in America,* ed. J. P. Mayer (Garden City, N.Y.: Anchor Books, 1969), 517, 518. John A. Hannigan aptly defines social movements as "collective attempts to articulate new grievances, construct new identities, and innovate new forms of association." John A. Hannigan, "Social Movement Theory and the Sociology of Religion: Toward a New Synthesis," *Sociological Analysis* 52 (1991): 326. I use Hannigan's basic definition when I refer to the holiness movement as a collective religious expression. Benedict Anderson, *Imagined Communities: Reflections on the Origins and Spread of Nationalism* (London: Verso, 1998), 36.

3. W. B. Godbey, *Autobiography of Rev. W. B. Godbey, A. M.* (Cincinnati: God's Revivalist Office, 1909), 10. "While the Bible must be your constant companion," Godbey wrote, reiterating a well-worn theme, "Holiness books constitute a loving cohort of faithful teachers on all lines of spiritual edification; while the good Holiness papers, like ministering angels, brighten your cottage with their pinions of light every week." W. B. Godbey, *Satan's Side-Tracks for Holiness People* (Nashville: Pentecostal Mission Publishing Company, n.d.), 40.

4. On the orality of holiness and pentecostal culture, see J. Lawrence Brasher, *The Sanctified South: John Lakin Brasher and the Holiness Movement* (Urbana: University of Illinois Press, 1994), xii, 69; Deborah Vansau McCauley, *Appalachian Mountain Religion: A History* (Urbana: University of Illinois Press, 1995), 257; Elmer T. Clark, *The Small Sects in America* (Nashville: Abingdon Press, 1965), 85, 98; Cheryl J. Sanders, *Saints in Exile: The Holiness-Pentecostal Experience in African American Religion and Culture* (New York: Oxford University Press, 1996), 49–52, 56; and Robert Mapes Anderson, *Vision of the Disinherited: The Making of American Pentecostalism* (New York: Oxford University Press, 1979), 223–227. For an examination of how readily radical evangelicals embraced modern advertising techniques, radio, and drama, see Betty A. DeBerg, *Ungodly Women: Gender and the First Wave of American Fundamentalism* (Minneapolis: Fortress Press, 1990); Douglas Carl Abrams, *Selling the Old-Time Religion: American Fundamentalists and Mass Culture, 1920–1940* (Athens: University of Georgia Press, 2001); Quintin J. Schultze, ed., *American Evangelicals and the Mass Media: Perspectives on the Relationship between American Evangelicals and the Mass Media* (Grand Rapids: Zondervan, 1990); Lillian Taiz, *Hallelujah Lads and Lasses: Remaking the Salvation Army in America, 1880–1930* (Chapel Hill: University of North Carolina Press, 2001), 4–5, 74–75, 79–90; Grant Wacker, "Searching for Eden with a Satellite Dish: Primitivism, Pragmatism, and the Pentecostal Character," in *Religion and American Culture,* ed. David G. Hackett (New York: Routledge, 1995), 445–446; and Edith Blumhofer, *Aimee Semple McPherson: Everybody's Sister* (Grand Rapids: William B. Eerdmans Publishing Company, 1993), 266–268. On holiness in particular, Roger Glenn Robins's work is most illuminating. Robins describes radical holiness men and women as "plainfolk modernists," by which he means they "expressed a vibrant strain of modernism, though one voiced in the idioms of plainfolk culture." Robins largely relates the holiness movement to "emerging social and economic transformations implied by the term, 'modernization' (evidenced most conspicuously in the rise of a market culture, entrepreneurial capitalism, and popular forms of mass discourse)." Roger Glenn Robins, "Plainfolk Modernist: The Radical Holiness World of A. J. Tomlinson" (Ph.D. diss., Duke University, 1999), 6, 7.

5. Anderson, *Imagined Communities,* 36, 32–35.

6. John F. Kasson, *Rudeness and Civility: Manners in Nineteenth-Century Urban America* (New York: Hill and Wang, 1990), 39, 37.

7. R. Laurence Moore, *Selling God: American Religion in the Marketplace of Ideas* (New York: Oxford University Press, 1994), 18–19. Nathan O. Hatch, *The Democratization of American Christianity* (New Haven: Yale University Press, 1989), 125–126.

8. Henry Smith Stroupe, *The Religious Press in the South Atlantic States, 1802–1865* (New York: AMS Press, 1956), 26.

9. On the rise of devotional literature, see Charles H. Lippy, *Being Religious, American Style: A History of Popular Religiosity in the United States* (Westport, Conn.: Praeger Publishers, 1994), 17, 147.

10. Hatch, *The Democratization of American Christianity*, 134.

11. Ibid., 141–142, 144–145.

12. Michael Emery, Edwin Emery, and Nancy L. Roberts, *The Press in America: An Interpretive History of the Mass Media* (Boston: Allyn and Bacon, 2000), 157. George H. Douglas, *The Golden Age of the Newspaper* (Westport, Conn.: Greenwood Press, 1999), 83–86. Kevin G. Barnhurst and John Nerone, *The Form of the News: A History* (New York: Guilford Press, 2001), 105–106.

13. For an examination of how the press influenced the First Great Awakening, see Frank Lambert, *Inventing the "Great Awakening"* (Princeton: Princeton University Press, 1999), 87–124; Harry S. Stout, *The Divine Dramatist: George Whitefield and the Rise of Modern Evangelicalism* (Grand Rapids: Eerdmans Publishing Company, 1991), 113–132; and T. H. Breen, "Retrieving Common Sense: Rights, Liberties, and the Religious Public Sphere in Late Eighteenth-Century America," in *To Secure the Blessings of Liberty: Rights in American History,* ed. Josephine F. Pacheco (Fairfax, Va.: George Mason University Press, 1993), 55–65. On the role played by the press in the Third Great Awakening, see Timothy L. Smith, *Revivalism and Social Reform: American Protestantism on the Eve of the Civil War* (Gloucester, Mass.: Peter Smith, 1976), 63–64, and Kathryn Long, *The Revival of 1857–58: Interpreting an American Religious Awakening* (New York: Oxford University Press, 1998), 26–45.

14. The term "movement culture" is used here to indicate what Rhys H. Williams and Susan M. Alexander describe as a "collection of ideas, symbols, meanings, and values that form a movement's self-identification. It builds solidarity within the movement and distinguishes the movement's 'we' from the opposition's 'they.'" Rhys H. Williams and Susan M. Alexander, "Religious Rhetoric in American Populism: Civil Religion as Move-

ment Ideology," *Journal for the Scientific Study of Religion* 33 (March 1994): 2.

15. "The Old Paths," *The Way of Holiness* (April 1876): 2.

16. Virginia Lieson Brereton, *From Sin to Salvation: Stories of Women's Conversions, 1800 to the Present* (Bloomington: Indiana University Press, 1991), 63.

17. "Sammy Hick on the Higher Life," *The Way of Holiness* (April 1876): 13.

18. "Ought Not Such to Profess Holiness" and "Editors Remarks," *The Way of Holiness* (April 1876): 12–13, 13–15.

19. In her study of conversion narratives, Virginia Lieson Brereton observes that the "altered understanding of sin and grace that emerged with holiness obviously required a different language. Those who wrote about holiness typically drew on a special vocabulary." Brereton, *From Sin to Salvation,* 64.

20. For excellent treatments of the theology and spiritual geography of holiness folk, see Charles Edwin Jones, *Perfectionist Persuasion: The Holiness Movement and American Methodism* (Metuchen, N.J.: Scarecrow Press, 1974), 35–46, and Steven D. Cooley, "Applying the Vagueness of Language: Poetic Strategies and Campmeeting Piety in the Mid-Nineteenth Century," *Church History* 36 (December 1994): 570–586.

21. J. B. Stevenson, "Where Am I Now?" *The Way of Holiness* (April 1876): 16, 17.

22. J. W. Baker, "Letter from Georgia," *The Way of Holiness* (May 1876): 22.

23. Long, *The Revival of 1857–58,* 27.

24. David W. Blight, *Race and Reunion: The Civil War in American Memory* (Cambridge, Mass.: Harvard University Press, 2001), 211, 216. For a study of Lost Cause ideology as a civil religion, see Charles Reagan Wilson, *Baptized in Blood: The Religion of the Lost Cause, 1865–1920* (Athens: University of Georgia Press, 1980). On the popularity and meaning of regional literature, see Richard H. Brodhead, *Cultures of Letters: Scenes of Reading and Writing in Nineteenth-Century America* (Chicago: University of Chicago Press, 1993), 115–141.

25. Nina Silber, *The Romance of Reunion: Northerners and the South, 1865–1900* (Chapel Hill: University of North Carolina Press, 1993), 66–67, 68.

26. "In the South," *The Christian Witness and Advocate of Bible Holiness,* 19 July 1883, 4.

27. "A Trip to Windsor, Fla.," *The Christian Witness and Advocate of Bible Holiness,* 21 February 1884, 5. "In the South," *The Christian Witness and Advocate of Bible Holiness,* 18 March 1886, 4.

28. "The Sunny South," *The Christian Witness and Advocate of Bible Holiness,* 12 May 1887, 2. "From Florida," *The Christian Witness and Advocate of Bible Holiness,* 28 April 1887, 6–7.

29. "From the South," *The Christian Witness and Advocate of Bible Holiness,* 22 September 1887, 8. See also C. M. Robeck Jr., "Pike, John Martin," in *The New International Dictionary of Pentecostal and Charismatic Movements,* ed. Stanley M. Burgess and Eduard M. Van Der Maas (Grand Rapids: Zondervan, 2002), 988–989.

30. "Advertisements," *The Way of Faith,* 5 August 1896, 4.

31. Briane Turley, *A Wheel within a Wheel: Southern Methodism and the Georgia Holiness Association* (Macon, Ga.: Mercer University Press, 1999), 93.

32. J. Wm. Garbutt, *William Asbury Dodge: Southern Holiness Pioneer,* ed. Kenneth O. Brown (1906; reprint, Hazelton, Pa.: Holiness Archives, 2001), 69, 43. In 1890 a one-year subscription to *The Way of Life* cost one dollar. "Some Popular Papers," *Atlanta Constitution,* 23 October 1892, 11.

33. Morrison first titled his paper *The Old Methodist,* indicating his primitivist agenda. His inaugural issue numbered 500 copies. In 1898 the paper claimed 20,000 subscribers. By 1934 Morrison's journal had a press run of 38,000. More surprising, four years after that, circulation climbed to 55,000. Percival A. Wesche, *Henry Clay Morrison: Crusader Saint* (Berne, Ind.: Herald Press, 1963), 52, 53, 62. I am indebted to William Kostlevy for providing me with this source. *The Pentecostal Herald,* 12 January 1898, 1, and 9 February 1898, 1.

34. Garbutt, *William Asbury Dodge,* 40. Dennis Rogers, *Holiness Pioneering in the Southland* (Hemet, Cal., 1944), 28. Thomas D. Clark, *The Rural Press and the New South* (Baton Rouge: Louisiana State University Press, 1948), 3–4. In January 1904 A. J. Tomlinson, one of the founders of the Church of God (Cleveland), purchased a small treadle press for $125. With this easy-to-operate machine he began publishing *The Way* from his home in Culberson, North Carolina. Joel R. Trammell, "Publishing the Gospel," *Church of God History and Heritage* (Winter 1998): 2. Years be-

fore M. M. Pinson helped establish the Assemblies of God, he bought a press and type in New Orleans for approximately $300. He intended to reach thousands with a planned holiness paper, until an insolvent business partner wrecked the venture. M. M. Pinson, "Sketch of the Life and Ministry of Mack M. Pinson," Flower Pentecostal Heritage Center, Springfield, Mo., 6 September 1949, 6.

35. Martin Wells Knapp, "The Revised Name," *God's Revivalist,* 3 January 1901, 1. On holiness adherents' use of pentecostal imagery, see Donald W. Dayton, *Theological Roots of Pentecostalism* (Metuchen, N.J.: Scarecrow Press, 1987), 174–175. See *The Revivalist* for January and June 1894 and January 1893. *Lightning Bolts from Pentecostal Skies, or Devices of the Devil Unmasked* was also the title of an influential book Knapp published in 1898. For the most incisive discussion of Knapp's role in the radical holiness movement, see William Kostlevy, "Nor Silver, Nor Gold: The Burning Bush Movement and the Communitarian Holiness Vision" (Ph.D. diss., University of Notre Dame, 1996), 21–48. See also Jones, *Perfectionist Persuasion,* 100.

36. Lloyd Raymond Day, "A History of God's Bible School in Cincinnati, 1900–1949" (M.A. thesis, University of Cincinnati, 1949), 22. Seth Cook Rees, a former Indiana Quaker who turned independent holiness evangelist, teamed up with Knapp and became one of the most widely read holiness writers. Rees considered *The Revivalist* critical to the movement's success. "It affords us an opportunity of speaking to thousands of souls which we could not reach by word of mouth," noted Rees. S. C. Rees, "A Stirring Appeal," *The Revivalist,* 16 February 1899, 9.

37. Edward L. Ayers, *The Promise of the New South: Life after Reconstruction* (New York: Oxford University Press, 1992), 418. Nonetheless, white southern literacy rates fell far below northern as well as national averages. In 1900 roughly 98 percent of northern whites were literate, as were 95 percent nationwide. C. Vann Woodward, *Origins of the New South, 1877–1913* (Baton Rouge: Louisiana State University Press, 1951), 400.

38. Evelyn Brooks Higginbotham's history of the women's movement in the black Baptist Church analyzes these changes and the church's role in facilitating them. "As black literacy rose from a mere 5 percent in 1860 to 70 percent in 1910," notes Higginbotham, "the church served as a major site of print production in black communities." She observes that "black literacy as well as the number of black students at secondary, college, and professional levels grew notably in the post-Reconstruction years because

of the combined role of black self-help and white philanthropy." Evelyn Brooks Higginbotham, *Righteous Discontent: The Women's Movement in the Black Baptist Church, 1880–1920* (Cambridge, Mass.: Harvard University Press, 1993), 11, 89. Sociologist Cheryl Townsend Gilkes demonstrates that the black sanctified church placed heavy emphasis on education and literacy. Educational goals of "general literacy, biblical literacy, advanced academic and professional achievement, and biblical expository skills" ranked second in priority after salvation and holiness. Cheryl Townsend Gilkes, "'Together and in Harness': Women's Traditions in the Sanctified Church," *Signs* 10 (Summer 1985): 687. On black papers in this era, see Steven Hahn, *A Nation under Our Feet: Black Political Struggles in the Rural South from Slavery to the Great Migration* (Cambridge, Mass.: Harvard University Press, 2003), 461–462. W. B. Godbey, like many other holiness ministers, told his readers, "You need a classical education to qualify you to successfully study the Bible." Holiness people, Godbey believed, must have at least a rudimentary knowledge of Hebrew and Greek in order to understand scriptures. Literacy in English was presumed indispensable. Godbey, *Autobiography*, 75, 76–77.

39. Combined circulation for several leading southern holiness papers indicates widespread literacy. In the 1890s, *The Way of Life, The Kentucky Methodist* (which became *The Pentecostal Herald*), *The Way of Faith,* and *The Revivalist* reported a combined total of approximately 51,000 copies in print at any one time. Garbutt, *William Asbury Dodge,* 69. Wesche, *Henry Clay Morrison,* 62. "Advertisements," *The Way of Faith,* 5 August 1896, 4. Day, "A History of God's Bible School in Cincinnati," 22. Since figures for many other popular holiness papers are unavailable, total circulation of perfectionist newspapers and journals in the South during the decade may well have exceeded 100,000.

40. John Leland Peters, *Christian Perfection and American Methodism* (New York: Abingdon Press, 1956), 139. B. F. Haynes, a southern Methodist minister in Tennessee, was typical of these small holiness publishers. After experiencing entire sanctification in 1894, he transformed his populist-style periodical *The Tennessee Methodist* into a holiness journal. The paper served the needs of holiness evangelists who carried the periodical into the hundreds of communities where they preached. Haynes also established the B. F. Haynes Publishing Company in Nashville as a subscription book business, which he then advertised in his newspaper. Under this company's rubric he published a volume of sermons and lectures by the

popular evangelist Sam Jones, titled *Thunderbolts.* Haynes's success was brief. Southern Methodist officials cracked down on the holiness entrepreneur for criticizing and then denouncing the MECS. As a result, Haynes's publishing ventures suffered. He first gave up his subscription business; then, after mortgaging his house to help support the paper, he eventually sold his interest in the journal, renamed *Zion's Outlook,* to another holiness group in Nashville. B. F. Haynes, *Tempest-Tossed on Methodist Seas; Or, A Sketch of My Life* (Louisville: Pentecostal Publishing Company, 1921), 228–229.

41. L. Pierce, *A Miscellaneous Essay on Entire Sanctification: Showing How It Was Lost from the Church and How It May and Must Be Regained* (Nashville: Publishing House of the M. E. Church, South, 1897), 39.

42. Frank Bartleman, *From Plow to Pulpit, From Maine to California* (Los Angeles: by the author, 1924), 41, 43, 44, 46, 48. *The Way of Faith,* 11 December 1895, 1.

43. D. A. Futrell, *A Backward Glance at Primitive Methodism* (Columbia, S.C.: Way of Faith Publishing House, 1895), 33.

44. Godbey, *Autobiography,* 499. John Wesley's *Plain Account of Christian Perfection* was possibly the most widely read text among southern holiness converts. It was repeatedly cited by advocates as their introduction to holiness.

45. Godbey, *Autobiography,* 498. Barry W. Hamilton, *William Baxter Godbey: Itinerant Apostle of the Holiness Movement* (Lewiston, N.Y.: Edwin Mellen Press, 2000), 95–96, 107, 109.

46. "Eighteenth National Camp Meeting," *Knoxville Daily Chronicle,* 19 September 1873, 4.

47. For an excellent contemporary example of the Wesleyan-holiness canon of saints and the types of books southern holiness enthusiasts read, see J. O. McClurkan, *Chosen Vessels: Twenty-one Biographical Sketches of Men and Women, Most of Whom Have Been Used of God in Pioneering Some Great Pentecostal Movement* (Louisville: Pickett Publishing Company, 1901). Among those McClurkan included were eighteenth-century evangelicals such as George Whitefield, Francis Asbury, William Carvosso, and Francis Asbury, as well as contemporaries such as Salvation Army founder William Booth, southern revivalist Sam Jones, and Frances Willard, leader of the Women's Christian Temperance Union. Before McClurkan compiled these sketches into one book, he published them in

his newspaper, *Zion's Outlook*. McClurkan emphasized the higher religious attainments of all and the role each played in the creation of the modern holiness movement. Holiness adherents read selectively. They were not interested in the full range of Wesley's works, especially his writings that seemed to make sanctification anything less than an instantaneous experience. Also, they frequently read Wesley through later holiness redactors who had significantly modified his theology. Hamilton, *William Baxter Godbey*, 126–134; Peters, *Christian Perfection and American Methodism*, 33. "Books and Tracts on Christian Holiness," *The Christian Witness and Advocate of Bible Holiness*, 5 November 1885, 7. "Our Book List," *The Way of Life*, 24 June 1891, 4. In one 1894 issue *The Way of Faith* posted eighty-five different holiness related books, tracts, and hymnals for sale. *The Way of Faith*, 17 October 1894, 7.

48. Martin Wells Knapp and L. L. Pickett, *Tears and Triumphs No. 2* (Louisville: Pickett Publishing Company, 1897).

49. "The Influence of Good Books," *The Way of Faith*, 12 February 1896, 1.

50. E. E. Shelhamer, *Popular and Radical Holiness, Contrasted* (Atlanta: by the author, 1906), preface.

51. Lawrence Goodwyn, *The Populist Movement: A Short History of the Agrarian Revolt in America* (New York: Oxford University Press, 1978), xvii. Woodward, *Origins of the New South*, 194, 247, 248.

52. Scholars have developed the theory of counterpublics in their critique of Jürgen Habermas, *The Structural Transformation of the Public Sphere: An Inquiry into the Category of Bourgeois Society*, trans. Thomas Burger and Frederick Lawrence (Cambridge, Mass.: MIT Press, 1989). Nancy Fraser argues that Habermas's notion of the public sphere (tied to the rise of the middle class and to public concern in the seventeenth and eighteenth centuries) neglects other nonliberal, nonbourgeois competing public spheres. From the beginning, Fraser writes, "counterpublics contested the exclusionary norms of the bourgeois public, elaborating alternative styles of political behavior and alternative norms of public speech." Nancy Fraser, "Rethinking the Public Sphere: A Contribution to the Critique of Actually Existing Democracy," *Social Texts* 25–26 (1990): 56, 57, 58, 61. Similarly, cultural critic Michael Warner contends that "the discourse that constitutes [a counterpublic] is not merely a different or alternative idiom, but one that in other contexts would be regarded with hostil-

ity or with a sense of indecorousness." Michael Warner, "Publics and Counterpublics," *Public Culture* 14 (Winter 2002): 86, 62. For an examination of the development of a counterpublic consciousness among the African American National Baptist Convention, see Higginbotham, *Righteous Discontent,* 11.

53. On the role of sectarian print culture in popular religion, see Peter W. Williams, *Popular Religion in America: Symbolic Change and the Modernization Process in Historical Perspective* (Englewood Cliffs, N.J.: Prentice-Hall, 1980), 17.

54. *Living Words,* April 1903, 7.

55. James D. Norris, *Advertising and the Transformation of American Society, 1865–1920* (New York: Greenwood Press, 1990), 29–30.

56. Virginia Lieson Brereton finds that leading evangelicals in the late nineteenth and early twentieth centuries often saw "themselves quite explicitly as sales persons needing to research the markets for their product and then choosing the best methods and messages with which to 'sell' to those markets." Brereton, *From Sin to Salvation,* 76. Roland Marchand and T. J. Jackson Lears describe how religious and secular advertisements had the power to realize consumers' dreams, linking them to a larger culture and giving them solace in the modern world. As Marchand argues, advertisements "contributed to the shaping of a 'community discourse,' an integrative common language shared by an otherwise diverse audience." T. J. Jackson Lears, *No Place of Grace: Antimodernism and the Transformation of American Culture, 1880–1920* (New York: Pantheon Books, 1981). T. J. Jackson Lears, "From Salvation to Self-Realization: Advertising and the Therapeutic Roots of the Consumer Culture, 1880–1930," in *The Culture of Consumption: Critical Essays in American History, 1880–1980,* ed. Richard Wightman Fox and T. J. Jackson Lears (New York: Pantheon Books, 1983), 3–38. Roland Marchand, *Advertising the American Dream: Making Way for Modernity, 1920–1940* (Berkeley: University of California Press, 1985), xx.

57. *The Pentecostal Herald,* 5 January 1898, 7.

58. *The Way of Life,* 11 September 1886, 3.

59. Haynes, *Tempest-Tossed on Methodist Seas,* 156, 157. John B. Culpepper, intro. to L. L. Pickett, *The Renewed Earth, or the Coming and Reign of Jesus Christ* (Louisville: Pickett Publishing Company, 1903), 3.

60. Turley, *Wheel within a Wheel,* 149–180, 65, 165.

61. "Young Harris, Ga.," *The Pentecostal Herald*, 11 August 1897, 3.

62. Murrill included in his list Hannah Whitall Smith's *The Christian's Secret of a Happy Life*, William McDonald's *New Testament Standard of Piety*, J. A. Wood's *Christian Perfection as Taught by Wesley*, as well as works by Carradine, Pickett, and Godbey. E. G. Murrill, "Some Suggestions to Holiness People," *The Way of Faith*, 17 October 1894, 2. This avid devotional reading was certainly nothing new. According to the religious historian David D. Hall, vernacular reading practices like this existed among seventeenth-century New England Protestants. Believers reread religious texts as a sign of their thorough devotion. The aura of books was "supremely 'precious' because it contained the gift of life," argues Hall. "Books spoke to the heart and aroused powerful emotions." They were "also channels for the Holy Spirit." David D. Hall, *Worlds of Wonder, Days of Judgment: Popular Religious Belief in Early New England* (Cambridge, Mass.: Harvard University Press, 1989), 42, 41. Murrill, "Some Suggestions to Holiness People," 2. See also B. L. Hill's testimony, "Improve Your Opportunities," *The Way of Faith*, 11 December 1895, 5. Hill, who made it his habit to read everything in *The Way of Faith*, declared that he received "more spiritual food from its pages than [from] any other paper."

63. In an 1896 issue of *The Revivalist*, a witness to the paper's power announced: "It fills me full of the Holy Ghost while reading. I study its theology as I would a book, especially Rev. W. B. Godbey's letters." *The Revivalist*, October 1896, 4. See also the experience of Lela G. McConnell, a native of Pennsylvania who would found the Kentucky Mountain Holiness Association. McConnell recalled having devoured her copies of the *Christian Standard*. Once she had gone through an issue from cover to cover, she would even read the advertisements. Lela G. McConnell, *The Pauline Ministry in the Kentucky Mountains or a Brief Account of the Kentucky Mountain Holiness Association* (Louisville: Pentecostal Publishing Company, 1942), 19.

64. The Church of God (Anderson, Indiana) paper *The Gospel Trumpet* boasted 60,000 subscriptions in 1908. To this the editor hoped to add another 140,000 by 1909. *The Gospel Trumpet*, 10 December 1908, 15. In 1900 the editor of *The Firebrand* (a Shenandoah, Iowa, radical holiness paper with a significant southern readership) reported a circulation of 10,000 issues, some for regular subscriptions and others for sample copies. *The Firebrand* (November 1900): 1. In a later period, the holiness-believing

Pentecostal Church of the Nazarene widely circulated its periodical literature in the first years of the denomination's existence. The fledgling church's publishing house in Kansas City, Missouri, served a large readership in Texas and the Southwest. Nine months after the founding of its publishing house in 1912, the denomination had sent out 938,825 copies of holiness periodicals. J. B. Chapman, *A History of the Church of the Nazarene* (Kansas City, Mo.: Nazarene Publishing House, 1926), 111–112. I am indebted to the archives of the Church of the Nazarene for this citation.

65. "Send Us a Card," *The Way of Life,* 24 June 1891, 2.

66. For an example of such a list, see "Evangelists' Directory," *The Pentecostal Herald,* 5 January 1898, 16. The directory contained over forty names, including H. C. Morrison, W. B. Godbey, L. L. Pickett, and W. A. Dodge as well as husband-and-wife teams. J. H. Padgett, an evangelist from Ennis, Texas, wrote to *The Way of Faith* in November 1896 to announce that he was collecting an extensive list of holiness evangelists. He asked for the "name, denomination and home address of each evangelist" who answered his request. He then planned to make the list available to holiness people living in "neglected localities where the doctrine of holiness has never been introduced." "Evangelists Please Take Notice," *The Way of Faith,* 25 November 1896, 1.

67. Otho B. Cobbins, *History of the Church of Christ (Holiness) U.S.A., 1895–1965* (New York: Vantage Press, 1966), 27.

68. Eva M. Watson, *George D. Watson, Fearless for the Truth* (1929; reprint, Salem, Ohio: Schmul Publishing Company, 2001), 54.

69. "Dr. Carradine's Book," *The Way of Faith,* 24 June 1891, 2, 3.

70. Robert Darnton, "What Is the History of Books?" in *Reading in America: Literature and Social History,* ed. Cathy N. Davidson (Baltimore: Johns Hopkins University Press, 1989), 44–45. Cultural historian Roger Chartier also stresses the formative aspect of texts. "Writing deploys strategies that are meant to produce effects, dictate a posture, and oblige the reader," he argues. "It lays traps which the reader falls into without even knowing it." Roger Chartier, *Forms and Meanings: Texts, Performances, and Audiences from Codex to Computer* (Philadelphia: University of Pennsylvania Press, 1995), 1. Conversion narratives, writes Virginia Lieson Brereton, were "highly formulaic, composed according to the requirements of a strictly defined convention." She finds that believers more than likely "perceived and shaped their experiences so that they were conformable

to the formula." Brereton, *From Sin to Salvation,* 16, xii. See also Rodger M. Payne, *The Self and the Sacred: Conversion and Autobiography in Early American Protestantism* (Knoxville: University of Tennessee Press, 1998).

71. *The Way of Faith,* 25 December 1895, 5.

72. *Live Coals of Fire,* 27 October 1899, 4.

73. Emma Christmas, "An Experience," *The Way of Faith,* 8 January 1896, 5, and 25 November 1895, 4. *The Way of Faith* solicited this help with ads calling on readers to circulate holiness papers and magazines. For one dime, agents' names would be added to the Holiness Exchange List, a document "sent to all publishers of holiness literature." These publishers would then mail sample copies to those on the list. *The Way of Faith,* 25 March 1896, 7. In January 1898 H. C. Morrison sent out five thousand sample copies of his paper. He asked those who received these free issues to "distribute them, and use their influence in getting the people to take the paper." Morrison thought such a canvassing strategy would be highly successful. Just a single copy sent to a southern town, Morrison recalled, was the means of one man's sanctification and numerous other conversions. *Pentecostal Herald,* 12 January 1898, 1.

74. W. C. Dunlap, *Life of S. Miller Willis: The Fire Baptized Lay Evangelist* (Atlanta: Constitution Publishing Company, 1892), 140.

75. "From South Carolina," *The Christian Witness and Advocate of Bible Holiness,* 7 May 1885, 8.

76. "Read and Lend," *The Revivalist,* October 1896, 4. See Louisiana native S. Childers's testimony, "Quiet Sowing," *The Revivalist,* October 1896, 4. David D. Hall notes the role of borrowing books in the spread of popular Protestantism in seventeenth-century New England. Book sharing became so common in some communities that "households without books (according to probate inventories) were able nonetheless to introduce their children to reading." Hall, *Worlds of Wonder,* 46. J. M. Pike was certainly aware of the power of lending papers and sending out sample copies. In 1896 the elated editor reported that whole families experienced sanctification and initiated revivals after a single issue of *The Way of Faith* entered their homes. "To Our Friends," *The Way of Faith,* 9 September 1896, 4.

77. I. E. Lowery, "The Colored Ministers and Bishop Taylor's Steamer," *The Christian Standard and Advocate of Bible Holiness,* 8

March 1887, 2. Growing numbers of African Americans also subscribed to *The Way of Faith* and *The Way of Life*. G. A. Mail [sic], "Holiness among the Colored People in North Carolina," *The Way of Faith*, 14 March 1900, 1. "Rev. W. A. Dodge's Work among the Colored People," *The Pentecostal Herald*, 24 February 1904, 4.

78. Fraser, "Rethinking the Public Sphere," 56, 57, 58, 61. Michael Warner, "Publics and Counterpublics," 86, 62.

79. J. W. Buckalew, *Incidents in the Life of J. W. Buckalew* (n.p., n.d.), 55.

80. Timothy L. Smith, *Called unto Holiness: The Story of the Nazarenes, the Formative Years* (Kansas City, Mo.: Nazarene Publishing House, 1962), 39.

81. *Alabama Christian Advocate*, 22 August 1895, 1.

82. "Denominational Loyalty," *Southern Christian Advocate*, 26 August 1886, 4.

83. "False Prophets," *Quarterly Review of the M. E. Church, South* (April 1892): 30. J. W. Rush, "Fair Play," *Alabama Christian Advocate*, 17 January 1895, 1. For a holiness response to such criticism, see "The Naughty Peddler," *The Way of Faith*, 4 December 1895, 4. The author of this piece defended the practice of circulating holiness books, tracts, and papers. John Wesley, the writer retorted, was the ultimate "peddler" of perfectionist literature.

84. "Bishops on Christian Perfection," *Quarterly Review of the M. E. Church, South* 40 (November–December 1894): 283.

85. By 1902 *Samson's Foxes* reached 620 subscribers. Trammell, "Publishing the Gospel," 1. A. J. Tomlinson, "Journal of Happenings: The Diary of A. J. Tomlinson, 1901–23," 18 August 1901, 11 December 1901, Dixon Pentecostal Research Center, Cleveland, Tenn.

86. "Our Attitude toward Exclusivists," *Christian Advocate*, 8 August 1889, 8. "The Leading of the Spirit," *Christian Advocate*, 2 July 1896, 1. The faithful did frequently use modern metaphors to illustrate how the Spirit spoke directly to individuals. G. D. Watson likened the relationship between a believer and the Spirit to the signal that is sent through a telegraph wire: the wire merely transmitted the unmediated message of the sender. Geo. D. Watson, "False Notions of Power," *Way of Faith*, 24 July 1895, 3.

87. "The Holiness Question," *Christian Advocate*, 12 December 1889, 9.

88. "'The Problem' and Its Critics," *Quarterly Review of the M. E. Church, South* (January 1893): 350.

89. *The Religious Herald,* 22 August 1907, 1.

4. SIGNS OF THE SECOND COMING

1. B. F. Haynes, *Tempest-Tossed on Methodist Seas; Or, A Sketch of My Life* (Louisville: Pentecostal Publishing Company, 1921), 232–233, 71–74.

2. As C. Vann Woodward noted, "It would have been difficult to find a climate more hostile to the cultivation of radical movements than the South of the 1890s." C. Vann Woodward, *Origins of the New South, 1877–1913* (Baton Rouge: Louisiana State University Press, 1951), 249.

3. *Atlanta Constitution,* 22 November 1887, quoted ibid., 198.

4. Paul Harvey, *Redeeming the South: Religious Cultures and Racial Identities among Southern Baptists, 1865–1925* (Chapel Hill: University of North Carolina Press, 1997), 94. "Delusions and Fallacies in the Higher Life Doctrine," *Religious Herald,* 28 June 1906, 2. Harvey, *Redeeming the South,* 94.

5. Hunter Dickson Farish, *The Circuit Rider Dismounts: A Social History of Southern Methodism, 1865–1900* (Richmond: Dietz Press, 1938), 25–27. Ralph E. Morrow, *Northern Methodism and Reconstruction* (East Lansing: Michigan State University Press, 1956), 237.

6. Briane Turley, *A Wheel within a Wheel: Southern Methodism and the Georgia Holiness Association* (Macon, Ga.: Mercer University Press, 1999), 104–105, 116, 123, 126. Vinson Synan, *The Holiness-Pentecostal Tradition: Charismatic Movements in the Twentieth Century* (Grand Rapids: William B. Eerdmans, 1997), 37–38. Geo. H. Pooser, "State Holiness Association," *Southern Christian Advocate,* 9 June 1887, 1.

7. *Wesleyan Christian Advocate,* 23 September 1885, 2–3, 5, quoted in Harold W. Mann, *Atticus Greene Haygood: Methodist Bishop, Editor, and Educator* (Athens: University of Georgia Press, 1965), 164–165.

8. L. L. Pickett and M. A. Smith, *The Pickett-Smith Debate on Entire Sanctification, a Second Blessing* (Louisville: Pickett Publishing Company, 1897), 28, 109.

9. Robert Stanley Ingersol, "Burden of Dissent: Mary Lee Cagle and the Southern Holiness Movement" (Ph.D. diss., Duke University, 1989), 110.

10. L. J. Montague, "Sanctification," *National Baptist Magazine* (April 1896): 90–92. Edward M. Brawley, ed., *The Negro Baptist Pulpit: A Collection of Sermons and Papers* (1890; reprint, Freeport, N.Y.: Books for Libraries Press, 1971), 94–95, 97. J. H. Eason, *Pulpit and Platform: Sanctification vs. Fanaticism* (Nashville: National Baptist Publishing Board, 1899), 10, 22–48. Harvey, *Redeeming the South,* 133.

11. John A. Thompson, "Evangelists," *Southern Christian Advocate,* 17 September 1891, 1.

12. "About Evangelists," *Alabama Christian Advocate,* quoted in *Southern Christian Advocate,* 17 September 1891, 1. See also "Teachers, True and False," *Christian Advocate,* 10 January 1895, 8; Farish, *The Circuit Rider Dismounts,* 73; and John Leland Peters, *Christian Perfection and American Methodism* (New York: Abingdon Press, 1956), 146–147.

13. "Resolution on Evangelism—South Georgia Conference," *Southern Christian Advocate,* 28 January 1892, 1. Timothy L. Smith, *Called unto Holiness: The Story of the Nazarenes, the Formative Years* (Kansas City, Mo.: Nazarene Publishing House, 1962), 153. Walter N. Vernon, Robert W. Sledge, Robert C. Monk, and Norman Spellman, *The Methodist Excitement in Texas: A History* (Dallas: Texas United Methodist Historical Society, 1984), 206.

14. "Bishop's Address," *Journal of the General Conference of the Methodist Episcopal Church, South, 1894,* quoted in J. Lawrence Brasher, *The Sanctified South: John Lakin Brasher and the Holiness Movement* (Urbana: University of Illinois Press, 1994), 39.

15. Robert H. Wiebe, *The Search for Order, 1877–1920* (New York: Hill and Wang, 1967), 113, 114, 117. T. J. Jackson Lears, *No Place of Grace: Antimodernism and the Transformation of American Culture, 1880–1920* (New York: Pantheon Books, 1981), 5, 9. T. J. Jackson Lears, "From Salvation to Self-Realization: Advertising and the Therapeutic Roots of the Consumer Culture, 1880–1930," in *The Culture of Consumption: Critical Essays in American History, 1880–1980,* ed. Richard Wightman Fox and T. J. Jackson Lears (New York: Pantheon Books, 1983), 6. On the professionalization of the Southern Baptist Convention, see Harvey, *Redeeming the South,* 101–102.

16. B. M. Messick, "Evangelists," *Christian Advocate,* 26 September 1895, 5.

17. Beverly Carradine, *Graphic Scenes* (1911; reprint, Salem, Ohio: Schmul Publishing Company, 1990), 173–174. Godbey recalled that "when

the fires of the Holy Ghost fell on me . . . those hallowed flames burned up the Free Mason, the Odd Fellow, the collegiate president, the big preacher, and the life insurance [sic]." W. B. Godbey, *Autobiography of Rev. W. B. Godbey, A. M.* (Cincinnati: God's Revivalist Office, 1909), 98. C. P. Jones spoke for the community of black holiness people in Mississippi when he declared: "My people loved beauty, but the beauty of the flesh is vain and deceiving and soon passes. They wanted to advance in the world; but worldly advantages proved only a snare." Quoted in Otho B. Cobbins, *History of the Church of Christ (Holiness) U.S.A., 1895–1965* (New York: Vantage Press, 1966), 24.

18. Carradine, *Graphic Scenes,* 174.

19. Peter W. Williams, *Popular Religion in America: Symbolic Change and the Modernization Process in Historical Perspective* (Englewood Cliffs, N.J.: Prentice-Hall, 1980), 17–18. See also Charles H. Lippy, *Being Religious, American Style: A History of Popular Religiosity in the United States* (Westport, Conn.: Praeger Publishers, 1994), 1–10, and Robert Orsi, "Everyday Miracles: The Study of Lived Religion," in *Lived Religion in America: Toward a History of Practice* (Princeton: Princeton University Press, 1997), 7, 15.

20. On the populist hermeneutics of holiness folk, see Stephen John Lennox, "Biblical Interpretation in the American Holiness Movement, 1875–1920" (Ph.D. diss., Drew University, 1992), 154. This spiritual egalitarianism was similar in many ways to that present in earlier revivals. The historian Paul Conkin writes that at the Cane Ridge, Kentucky, revival "almost anyone, including those who rose from the ground as well as child converts, might burst out with an exhortation." Paul K. Conkin, *Cane Ridge: America's Pentecost* (Madison: University of Wisconsin Press, 1990), 94.

21. Phoebe Palmer, *Pioneer Experiences, or, the Gift of Power Received by Faith* (1868; reprint, New York: Garland Publishing, 1984), vi. Herbert F. Stevenson, ed., *Keswick's Authentic Voice* (Grand Rapids: Zondervan Publishing House, 1959), 470.

22. Tom Lutz, *American Nervousness, 1903: An Anecdotal History* (Ithaca, N.Y.: Cornell University Press, 1991), 19–20, 25. Lears, *No Place of Grace,* 47. See also Gail Bederman, *Manliness and Civilization: A Cultural History of Gender and Race in the United States, 1880–1917* (Chicago: University of Chicago Press, 1995), 14.

23. A. M. Hills, *Holiness and Power for the Church and the Ministry* (Cincinnati: Revivalist Office, 1897), 29.

24. D. William Faupel, *The Everlasting Gospel: The Significance of Eschatology in the Development of Pentecostal Thought* (Sheffield, England: Sheffield Academic Press, 1996), 79, 82. On the use of a new pentecostal vocabulary that accompanied the focus on the Holy Spirit, see Donald W. Dayton, *Theological Roots of Pentecostalism* (Metuchen, N.J.: Scarecrow Press, 1987), 78–79. For an examination of the wave of interest in the Holy Spirit among other late-nineteenth-century Protestants, see Grant Wacker, "The Holy Spirit and the Spirit of the Age in American Protestantism, 1880–1910," *Journal of American History* 72 (June 1985): 45–62.

25. Martin Wells Knapp, *The Double Cure* (Cincinnati: God's Revivalist Office, 1895), 16–17. James F. Findlay Jr., *Dwight L. Moody: American Evangelist, 1837–1899* (Chicago: University of Chicago Press, 1969), 238. N. J. Holmes and Wife, *Life Sketches and Sermons* (Royston, Ga.: Press of the Pentecostal Holiness Church, 1920), 68–69. A. M. Hills also pointed out the practical results of Holy Ghost baptism: it gave believers divine courage and "a power of utterance to the lips to say what God wants his witnesses to say." Hills, *Holiness and Power,* 313, 310. For an overview of Holy Spirit empowerment, see John Fea, "Power from on High in an Age of Ecclesiastical Impotence: The 'Enduement of the Holy Spirit' in American Fundamentalist Thought, 1880–1936," *Fides et Historia* 1 (Summer 1994): 23–35. See also Ann Taves, *Fits, Trances, and Visions: Experiencing Religion and Explaining Experience from Wesley to James* (Princeton: Princeton University Press, 1999), 4.

26. David Douglas Daniels, "The Cultural Renewal of Slave Religion: Charles Price Jones and the Emergence of the Holiness Movement in Mississippi" (Ph.D. diss., Union Theological Seminary, 1992). Zora Neale Hurston, *The Sanctified Church* (Berkeley: Turtle Island, 1983), 103. For more on the black holiness protest against mainline black denominations, see Hans A. Baer, "The Socio-Religious Development of the Church of God in Christ," in *African Americans in the South: Issues of Race, Class, and Gender,* ed. Hans A. Baer and Yvonne Jones (Athens: University of Georgia Press, 1992), 111. W. F. Graham, "Religious Superstition," *National Baptist Union,* 21 June 1902, 5. "Pretentiousness in the Ministry," *National Baptist Magazine* (August 1901): 335–336.

27. W. E. Robinson, "Specific Theological Apostasy," *The National Bap-*

tist Magazine (October 1897): 452. Daniel Alexander Payne, *Recollections of Seventy Years* (1886; reprint, New York: Arno Press and the New York Times, 1969), 253.

28. George D. Watson, "Aunt Nellie's Vision," *The Holiness Advocate,* 15 May 1907, 3. Mary Mason, *The History and Life Work of Elder C. H. Mason, Chief Apostle, and His Co-Laborers* (n.p., 1924), 19, 15–17. Ithiel C. Clemmons, *Bishop C. H. Mason and the Roots of the Church of God in Christ* (Bakersfield, Calif.: Pneuma Life Publishing, 1996), 17–18, 21, 31. Daniels, "The Cultural Renewal of Slave Religion," 89, 93. Mason, *The History and Life Work of Elder C. H. Mason,* 54. For an examination of the ring-shout in African American religion, see Albert J. Raboteau, *Slave Religion: The "Invisible Institution" in the Antebellum South* (New York: Oxford University Press, 1978), 68–73.

29. "Primitivism," argues the religious historian Richard T. Hughes, "suggests that 'first times' are in some sense normative or jurisdictional for contemporary belief and behavior." For Hughes, restorationism "more closely conforms to 'chronological primitivism' wherein the greatest excellence and happiness existed at the fount of time." Richard T. Hughes, "Introduction: On Recovering the Theme of Recovery," in *The American Quest for the Primitive Church,* ed. Richard T. Hughes (Urbana: University of Illinois Press, 1988), 1, 3. Nathan O. Hatch, *The Democratization of American Christianity* (New Haven: Yale University Press, 1989), 167, 169, 179.

30. Steven Lee Ware, "Restoring the New Testament Church: Some Varieties of Restorationism in the Holiness Movement of the Late Nineteenth and Early Twentieth Centuries" (Ph.D. diss., Drew University, 1998), 2–3.

31. W. B. Godbey and Seth Cook Rees, *The Return of Jesus* (Cincinnati: God's Revivalist Office, 1898), 50.

32. Cobbins, *History of the Church of Christ,* 28–29. The black Baptist official J. H. Eason condemned the sort of sanctification that led to sectarianism as "'crazification' and fanaticism." Eason, *Pulpit and Platform,* 57.

33. R. G. Spurling, *The Lost Link* (Turtletown, Tenn.: by the author, 1920).

34. "Pentecostal Power and Glory Now," *Christian Advocate,* 22 August 1889, 1.

35. "Affray at a Meeting," *Dallas Morning News,* 21 July 1903, 4.

36. "To the Holiness People," *The Way of Faith,* 11 December 1895, 2.

37. J. Wm. Garbutt, *William Asbury Dodge: Southern Holiness Pioneer,* ed. Kenneth O. Brown (1906; reprint, Hazelton, Pa.: Holiness Archives, 2001), 88, 104. Turley, *Wheel within a Wheel,* 144.

38. Turley, *Wheel within a Wheel,* 144. A. J. Jarrell to George G. Smith, 16 October 1894, C. C Papers, Woodruff Library, Emory University, Atlanta, quoted ibid., 146. On the success of Haygood's campaign to defeat the holiness movement, see Mann, *Atticus Greene Haygood,* 165–167.

39. Joseph H. King, *Yet Speaketh: Memoirs of the Late Bishop Joseph H. King* (Franklin Springs, Ga.: Publishing House of the Pentecostal Holiness Church, 1949), 41–42.

40. William Clair Turner, "The United Holy Church of America: A Study in Black Holiness-Pentecostalism" (Ph.D. diss., Duke University, 1984), 58. Charles Edwin Jones, *Perfectionist Persuasion: The Holiness Movement and American Methodism* (Metuchen, N.J.: Scarecrow Press, 1974), 93. Percival A. Wesche, *Henry Clay Morrison: Crusader Saint* (Berne, Ind.: Herald Press, 1963), 82–86.

41. Smith, *Called unto Holiness,* 160.

42. Daniels, "The Cultural Renewal of Slave Religion," 33–34, 46–47, 100–102.

43. George W. Stanley, *My Life's Experiences with God* (Franklin Springs, Ga.: Publishing House of the Pentecostal Holiness Church, n.d.), 15.

44. Deborah Vansau McCauley, *Appalachian Mountain Religion: A History* (Urbana: University of Illinois Press, 1995), 281–283.

45. Smith, *Called unto Holiness,* 37.

46. Jones, *Perfectionist Persuasion,* 57.

47. Melvin Easterday Dieter, *The Holiness Revival of the Nineteenth Century* (Lanham, Md.: Scarecrow Press, 1996), 208–216. Synan, *The Holiness-Pentecostal Tradition,* 35–37. Smith, *Called unto Holiness,* 28–38.

48. *Christian Perfection: An Address by the Southern Holiness Association* (La Grange, Ga.: A. J. Jarrell, n.d.), 19–20. In the late 1890s this older generation of loyalists used the holiness press to excoriate the western and later southern "come-outers." See P. Tower, "Come-outism Perilous to Holiness," *The Christian Witness and Advocate of Bible Holiness,* 2 July 1885, 2; "The Call for a Convention," *The Way of Faith,* 21 October 1896, 4; and "Dr. Carradine's Letter," *The Way of Faith,* 21 October 1896, 4.

49. Vinson Synan, *Old Time Power: A Centennial History of the International Pentecostal Holiness Church* (Franklin Springs, Ga.: LifeSprings Resources, 1998), 74.

50. *The Discipline of the Holiness Church* (Goldsboro, N.C.: Nash Brothers, Book and Job Printing, 1902), 3. Both Crumpler's Holiness Church and a Holiness Church founded in Donalsonville, Georgia, several years earlier borrowed heavily from the Methodist discipline, adding articles on holiness, divine healing, the second coming of Christ, and strict church rules. *The Discipline of the Holiness Church* (Louisville: Pentecostal Herald Press, ca. 1897).

51. Synan, *The Holiness-Pentecostal Tradition,* 41–43, 69–77.

52. Brasher, *The Sanctified South,* 38. Godbey and Rees, *The Return of Jesus,* 16.

53. Historian Timothy Weber describes the doctrine of premillennialism as "not so much a theology as it is a particular view of history. Premillennialists reject popular notions of human progress and believe that history is a game that the righteous cannot win." Timothy P. Weber, "Premillennialism and the Branches of Evangelicalism," in *The Variety of American Evangelicalism,* ed. Donald W. Dayton and Robert K. Johnston (Downer's Grove, Ill.: InterVarsity Press, 1991), 6. George Marsden's classic study of American fundamentalism identifies the Baconian underpinnings of dispensational premillennialism. This theology enabled conservative Protestants to "look at things scientifically." For individuals who held to these views, the Bible became an "encyclopedic puzzle," Marsden argues. "It was a dictionary of the facts that had been progressively revealed in various historical circumstances and literary genres and still needed to be sorted out and arranged." George M. Marsden, *Fundamentalism and American Culture: The Shaping of Twentieth-Century Evangelicalism, 1870–1925* (New York: Oxford University Press, 1980), 58.

54. On the Bible Conference movement, see Ernest R. Sandeen, *The Roots of Fundamentalism: British and American Millenarianism, 1800–1930* (Chicago: University of Chicago Press, 1970), 132–161. These gatherings paralleled the National Holiness Association revivals in structure and popularity. On the pessimistic aspect of premillennialism, see Timothy P. Weber, *Living in the Shadow of the Second Coming: American Premillennialism, 1875–1925* (Chicago: University of Chicago Press, 1987), 10, and Sandeen, *The Roots of Fundamentalism,* xvii, 13, 41, 161. Dwight L.

Moody, *New Sermons* (New York: Henry S. Goodspeed, 1880), 535. For a treatment of the anti-immigrant aspect of holiness, see Smith, *Called unto Holiness,* 201. Moody's lifeboat metaphor was later taken up by W. B. Godbey. In his *Appeal to Postmillennialists,* Godbey shouted down his opponents and implored them, "I want you to see that the Bible is true which describes humanity as an old, unseaworthy, ruined bark, ready to founder; while Christ is the lifeboat, calling us all to forsake the old wreck, leap on board and ride away to glory." Godbey, *An Appeal to Postmillennialists* (Nashville: Pentecostal Mission Publishing Co., n.d.), 15.

55. Holmes and Wife, *Life Sketches and Sermons,* 70–72. J. O. McClurkan confessed that his *Behold He Cometh!* amounted to little more than a compilation of the work of his favorite premillennial theologians. McClurkan quoted liberally from the books of C. I. Scofield, Jennie Bland Beauchamp, W. E. Blackstone, D. T. Taylor, A. J. Gordon, and A. B. Simpson. McClurkan, *Behold He Cometh! A Series of Brief Lessons on the Second Coming of Christ* (Nashville: Pentecostal Book and Tract Depository, 1901), 5.

56. Haynes, *Tempest-Tossed on Methodist Seas,* 82. Nathaniel West, an "Old School" Presbyterian minister, also shaped the theology of many a southern perfectionist through his short book *John Wesley and Premillennialism,* which was reprinted by H. C. Morrison's Pentecostal Publishing Company. Wesley would not have sympathized with this pessimistic eschatology, but West held that "Wesley and the Oxford Methodists were lovers of premillennial doctrine." West, *John Wesley and Premillennialism* (188?; reprint, Louisville: Pentecostal Publishing Company, 1894), 5. On Wesley's battle with what he considered to be Adventist fanatics, see Peters, *Christian Perfection and American Methodism,* 67–69. G. F. Taylor, a founder of the Pentecostal Holiness Church, so admired the work of J. A. Seiss that he even named one of his sons after this premillennial divine. Vinson Synan, "George Floyd Taylor, Conflicts and Crowns," in *Portraits of a Generation: Early Pentecostal Leaders,* ed. James R. Goff and Grant Wacker (Fayetteville: University of Arkansas Press, 2002), 330.

57. Mason, *History and Life Work of Elder C. H. Mason,* 35, 94.

58. Milton G. Sernett, "Black Religion and the Question of Evangelical Identity," in *The Variety of American Evangelicalism,* 135, 142. See also Dayton, *Theological Roots of Pentecostalism,* 146.

59. "W. E. Fuller's (Colored) Letter," *Live Coals of Fire,* 26 January

1900, 1. "W. E. Fuller's (Colored) Letter," *Live Coals of Fire,* 1 June 1900, 8. G. A. Mail [sic], "Holiness among the Colored People in North Carolina," *The Way of Faith,* 14 March 1900, 1.

60. On Simpson's influence, see Smith, *Called unto Holiness,* 184, 189.

61. See articles from the *Atlanta Constitution,* 17–28 August 1899, including "Camp Meeting Is at an End," 28 August, 4, and "Campmeeting at Exposition Park," 17 August, 10.

62. Clement C. Cary, *The Second Coming of Christ: Showing Pre-Millennialism to be Unscriptural and Unreasonable* (Atlanta: Doctor Blosser Company, 1902), 3.

63. Clifford Geertz, *The Interpretation of Cultures: Selected Essays* (New York: Basic Books, 1973), 124, 93, 119.

64. Edward L. Ayers, *The Promise of the New South: Life after Reconstruction* (New York: Oxford University Press, 1992), 283, 298, 309. C. Vann Woodward, *Tom Watson: Agrarian Rebel* (New York: Oxford University Press, 1963), 331. The widely popular preacher and author G. D. Watson serves as an excellent example. He suffered from the financial failures of the era after his land speculation schemes fell apart. Worse yet, a freeze in 1894 destroyed his citrus grove in Windsor, Florida. Charges of marital infidelity and the subsequent scandal in the MECS only added to his many other woes. Not long after this string of disasters, Watson embraced pre-millennialism. William C. Kostlevy, "Watson, G(eorge) D(ouglas)," in *Historical Dictionary of the Holiness Movement,* ed. William C. Kostlevy (Lanham, Md.: Scarecrow Press, 2001), 265–266. Eva M. Watson, *George D. Watson, Fearless for the Truth* (1929; reprint, Salem, Ohio: Schmul Publishing Company, 2001), 57, 83. Francis Cooley, "Immigration a Menace to American Institutions," *The Pentecostal Herald,* 23 May 1906, 2. Wiebe, *The Search for Order,* 45, 105. Concerning this period, T. J. Jackson Lears remarks, "An entire range of human experience lay beyond the boundaries of official optimism." Lears, *No Place of Grace,* 4. For an imaginative look at the psychic crisis of the 1890s in rural Wisconsin, see Michael Lesy, *Wisconsin Death Trip* (London: Allen Lane, 1973).

65. Haynes, *Tempest-Tossed on Methodist Seas,* 73.

66. William Kostlevy, "Nor Silver, Nor Gold: The Burning Bush Movement and the Communitarian Holiness Vision" (Ph.D. diss., University of Notre Dame, 1996), 21. Brasher, *The Sanctified South,* 62–63. Turley, *Wheel within a Wheel,* 196–198.

67. "A Post Millennial Fallacy," *The Revivalist* (March 1897): 2.

68. W. E. Blackstone, *Jesus Is Coming* (New York: Fleming H. Revell, 1908), 25.

69. 2 Peter 3:3–4. W. B. Godbey, "The Sign of His Coming—The Holiness Movement," *The Way of Faith,* 6 October 1896, 13. Joseph Cadwallader, "To Hasten His Coming," *The Way of Faith,* 25 March 1895, 3. The faithful pictured the growth of perfectionist missions in the United States and abroad as well as the special role that women ministers played in the movement as miraculous signs of the "eleventh hour." One observer noted that "humble girls are being called into work, and the Spirit is resting mightily upon the 'daughters' and 'handmaidens,' according to Joel's prophecy." J. O. McClurkan, *Chosen Vessels: Twenty-one Biographical Sketches of Men and Women, Most of Whom Have Been Used of God in Pioneering Some Great Pentecostal Movement* (Louisville: Pickett Publishing Company, 1901), 196. See also C. B. Jernigan, *Pioneer Days of the Holiness Movement in the Southwest* (Kansas City, Mo.: Pentecostal Publishing House, 1919), 146–147.

70. Cary, *Second Coming of Christ,* 3. See *The Way of Faith,* 23 September 1896, 4; 14 October 1896, 4; 21 October 1896, 4; and 28 October 1896, 4.

71. Mason, *History and Life Work of Elder C. H. Mason,* 92, 95. See also Leonard Lovett, "The Spiritual Legacy and Role of Black Holiness-Pentecostalism in the Development of American Culture," *One in Christ* 23 (1987): 148–149.

72. R. L. Harris, *Why We Left the M. E. Church, South* (Milan, Tenn.: by the author, 1894), 14–15. Godbey and Rees, *The Return of Jesus,* 75. Haynes, *Tempest-Tossed on Methodist Seas,* 71–73. Geo. L. Miller, "State of the Churches at the Present Time," *The Way of Faith,* 29 January 1896, 6.

73. The movement's championing of a degree of gender and racial equality was largely isolated from the realm of politics. Gari-Anne Patzwald and William C. Kostlevy, "Carradine, Beverly," in *Historical Dictionary of the Holiness Movement,* 42. Roger Glenn Robins, "Plainfolk Modernist: The Radical Holiness World of A. J. Tomlinson" (Ph.D. diss., Duke University, 1999), 234, 246. The experience of B. F. Haynes was much the same as Carradine's and Tomlinson's. Haynes, *Tempest-Tossed on Methodist Seas,* 155–156.

74. On what some historians refer to as the "great reversal" of evangelicalism, from a focus on societal to personal sin, see David O. Moberg, *The Great Reversal: Evangelism versus Social Concern* (Philadelphia: J. B.

Lippincott, 1972), 20, 26, 34; Donald W. Dayton, *Discovering an Evangelical Heritage* (Peabody, Mass.: Hendrickson, 1976), 126, 163, 166–167; Dieter, *The Holiness Revival of the Nineteenth Century,* 259; R. Lawrence Moore, *Religious Outsiders and the Making of Americans* (New York: Oxford University Press, 1986), 128–129; Weber, *Living in the Shadow of the Second Coming,* 93, 99; and Marsden, *Fundamentalism and American Culture,* 85–93.

75. Cary, *The Second Coming of Christ,* 35.

76. *The Revivalist,* May 1894, 4. See also "Don't Get Excited over Politics," *The Pentecostal Herald,* 20 September 1899, 9. On this point, Samuel Hill's analysis of southern Baptists and Methodists is particularly appropriate. Even more than other conservative evangelicals, holiness and, later, pentecostal adherents considered the conversion and Spirit baptism of individuals to be virtually the sole task of the church. That "Great Commission" took priority. All other interests—political, social, or cultural—were either peripheral or antithetical to these primary goals. Samuel S. Hill Jr., *Southern Churches in Crisis* (New York: Holt, Rinehart, and Winston, 1967), 73, 77–81. See also "John Dull's Letter," *Live Coals of Fire,* 15 December 1899, 7.

77. Martin Wells Knapp and L. L. Pickett, "The Rapture," in *Tears and Triumphs No. 2,* ed. Knapp and Pickett (Louisville: Pickett Publishing Company, 1897), hymn no. 65.

78. Sandeen, *The Roots of Fundamentalism,* 166. Historian William R. Glass notes the paucity of southern premillennialists in his study of southern fundamentalism. According to Glass, "premillennialism, particularly of the dispensational variety, was an important stumbling block to fundamentalist recruiting efforts among Southern Protestants." This remained the case until fundamentalism later won a significant following in the region. William R. Glass, *Strangers in Zion: Fundamentalism in the South, 1900–1950* (Macon, Ga.: Mercer University Press, 2001), xvii.

79. "Is the World Growing Worse?" *Christian Advocate,* 14 March 1895, 4. W. F. Packard, "Two Kinds of Preaching," *Christian Advocate,* 18 June 1896, 3.

80. "Forces That Make for Righteousness," *The Southern Witness,* 16 March 1905, 6. Warren A. Candler, *Great Revivals and the Great Republic* (1904; reprint, Nashville: Publishing House of the M. E. Church South, 1924), 328. W. W. Gaines, "Signs of the Times," *National Baptist Magazine* (June 1901): 289–292.

81. W. W. Landrum, "The Second Coming of Christ," *Christian Index,* 30 March 1899, 3, quoted in Glass, *Strangers in Zion,* 48.

82. George Washington Wilson, *The Sign of Thy Coming; or, Premillennialism, Unscriptural and Unreasonable* (Boston: Christian Witness, 1899). Daniel Steele, *Jesus Exultant, or Christ, No Pessimist* (Boston: Christian Witness, 1899). Smith, *Called unto Holiness,* 35, 193–195, 214. John T. Benson, *A History, 1898–1915, of the Pentecostal Mission, Inc., Nashville, Tennessee* (Nashville: Trevecca Press, 1977). In 1969 H. Ray Dunning argued that the southern wing of the denomination tended toward legalism, or what he called "scriptural casuistry." Unlike their eastern and western brethren, southerners embraced a kind of proto-fundamentalism. They held out no hope for societal change, were more literalistic in their interpretation of scripture, and maintained strict behavioral standards. Dunning, "Nazarene Ethics as Seen in a Theological, Historical, and Sociological Context" (Ph.D. diss., Vanderbilt University, 1969), 99, 106–118.

83. Kostlevy, "Nor Silver, Nor Gold," 19, 21, 42. Smith, *Called unto Holiness,* 35.

84. L. L. Pickett, *The Renewed Earth: Or the Coming Reign of Jesus Christ* (Louisville: Pickett Publishing Company, 1903), 305–306.

85. For overviews of the healing revival in the holiness movement, see Raymond J. Cunningham, "From Holiness to Healing: The Faith Cure in America, 1872–1892," *Church History* 43 (September 1974): 499–513, and Jonathan R. Baer, "Redeemed Bodies: The Functions of Divine Healing in Incipient Pentecostalism," *Church History* 70 (December 2001): 735–771. In 1895 E. M. Murrill, a holiness preacher in Mount Pleasant, Texas, read A. B. Simpson's *Gospel of Healing.* "It was the instrument used by the Spirit," Murrill testified in *The Way of Faith,* "to open my eyes to see divine healing as much provided for in the plan of our salvation as are forgiveness and sanctification." E. M. Murrill, "Divine Healing," *The Way of Faith,* 8 July 1896, 3. R. C. Oliver, "Sin and Sickness," *The Christian Witness and Advocate of Bible Holiness,* 20 March 1884, 2. Mattie Perry, "Divine Healing," *The Way of Faith,* 25 December 1895, 3. Jonathan Baer argues that healing was central to the lives of those he dubs "incipient pentecostals." Healing represented the direct intervention of God in believers' lives. Baer, "Redeemed Bodies," 736, 763, 770.

86. W. B. Godbey, *Spiritual Gifts and Graces* (Cincinnati: God's Revivalist Office, 1895), 10.

87. David D. Hall, *Worlds of Wonder, Days of Judgment: Popular Religious Belief in Early New England* (Cambridge, Mass.: Harvard University Press, 1989), 71–72, 111.

88. See *The Way of Faith,* 27 November 1895, 3; 18 December 1895, 3; and 25 December 1895, 3. "Valuable Books on Divine Healing," *The Way of Faith,* 25 March 1895, 3. C. P. Jones and C. H. Mason considered healing a result of the restoration of scriptural Christianity. Cobbins, *History of the Church of Christ,* 31, 156. Daniels, "The Cultural Renewal of Slave Religion," 195–196.

89. *Live Coals of Fire,* 10 November 1899, 1. Joel 2:28. Acts 2:19–20 also served as a seminal text for followers of radical holiness: "And I will shew wonders in heaven above, and signs in the earth beneath; blood, and fire, and vapour of smoke: The sun shall be turned into darkness, and the moon into blood, before that great and notable day of the Lord come." M. B. Woodworth-Etter, *Signs and Wonders God Wrought in the Ministry for Forty Years* (Indianapolis: by the author, 1916), 534–535, quoted in Faupel, *The Everlasting Gospel,* 39. Baer, "Redeemed Bodies," 748.

90. Jernigan, *Pioneer Days of the Holiness Movement in the Southwest,* 45. See "Vision of M. J. Womack" and "Vision of Mrs. S. A. McNeely," *Live Coals of Fire,* 23 February 1900, 6, and G. D. Watson's account of a former slave woman's vision, Watson, "Aunt Nellie's Vision," 3.

91. Duncan Aikman, "Holy Rollers," *American Mercury* 15 (October 1928): 181.

92. W. C. Dunlap, *Life of S. Miller Willis: The Fire Baptized Lay Evangelist* (Atlanta: Constitution Publishing Company, 1892), 79.

93. George W. Stanley, *My Life's Experiences with God* (Franklin Springs, Ga.: Publishing House of the Pentecostal Holiness Church, n.d.), 15–16.

94. Jernigan, *Pioneer Days,* 42. At another meeting, held in Sunset, Texas, in 1897, a Methodist minister testified against second blessing holiness. At that moment, Jernigan recalled, the minister "groaned and swayed backward and fell in a heap on the floor." The meeting degenerated into chaos as congregants rushed to aid him. According to Jernigan, the holiness ministers officiating knew that "it was nothing but the power of God that had laid him out." Ibid., 38–39.

95. James Benjamin Hilson, *History of the South Carolina Conference of the Wesleyan Methodist Church of America: Fifty Years of Wesleyan*

Methodism in South Carolina (Winona Lake, Ind.: Light and Life Press, 1950), 65–66. Mason, *The History and Life Work of Elder C. H. Mason*, 96, 97. For other instances of African American holiness lore, see Cobbins, *History of the Church of Christ*, 143, 146.

96. Jernigan, *Pioneer Days of the Holiness Movement in the Southwest*, 39, 42, 44. E. E. Shelhamer, *Sixty Years of Thorns and Roses* (Cincinnati: God's Bible School and Revivalist, 193?), 66. See also A. B. Crumpler, "Dunn, N. C.," *The Way of Faith*, 17 June 1896, 1; Florence Goff, *Fifty Years on the Battlefield for God* (Falcon, N.C., n.d.), 19; and "History of Pentecost," *The Faithful Standard* (September 1922): 6. For contemporary criticism of various movements of the Spirit, see Taves, *Fits, Trances, and Visions*, 3, 121–127, 164, 247–249, and Leigh Eric Schmidt, *Hearing Things: Religion, Illusions, and American Enlightenment* (Cambridge, Mass.: Harvard University Press, 2000), 4–5, 9.

97. Godbey, *Spiritual Gifts and Graces*. Martin Wells Knapp, *Lightning Bolts from Pentecostal Skies; Or, Devices of the Devil Unmasked* (Cincinnati: Office of the Revivalist, 1898), 82–84. George D. Watson, *Live Coals: Being Expositions of Scripture on the Doctrine, Experience, and Practice of Christian Holiness* (Cincinnati: God's Revivalist Office, 1886). G. D. Watson, "Burning Love," *The Way of Faith*, 16 September 1896, 1. T. J. Jackson Lears discusses the "fables of abundance" which advertising culture fostered during this same period. Just as holiness leaders championed further works of the Spirit, advertising agents created a therapeutic world of plenty, promising to meet the needs of consumers. An earlier age of "scarcity" gave way to an era of measured excess and willful indulgence. In the early twentieth century, "corporate advertising," Lears contends, "brought a disembodiment of abundance imagery, as the carnivalesque celebration of fleshy excess was streamlined into an exaltation of industrial efficiency." T. J. Jackson Lears, *Fables of Abundance: A Cultural History of Advertising in America* (New York: Basic Books, 1994), 18.

98. Godbey, *Spiritual Gifts and Graces*, 12, 25.

99. Watson urged readers of *The Way of Faith*, Irwin among them, to seek God's refining fire, which would "purge away indwelling sin" and "the carnal mind." G. D. Watson, "Rejoicing," *The Way of Faith*, 6 November 1895, 2. William T. Puriton, "Red Hot Holiness: B. H. Irwin and the Fire-Baptized Holiness Tradition," paper delivered at the Annual Meeting of the Society for Pentecostal Studies, Church of God Theological Seminary,

Cleveland, Tenn., 1998, 2–5. Vinson Synan, *Old Time Power: A Centennial History of the International Pentecostal Holiness Church* (Franklin Springs, Ga.: LifeSprings Resources, 1998), 45.

100. B. H. Irwin, "The Baptism of Fire," *The Way of Faith,* 13 November 1895, 2. He later reprinted his searing testimony as a pamphlet, which a few perfectionist periodicals offered for sale at two cents per copy.

101. "A Murderous Assault on Evangelist B. H. Irwin," *The Way of Faith,* 12 August 1896, 1. B. H. Irwin, "Coon Rapids Iowa," *The Way of Faith,* 29 July 1896, 4. On persecution and mob violence, see also *Live Coals of Fire,* 6 October 1899, 1, and W. M. Hayes, *Memoirs of Richard Baxter Hayes* (Greer, S.C., 1945), 28.

102. J. H. King, "Eschatology," *Live Coals of Fire,* 10 November 1899, 6. King, *Yet Speaketh,* 80–81. "Aunt Nancy's Experience," *Live Coals of Fire,* 4 May 1900, 6. "W. E. Fuller's (Colored) Letter," *Live Coals of Fire,* 26 January 1900, 1. See also "The Baptism of Fire," *The Way of Faith,* 23 December 1896, 1, and "Mrs. E. M. Pafford's Testimony," *Live Coals of Fire,* 18 May 1900, 5.

103. Synan, *Old Time Power,* 48–51. Only one ordained minister resided outside North America, in Capetown, South Africa. "Official List of the Fire-Baptized Holiness Association of America," *Live Coals of Fire,* 9 March 1900, 8.

104. "The Baptism of Fire," *The Way of Faith,* 13 November 1895, 4.

105. Stephen H. Webb, *Blessed Excess: Religion and the Hyperbolic Imagination* (Albany: State University of New York Press, 1993), xiii.

106. Godbey, *Autobiography,* 127–129. The Nazarene minister W. C. Wilson faulted Godbey for introducing this strange new doctrine. Godbey's translation, Wilson angrily protested, "has many times encouraged people to believe that the incoming of the Holy Spirit is always a spectacular, explosive experience, creating, as it were, a big noise and a big smoke." W. C. Wilson, "Well Glory!" manuscript, Church of the Nazarene Archives, Kansas City, Mo., 59.

107. "The Dynamite," *Live Coals of Fire,* 10 November 1899, 2. Edward Kelley, "Dynamite," 20 April 1900, 6. The historians Carl Smith and Paul Avrich highlight the performative aspects of bomb talk among late-century Chicago anarchists. According to Avrich, "week after week" dynamite's "virtues were glorified in articles, editorials, and even verse." Carl Smith, *Urban Disorder and the Shape of Belief: The Chicago Fire, the Haymarket Bomb, and the Model Town of Pullman* (Chicago: University of Chicago

Press, 1995), 115–118. Avrich, *The Haymarket Tragedy* (Princeton: Princeton University Press, 1984), 167, 160–177. Synan, *The Holiness-Pentecostal Tradition,* 57. On subsequent baptisms, see "Editorial Correspondence," *Live Coals of Fire,* 23 February 1900, 4.

108. Hilson, *History of the South Carolina Conference of the Wesleyan Methodist Church of America,* 45, 50.

109. *Telephone* quoted in "The Waco, Texas, Camp-Meeting," *The Pentecostal Herald,* 11 August 1897, 4. *Christian Advocate,* 3 March 1898, 8. E. D. Wells, "The Carnal Heart," *Live Coals of Fire,* 26 January 1900, 3.

110. J. A. Porter, "Is a Third Blessing Necessary?" *The Way of Faith,* 11 November 1896, 4. Synan, *The Holiness-Pentecostal Tradition,* 57. On the feuds that shook camp meetings, see Dennis Rogers, *Holiness Pioneering in the Southland* (Hemet, Calif., 1944), 26; Jernigan, *Pioneer Days,* 152–154, 156; and "Demorest, Georgia," *The Repairer and Holiness Advocate* (April 1900): 4. A. M. Hills, "Fanaticism among Holiness People," *The Holiness Advocate,* 1 April 1903, 5.

111. C. E. Jones, "Irwin, B(enjamin) H(ardin)," in *Dictionary of Christianity in America,* ed. Robert D. Linder, Daniel G. Reid, Bruce L. Shelley, and Harry S. Stout (Downers Grove, Ill.: InterVarsity Press, 1990), 583.

112. Dayton, *Theological Roots of Pentecostalism,* 174. C. T. S., "Trim Your Lamps," in *Blood and Fire Songs,* ed. C. T. Stevens (Shott, Mo., 1897), hymn no. 35.

5. The Emergence of Southern Pentecostalism

1. G. B. Cashwell, "Pentecost in the South," *The Apostolic Faith* (April 1907): 4.

2. See the comments of a leading Church of God (Cleveland) author in "History of Pentecost: The Shout Heard Round the World," *The Faithful Standard* (October 1922): 9.

3. Robert Mapes Anderson, *Vision of the Disinherited: The Making of American Pentecostalism* (New York: Oxford University Press, 1979), 47–48. James R. Goff Jr., *Fields White unto Harvest: Charles F. Parham and the Missionary Origins of Pentecostalism* (Fayetteville: University of Arkansas Press, 1988), 17–61.

4. Goff, *Fields White unto Harvest,* 54–56.

5. Acts 2:4.

6. "New Sect in Kansas Speaks with Strange Tongues," *St. Louis Post*

Dispatch, 25 January 1901. "Parham's New Religion Practiced at 'Stone's Folly,'" *Kansas City Times,* 27 January 1901. See also *Topeka Daily Capital,* 6 January 1901, 2, and *Topeka State Journal,* 7 January 1901, 4. Goff, *Fields White unto Harvest,* 79–83. Sarah E. Parham, *The Life of Charles F. Parham: Founder of the Apostolic Faith Movement* (1930; reprint, New York: Garland Publishing, 1985), 59–66.

7. Chas. F. Parham, *A Voice Crying in the Wilderness,* in *The Sermons of Charles F. Parham,* ed. Donald W. Dayton (1902; reprint, New York: Garland Publishing, 1985), 31. On the millennial hopes of the early tongues speakers, see Goff, *Fields White unto Harvest,* 15, 62, 164, and Vinson Synan, *The Holiness-Pentecostal Tradition: Charismatic Movements in the Twentieth Century* (Grand Rapids: William B. Eerdmans, 1997), 92.

8. Anderson, *Vision of the Disinherited,* 58.

9. C. W. Shumway, "A Study of 'The Gift of Tongues'" (A.B. thesis, University of Southern California, 1914), 173. Douglas J. Nelson, "For Such a Time as This: The Story of William J. Seymour and the Azusa Street Revival" (Ph.D. diss., University of Birmingham, 1981), 31–39. Douglas Jacobsen, *Thinking in the Spirit: Theologies of the Early Pentecostal Movement* (Bloomington: Indiana University Press, 2003), 59–65. M. Robeck, "Seymour, William Joseph," in *The New International Dictionary of Pentecostal and Charismatic Movements,* ed. Stanley M. Burgess and Eduard M. Van Der Maas (Grand Rapids: Zondervan, 2002), 1054–55. Dale T. Irvin, "Charles Price Jones: Image of Holiness," in *Portraits of a Generation: Early Pentecostal Leaders,* ed. James R. Goff and Grant Wacker (Fayetteville: University of Arkansas Press, 2002), 44. On former slaves reconnecting with lost kin, see Steven Hahn, *A Nation under Our Feet: Black Political Struggles in the Rural South from Slavery to the Great Migration* (Cambridge, Mass.: Harvard University Press, 2003), 166.

10. *Los Angeles Daily Times,* 18 April 1906, sec. 2, 1. *Los Angeles Daily Times,* 19 April 1906, sec. 2, 4. *Los Angeles Herald,* 10 September 1906, 7. *Los Angeles Herald,* 24 September 1906, 7. *Topeka Daily State Journal,* 25 July 1906, 6. *St. Louis Post Dispatch,* 2 August 1906, sec. 2, 11. Frank Bartleman, *Azusa Street* (1925; reprint, South Plainfield, N.J.: Bridge Publishing, 1980), 48. On the global significance of Azusa, see D. William Faupel, *The Everlasting Gospel: The Significance of Eschatology in the Development of Pentecostal Thought* (Sheffield, England: Sheffield Academic Press, 1996), 187–227.

11. Anderson, *Vision of the Disinherited*, 10–27, 44–46. Parham, *A Voice Crying in the Wilderness*, 29. Harold Hunter argues that the revival in North Carolina should not be confused with a "fully developed American Classical Pentecostal position," most significantly, because enthusiasts there did not make the connection between Holy Ghost baptism and the gift of tongues. Harold Hunter, "Spirit Baptism and the 1896 Revival in Cherokee County, North Carolina," *Pneuma* 5 (Fall 1983): 8–9.

12. On the connection between tongues speech and millennialism, see James R. Goff Jr., "Charles Parham and the Problem of History," in *All Together and in One Place: Theological Papers from the Brighton Conference on World Evangelism*, ed. Harold D. Hunter and Peter D. Hocken (Sheffield, England: Sheffield Academic Press, 1993), 189.

13. Robert Mapes Anderson posits that "speaking in tongues, miraculous healings, exorcisms, and other ecstatic practices are best understood in relationship to" millennialism. Anderson, *Vision of the Disinherited*, xiii, 79–80. See also Faupel, *The Everlasting Gospel*, 18.

14. Shumway, "Study of 'The Gift of Tongues,'" 20, 21.

15. Joe Creech contends that Azusa was only one of many historical points of origin for pentecostalism, although he acknowledges its symbolic and theological importance. Joe Creech, "Visions of Glory: The Place of the Azusa Street Revival in Pentecostal History," *Church History* 65 (September 1996): 406–408, 420. On the massive impact of the Azusa Street meeting, see Cecil M. Roebeck Jr., "Pentecostal Origins from a Global Perspective," in *All Together and in One Place*, 166–180. Anderson, *Vision of the Disinherited*, 74.

16. "A Message Concerning His Coming," *The Apostolic Faith* (October 1906): 3. See *The Apostolic Faith* (December 1906): 4; (January 1907): 2; (February–March 1907): 4; (April 1907): 3; (May 1907): 2, 3; (September 1907): 4.

17. On the pentecostal use of the "latter rain" metaphor, see Donald W. Dayton, *Theological Roots of Pentecostalism* (Metuchen, N.J.: Scarecrow Press, 1987), 26–28, and "The Pentecostal Baptism Restored," *The Apostolic Faith* (October 1906): 1. Some holiness authors had employed the "latter rain" concept at least since the 1880s. W. R. Monroe, "'The Early and Latter Rain'; Or Pentecost to Be Repeated," *The Christian Witness and Advocate of Bible Holiness*, 19 May 1887, 5. But the metaphor certainly took on greater meaning for pentecostals.

18. Grant Wacker argues that pentecostal periodicals "constituted by

far the most important technique for sustaining national and world consciousness." Grant Wacker, *Heaven Below: Early Pentecostals and American Culture* (Cambridge, Mass.: Harvard University Press, 2001), 264. F. L. Bramblett, D. R. Brown, and Hugh Bowling, "Report of Committee on Books and Periodicals," in *Minutes of the Fifth Annual Session of the Georgia and Upper South Carolina Convention of the Pentecostal Holiness Church Held at Canon, Ga., Nov. 17–19, 1915* (n.p., 1915), 8–9. A. J. Tomlinson, *The Last Great Conflict* (Cleveland, Tenn.: Press of Walter E. Rodgers, 1913), 118.

19. *The Apostolic Faith* (November 1906): 3, and (January 1907): 4. Bartleman, *Azusa Street,* 153.

20. Joseph H. King, *Yet Speaketh: Memoirs of the Late Bishop Joseph H. King* (Franklin Springs, Ga.: Publishing House of the Pentecostal Holiness Church, 1949), 112–113. J. H. King, "Transformed by the Holy Ghost," *The Apostolic Faith* (February–March 1907): 5. N. J. Holmes and Wife, *Life Sketches and Sermons* (Royston, Ga.: Press of the Pentecostal Holiness Church, 1920), 136–138, 140.

21. *The Gospel Witness* quoted in "Work Increasing," *The Apostolic Faith* (February–March 1907): 5.

22. On print culture and the formation of community, see Benedict Anderson, *Imagined Communities: Reflections on the Origins and Spread of Nationalism* (London: Verso, 1998), 32–36; Evelyn Brooks Higginbotham, *Righteous Discontent: The Women's Movement in the Black Baptist Church, 1880–1920* (Cambridge, Mass.: Harvard University Press, 1993), 11; and Nathan O. Hatch, *The Democratization of American Christianity* (New Haven: Yale University Press, 1989), 73, 75, 76, 146.

23. Over the course of his career, Bartleman authored more than 550 articles, 100 tracts, and 6 books. C. M. Robeck Jr., "Bartleman, Frank," in *The New International Dictionary of Pentecostal and Charismatic Movements,* 366. *The Apostolic Faith* (February–March 1907): 1.

24. Edward Ayers notes that new musical styles (jazz, the blues, and country music) entered the South at roughly the same time as holiness and pentecostalism did: "Those who played and those who preached incorporated new ideas and styles from outside the South into their own distinctly Southern vocabularies." Edward L. Ayers, *The Promise of the New South: Life after Reconstruction* (New York: Oxford University Press, 1992), 373.

25. As Wacker notes, believers occasionally "proved so respectful—or fearful—of the supernatural power embedded in their periodicals that per-

sons who had not received Holy Spirit baptism were not allowed to touch them." Wacker, *Heaven Below,* 94. A publication's power and reach were not limited by space or time. For instance, the Los Angeles–based *The Upper Room* reported that an overseas reader was instantly cured by reading it. "Healed While Reading This Paper," *The Upper Room* (July 1910): 1. Robert Mapes Anderson estimates that pentecostals published as many as seventy-four different newspapers in the early years of the movement. Anderson, *Vision of the Disinherited,* 75.

26. "Press the Revival—Reject the Counterfeit," *The Holiness Advocate,* 15 May 1907, 4. Crumpler later rejected the pentecostal faction and eventually returned to the Methodist Episcopal Church, South.

27. Alice Taylor, "In New Orleans," *The Apostolic Faith* (September 1907): 1.

28. Clark Eckert, "Pentecostal Work at Cocoanut Grove, Fla.," *The Bridegroom's Messenger,* 1 December 1908, 2. See also Berta Maxwell, "My Testimony," *The Holiness Advocate,* 1 June 1907, 6; R. F. Wellons, "My Experience," *The Holiness Advocate,* 8; H. E. Moulton, "Atlanta, Ga.," *The Bridegroom's Messenger,* 15 December 1907, 4; *The Bridegroom's Messenger,* 1 March 1908, 3; and Gary Don McElhany, "The South Aflame: A History of the Assemblies of God in the Gulf Region" (Ph.D. diss., Mississippi State University, 1996), 136–137.

29. M. H. Alexander, "Pasley, N. C., March 19, 1908," *The Bridegroom's Messenger,* 15 April 1908, 3. The Cane Ridge revival in Kentucky, which occurred more than one hundred years before Azusa, owed its success to similar modes of transmission. Historian Paul Conkin observes that ministers who participated in the ecstatic outdoor meetings spread the word through the pulpits of numerous southern congregations. Ministers retold the story of the revival to their audiences. As a result, physical exercises similar to those being described occurred among the laity. Paul K. Conkin, *Cane Ridge: America's Pentecost* (Madison: University of Wisconsin Press, 1990), 69–70.

30. F. L. Juillerat, "Durant, Fla.," *The Bridegroom's Messenger,* 1 December 1907, 3.

31. G. B. Cashwell, "Came 3,000 Miles for His Pentecost," *The Apostolic Faith,* 6 December 1907, 3.

32. Synan, *The Holiness-Pentecostal Tradition,* 113–114.

33. James R. Goff Jr., "The Pentecostal Catalyst to the South: G. B. Cashwell (1906–1909)," paper at the Flower Pentecostal Heritage Center,

Springfield, Mo., 2. "Well Adapted to Tobacco," *Atlanta Constitution,* 27 October 1893, 2.

34. McElhany, "The South Aflame," 30–31, 58, 62. G. B. Cashwell, "Pentecost in North Carolina," *The Apostolic Faith* (January 1907): 1. Vinson Synan, *Old Time Power: A Centennial History of the International Pentecostal Holiness Church* (Franklin Springs, Ga.: LifeSprings Resources, 1998), 98–101. "Fire Baptized Holiness Church Meet at Royston," *Atlanta Constitution,* 3 March 1907, B3. G. B. Cashwell, "An Explanation," *The Bridegroom's Messenger,* 1 October 1907, 1.

35. "The Bridegroom's Messenger, One Year Old Oct. 1," *The Bridegroom's Messenger,* 15 September 1908, 1. Cashwell also asked his regular subscribers to become agents for the paper. For twenty-five cents, readers would be given a bundle of papers to distribute to anyone who showed interest. In addition, Cashwell urged his readers to "send us names [of those] who are not able to pay that we may add them to our subscription list." "Are You Interested," *The Bridegroom's Messenger,* 1 October 1908, 2.

36. Bartleman, *Azusa Street,* 53. "Apostolic Faith Mission Church of God," in *Encyclopedia of African American Religions,* ed. Larry G. Murphy, J. Gordon Melton, and Gary L. Ward (New York: Garland Publishing, 1993), 51. C. H. Mason, "Tennessee Evangelist Witnesses," *The Apostolic Faith* (February–March 1907): 7.

37. G. F. Taylor, *The Spirit and the Bride* (Dunn, N.C., 1907), 98. By 1908 Cashwell's newspaper was regularly advertising Taylor's book. *The Bridegroom's Messenger,* 15 January 1908, 1.

38. "Revival at Texarkana," *Dallas Morning News,* 14 September 1908, 2. R. B. Hayes, "Perilous Times," *The Bridegroom's Messenger,* 15 January 1908, 1. B. Dinnick, "A Sign of His Coming," *The Holiness Advocate,* 1 June 1907, 3. E. A. Sexton, "Jesus Is Coming," *The Bridegroom's Messenger,* 1 February 1908, 1. Elizabeth A. Sexton, "And Hath Raised Us Up Together, and Made Us to Sit Together in Heavenly Places in Christ Jesus," *The Bridegroom's Messenger,* 1 March 1908, 1. See also Wm. A. Gurganus, *A Sketch of My Early Experience* (Norfolk, Va.: by the author, n.d.), 3.

39. J. B. Keeling, "Religious Fervor Drives Devotees to Strange Antics," *Birmingham Age-Herald,* 23 June 1907, 27. Allan Anderson, *An Introduction to Pentecostalism: Global Charismatic Christianity* (Cambridge: Cambridge University Press, 2004), 217, 219.

40. "Colleges vs. Gifts of Tongues," *The Bridegroom's Messenger,* 1 October 1907, 1. "Sept. 6th 5 A.M.," *The Bridegroom's Messenger,* 1 October

1907, 1. "T. A. Cary's Letter," *Live Coals,* 13 February 1907, 4. Florence Goff, *Fifty Years on the Battlefield for God* (Falcon, N.C., n.d.), 51.

41. Frederick Hencke, "The Gift of Tongues and Related Phenomena at the Present Day," *American Journal of Theology* 13 (April 1909): 198–199, 202.

42. Anderson, *Vision of the Disinherited,* 99, 101, 113. Wacker, *Heaven Below,* 202–205, 208–211. See also the demographic research of Robert Francis Martin. In his 1975 study of early pentecostals, Martin discovered few social, cultural, or economic differences between pentecostals and their nonpentecostal neighbors in the South. Robert Francis Martin, "The Early Years of American Pentecostalism, 1900–1940: Survey of a Social Movement" (Ph.D. diss., University of North Carolina, 1975), 122–152. The historian Daniel Woods found that pentecostals in western Virginia and southern West Virginia typically came from the middle to upper range of the working classes, what he calls the "aspiring working class." Daniel Glenn Woods, "Living in the Presence of God: Enthusiasm, Authority, and Negotiation in the Practice of Pentecostal Holiness" (Ph.D. diss., University of Mississippi, 1997), 139–143.

43. Anderson, *Vision of the Disinherited,* 109. Wacker, *Heaven Below,* 213–216. Shumway, "Study of 'The Gift of Tongues,'" 192. "Questions about Speaking with Tongues Answered," *The Wesleyan Methodist,* 18 March 1908, 8–9.

44. Wacker, *Heaven Below,* 215. D. Woods, "Awrey, Daniel P.," in *New International Dictionary of Pentecostal and Charismatic Movements,* 344. D. C. Opperman, another traveling evangelist-educator, ministered throughout the South and Southwest. Moving about the country constantly, Opperman established numerous short-term Bible schools. E. L. Blumhofer, "Opperman, Daniel Charles Owen," *New International Dictionary of Pentecostal and Charismatic Movements,* 946.

45. Quoted in Anderson, *Vision of the Disinherited,* 69. Keeling, "Religious Fervor Drives Devotees to Strange Antics," 27.

46. Edith Blumhofer, *Restoring the Faith: The Assemblies of God, Pentecostalism, and American Culture* (Urbana: University of Illinois Press, 1993), 71–72. *The Holiness Advocate,* 15 May 1907, 8. "Children's Corner," *The Holiness Advocate,* 1 June 1907, 2. Wacker, *Heaven Below,* 48.

47. "Services Held by New Sect in Gate City," *Atlanta Constitution,* 11 July 1907, 1.

48. For a discussion of the role of women leaders in the holiness movement, see Lucille Sider Dayton and Donald W. Dayton, "'Your Daughters Shall Prophesy': Feminism in the Holiness Movement," *Methodist History* 14 (January 1976): 67–92. Nowhere was this more clear perhaps than in the Church of God, Anderson, which struggled to maintain interracial communion and some degree of gender equality throughout its history. Cheryl J. Sanders writes that blacks make up 20 percent of current COG Anderson membership. Equally astonishing, the first black congregation in the denomination was founded and pastored by a woman, Jane Williams, in Charleston, South Carolina, in 1886. Cheryl J. Sanders, *Saints in Exile: The Holiness-Pentecostal Experience in African American Religion and Culture* (New York: Oxford University Press, 1996), 22, 33.

49. Wayne E. Warner, *The Women Evangelist: The Life and Times of Charismatic Evangelist Maria B. Woodworth-Etter* (Metuchen, N.J.: Scarecrow Press, 1986).

50. Anna Kelly, "More about Women Preaching," *The Holiness Advocate,* 1 March 1906, 5. On gender equality at Azusa, see Nelson, "For Such a Time as This," 197–198, 204. This equality stands in sharp contrast to the prevailing view of southern Methodists at this time. Representative of an earlier southern mainline opinion, one leader of the MECS noted, "If Christ had intended that women should preach, it seems likely that he would have chosen some of them to be apostles." W. A. McCarty, "Emancipated Woman," *Christian Advocate,* 30 May 1895, 3.

51. Joe Creech argues that the Church of God (Cleveland), even after it became pentecostal, remained antagonistic to "racial mingling, and women had little place in the COG hierarchy." Creech, "Visions of Glory," 415. Furthermore, David G. Roebuck posits that the COG limited the roles of women ministers because "the original premise upon which they ministered—that Spirit-baptism in these 'last days' equips women for ministry—failed to impute authority to women." David G. Roebuck, "Limiting Liberty: The Church of God and Women Ministers, 1886–1996" (Ph.D. diss., Vanderbilt University, 1997), 4. Wacker, too, observes that "other priorities eclipsed self-conscious gender concerns of any sort—traditional, progressive, or otherwise." Wacker, *Heaven Below,* 176.

52. Wacker, *Heaven Below,* 234.

53. William Archer, *An English Reading of the Race Problem* (New York: E. P. Dutton, 1910), 73–75. For an example of the racist tirades that

dotted the front pages of white southern denominational papers, see *The Baptist Record* (Jackson, Mississippi), 17 January 1907, 1.

54. Quote from A. A. Boddy, "The Southern States," *Confidence* (September 1912): 209, reprinted in *The Bridegroom's Messenger*, 1 September 1912, 1. *The Apostolic Faith* (February–March 1907): 7. Bartleman, *Azusa Street*, 54. Jacobsen, *Thinking in the Spirit*, 260–263.

55. Ethel E. Goss, *The Winds of God: The Story of the Early Pentecostal Movement (1901–1914) in the Life of Howard A. Goss* (1958; reprint, Hazelwood, Mo.: Word Aflame Press, 1985), 98.

56. "Ba Ba Bharati Says Not a Language," *Los Angeles Times*, 19 September 1906, 1.

57. *The Apostolic Faith* (Kansas), October 1912, 6. Chas. F. Parham, "Free-Love," *The Apostolic Faith* (Kansas), December 1912, 4. Charles F. Parham, *The Everlasting Gospel*, in *Sermons of Charles F. Parham*, 118. See also the racist arguments of Alma White, a holiness evangelist who would later sympathize with the Ku Klux Klan. White depicted Azusa and its southern outposts as mongrelized carnivals of free love. Alma White, *Demons and Tongues* (1936; reprint, Zarephath, N.J.: Pillar of Fire Publishers, 1949), 67, 72–73, 82.

58. W. B. McCafferty, *Pioneer Incidents*, 3, quoted in McElhany, "The South Aflame," 192.

59. F. F. Bosworth, *Bosworth's Life Story: The Life Story of Evangelist F. F. Bosworth, as Told by Himself in the Alliance Tabernacle, Toronto* (Toronto: Alliance Book Room, n.d.), 12–13. F. F. Bosworth, to "Mother and All," 21 August 1911, Flower Pentecostal Heritage Center, Springfield, Mo. F. F. Bosworth to "Mr. B. B. Bosworth," September 1912, Flower Pentecostal Heritage Center, Springfield, Mo.

60. M. M. Pinson, "Sketch of the Life and Ministry of Mack M. Pinson," manuscript, Flower Pentecostal Heritage Center, Springfield, Mo., 6 September 1949, 9, 13. Edith Blumhofer notes that for every story of women being affirmed in leadership there is also one of frustration and suppression. Edith L. Blumhofer, "Women in American Pentecostalism," *Pneuma* 17 (Spring 1995): 19. The pentecostal press occasionally sent mixed signals, elevating women to leadership status while relegating them to a subservient role. In the same issue of *The Church of God Evangel*, J. A. Giddens advocated women's right to preach, while E. B. Culpepper cautioned women: "You will have all you can do without running [your] hus-

band's [business] or [the] business of the church." E. B. Culpepper, "Who Is Head of the Family, Husband or Wife?" *The Church of God Evangel,* 6 May 1916, 4. On this ambiguous legacy, Cheryl Townsend Gilkes, drawing on oral tradition, remarks that although the major black pentecostal bodies denied women ordination, women nonetheless assumed powerful roles as exhorters, church mothers, missionaries, teachers, and deaconesses. Cheryl Townsend Gilkes, "'Together and in Harness': Women's Traditions in the Sanctified Church," *Signs* 10, no. 4 (Summer 1985): 683.

61. The historian Jarod H. Roll, however, draws connections between pentecostalism and socialism in Missouri. In the 1910s several Church of God (Cleveland) preachers were believed to be socialists, and newspapers in the Bootheel linked "holy roller" religion with political radicalism. Roll observes that both "were new and radical; neither advocated a return to old standards. Whatever the case, both movements empowered the rural working class to transfer that energy into public broadcasts of faith and hope." Jarod H. Roll, "From Revolution to Reaction: Early Pentecostalism, Radicalism, and Race in Southeast Missouri, 1910–1930," *Radical History Review* 90 (Fall 2004): 17. I have found little evidence of this link in my research. Pentecostals' challenge to mainstream culture was largely apolitical. Consequently some scholars have been quick to criticize or dismiss the movement. In the 1940s Liston Pope's study of labor unrest in Gaston County, North Carolina, indicted church leaders for not standing "in opposition to the prevailing economic arrangements or to the drastic methods employed for their preservation." Liston Pope, *Millhands and Preachers: A Study of Gastonia* (New Haven: Yale University Press, 1942), 330. Robert Mapes Anderson concludes that pentecostalism represented a dysfunctional and maladjusted reaction to social pressures. Because of pentecostals' negative appraisal of society and their pessimistic outlook, they were an apolitical, "conservative bulwark of the status quo" who channeled their social protest "into the harmless backwaters of religious ideology." Anderson, *Vision of the Disinherited,* 239. Similarly, R. Laurence Moore argues that the otherworldliness of pentecostals cut off social protest by defusing class hostilities. R. Laurence Moore, *Religious Outsiders and the Making of Americans* (New York: Oxford University Press, 1986), 140–142. For a counter to these appraisals, see Clifford Geertz, *The Interpretation of Cultures: Selected Essays* (New York: Basic Books, 1973), 124, 93, 119. For an assessment of the positive role of faith in pentecostalism, see Grant Wacker,

"The Functions of Faith in Primitive Pentecostalism," *Harvard Theological Review* 77 (1984): 355, 356, 363.

62. "R. B. Hayes' Letter," *The Bridegroom's Messenger,* 1 October 1907, 2. M. M. Pinson, "Birmingham Report," *The Bridegroom's Messenger,* 1 December 1907, 1. See also B. F. Lawrence, *The Apostolic Faith Restored,* in *Three Early Pentecostal Tracts,* ed. Donald Dayton (1916; reprint, New York: Garland Publishing,, 1985), 12.

63. "Mrs. Anna Kelly's Letter," *The Apostolic Evangel,* 3 April 1907, 4. On direct communication with God, see Woods, "Living in the Presence of God," 24. "Above all else," Woods argues, "pentecostals desired the assurance and guidance that comes from hearing the voice of God." Woods, "Living in the Presence of God," 29, 85.

64. Pinson, "Sketch of the Life and Ministry of Mack M. Pinson," 9. Goss, *The Winds of God,* 80. Holmes, *Life Sketches and Sermons,* 144–145. For an examination of the exuberant new musical styles of black holiness and pentecostalism, see Paul Oliver, *Songsters and Saints: Vocal Traditions on Race Records* (Cambridge: Cambridge University Press, 1984), 169–198.

65. Wacker, *Heaven Below,* 49. For more on the failure of foreign tongues (xenolalia), see Anderson, *Vision of the Disinherited,* 16–19, 90–92; Goff, *Fields White unto Harvest,* 154; and Gary B. McGee, "'Latter Rain' Falling in the East: Early-Twentieth-Century Pentecostalism in India and the Debate over Speaking in Tongues," *Church History* 68 (September 1999): 660–661. The University of Southern California researcher C. W. Shumway could not track down or verify any actual incidents of xenolalia. Shumway, "Study of 'The Gift of Tongues,'" 42, 45, 170. Ann Taves, *Fits, Trances, and Visions: Experiencing Religion and Explaining Experience from Wesley to James* (Princeton: Princeton University Press, 1999), 9, 332–334.

66. James R. Goff, "The Limits of Acculturation: Thomas Hampton Gourley and American Pentecostalism," *Pnuema* 8 (Fall 1996): 171. Duncan Aikman, "Holy Rollers," *American Mercury* 15 (October 1928): 186. Goss, *The Winds of God,* 150.

67. See selections from *Gadsen Evening Journal* and *Gadsen Daily News* in Dorothy Womack Oden, *The History of the Alabama City Church of God* (Montgomery: Herff Jones, 1988), 9–13. I. A. Newby, *Plain Folk in the New South: Social Change and Cultural Persistence, 1880–1915* (Baton Rouge: Louisiana State University Press, 1989), 406. For other instances of

persecution, see T. J. McIntosh, "A Note from Brother McIntosh," *The Way of Faith,* 4 October 1909, 8; Ayers, *The Promise of the New South,* 400–401; and George W. Stanley, *My Life's Experiences with God* (Franklin Springs, Ga.: Publishing House of the Pentecostal Holiness Church, n.d.), 24–25.

68. "Holy Roller Preacher Was Struck in the Face," *Atlanta Constitution,* 17 January 1908, 3.

69. "Letter of a Baptist Preacher to His Wife Describing a Pentecostal Meeting at Durant, Fla.,'" *The Evening Light and Church of God Evangel,* 1 July 1910, 2. "Report from Florida," *The Way of Faith,* 23 July 1908, 13.

70. Rev. E. J. Hardee, "Wauchula Letter," *The Florida Christian Advocate,* 20 August 1907, 3. "Presbyterian Church," *The Champion,* 12 November 1908, 4.

71. John G. Logan, "The Pentecostal Tongues," *Toccoa Record,* 7 March 1907, 4. The official organ of southern Methodism, the *Christian Advocate,* also predicted the demise of what it depicted as regressive pentecostal sects. The modern miracles of science, travel, and worldwide progress, one editorial declared, would sweep away the primitive superstitions of pentecostalism. "Miracles of Healing," *The Christian Advocate,* 1 January 1909, 4. "Toccoa City Council Proceedings," *Toccoa Record,* 7 March 1907, 5.

72. *Biblical Recorder* quoted in *The Christian Index,* 11 April 1907, 1. S. C. Todd, "Some Sad Failures of Tongues in Mission Fields," *Baptist Argus,* 23 January 1908, 1–2. For an example of a prominent evangelical's public condemnation of pentecostalism, see A. C. Dixon, *Speaking with Tongues* (Los Angeles: Biola Book Room, n.d.).

73. Sigmund Freud, *Civilization and Its Discontents,* trans. James Strachey (New York: W. W. Norton and Company, 1962), 61–62.

74. Grover C. Loud, *Evangelized America* (1928; reprint, Freeport, N.Y.: Books for Libraries Press, 1971), 280. This "freedom of the Spirit" motif, as Samuel Hill points out, had long permeated southern religious history. If spiritual freedom was imperiled, then, as evangelicals frequently maintained, the act of leaving mainline churches was justified. Baptists in the eighteenth century and O'Kellyites, Stoneites, Campbellites, and Antimission Baptists in the early nineteenth century all made the exodus, at least in part, in the interests of practicing according to their own beliefs. Samuel S. Hill, *One Name but Several Faces: Variety in Popular Christian Denominations in Southern History* (Athens: University of Georgia Press, 1996), 80, 81.

75. As early as 1902 Charles Parham argued that even John Wesley, the patron saint of perfectionism, did not have the baptism of the Spirit since he never spoke in tongues. Parham, *A Voice Crying in the Wilderness*, 32, 35. Grant Wacker, "Travail of a Broken Family: Evangelical Responses to Pentecostalism in America, 1906–1916," *Journal of Ecclesiastical History* 47 (July 1996): 526, 505–528. Wacker, *Heaven Below*, 183. J. H. King, intro. to Taylor, *The Spirit and the Bride*. See also D. Beaufort Causey, "Silver, S. C.," *The Bridegroom's Messenger,* 15 April 1908, 3. Goff, *Fifty Years on the Battlefield for God,* 51. G. B. Cashwell, like many first-generation southern pentecostals, could "not see how any honest man or woman can claim to have the pentecostal baptism and not have the pentecostal evidence [speaking in tongues]." G. B. Cashwell, "Pentecostal Evidence," *The Apostolic Evangel,* 3 April 1907, 3.

76. As the historian Charles Edwin Jones points out, pentecostals believed that speaking in tongues was the initial evidence of Holy Spirit baptism. This thoroughly offended holiness adherents who did not possess "the gift." Charles Edwin Jones, "Tongues-Speaking and the Wesleyan-Holiness Quest for Assurance of Sanctification," *Wesleyan Theological Journal* 22 (Fall 1987): 117–124.

77. B. F. Haynes, "Fanaticism and Its Progeny," *The Pentecostal Advocate,* 10 February 1910, 2. Winfred R. Cox, "An Open Door for Heresy," *God's Revivalist and Bible Advocate,* 23 May 1907, 10. Oswald Chambers, "Third Work of Grace–A Confusion of the Devil," *God's Revivalist and Bible Advocate,* 14 February 1907, 1. "BORDER LAND HOLINESS PEOPLE," *Nazarene Messenger,* 15 April 1909, 12. Amanda Coulson, "The Tongues People as I Saw Them," *The Pentecostal Advocate,* 18 May 1911, 7.

78. P. B. Campbell, "The Gift of Tongues," *The Wesleyan Methodist,* 13 February 1907, 8. S. A. Manwell, "Speaking with Tongues," *The Wesleyan Methodist,* 6 March 1907.

79. Anderson, *Vision of the Disinherited,* 151. William H. Budd, *The Bible Gift of Tongues vs. the Modern Gift of Unknown Tongues* (1909; reprint, Louisville: Pentecostal Publishing House, 193?), 15.

80. "The Tongues Movement," *The Holiness Evangel,* 16 September 1908, 2. For a similar account, see G. C. Mendenhall, "North Carolina," *The Wesleyan Methodist,* 16 October 1907, 5. Goss, *The Winds of God,* 207, 208. For other lurid descriptions of pentecostal revivals in holiness papers, see "More about Satisfactory Evidence," *The Wesleyan Methodist,* 21 September 1910, 11, and T. M. Coon, "Georgia," *The Wesleyan Methodist,* 21

September 1910, 11. On the fear of being confused with pentecostals, see James Benjamin Hilson, *History of the South Carolina Conference of the Wesleyan Methodist Church of America: Fifty Years of Wesleyan Methodism in South Carolina* (Winona Lake, Ind.: Light and Life Press, 1950), 85.

81. W. B. Godbey, *Tongue Movement, Satanic* (Zarephath, N.J.: Pillar of Fire, 1918), 4–5. W. B. Godbey, *Spiritualism, Devil-Worship and the Tongues Movement* (Cincinnati: God's Revivalist Press, n.d.), 26. Barry W. Hamilton, *William Baxter Godbey: Itinerant Apostle of the Holiness Movement* (Lewiston, N.Y.: Edwin Mellen Press, 2000), 259–264. The issue of tongues speech ultimately divided holiness and pentecostal believers. First-generation pentecostals' identity almost always hinged on Holy Ghost baptism, signified by tongues speech. This was the case even though some anecdotal evidence suggests that only one in two pentecostals actually spoke in tongues. Wacker, *Heaven Below*, 35, 41. Unlike Wacker, the historian Donald Dayton does not acknowledge the central role played by tongues speech. Dayton, *Theological Roots of Pentecostalism*, 15, 16.

82. On the fourfold gospel, see Dayton, *Theological Roots of Pentecostalism*, 21.

83. See "Is the World Growing Better?" *The Wesleyan Methodist*, 11 September 1907, 1, and "A Sad Compromise," *The Wesleyan Methodist*, 11 December 1907, 8. C. W. Ruth, "The Gift of Tongues," *The Pentecostal Messenger*, 1 November 1912, 2.

84. Goff, *Fifty Years on the Battlefield for God*, 52. McElhany, "The South Aflame," 110. John T. Benson, *A History, 1898–1915, of the Pentecostal Mission, Inc., Nashville, Tennessee* (Nashville: Trevecca Press, 1977), 94.

85. Synan, *Old Time Power*, 107. On Crumpler's break with N. J. Holmes's pentecostal school, see A. B. Crumpler, unaddressed letter, 2 June 1909, International Pentecostal Holiness Church Archives, Oklahoma City.

86. Ithiel C. Clemmons, *Bishop C. H. Mason and the Roots of the Church of God in Christ* (Bakersfield, CA.: Pneuma Life Pub., 1996), 65–66.

87. Timothy L. Smith, *Called unto Holiness: The Story of the Nazarenes, the Formative Years* (Kansas City, Mo.: Nazarene Publishing House, 1962), 320. "Monterey, Tenn.," *The Pentecostal Advocate*, 8 April 1909, 10. Pentecostal Church of the Nazarene, Arkansas District, *Journal* (n.p., 1910), 34. C. B. Jernigan, *Pioneer Days of the Holiness Movement in the Southwest* (Kansas City, Mo.: Pentecostal Publishing House, 1919), 84. "Tongues," *The Pentecostal Advocate* (Peniel, Tex.), 25 November 1909, 5.

As of 2001, southerners made up only 13 percent of the denomination's total U.S. membership. See John L. Brasher, "Church of the Nazarene" in *Encyclopedia of Religion in the South, Revised,* ed. Samuel Hill and Charles H. Lippy (Macon, Ga.: Mercer University Press, 2005), 207–209.

88. B. L. Padgett, "South Carolina," *The Wesleyan Methodist,* 27 March 1907, 4. J. R. George, "South Carolina," *The Wesleyan Methodist,* 8 April 1907, 9. On membership losses, see Hilson, *History of the South Carolina Conference of the Wesleyan Methodist Church of America,* 84, 91. For examples of other bitter encounters between Wesleyans and pentecostals, see these items from *The Wesleyan Methodist:* G. C. Mendenhall, "North Carolina," 16 October 1907, 5; B. L. Padgett and J. C. Brewington, "Long Shoals," 2 September 1908, 12; H. S. Dixon, "The Work in Georgia," 14 October 1908, 4; and H. S. Dixon, "Georgia," 30 June 1909, 4. For a suggestive account of Wesleyan losses in the region, see Ira Ford McLeister and Roy Stephen Nicholson, *History of the Wesleyan Methodist Church of America* (Marion, Ind.: Wesley Press, 1959), 462.

89. A. J. Tomlinson, "Journal of Happenings: The Diary of A. J. Tomlinson, 1901–23," 25 September 1908, 56, Dixon Pentecostal Research Center, Cleveland, Tenn.

90. Shumway, "A Study of 'The Gift of Tongues,'" 191.

91. Anderson, *Vision of the Disinherited,* 114, 268, note 2. U.S. Bureau of the Census, *Religious Bodies, 1916,* vol. 2 (Washington, D.C.: Government Printing Office, 1919), 41, 211, 218, 219, 275. The 1936 census of religious bodies reported 356,329 pentecostals in the United States. Roughly one out of every two lived in the South. Anderson, *Vision of the Disinherited,* 114.

6. THE EAGLE SOARS

1. C. W. Shumway, "A Study of 'The Gift of Tongues'" (A.B. thesis, University of Southern California, 1914), 191. Robert Mapes Anderson, *Vision of the Disinherited: The Making of American Pentecostalism* (New York: Oxford University Press, 1979), 170. Grant Wacker, *Heaven Below: Early Pentecostals and American Culture* (Cambridge, Mass.: Harvard University Press, 2001), 271. "Pentecostalism and the 100th Anniversary of the Azusa Street Revival," pewforum.org (accessed 8/23/06). The American South still contains the largest concentration of committed evangelical Protestants. These are Christians who regularly attend worship services

and hold traditional beliefs. Baptists and pentecostals are good examples of this group, which accounts for 52 percent of the South's population. Andrew Kohut, John C. Green, Scott Keeter, and Robert C. Toth, *The Diminishing Divide: Religion's Changing Role in American Politics* (Washington, D.C.: Brookings Institution Press, 2000), 130.

2. "The Third Force in Christendom," *Life*, 6 June 1958, 113.

3. William A. Clark, "Sanctification in Negro Religion," *Social Forces* 15 (May 1937): 546, 549.

4. Will Herberg, *Protestant-Catholic-Jew: An Essay in American Religious Sociology* (Chicago: University of Chicago Press, 1983), 123. "The Third Force in Christendom," 116.

5. Lisa McGirr, *Suburban Warriors: The Origins of the New American Right* (Princeton: Princeton University Press, 2001), 48–53. For a fascinating account of one such pentecostal family, see Dan Morgan, *Rising in the West: The True Story of an "Okie" Family from the Great Depression through the Reagan Years* (New York: Alfred A. Knopf, 1992). Originating in Arkansas in 1914 with only six thousand members, the Assemblies of God would grow to 2.2 million by 1990. By then most members lived in the Midwest and West. Brett Carroll, *The Routledge Historical Atlas of Religion in America* (New York: Routledge, 2000), 118–119.

6. James Baldwin, *Go Tell It on the Mountain* (1952; reprint, New York: Laurel, 1985), 12, 18. On the emergence of African American storefront churches in Chicago, see James R. Grossman, *Land of Hope: Chicago, Black Southerners, and the Great Migration* (Chicago: University of Chicago Press, 1991), 94–95, 131, 158–159. See also Anthea D. Butler, "Church Mothers and Migration in the Church of God in Christ," in *Religion in the American South: Protestants and Others in History and Culture*, ed. Beth Barton Schweiger and Donald G. Mathews (Chapel Hill: University of North Carolina Press, 2004), 195–218, and Arthur E. Paris, *Black Pentecostalism: Southern Religion in an Urban World* (Amherst: University of Massachusetts Press, 1982).

7. "History of Pentecost: The Shout Heard around the World," *The Faithful Standard* (October 1922): 15.

8. Zachary M. Tackett, "Signs of the Times: Premillennialism in the *Pentecostal Evangel*, 1914–2001," paper delivered at the Annual Meeting of the Society for Pentecostal Studies, Regent University, Virginia Beach, Va., March 2005, 3–4. William W. Menzies, *Anointed to Serve: The Story of the Assemblies of God* (Springfield, Mo.: Gospel Publishing House, 1971), 328–

329. "Requirements for the Rapture," General Presbytery Minutes of the Assemblies of God, 1946, 12, Flower Pentecostal Heritage Center, Springfield, Mo.

9. See, for instance, the creed of the African American pentecostal denomination the Bible Way Church of Our Lord Jesus Christ. One of that group's chief tenets concerned "the resurrection and rapture of the true Church of God." "What We Believe and Preach," *The Bible Way News Voice* (Washington, D.C.) (December–January 1950–51): 2. The Church of God in Christ also includes a section on the second coming in its principal doctrines, although, like some other African American groups, the church does not emphasize premillennialism and the rapture to the extent that white organizations do. "The Doctrines of the Church of God in Christ," cogic.org (accessed 8/16/06). For the church's earlier view on the rapture, see *ChoG in Christ,* Year Book, 44th Annual Convention (1951), 88–89, quoted in Walter J. Hollenweger, "Black Pentecostal Concept," *Concept* 30 (June 1970): 32; for the views of a host of other black churches in the years before 1970, see 35–66. The current doctrinal statement of the African American Fire-Baptized Church of God of the Americas is more specific than the Church of God in Christ's: "We Believe . . . in the imminent personal pre-millenial second coming of our Lord Jesus Christ (1 Thessalonians 4:15–18; Titus 2:13; 2 Peter 3:1–14; Matthew 24:20–24), and we love and await for His appearing (2 Timothy 4:8)." "What We Believe," fbhchurch.org (accessed 8/16/06). The Memphis-based African American World Overcomers Outreach Ministries Church is also explicit: "WE BELIEVE in the imminent RETURN OF JESUS CHRIST and bodily rapture or resurrection of the church (Acts 1:11; 1 Thessalonians 4:13–17)." "What We Believe," worldovercomers.org (accessed 8/28/06). The Assemblies of God's doctrine of premillennialism is similar, if even more precise: "The Assemblies of God preaches a clear message that Jesus is coming soon, and we will preach that message without apology, no matter how long the Lord delays His coming." The church includes detailed sections on the rapture and the tribulation in its doctrinal statement. "End-Time Events," ag.org (accessed 8/16/06). On the millennial views of other pentecostal groups, see "Our Story," pawinc.org (accessed 8/16/06); "Coming of the Lord," arc.iphc.org (accessed 8/16/06); and "Doctrinal Commitments," churchofgod.cc (accessed 8/16/06). *Spirit and Power: A 10-Country Survey of Pentecostals* (Washington, D.C.: The Pew Forum on Religion and Public Life), 24, pewforum.org (accessed 11/22/2006).

10. Vinson Synan, *The Holiness-Pentecostal Tradition: Charismatic Movements in the Twentieth Century* (Grand Rapids: William B. Eerdmans, 1997), 153, 196. On African American churches, see L. Lovett, "Black Holiness Pentecostalism," in *The New International Dictionary of Pentecostal and Charismatic Movements,* ed. Stanley M. Burgess and Eduard M. Van Der Maas (Grand Rapids: Zondervan, 2002), 424–427.

11. The Church of God of Prophecy built a religious theme park in Cherokee County, North Carolina, known as Fields of the Wood. Commemorating the place where A. J. Tomlinson "prevailed in prayer," the 216-acre shrine boasts the world's largest reproduction of the Ten Commandments, built into the side of a mountain. The denomination claims that Fields of the Wood is the site where all nations of the world will one day recognize the authority of the Church of God. Synan, *The Holiness-Pentecostal Tradition,* 199. H. D. Hunter, "Fields of the Wood," in *The New International Dictionary of Pentecostal and Charismatic Movements,* 636–637.

12. Vinson Synan, *Old Time Power: A Centennial History of the International Pentecostal Holiness Church* (Franklin Springs, Ga.: LifeSprings Resources, 1998), 110. M. M. Pinson, Oildale, Calif., to Rev. J. R. Flower, Springfield, Mo., 10 January 1951, Flower Pentecostal Heritage Center, Springfield, Mo.

13. James R. Goff Jr., *Fields White unto Harvest: Charles F. Parham and the Missionary Origins of Pentecostalism* (Fayetteville: University of Arkansas Press, 1988), 152.

14. Anderson, *Vision of the Disinherited,* 169, 175, 170. Synan, *The Holiness-Pentecostal Tradition,* 152.

15. "'Rollers' Have No Color Line," *Atlanta Constitution,* 30 June 1912, 12.

16. "Preacher Held in Man's Death at Tent Meeting," *Atlanta Constitution,* 13 August 1922, 1. "Farmer Admits Pulpit Killing," *Atlanta Constitution,* 15 August 1922, 1.

17. Anderson, *Vision of the Disinherited,* 188–192.

18. Quoted in David Edwin Harrell Jr., *White Sects and Black Men in the Recent South* (Nashville: Vanderbilt University Press, 1971), 95–96. Harold D. Hunter, "A Journey toward Racial Reconciliation: Race Mixing in the CGP," paper delivered at the Annual Meeting of the Society for Pentecostal Studies, Marquette University, Milwaukee, March 2004, 8–9.

19. "All Races Essentially Alike, Report of Eight Scientists," *The Bible Way News Voice* (December–January 1950–51): 1. "Elder Williams Helps Interracial Group to Fight Discrimination," *The Bible Way News Voice* (September–October 1950): 1. Elder Williams, "Pastor's Prophecy of Death Fulfilled," *The Bible Way News Voice* (November–December 1947): 1–2. In 1952 the African American minister R. C. Lawson, founder of the Church of Our Lord Jesus Christ, wrote his scathing "Letter to a Southern White Preacher" in which he challenged segregationists by tracing the ancestry of Christ to an African line. Robert C. Spellman, "Issues of Consensus and Controversy amongst Mainline Predominantly Black Pentecostal Church Organizations," paper delivered at the Annual Meeting of the Society for Pentecostal Studies, Christ for The Nations Institute, Dallas, 1990, J35.

20. James L. Delk, "Miscellanea: A Tribute to Bishop Mason and the Church of God in Christ," n.d., 7, 11, Flower Pentecostal Heritage Center, Springfield, Mo.

21. Allison Calhoun-Brown, "While Marching to Zion: Other-worldliness and Racial Empowerment in the Black Community," *Journal for the Scientific Study of Religion* 37 (September 1998): 432. George Eaton Simpson, "Black Pentecostalism in the United States," *Phylon* 35 (2nd quarter 1974): 210. On C. H. Mason, see Vinson Synan, "The Quiet Rise of Black Pentecostals," *Charisma* (June 1986): 48. David D. Daniels III, "'Doing All the Good We Can': The Political Witness of African American Holiness and Pentecostal Churches in the Post–Civil Rights Era," in *New Day Begun: African American Churches and Civic Culture in Post–Civil Rights America* (Durham, N.C.: Duke University Press, 2003), 164–165, 168–169, 171–173.

22. U.S. Federal Bureau of Investigation, "Unsubs; Burning of the Sanctified Pentecostal Church," FD-304, 4 February 1965, Dupree African-American Pentecostal and Holiness Collection, Schomburg Center for Research in Black Culture, New York Public Library.

23. Quoted in Daniels, "'Doing All the Good We Can,'" 170. David J. Garrow, *Bearing the Cross: Martin Luther King, Jr., and the Southern Christian Leadership Conference* (New York: Vintage Books, 1986), 620–621. Andrew Billingsley, *Mighty Like a River: The Black Church and Social Reform* (New York: Oxford University Press, 1999), 97.

24. W. F. Carothers, "Attitudes of Pentecostal Whites to the Colored Brethren in the South," *The Weekly Evangel,* 14 August 1915, 2.

25. Mark Newman, *Getting Right with God: Southern Baptists and Desegregation, 1945–1995* (Tuscaloosa: University of Alabama Press, 2001), 171, 182–183.

26. "Our Colored Brethren," *The Pentecostal Evangel,* 12 January 1946, 12. Ralph M. Riggs, Springfield, Mo., to Rev. Nicholas B. H. Bhengu, East London, South Africa, 23 February 1955, Flower Pentecostal Heritage Center, Springfield, Mo. See also Riggs, Springfield, Mo., to Reverend Kenneth Roper, Covelo, Calif., 24 January 1956, Flower Pentecostal Heritage Center, Springfield, Mo.

27. Edith Blumhofer, *Restoring the Faith: The Assemblies of God, Pentecostalism, and American Culture* (Urbana: University of Illinois Press, 1993), 246–247. E. S. Williams quoted in James S. Tinney, "Pentecostal Origins: James S. Tinney Interviews E. S. Williams," *Agora* 2 (Winter 1979): 5. Joseph L. Gerhart, Santa Cruz, Calif., to Thomas F. Zimmerman, Springfield, Mo., 2 November 1960, Flower Pentecostal Heritage Center, Springfield, Mo. Velma Clyde, "Black Pastor Recalls Discrimination," *The Oregonian,* 27 January 1973, 3M. Bob Harrison with Jim Montgomery, *When God Was Black* (Grand Rapids: Zondervan Publishing House, 1971), 15, 5. Dawn Ministries, dawnministries.org (accessed 8/14/06). Howard N. Kenyon, "An Analysis of Ethical Issues in the History of the Assemblies of God" (Ph.D. diss., Baylor University, 1988), 96–104.

28. L. Calvin Bacon, "Eyewitness at a Funeral," *The Pentecostal Evangel,* 14 July 1968, 20, 21. Concerning King's death, Bacon focused much of his attention on the violence and lawlessness it produced. See also LeRoy Johnson, "Civil Disobedience," *The Pentecostal Evangel,* 14 July 1968, 8. Southern members of the majority-white holiness Church of the Nazarene reflected on King's death in similar fashion. Writing to that denomination's chief publication, Memphis resident Jacklyn W. Shockley was disturbed primarily that violence could take place in her "fair city." She did question the complacency and indifference of the church, asking, "Will our beautiful church stand silent?" But like Bacon, Shockley concluded that the gospel was the only answer. Jacklyn W. Shockley, "Memphis: It Can't Happen Here," *Herald of Holiness,* 1 May 1968, 8. Stan Ingersol, denominational archivist, Church of the Nazarene Archives, telephone interview with author, 1 August 2006.

29. B. E. Underwood quoted in David Waters, "Pentecostals Will End Racial Split," *The Commercial Appeal,* 12 January 1994, B2. Assemblies of God resolution quoted in Blumhofer, *Restoring the Faith,* 250.

30. The progressive pentecostal magazine *Agora,* published from 1977 to 1981, revealed the rising social conscience among adherents of both races. "The Agenda," *Agora* 1 (Summer 1977): 4–5. B. E. Underwood quoted in David Waters, "Pentecostals Will End Racial Split," B2. David Waters, "Pentecostals Prepare to Heal Rift," *The Commercial Appeal,* 17 October 1994, B1. Vinson Synan, "Strategy for the Future," *Ministries Today* (January–February 1995): 71. "The Memphis Miracle," *Ministries Today* (January–February 1995): 36–73.

31. "The Memphis Manifesto," *Ministries Today* (January–February 1995): 38. Synan, *The Holiness-Pentecostal Tradition,* 186.

32. K. Connie Kang, "Pentecostal Enthusiasm Is Spreading," *Los Angeles Times,* 28 April 2006, B1, 3. Melissa Black and Robert Siegel, "Pentecostals Mark 100 Years of Worship," National Public Radio's *All Things Considered,* 26 April 2006. "Pentecostalism at 100," *Christian Science Monitor,* 24 April 2006, 1. Richard Vara, "Azusa Centennial," *Houston Chronicle,* 22 April 2006, 1.

33. Marshall Allen, "Pentecostal Movement Celebrates Humble Roots," *Washington Post,* 15 April 2006, B9.

34. See David G. Roebuck, "Limiting Liberty: The Church of God and Women Ministers, 1886–1996" (Ph.D. diss., Vanderbilt University, 1997); Wacker, *Heaven Below,* 176; Blumhofer, *Restoring the Faith,* 164–179.

35. *The Book of Doctrines: Issued in the Interest of the Church of God* (Cleveland, Tenn.: Church of God Publishing House, 1922), 113, 114.

36. R. H. Gause, *Church of God Polity* (Cleveland, Tenn.: Pathway Press, 1973), 190, 85, 86, quoted in Paul K. Jewett, "The Ordination of Women," paper delivered at the Annual Meeting of the Society for Pentecostal Studies, Church of God School of Theology, Cleveland, Tenn., November 1983, F9.

37. Billingsley, *Mighty Like a River,* 137, 141. Butler, "Church Mothers and Migration," 196–198. Cheryl J. Sanders, *Saints in Exile: The Holiness-Pentecostal Experience in African American Religion and Culture* (New York: Oxford University Press, 1996), 33. COGIC manual quoted in Felton Best, "Loosing the Women: African American Women and Leadership in the Pentecostal Church, 1890–Present," paper delivered at the Annual Meeting of the Society for Pentecostal Studies, Wheaton College, Wheaton, Ill., November 1994, 17.

38. Blumhofer, *Restoring the Faith,* 171–177. R. M. Griffith and D.

Roebuck, "Women, Role of," in *The New International Dictionary of Pentecostal and Charismatic Movements,* 1204–1206.

39. Norma T. Mitchell, "Women in Religion," in *Encyclopedia of Religion in the South, Revised,* ed. Samuel Hill and Charles H. Lippy (Macon, Ga.: Mercer University Press, 2005), 846. Brad Liston and Michael Paulson, "Southern Baptists Deliver a 'No' on Women as Pastors," *Boston Globe,* 15 June 2000, A1. Nancy A. Hardesty, *Women Called to Witness: Evangelical Feminism in the Nineteenth Century* (Nashville: Abingdon Press, 1984), 158.

40. Catherine F. Hitchings, "Rowena Morse Mann: First Woman Doctor of Philosophy, 1870–1958," harvardsquarelibrary.org, (accessed 8/16/06).

41. Jewett, "The Ordination of Women," F1, 3. David G. Roebuck, "Limiting Liberty," 4.

42. Sanders, *Saints in Exile,* 33. Lucille Sider Dayton and Donald Dayton, "'Your Daughters Shall Prophesy': Feminism in the Holiness Movement," in *Modern American Protestantism and Its World: Historical Articles on Protestantism in American Religious Life,* vol. 12, ed. Martin E. Marty (Munich: K. G. Saur, 1993), 259. Edith Blumhofer, "The Role of Women in the Pentecostal Ministry," *Assemblies of God Heritage* (Spring 1985–86): 11, 14. Hardesty, *Women Called to Witness,* 159–161. Synan, *The Holiness-Pentecostal Tradition,* 190–191.

43. "Worship with Snake," *Washington Post,* 20 October 1914, 4.

44. Homer A. Tomlinson, *The Shout of a King* (Queens, N.Y.: Church of God, U.S.A., Headquarters, 1968), 41. Weston La Barre, *They Shall Take up Serpents: Psychology of the Southern Snake-Handling Cult* (Minneapolis: University of Minnesota Press, 1962), 36. For a fascinating account of George Hensley's services, see Steven M. Kane, "Snake Handlers of Southern Appalachia" (Ph.D. diss., Princeton University, 1979), 33. David L. Kimbrough, *Taking up Serpents: Snake Handlers of Eastern Kentucky* (Chapel Hill: University of North Carolina Press, 1995), 39–48.

45. Ralph W. Hood and Steven M. Kane, "Serpent Handlers," in *Encyclopedia of Religion in the South,* ed. Samuel S. Hill and Charles H. Lippy (Macon, Ga.: Mercer University Press, 2005), 719.

46. A. J. Tomlinson, *The Signs that Follow,* undated pamphlet from the Flower Pentecostal Heritage Center, Springfield, Mo., 3.

47. "Lets Rattlesnake Bite Him; Is Dead," *Washington Post,* 14 July 1919, 1. "Holy Roller Creed Fails to Save Baby from Rattlesnake," *Atlanta*

Constitution, 15 August 1920, 1A. "Snake Shatters One Man's Faith in Holy Rollers," *Atlanta Constitution,* 16 June 1924, 1.

48. *Book of Minutes: A Compiled History of the Work of the General Assemblies of the Church of God* (Cleveland, Tenn.: Church of God Publishing House, 1922), 297. Mickey Crews, *The Church of God: A Social History* (Knoxville: University of Tennessee Press, 1990), 86–90. On secular and denominational press coverage of the controversy, see Kane, "Snake Handlers of Southern Appalachia," 37–64.

49. Sarah Posner, "Pastor Strangelove," prospect.org, 6 June 2006 (accessed 8/25/06). "TBN Newsletter," tbn.org, May 2000 (accessed 8/25/06). Shayne Lee, *T. D. Jakes: America's New Preacher* (New York: New York University Press, 2005), 1–3, 158–177. *Spirit and Power,* 20. Jerma Jackson, "Sister Rosetta Tharpe and the Evolution of Gospel Music," in *Religion in the American South,* 219–222, 230–232. Paul Oliver, *Songsters and Saints: Vocal Traditions on Race Records* (Cambridge: Cambridge University Press, 1984), 170–171, 188–189, 197–198.

50. Stephen R. Tucker, "Pentecostalism and Popular Culture in the South: A Study of Four Musicians," *Journal of Popular Culture* 16 (Winter 1982): 68–78. Jimmy Wayne Jones Jr., "Modern American Pentecostalism: The Significance of Race, Class, and Culture in Charismatic Growth, 1900–2000" (Ph.D. diss., University of Arkansas, 2002), 130–154. Johnny Cash, *Man in Black* (Grand Rapids: Zondervan, 1975), 25. Tammy Wynette with Joan Dew, *Stand by Your Man* (New York: Simon and Schuster, 1979), 23–24. Charles Sawyer, *The Arrival of B. B. King* (Garden City, N.Y.: Doubleday and Company, 1980), 39–40. Myra Lewis with Murray Silver, *Great Balls of Fire: The Uncensored Story of Jerry Lee Lewis* (New York: William Murrow and Company, 1982), 34–35, 308–311. Little Richard quoted in Charles White, *The Life and Times of Little Richard: The Quasar of Rock* (New York: Da Capo Press, 1994), 16. Marvin Gaye and Dolly Parton also attended pentecostal churches in their youth.

51. Vince Staten, *The Real Elvis: Good Old Boy* (Dayton, Ohio: Media Ventures, 1978), 47–48. Van K. Brock, "Assemblies of God: Elvis and Pentecostalism," *Bulletin of the Center for the Study of Southern Culture and Religion* 3 (June 1979): 9–15. On Elvis's relationship with the Blackwood Brothers, see James R. Goff Jr., *Close Harmony: A History of Southern Gospel* (Chapel Hill: University of North Carolina Press, 2002), 237–238. Saul Pett, "Why Do the Girls Love Elvis?" *Richmond Times-Dispatch,* 22 July 1956, L7. "Elvis Says Jumping 'Arown' Comes Natural When He

Sings"; Saul Pett, "'It's Just the Way Ah Feel,' Says Young Elvis"; Louella O. Parsons, "What Makes Elvis Rock?"; Saul Pett, "I Don't Feel Sexy When I Sing, Pleads Diamond Loaded Elvis" (newspaper clippings at the Flower Pentecostal Heritage Center, Springfield, Mo.). Elvis learned about music and performance from other musicians, too. He fused various traditions in ways that had been unthinkable a decade before. As a young man Elvis would slip out of First Assembly with friends to attend a black church down the road. The singing and preaching there made a lasting impression. Peter Guralnick, *Last Train to Memphis: The Rise of Elvis Presley* (Boston: Little, Brown, 1994), 17, 67, 75.

52. Mrs. Earl H. Clements, Richmond, Va., to Mr. Ralph M. Riggs, Springfield, Mo., 4 August 1956; Mrs. George Arnold, Macon, Ga., to Mr. Riggs, Springfield, Mo., 29 September 1956; G. P. Hertweck, Hattiesburg, Miss., to Reverend Ralph M. Riggs, Springfield, Mo., 20 August 1956, Flower Pentecostal Heritage Center, Springfield, Mo. Brian Ward, *Just My Soul Responding: Rhythm and Blues, Black Consciousness, and Race Relations* (London: UCL Press, 1998), 100.

53. David Wilkerson, "Rock and Roll: The Devil's Heartbeat," *Pentecostal Evangel,* 12 July 1959, 4. Tomlinson, *The Shout of a King,* 21. Pett, "Why Do the Girls Love Elvis?" L7.

54. Ashcroft quoted in Dan Betzer, *Destiny: The Story of John Ashcroft* (Springfield, Mo.: Revivaltime Media Ministries, 1988), 15.

55. Liston Pope, *Millhands and Preachers: A Study of Gastonia* (New Haven: Yale University Press, 1942), 164, 165.

56. Pope, *Millhands and Preachers,* 56. For a counter to Pope, see Jarod H. Roll, "From Revolution to Reaction: Early Pentecostalism, Radicalism, and Race in Southeast Missouri, 1910–1930," *Radical History Review* 90 (Fall 2004): 5–30. Pentecostal Assemblies of the World, 1963 Minute Book of the PAoW, 9–12, 25, quoted in Hollenweger, "Black Pentecostal Concept," 63, 66. For a discussion of the early views of the Pentecostal Holiness Church on unions, see Vivian E. Deno, "Holy Ghost Nation: Race, Gender, and Working-Class Pentecostalism, 1906–1926" (Ph.D. diss., University of California, Irvine, 2002), 135–137. "Religion as Strike Cause," *Boston Daily Globe,* 10 May 1913, 2. *Book of Minutes,* 184.

57. Crews, *The Church of God,* 109–120. "The Pentecostal Movement and the Conscription Law," *The Weekly Evangel,* 4 August 1917, 6. Blumhofer, *Restoring the Faith,* 144–145. Roger Robins, "Attitudes toward

War and Peace in the Assemblies of God: 1914–1918," paper at the Flower Pentecostal Heritage Center, Springfield, Mo.

58. "Holy Roller Held for Not Registering," *Dallas Morning News*, 15 June 1917, 3. "'Holy Roller' Guilty of Opposing the Draft," *Atlanta Constitution*, 26 June 1918, 9. Robert Shuler, "I Have in My Possession," *Bob Shuler's Freelance*, n.d (newspaper clipping at the Flower Pentecostal Heritage Center, Springfield, Mo.). Billy Sunday quoted in George M. Marsden, *Fundamentalism and American Culture: The Shaping of Twentieth-Century Evangelicalism, 1870–1925* (New York: Oxford University Press, 1980), 142.

59. "Holy Roller Preacher Arrested as Pro-German, Thanks God For Jail," *Atlanta Constitution*, 1 July 1918, 7. Crews, *The Church of God*, 117–122.

60. See "Mason, Charles Harrison—Espionage Act, 29 June 1918," and "Mason, Charles Harrison (Rev.)," in Sherry Sherrod Dupree and Herbert C. Dupree, *Exposed!!! Federal Bureau of Investigation (FBI) Unclassified Reports on Churches and Church Leaders* (Washington, D.C.: Middle Atlantic Regional Press, 1993), 31–32. Theodore Kornweibel Jr., "Bishop C. H. Mason and the Church of God in Christ during World War I: The Perils of Conscientious Objection," *Southern Studies: An Interdisciplinary Journal of the South* 26 (Winter 1987): 266.

61. Blumhofer, *Restoring the Faith*, 148–149. Wacker, *Heaven Below*, 246–250. Crews, *The Church of God*, 123–127. Delk, "Miscellanea," 10.

62. Murray W. Dempster, "Reassessing the Moral Rhetoric of Early American Pentecostal Pacifism," *Crux* 26 (March 1990): 33. Menzies, *Anointed to Serve*, 328. Murray W. Dempster, "Peacetime Draft Registration and Pentecostal Moral Conscience," *Agora* 5 (Summer 1981): 5.

63. Daniels, "Doing All the Good We Can," 174–175. Hans A. Baer, "The Socio-Religious Development of the Church of God in Christ," in *African Americans in the South: Issues of Race, Class, and Gender*, ed. Hans A. Baer and Yvonne Jones (Athens: University of Georgia Press, 1992), 120–121. Fredrick C. Harris, *Something Within: Religion in African-American Political Activism* (New York: Oxford University Press, 1999), 58, 61–62, 182. Augustus Cerillo Jr., "Pentecostals and the Presidential Election," *Agora* 4 (Winter 1981): 3. Glenn H. Utter and James L. True, *Conservative Christians and Political Participation: A Reference Handbook* (Santa Barbara, Calif.: ABC CLIO, 2004), 131. In the 1960s the official publica-

tions of the Pentecostal Holiness Church seldom dealt with the upheavals of the era unless it was to condemn Black Panthers, drug users, and draft dodgers. Synan, *Old Time Power,* 254.

64. Allan Anderson, *An Introduction to Pentecostalism: Global Charismatic Christianity* (Cambridge: Cambridge University Press, 2004), 259. Russell P. Spittler, "Are Pentecostals and Charismatics Fundamentalists? A Review of American Uses of These Categories," in *Charismatic Christianity as a Global Culture,* ed. Karla Poewe (Columbia: University of South Carolina Press, 1994), 108–109. Marsden, *Fundamentalism and American Culture,* 94. Farnum St. John, "Fundamentalism in a Word," *The Herald of Truth,* n.d., 5 (newspaper in the International Pentecostal Holiness Church Archives and Research Center, Oklahoma City).

65. Utter and True, *Conservative Christians and Political Participation,* 23, 25.

66. Anderson, *Introduction to Pentecostalism,* 258. *General Council Minutes,* 1963, quoted in Menzies, *Anointed to Serve,* 330. Crews, *The Church of God,* 149–150.

67. Gordon Lindsay, *Red Moon over America!* (Dallas: Voice of Healing Publishing Company, 1957), 7. For a similar view from a pentecostal representative of the National Association of Evangelicals, see Frank W. Smith, *What Is Communism?* (Springfield, Mo.: Gospel Publishing House, n.d.).

68. "Elder Solomon Michaux Dies," *New York Times,* 21 October 1968, 47. J. Gordon Melton, *The Encyclopedia of American Religion,* vol. 1 (Tarrytown, N.Y.: Triumph Books, 1991), 223. "Dr. King to Press New Voter Drive," *New York Times,* 2 April 1965, 24. Elder L. S. Michaux, Washington, D.C., to Rev. Martin Luther King, Atlanta, 22 December 1964; J. Edgar Hoover, Washington, D.C., to Elder L. S. Michaux, Washington., D.C.; and "Michaux Airs Views on King-Hoover Feud," all in Dupree and Dupree, *Exposed!!!,* 16–19, 21, 20. Donald W. Dayton, *Discovering an Evangelical Heritage* (Peabody, Mass.: Hendrickson Publishers, 1976), 3.

69. Synan, *Old Time Power,* 256–257. "Assemblies of God Opposes Kennedy," *Leader and Press,* n.d., newspaper clipping at the Flower Pentecostal Heritage Center, Springfield, Mo. Crews, *The Church of God,* 161.

70. Grant Wacker, "Searching for Norman Rockwell: Popular Evangelicalism in Contemporary America," in *The Evangelical Tradition in*

America (Macon, Ga.: Mercer University Press, 1984), 294, 301, 307–309. Robert C. Cunningham, "Signs of His Return," *The Pentecostal Evangel,* 7 January 1968, 4. Kenneth J. Heineman, *God Is a Conservative: Religion, Politics, and Morality in Contemporary America* (New York: New York University Press, 1998), 21–22, 28, 34, 172. Robert C. Liebman and Robert Wuthnow, *The New Christian Right: Mobilization and Legitimization* (New York: Aldine Publishing Company, 1983), 52–53. On the gradual politicization of the Assemblies of God, see Jones, "Modern American Pentecostalism," 171–183. By the end of the century, denominations such as the Assemblies of God were issuing far-right edicts on a range of political issues: environmentalism, feminism, human cloning, abortion, the law and crime, capital punishment, and euthanasia. *Contemporary Issues: Social, Medical, and Political* (Springfield, Mo.: Assemblies of God Office of Public Relations, 1995), 2–46.

71. David Edwin Harrell Jr., *Pat Robertson: A Personal, Political, and Religious Portrait* (San Francisco: Harper and Row, 1987), 131–137. Utter and True, *Conservative Christians and Political Participation,* 167. Pat Robertson quoted in David Nyhan, "Mr. Pray-TV Bombs in Michigan," *Boston Globe,* 10 August 1986, A21.

72. Dudley Clendinen, "Robertson's Camp Hopes to Capture Vast TV Evangelical Vote in Nation," *New York Times,* 30 September 1986, B4. Mark D. Regnerus, David Sikkink, and Christian Smith, "Voting with the Christian Right: Contextual and Individual Patterns of Electoral Influence," *Social Forces* 77 (June 1999): 1378–79, 1385. Harrell, *Pat Robertson,* 137. Heineman, *God Is a Conservative,* 173. Paul S. Boyer, "Make Believe: The Strange World of Conspiracy Theorists," *The Christian Century,* 7 July 2004, 32. Christopher Buckley, "Apocalypse Soon," *New York Times,* 11 February 1996, BR8.

73. "Pastors Reveal Major Influences on Churches," barna.org, 14 January 2005 (accessed 8/28/06). Julia Duin, "Christian Group to Advocate More Support for Israel," washingtontimes.com, 13 July 2006 (accessed 8/28/06). Guy Raz, "Pro-Israel Christians Lobby in Washington," npr.org, 17 July 2006 (accessed 8/28/06). Posner, "Pastor Strangelove." On the lasting appeal of premillennialism among conservative Protestants, see Timothy P. Weber, *Living in the Shadow of the Second Coming: American Premillennialism, 1875–1925* (Chicago: University of Chicago Press, 1987), 231–244. The Pew Forum's 2006 study showed that 60 percent of pentecostals

surveyed sympathized with "Israel rather than with Palestinians." Only 40 percent of nonpentecostal Christians surveyed said the same. *Spirit and Power,* 67.

74. John Hagee, "Bible Positions on Political Issues," *JHMagazine* 16 (September–October 2004): 4. John Hagee, "Frequently Asked Questions," jhm.org (accessed 8/28/06). "Homosexuality," icmnet.org (accessed 8/28/06). Ed Gordon, "GOP Steps Up Efforts to Court Black Conservatives," npr.org, 9 February 2005, (accessed 8/28/06).

75. Shaila Dewan, "Lady Liberty Trades in Some Trappings," nytimes.com, 4 July 2006 (accessed 7/5/06). "What We Believe," worldovercomers.org. Harvey Cox, *Fire from Heaven: The Rise of Pentecostal Spirituality and the Reshaping of Religion in the Twenty-first Century* (Reading, Mass.: Addison-Wesley, 1995), 17.

76. As of August 2006 only one of the incoming freshmen at Yale University was a self-identified pentecostal. Gale Iannone of the Yale University chaplain's office, phone interview with author, 10 August 2006. Vicki Haddock, "Son of a Preacher Man: How John Ashcroft's Religion Shapes His Public Service," sfgate.com, 4 August 2002 (accessed 8/10/06).

77. John Ashcroft with Gary Thomas, *On My Honor: The Beliefs That Shape My Life* (Nashville: Thomas Nelson Publishers, 1998), 184–186.

78. Haddock, "Son of a Preacher Man."

79. "Bob Jones University Ends Ban on Interracial Dating," archives.cnn.com, 4 March 2000 (accessed 8/10/06). "Larry King Live: What Did John Ashcroft Say at Bob Jones University?" transcripts.cnn.com, 12 January 2001 (accessed 8/10/06).

80. Ashcroft, *On My Honor,* 185.

81. For criticism of Attorney General Ashcroft, see Jeffrey Toobin, "Ashcroft's Ascent: How Far Will the Attorney General Go?" *New Yorker,* 15 April 2002, 57–63. "Senator John Ashcroft: Missouri's Champion of States' Rights and Traditional Southern Values," *Southern Partisan* (2nd quarter 1998): 28. "Ashcroft's Flirtation with the Racist Right," *Boston Globe,* 10 January 2001, A19.

82. Julian Bond quoted in Haddock, "Son of a Preacher Man."

83. "Ashcroft Sings," cnn.com, 25 February 2002 (accessed 8/6/06).

84. Katty Kay, "Ashcroft Rallies Troops with Song," news.bbc.co.uk, 4 March 2002 (accessed 8/6/06).

85. Philip Shabecoff, "Senate Confirms Clark as Secretary of Interior," *New York Times,* 19 November 1983, 12. Born in Lusk, Wyoming, Watt

was one of the first pentecostals to serve in such an important political office. James Watt and Caspar Weinberger quotes from Paul Boyer, *When Time Shall Be No More: Prophecy Belief in Modern American Culture* (Cambridge, Mass.: Harvard University Press, 1992), 141.

86. John Herbers, "Armageddon View Prompts a Debate," *New York Times,* 24 October 1984, A1, 25.

87. Walter Goodman, "Religious Debate Fueled by Politics," *New York Times,* 28 October 1984, 31; John Herbers, "Religious Leaders Tell of Worry on Armageddon View Ascribed to Reagan," *New York Times,* 21 October 1984, 32; "On the Record: 3 Views of Armageddon," *New York Times,* 24 October 1984, A25. Boyer, *When Time Shall Be No More,* 142.

88. Jane Lampman, "The End of the World," csmonitor.com, 18 February 2004 (accessed 8/11/06). "A Half-Century of Evangelical Influence in U.S.," *Hartford Courant,* 30 July 2006, 5. Ann Banks, "In a Nervous World, a Series of Apocalyptic Thrillers Continues to Dominate Bestseller Lists," *Washington Post,* 17 October 2004, T10. Amy Johnson Frykholm, *Rapture Culture: Left Behind in Evangelical America* (New York: Oxford University Press, 2004), 3–4.

89. L. F. Wilson, "Bible Institutes, Colleges, Universities," in *The New International Dictionary of Pentecostal and Charismatic Movements,* 372–381. Menzies, *Anointed to Serve,* 372–373. James S. Tinney, "Pentecostals Refurbish Upper Room," *Christianity Today,* 1 April 1966, 47–48. On COGIC members' rising affluence, see Baer, "The Socio-Religious Development of the Church of God in Christ," 119.

90. John A. Sims quoted in Harrell, *Pat Robertson,* 132–133.

91. Sridhar Pappu, "The Preacher," theatlantic.com, March 2006 (accessed 8/28/06). Lauren F. Winner, "T. D. Jakes Feels Your Pain," christianitytoday.com, 7 February 2000 (accessed 8/28/06). Lee, *T. D. Jakes,* 106–122. Hagee, "Frequently Asked Questions," *Book of Minutes,* 209. For an African American critique of word of faith theology, see "Megachurches Have Wrong Focus, Black Leaders Say," *Houston Chronicle,* 2 July 2006, 5. The Pew Forum's 2006 survey revealed that pentecostals are much more likely than other Christians to claim that faith is a key to success and that God grants health and wealth to believers. *Spirit and Power,* 29, 53.

92. R. Laurence Moore, *Religious Outsiders and the Making of Americans* (New York: Oxford University Press, 1986), 142. Wacker, *Heaven Below,* 267.

93. *The Apostle,* DVD, directed by Robert Duvall (1997; West Hollywood, Calif.: Butchers Run Films, 2002).

Illustration Credits

16   George D. Watson, *Love Abounding and Other Expositions on the Spiritual Life* (Boston: McDonald, Gill and Company, 1891), frontispiece.

19   Library of Congress Prints and Photographs Division (reproduction number LC-USZ62-15600).

23   William T. Smithson, *Methodist Pulpit South* (Washington, D.C.: Henry Polkinhorn, 1859), 189.

33   Matthew Simpson, *Cyclopaedia of Methodism: Embracing Sketches of Its Rise, Progress, and Present Condition, with Biographical Notices and Numerous Illustrations* (Philadelphia: Everts and Stewart, 1878), 692.

60   Bud Robinson, *Sunshine and Smiles: Life Story, Flash Lights, Sayings, and Sermons* (Chicago: Christian Witness Company, 1904), 53.

70   Martin Wells Knapp, *Lightning Bolts from Pentecostal Skies, or Devices of the Devil Unmasked* (Cincinnati: Office of the Revivalist, 1898), 33.

78   Flower Pentecostal Heritage Center, Springfield, Mo.

83   Church of the Nazarene Archives, Kansas City, Mo.

96   Church of the Nazarene Archives, Kansas City, Mo.

107   I. E. Lowery, *Life on the Old Plantation in Ante-Bellum Days: Or, a Story Based on Facts* (Columbia, S.C.: State Company Printers, 1911), frontispiece.

112   Church of the Nazarene Archives, Kansas City, Mo.

114   Martin Wells Knapp, *Lightning Bolts from Pentecostal Skies, or De-*

vices of the Devil Unmasked (Cincinnati: Office of the Revivalist, 1898), frontispiece.

119 Edgar P. Ellyson, *Holding Out: Written Especially for Young Converts; Also for New Arrivals in the Land of Canaan* (Cincinnati: Revivalist Office, 1896), 7.

124 L. L. Pickett and W. N. Matheney, *Bible Fruit, Being a Series of Bible Readings* (Louisville: Pickett Publishing Company, 1899), frontispiece.

132 Church of the Nazarene Archives, Kansas City, Mo.

138 B. F. Haynes, *Tempest-Tossed on Methodist Seas: Or, a Sketch of My Life* (Louisville: Pentecostal Publishing Company, 1921), frontispiece.

151 Martin Wells Knapp, *Lightning Bolts from Pentecostal Skies, or Devices of the Devil Unmasked* (Cincinnati: Office of the Revivalist, 1898), 188.

153 Matthew Simpson, *Cyclopaedia of Methodism: Embracing Sketches of Its Rise, Progress, and Present Condition, with Biographical Notices and Numerous Illustrations* (Philadelphia: Everts and Stewart, 1878), 66.

160 C. B. Jernigan, *Pioneer Days of the Holiness Movement in the Southwest* (Kansas City, Mo.: Pentecostal Nazarene Publishing House, 1915), 112.

160 Church of the Nazarene Archives, Kansas City, Mo.

163 W. R. Moody, *The Life of Dwight L. Moody* (London: Morgan and Scott, 1900), 392.

166 "Camp Meeting Has Commenced," *Atlanta Constitution,* 19 August 1899, 5.

194 Flower Pentecostal Heritage Center, Springfield, Mo.

197 Martin Wells Knapp, *Lightning Bolts from Pentecostal Skies, or Devices of the Devil Unmasked* (Cincinnati: Office of the Revivalist, 1898), 160.

212 "Holy Rollers Worship in the Police Court," *Atlanta Constitution,* 10 November 1908, 7.

225 Flower Pentecostal Heritage Center, Springfield, Mo.

233 Library of Congress Prints and Photographs Division (reproduction number LC-USZ62-107501).

246 Flower Pentecostal Heritage Center, Springfield, Mo.

269 Flower Pentecostal Heritage Center, Springfield, Mo.

275 Flower Pentecostal Heritage Center, Springfield, Mo.

Index

Durham, William C., 236
Duvall, Robert, 282

Eaton, Clement, 35
Edmonds, Richard, 52
education, 113. *See also* schools and colleges
Elizabeth City, N.C., revivals at, 158
Elliott, T. M., 123
emotionalism, 223
The End of the Age (Robertson), 270
endtime theology. *See* apocalyptic (end of world theology)
Engel v. Vitale, 267
Episcopalians, 18, 249
Epps, James, Jr., 84
The Evangel, 262
evangelicals: contemporary, 4, 5; oppose premillennialism, 172–173; in the South, 24–25
evangelism, and print culture, 100–101, 102–103, 115, 128–129
evangelist, denominational opposition to, 143
Evans, C. A., 81–82
The Evening Light and Church of God Evangel, 218–219
Evening Light Saints, 192
evolution, 14, 265, 267
Experimental Religion (Rosser), 116

The Faithful Standard, 234
Falwell, Jerry, 270, 271
Farber, Raphael, 269
farmers, 64–65

Farrow, Lucy, 192, 211
Federal Bureau of Investigation (FBI), 241, 262, 266
finished work controversy, 237, 238, 239–240
Finney, Charles Grandison, 29, 31; and northern revivals, 26–27
Fire-Baptism (Fire-Baptized Holiness Church), 164, 180–184, 187, 203, 239
Fire-Baptized Holiness Association, 180, 185
Fisher, Annie May, 94
Fletcher, John, 29, 117, 179
Florida: camp meetings in, 108, 226; pentecostal evangelists in, 236; pentecostalism in, 200, 219–220, 227
Flower, J. Roswell, 259
fourfold gospel, 165, 224
Fourth Great Awakening, 4
Freedmen's Aid Society, 41
Free Methodist Church, 46, 48, 76, 157
Freud, Sigmund, 11, 221
Fuller, W. E., 164, 181
fundamentalism, 41–42, 264–265
Futrell, D. A., 115–116

Gaddis, Merrill Elmer, 58–59
Gaines, W. W., 173
gambling, 242
Garr, A. G., 216
Garrison, William Lloyd, 31
Gaston County, N.C., 6
gender equality, 58, 209–214
Georgia: holiness movement in,

literacy, 103, 113

literature: apocalyptic, 137; and Lost Cause, 107–108

Little Richard, 4, 256

Live Coals of Fire (Ga.), 125, 128

Live Coals of Fire (Neb.), 180–181

Lively, J. W., 155

Livesey, J., 86–87

Living Waters (publishing house), 116

Living Word (Nashville), 159

Living Words (Pittsburgh), 120

Logan, John G., 220

Los Angeles: Azusa Street revival's 100th anniversary (2006), 245–247; Cashwell's revival at, 1; *1906* revival at, 5, 10–11, 186

Los Angeles Times, 193

Lost Cause, 13, 79, 81, 107, 275

The Lost Link, 150

Loud, Grover C., 221

Louisiana: and holiness movement, 66; missionaries in, 41–42

Lowery, Irving E.: and interracial ministry, 77–78, 84; and mainline churches, 157; and northern holiness, 47, 106–107; and print culture, 92, 129; and sanctification, 54

Lowney, Elijah, 47

Lowrey, Asbury, 19

Lutherans, 36

lynching, 37, 46, 85, 90, 91, 168, 171, 177, 253

Macon Daily Telegraph, 39

magazines, 8

Mahan, Asa, 29

mainline churches. *See specific denominations*

Mason, Charles Harrison: biography of, 178; and draft, 262; and holiness ministry, 46; itinerant holiness of, 77, 78; and pentecostalism, 204, 226, 235; and premillennialism, 164, 169; and racism, 241; and ringshout, 149

Mason, Eliza, 149

Mason, Mary, 178

materialism: acceptance of, 279–281; criticism of, 20, 21, 281

McAlister, R. E., 237

McBride, Jesse, 37

McCafferty, Burt, 213

McClurkan, J. O.: and anti-tongues, 225–226; and holiness ministry, 56, 159–161; and interracial ministry, 92; and premillennialism, 165, 174

McDonald, William, 53, 106, 108

McLain, Thomas, 251

McLaughlin, Sister, 208–209

McMaree, Horton, 239

McMinnville Enterprise, 43

McPherson, Aimee Semple, 254

medical profession, 144

Mehlman, Ken, 271

Memphis, Tenn.: pentecostal churches in, 257; pentecostal gathering at, 244–246

Memphis Miracle, 245–247

Mencken, H. L., *American Mercury*, 5–6

Mennonites, 261

Merritt, Timothy, 29; *Guide to Christian Perfection*, 31

Messick, B. M., 144–145

The Methodist, 110–111, 130

Methodist Episcopal Church, South (MECS): and authority, 145–146; division with northern, 17–18, 76–77, 140–142; and effect of Civil War, 40, 67; General Conference, 21, 143–144; ministers in, 61, 155; North Alabama Conference, 105; oppose holiness movement, 133, 140–145; and racism, 90–91; and southern dissenters, 157; subject matter of, 8

Methodists: and anti-tongues, 12; and entire sanctification, 22–23; Free Will, 47–48, 76; and gender issues, 95–96; and holiness ministers, 152–155; internal division among, 141; in Jacksonian era, 20–21, 22; and Lost Cause, 81; northern, 17–18, 40–41, 46–47, 77–78; oppose perfectionists, 130–134, 136–137; and pentecostals, 216, 219–220; and postbellum years, 40–41; primitive, 25; Wesleyan, 36, 76

Mials, G. A., 164

Michaux, Solomon Lightfoot, 266

Milan Exchange, 142

militancy, 233

millennialism. *See* postmillennialism; premillennialism

Miller, G. G., 218–219

Miller, William, 162

mill workers ("millbillies"), 59, 62, 217

ministers: African American, 243; and denominational controls, 152–157; holiness, 155–157; MECS, 61, 152–155; northern, 17, 18; of radical holiness, 10, 83, 114, 158, 188, 192, 207, 228

missionaries, northern, 17, 41, 52, 77

missionary journals, 102, 221

missions, 63

Mississippi: and antebellum religion, 25; and print culture, 113; revivals in, 125

Missouri, 116, 158, 179, 191, 235, 259, 273

modern culture, and threat to holiness movement, 10, 69–72

Mondale, Walter F., 278

Moody, Dwight L., 147–148, 162–163, 164

Moore, Joanna P., 45–46, 47, 77

Moore, Michael, 276

morality, national, 268

Morgan, G. Campbell, 146

Mormonism, 50

Morrison, Henry Clay: author of *From the Pulpit to Perdition*, 71–72; expelled by MECS, 155, 169; and Fire Baptism, 183; and holiness ministry, 56; and interracial ministry, 84; and mainline church, 157; and print culture, 87–88, 110–111, 115, 121

movement culture, 120–121

Murphy, Mary A., 126

Murrah, E. G., 110
Murrill, E. M., 123, 152
music: black gospel, 255; country,
256; jazz, 255; pentecostal, 255–
256, 256–257; rock 'n' roll, 256–
258. *See also* hymnals; hymns
Myrick, Luther, 35

Nashville, Tenn.: and effect of
Civil War, 40; and holiness
journals, 81, 82, 91, 92, 95, 102,
125, 134, 141, 159
National Baptist Magazine, 142,
173
National Camp Meeting Association for the Promotion of Holiness (NCMAPH), 43, 45, 50, 51,
110
National Camp Meetings, 52, 106,
117
National Economist, 120
National Farmers Alliance, 74
National Holiness Association, 18,
43, 51, 53, 173, 174
National Religious Broadcasters,
275
neckties, prohibition against, 69
neurasthenia, 146–147
New England, and conventional
theology, 30
New Jersey, revival in, 42–43, 53
New School Presbyterianism, 27
New South creed, 52, 172
newspapers: holiness, 1, 8–9, 32,
33, 35, 43, 100, 103; pentecostal,
200–203, 204; and tongues
speaking, 196–199

New Testament Church of Christ,
159
Niagara Conference, 162
North: and holiness literature, 8;
perfectionism in, 8, 16, 30–31;
and premillennialism, 163–164,
168; and romanticism of South,
108–109; and roots of holiness
movement, 13, 16–17, 29–35,
51–52
North Carolina: missionaries in,
36, 41–42; and northern Methodist agitation, 40–41; pentecostalism in, 227; revivals in,
1–2, 3, 6, 158, 202, 205–206
northern missionaries, 17, 41, 52,
77
North Georgia Conference, 62, 154

Oberlin College, 31
Ocean Grove, N.J., holiness re-
vival at, 53
O'Connor, Flannery, 282
Ohio, 18, 32, 79–80
Okey records, 255
The Old Methodist, 88
Old School Presbyterians, 27
Oliver, R. C., 44, 61, 104, 106, 109
oneness pentecostalism, 237, 238,
240
orality, of holiness movement, 101
orphanages, 63

pacifism, 261–263
Padgett, B. L., 227
Pafford, E. M., 127–128
Page, Thomas Nelson, 107

Platt, Trena, 96
Plessy v. Ferguson, 90
Plymouth Brethren sect, 50
pneumatology, 147
poisoning, 251, 252
politics: advocated by pentecostals, 265–283; rejected by pentecostals, 214, 259; rejected by holiness movement, 10, 170
Pope, Liston, 6, 259–260, 260, 261
Popular and Radical Holiness, Contrasted (Shelhamer), 118
Populism: and holiness movement, 57, 62, 64, 67; and national organization, 74, 139; and print culture, 102, 118–120
pork, prohibition against, 69
postmillennialism, 31, 167–168, 172, 174
poverty, and holiness movement, 59–61, 62
power, and holiness movement, 146–148
preaching: and holiness movement, 47, 51, 67, 94, 101, 115, 143, 155, 179, 180, 201, 207; and pentecostalism, 190, 191, 192, 203, 204, 209, 226, 256
premillennialism: and holiness movement, 5, 9–10, 138–139, 161–185, 224; and pentecostals, 187, 195–196, 204–206, 228, 234–235, 270, 271; and politicians, 277–279
Presbyterians, 18, 25, 27, 250
Presley, Elvis, 4, 257
Price, Judge, 126
printing press, 101–102, 111–112

professionalism, 144
prohibition: against alcohol, 66, 167, 171, 184, 242, 273; against church entertainment, 71; against Coca-Cola, 123, 181; against coffee, 123, 184; against dancing, 123, 273; against neckties, 69; against pork, 69; against theater, 57, 68, 71, 123; against tobacco, 69, 70, 123, 171, 202
prophecies, 3, 196
Protestants, Southern, 5, 12–13
provincialism, 75
publishing, and holiness movement, 113–117

Quakers, 37, 261
Quarterly Review, 35
Quarterly Review of the M. E. Church, South, 140

race: and holiness movement, 46, 82–92; and integration of holiness churches, 9, 13; and pentecostal movement, 209–214, 235, 238–239; and pentecostal reconciliation, 244–247
race mixing, 212, 237–239
radical holiness: advertisements, 119; Fire-Baptized, 182; ministers of, 10, 83, 114, 158, 188, 192, 207, 228; and premillennialism, 12, 164; press, 118, 133, 196, 199
radio, 230, 254, 266, 282
rapture: and hymns, 196; and pentecostals, 197, 206, 234–235,

279; and second coming, 161, 164
Reagan, Ronald, 264, 278
Rees, Seth Cook, 149–150
regionalism, 64–66, 72–73
Reid, Isaiah, 174, 180
Religious Herald (Richmond), 81, 135, 139
The Repairer and Holiness Advocate, 118
Republican Party: and agrarianism, 64–66; and holiness movement, 13–14; and pentecostals, 271
restorationism, 48, 67, 139, 149–150, 158, 159, 214–215
The Revivalist, 112–113, 117, 129, 171
revivals: Azusa, 7, 110, 186, 200, 245–246; at Birmingham, 208; at Cane Ridge, 24; at Charleston, 43, 110, 128–129; in Ga., 110; at Knoxville, 17, 18–19, 22, 43, 54; in N.C., 1–2, 3, 6, 158, 202, 205–206; northern, 26–27, 42–43, 53; at Richmond, 43; and tongues speaking, 12
Riggs, Ralph M., 242–243, 258
ring-shout, 149
Roberson, Lizzie, 46
Roberts, Oral, 230
Robertson, Pat, 268–270, 271, 274
Robinson, "Uncle Bud," 54, 56, 59–60, 62–63, 76
Robinson, W. E., 148
rock 'n' roll, 256–258
Rodgers, H. G., 226
Roe v. Wade, 267

Rogers, Denis, 111
Roman Catholicism, 4, 30
Roosevelt, Franklin D., 266
Rosser, Leonidas, 116
rural society, 24, 67–68
Rush, J. W., 131
Russell, Robert, 261
Ruth, C. W., 224

Safire, William, 268
salvation. *See* conversion
Samson's Foxes, 133
sanctification, entire: and African Americans, 46, 47, 88, 92; and antebellum South, 8, 16, 22–23, 31; and holiness movement, 2, 34, 35, 52, 53, 77, 104, 147, 175; and mainline church, 21, 35, 49, 51, 76, 142, 156; and northerners, 17; and pentecostals, 224; and print culture, 34, 44–45, 70, 106, 117, 125–126, 128, 134; testimonials of, 105; Wesley on, 29–30
Sanctification (Godbey), 116
Sandford, Frank W., 189
Santorum, Rick, 271
Satan: and modernism, 10; and pentecostalism, 222; and rock 'n' roll, 258; and communism, 266
Savannah, Georgia, revivals at, 110
school prayer, 14, 267, 273
schools and colleges, 31, 73, 79, 274
Scopes trial, 265
Scott, Orange, 36

Swaggart, Jimmy, 230, 270
Synan, Vinson, 6, 245

tax law, 267
Taylor, G. F., 204, 205
Tears and Triumphs (hymnal), 117
technology, and print culture, 101–102, 103
televangelism, 254–255, 268–271
temperance, 27, 37, 69, 74
Tennessee: Methodists in, 18; missionaries in, 41–42; and northern Methodist agitation, 40–41; pentecostal evangelists in, 236; pentecostalism in, 200, 244–246, 257; and religious dissent, 65; revivals in, 17, 18–19, 22, 43, 54
Tennessee Methodist, 66, 90, 131
terror, war on, 271, 275
testimonials, 127, 199–201, 203, 210
Texas: and antiholiness, 143; holiness ministers in, 155; holiness movement in, 47–50, 160; pentecostalism in, 191; revivals in, 152, 183, 205
Texas Christian Advocate, 49
Texas Holiness Association, 48
Tharpe, Sister Rosetta, 255
theater, prohibition against, 57, 68, 71
third blessing. *See* Fire-Baptism (Fire-Baptized Holy Church)
Thompson, John A., 142
Thornwell, James Henley, 27–28, 39

Tillet, Wilbur F., 140
Tillman, Charlie, 92
Tilton, Robert, 280
Tinney, James S., 279–280
tobacco, prohibition against, 69, 70, 123, 171, 202
Tocqueville, Alexis de, 100
Todd, Jacob, 52
Todd, S. C., 165
Toiler's Friend, 120
Tomlinson, A. J.: founder of Church of God, 170, 236; and pacifism, 262; on pentecostal origins, 227, 281; on political organizations, 260–261; and print culture, 133–134, 198; on serpent handling, 251–252, 253
Tomlinson, Homer A., 251–252, 258–259
Tongue of Fire, 110
tongues movement, detractors of, 186–187
tongues speaking: critics of, 221, 264–265; and evidence of Holy Ghost, 3, 5, 10–11, 187, 215; and foreign language, 216; movement of, 1, 2, 193–195, 224, 227–228; and Parham, 189–192, 193, 194–195, 206, 228; in the South, 202, 204–206, 227
Topeka, Ks., and Parham's school, 189–191
Touching Incidents and Remarkable Answers to Prayer, 117–118

223, 226–227; and premillennialism, 224

Wesleyan Methodist Connection, 76

West, and "tongues" movement, 13, 196

Weyrich, Paul, 270

Wheaton, "Mother" Elizabeth, 86

White, J. Wofford, 2–3

White, Robert, 62

White League, 46

whites, and conversion, 24

white supremacy, 91

Whittier, True, 47

The Whole Truth, 204, 210

Wilkerson, David, 258

Willard, Frances, 32

Williams, Alton R., 272–273

Williams, F. W., 203–204

Williams, J. A., 88–89

Williams, Smallwood E., 240

Willis, Miller, 80, 128, 177

Wilson, George W., 173

Windsor, Fla., 108

women: and church leadership, 9, 93–98, 209, 247–249; and gen-der roles, 93; homes for, 63; ordination of, 247–250; and revivals, 26; and rights organization, 74

Women's Christian Temperance Union, 109

women's suffrage, 167

Wood, J. A., 42, 44, 122

Woodworth-Etter, Maria, 176, 209

Wool Hat, 120

"word of faith" theology, 280–281

World's Christian Fundamentals Association, 264–265

World War I, 234, 261

World War II, 14, 234, 261–263

Worrell, A. S., 199

worship style, 59, 149, 187, 215, 223, 231

Worth, Daniel, 37, 38

Wyatt-Brown, Bertram, 35

Wynette, Tammy, 4, 256

xenoglossy, 189

Zimmerman, Thomas, 265

Zion's Outlook, 82, 91, 92, 125, 168